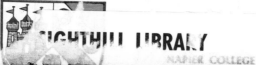

Harvard Business School

Research Colloquium

Contributors

Vincent P. Barabba
David K. Braun
Robert D. Buzzell
John F. Cady
E. Raymond Corey
Michael Drexler
Stephan H. Haeckel
John R. Hauser
Mary Gardiner Jones
Patrick J. Kaufmann
Theodore Levitt
Charles M. Lillis
Bonnie J. McIvor
Michael J. Naples
John A. Quelch
Michael L. Ray
Walter J. Salmon
V. Srinivasan
Louis W. Stern
Rudolph W. Struse III
Eric von Hippel
William F. Waters
Boris C. G. Wilenkin
George S. Yip

Marketing in an Electronic Age

Edited by **Robert D. Buzzell**

Harvard Business School Press

Boston, Massachusetts

Harvard Business School Press
© 1985 by the President and Fellows of Harvard College.
All rights reserved.
Printed in the United States of America.

88 87 86 85   5 4 3 2

Library of Congress Cataloging in Publication Data
Main entry under title:

Marketing in an electronic age.

Includes bibliographical references and index.
1. Electronic marketing—Addresses, essays, lectures.
2. Electronic marketing—United States—Addresses,
essays, lectures.   I. Buzzell, Robert D. (Robert Dow),
1933–
HF5415.122.M425   1985   658.8′5   84-25166
ISBN 0-87584-159-7

Contents

Foreword

Founded in 1908, the Harvard University Graduate School of Business Administration celebrated its seventy-fifth anniversary in the academic year 1983–84. We chose to take this opportunity to involve our faculty in thinking seriously about the challenges and opportunities ahead in important fields of management research and teaching.

Field-based empirical research, within and across organizations, has always been fundamental to Harvard Business School's ability to meet its objectives of educating business managers and helping to improve the practice of management. In some respects, we are creating a distinctive model of research. We have often broken through the bounds of traditional disciplines and methodologies to borrow whatever tools and concepts were needed for a particular inquiry. In addition, we have been less concerned with testing existing theory than with generating new insights. And while we often find ourselves drawn to problems that are broad in scope, we strive for results that are operationally significant to managers.

Because Harvard Business School faculty members are committed to pursuing research on the way business actually *does* function, as well as theoretical explorations of how it perhaps *should* function, they can give students and practitioners a vital perspective on the real world of professional practice. Their continuing close contact with operating businesses keeps Harvard Business School faculty at the frontiers of management practice. Research conducted by the faculty often yields insights that are of considerable practical benefit to managers in both day-to-day operations and longer-range planning.

In sponsoring the colloquium series of 1983–84, we hoped to set the course for research development over the next decade, and in particular to encourage greater emphasis on multiperson, multiyear studies of major issues. The complexity of many issues confronting business today almost requires that academicians find more effective forms of collaboration in doing our research. The problems we study are often beyond the capacity of any individual researcher.

In addition to encouraging a reshaping of researchers' work habits, the conferences promised to help strengthen the ties between Harvard Business School and the outside academic and business leadership communities. The series comprised sixteen conferences held at the Harvard Business School campus, each lasting two to five days. Papers were presented by eighty members of the HBS faculty and an approximately equal number of practitioners and academics from other institutions. Altogether, some 450 academics and practitioners were involved as discussants and participants.

Some of these colloquia focused on current research topics, such as U.S. competitiveness in the world economy, productivity and technology, global competition, and world food policy. Others concentrated on establishing agendas for the coming decade's research and course development in a particular field. Clearly, these were not tasks to be attempted in isolation. Rather we wanted to work jointly with others in business, government, and the academic world who could contribute and would themselves gain from the undertaking. The papers presented in this volume have all benefited from the thoughtful discussion they received at the colloquium.

Beyond exploring research findings in particular areas, we hoped that these colloquia would sustain and enliven the continuing dialogue between students and practitioners of management. From that melding of perspectives, we have found, insights emerge that can revitalize the education of future managers and refine current professional practice. In that spirit of cooperative endeavor, I am proud to introduce this collection of essays.

JOHN H. MCARTHUR
Dean of the Faculty
Harvard Business School

Acknowledgments

The planning and organization of the HBS colloquium "Marketing and the New Information/Communication Technologies" was a cooperative enterprise that required the efforts of many people. The first to be recruited were the chairpeople of the five half-day sessions: E. Raymond Corey, John D. C. Little, Stephen A. Greyser, John F. Cady, and Theodore Levitt. Each of the chairpeople provided essential leadership in planning the content of his session and in selecting speakers. The speakers, of course, created the papers that constituted the program for the meeting.

For most of the sessions, discussants were recruited and prepared comments in advance. Some of them went further and prepared full-blown papers: these have been included in this volume (Chapters 13, 14, and 18). Other discussants, whose contributions were no less valuable, included Darral G. Clarke, J. Phillip Samper, Paul A. Strassman, Clarence Selin, F. Kent Mitchel, and Frank M. Bass.

Several corporations provided much-needed assistance to the colloquium chairpeople and speakers. Some of these are acknowledged in the papers in this collection. Others included the International Business Machines Corporation; American Bell, Inc. (as it was then still called); BBDO International; Eastman Kodak Company; Frost & Sullivan, Inc.; Management Horizons; Booz Allen & Hamilton, Inc.; Xerox Corporation; and Datapro Research Corporation.

I would also like to acknowledge the efforts of the following people, whose research for Chapter 4 by Walter J. Salmon was invaluable: Jose Abete, Matt Czajkowski, John Hoagland, Laurence Lepard, Rich Schlesinger, Dennis Wong, and Marci Dew.

On the administrative side, I was ably assisted by Paul Schwartz. The staff of Harvard Business School's Division of Research provided administrative and editorial support for me and for the speakers and participants. Needless to say, the budgetary support of the Division of Research was also a *sine qua non* of the colloquium. Arrangements for the meeting itself, meals, and living quarters were efficiently managed by Paula Alexander.

Susan Oleksiw edited the colloquium papers and made them significantly more intelligible.

Finally, throughout the nearly two years of planning the colloquium and preparing this publication, Renee Young has provided vital assistance. It was she who organized the files, set up meetings, remembered the deadlines, and called speakers to nag them.

To all of these contributors, many thanks for your efforts. I believe the results justify the many hours of work that have gone into the project.

Marketing in an Electronic Age

INTRODUCTION

Marketing 1995, A Scenario for the Future

Robert D. Buzzell

Harvard Business School

Throughout history, marketing methods and institutions have been shaped by changes in the technologies available for obtaining, analyzing, and communicating information. The systems used in the 1980s for selling, advertising, and marketing research would be inconceivable without the telephone, television, and computers. In the future, equally great changes will no doubt take place, as new systems for home information and entertainment, office automation, and financial services evolve. The new systems that are envisioned for the 1990s will be based on the emerging, integrated technology of "information/communications," which has yet to find a name. Some have called it "compunications." Whatever term is used, the new technology—rooted in microelectronics—is certain to reshape today's marketing systems between now and the end of the century.

How will marketing change? As a way of exploring the possibilities, let's imagine how the introduction of a new product might be handled in 1995.[1]

Marketing in 1995: A Scenario

In early March 1995, Jane Ferguson and Tom Fitzgerald sat before Ferguson's electronic work station, looking at the last of a series of graphic displays.[2] Ferguson was project manager for ICON, a new electronic photography system developed by Universal Electronics Corporation, while Fitzgerald was Universal's manager for decision support services. The graphs they were studying depicted projections of sales, expenses, profits, and investment requirements for a new line of cameras and film based on the ICON technology.

Ferguson's work station combined the functions of a powerful self-contained computer; a terminal through which she could access the main computer system of the company's Consumer Division; a word processor; an electronic mail system for sending and receiving voice and nonvoice messages; and an office copier. Earlier that day she had reviewed stored messages from the members of her project team, reporting the status of various parts of the ICON program.

Ferguson's responsibility was to recommend an introductory business plan to the company's New Products Committee, including initial investments in tooling; production quantities for the first three months; the models and features to be included in the product line; pricing; and first-year budgets for sales, advertising and promotion, and customer service. Fitzgerald's role was to provide all of the estimates and forecasts needed for the business plan, and to ensure that the data were properly analyzed. Occasionally, he found himself in disagreement with Ferguson and other line managers at Universal when they "stretched" interpretations of marketing research to fit their own preconceptions. But for the ICON project, the picture seemed clear: Ferguson and Fitzgerald agreed that the introductory plan should include both a line of several amateur cameras and a medical imaging system for use by surgeons. Simulations of financial results indicated an expected pretax internal rate of return on the program of 32.6 percent, and only a 12 percent chance that the rate of return would fall below Universal's minimum requirement of 20 percent.

The financial simulations used to project sales and profit performance were produced by one module of a decision support system (DSS) available to Universal's executives. The DSS included several internal data banks, a collection of programs for statistical analysis, standard financial statement programs, and an array of computer graphics capabilities. Through her console, Ferguson could also review information from several syndicated data base services, including historical industry data and current information such as weather forecasts, airline schedules, and stock market reports.

Ferguson switched her data terminal to report preparation and wrote a brief memorandum summarizing her recommendations. Then, she specified the tables and graphs supporting her conclusions and listed the names of the New Products Committee members as recipients of the memorandum. Although the eight members of the committee were located in five different cities, including Tokyo and Munich, all would have copies of the report on their desks by the following morning and a final decision would be forthcoming soon. She doubted that the committee would delay the program by postponing their decision until their next in-person meeting, which in recent years had been held annually.

The information used by Ferguson and Fitzgerald in their analysis of the ICON program came from a wide variety of sources. Universal regularly updated its forecasts of the size and composition of the imaging systems market, using econometric models developed by Eco Research Institute (ERI), a specialized forecasting organization. ERI's models and data banks related the industry's performance to population, consumer employment and income, prices, and other factors that affected the highly discretionary purchases of imaging equipment and consumable supplies. By 1995, ERI's statistics covered almost fifty years of the industry's history, beginning with the introduction of instant photography by Polaroid in 1948 and including all of the successive "revolutions" in imaging technology: color film, the Kodak Instamatic, color instant photography, the Pocket Instamatic, the Disc Camera, and the early electronic systems introduced by a Japanese company in the late 1980s. This extensive statistical series, along with the increasingly detailed economic and demographic data available to ERI, enabled them to produce more and more accurate forecasts during the 1980s and early 1990s. Fitzgerald's staff at Universal received quarterly updates from ERI through dedicated computer terminals. Even small companies could and did utilize a simplified ERI forecasting service; many retailers, for example, accessed the service via their microcomputers, which also provided them with data from their trade association's annual survey of operating results.

Besides the econometric forecasts of industry sales and prices, Ferguson and Fitzgerald had conducted an extensive program of consumer and market research on the proposed ICON products. Product concept studies, for example, had been conducted through traditional focus group interview sessions with consumers and with surgeons who might use the professional versions of the system, and through Cable Feedback, a relatively new form of customer research.

Cable Feedback obtained customer reactions to new products, packages, and advertisements by displaying them to a sample of households equipped with two-way cable television. The respondents in these studies communicated their reactions by pushing buttons on keyboards attached to their TV sets. The responses were recorded directly by Cable Feedback's headquarters computer and tabulated within minutes after the completion of the test. The data were then transmitted to Universal's computer system and were available to Fitzgerald's research analysts the following morning. Although the two companies had different makes of computers, the Universal Data Network Standards adopted during the 1980s permitted the systems to "talk" to each other.

While the two-way cable studies were helpful to the Universal managers in screening basic product design alternatives, even in 1995 they did not provide a representative sample of consumers. Consequently, once the product concepts had been narrowed down, Fitzgerald commissioned additional research. Telephone surveys were carried out in several countries to determine the most likely uses for the cameras.

In the telephone surveys, interviewers sat at consoles in which their "questionnaires" were displayed on TV screens. Households were selected for calling by a computerized random dialing system. As consumers responded to the questions, the interviewers keyed in their answers, which were recorded and, soon afterward, analyzed by the minicomputer to which the consoles were attached. The entire system was controlled by a Call Control program that automatically compiled measures of interviewer efficiency and tested each consumer's responses for consistency and plausibility.

Still another study was designed to test alternative television commercial concepts. ADCOMP, a specialized research supplier, utilized a "split cable" TV system to show several different commercials simultaneously to matched groups of households within three cable TV networks. Reactions were then obtained through telephone interviews.

As Ferguson and Fitzgerald had anticipated, the New Products Committee accepted their recommended business plan with only minor modifications. During late March and April, as the Manufacturing Division was completing preparations for full-scale production, Ferguson worked on plans for introducing the product line to the sales force and, soon afterward, to distributors and dealers. On May 15, Ferguson officially announced the new product line in a teleconference.

Universal maintained its own private teleconferencing facilities at its New York, San Francisco, London, and Tokyo offices. Elsewhere, company salespeople participated by going to rented facilities at units of the Elite Hotels chain. The teleconference was, in effect, a live video program in which Ferguson displayed the product line and outlined the introductory marketing campaign. After the presentation, participants asked questions; video cameras transmitted pictures of the questioners so that everyone at the twenty locations could see as well as hear the question-and-answer exchanges. Occasionally, lists and calculations were exchanged via "electronic black-boards" installed in each location.

Ferguson turned the telemeeting over to Bill Ramirez, the national sales manager. Ramirez explained to the sales representatives that they would soon receive videodiscs containing sales training material and presentations to be used with retailers. Each of Universal's salespeople had a portable videodisc player, which could be used to view communications from headquarters and to show retailers programs describing promotions, new products, and so on. Once the sales reps had made their presentations to major account buyers, the introductory campaign called for a "telemarketing blitz," in which telephone sales assistants would solicit orders from smaller retailers.

While Ferguson and Ramirez were preparing the sales force for the ICON introduction, across town another part of the program was taking shape. In the offices of Boyle, Barton, and Bates (Three Bs), a leading advertising agency, Tony Boyle was reviewing the media plan for the ICON products. Renee Sexton, the account executive for Universal, had used Three Bs' computerized media model to test a variety of media schedules and budgets. Her recommendations for the first phase of the campaign included commercials on several cable networks as well as all four major broadcast networks in the United States. She also proposed to advertise ICON in Europe on programs beamed to consumers via direct broadcast satellite television systems. For the medical version of the product line, she had produced a completely separate campaign to reach surgeons via the Worldwide Hospital Network, a cable TV system that was confined to hospitals and surgical clinics. Sexton's plan also included a specialized campaign aimed at the parents of infants and young children, always a prime market segment for picture taking. Commercials tailored to this segment would be "narrowcast" over *Parenting* magazine's special interest cable channel.

By 1995, 80 percent of U.S. households, and comparable proportions of other industrialized nations, were equipped with cable TV systems. On average, each household could receive more than fifty channels. Some of these channels offered very specialized programming, such as that aimed at parents of infants and toddlers. Others were very localized in coverage and appeal and were used heavily by retailers for local area advertising. Still other channels were available only to physicians, educators, and other professional groups.

Bruce and Margie Charles were especially interested in the new ICON cameras because their new baby, Cathie, was growing so fast. They wanted to preserve through photographs each new accomplishment in Cathie's young life. After seeing several commercials, the couple decided to get more details and used their cable TV system to view a five-minute "infomercial" sponsored by Universal. Then, to get a disinterested viewpoint, they switched to another cable channel and consulted an evaluation of ICON prepared by Consumer Resource, an independent testing agency. All of this information seemed favorable to Bruce and Margie, and they decided to purchase the top-of-the-line Zeus model complete with twelve tape cassettes and an electronic zoom lens.

Margie wanted to buy the camera immediately, and she switched the console to Videomall, a home shopping service. Here she requested a display of model numbers and prices, and was informed that the Zeus model could be obtained for $169.95, with shipment within ten days by Continental Express. The display asked her simply to key in the Charles's OmniCard number, and payment would be made directly from their BalanceSheet Manager Account at Hemispheric Bank, Investment and Credit Corporation to the participating retailer, Discatalog Shippers, Inc. Before making a final decision, however, she decided to review the Charles's family budget, which was stored in the computer module of their Home Information/Communication/Security/Management System.

> The systems used by the Charles family evolved from the teletext and videotex systems first developed and tested in the early 1980s. By the mid-1990s, a common package of services in an upper-middle-income U.S. household might include (besides cable TV) teleshopping; home banking; access to data banks including news, classified ads, and weather; a home fire/burglar alarm system; and household management/control systems such as energy management, scheduling, and budgeting.

Despite the convenience of in-home shopping, Bruce, an engineer, wanted to try the product before buying. The following day, he went to a nearby branch of Fearless Foto, a national chain of stores specializing in home entertainment products and services. In the store he watched a demonstration on a videodisc player and discovered that Fearless was offering, as an introductory special, *two* dozen tape cassettes with the Zeus model—all for $164.44. As Bruce paid for his purchase at the store's checkout counter, using his OmniCard, the transaction was recorded—along with the Charles's Zip code and ID number—on a point-of-sale (POS) terminal.

Ten days after the new ICON cameras went on sale, the Fearless Foto chain reviewed sales results. The company's on-line POS system provided sales and gross profit data, by model, for each of the

217 Fearless outlets around the United States. The system also yielded estimates of price elasticity and response to local promotion, based on results obtained with nine different combinations of retail prices and levels of promotional support. It was clear to the buyer for Fearless that ICON would be a big success, and that he should reorder as soon as possible. Turning to an order entry terminal, the buyer placed an order with Universal's Western Division warehouse for immediate shipment. A return message confirmed the receipt of the order and indicated the date of shipment almost instantaneously, and a voice signal thanked Fearless for its purchase.

Fearless Foto's point-of-sale system was typical of those used by large retailers by the mid-1990s. Not only did the system handle credit authorization and record and control sales receipts, it also produced very detailed merchandising data as a basis for controlling inventories, scheduling personnel requirements, and measuring the effects of space allocation, promotion, and pricing. Order entry terminals like that used by Fearless Foto to place its reorder were also widely employed by retailers, wholesalers, and manufacturers. These terminals facilitated rapid communications between buyers and sellers, provided input data to inventory records for both parties, and at the same time permitted direct transfer of funds from the buyer's bank account to that of the seller.

In mid-December 1995, Jane Ferguson, Tom Fitzgerald, and Bill Ramirez met to celebrate. All three had just been informed that their bonuses would be large ones because of the successful market introduction of the ICON products. The day before, Fitzgerald had run a new set of sales projections based on data obtained from Universal's panel of POS-equipped retailers. Overall, the forecast for 1996 was 20 percent ahead of the original business plan figure. The store data also gave a clear picture of the demographic characteristics of buyers, and indicated that the rate of usage of tape cassettes per camera would probably be even higher than the last revised forecast. Early sales results for ICON Medical Imagers were also favorable, according to figures obtained from MedPanels, Ltd.

Later that evening, the three managers were happy but tired. All agreed that the next day would be an ideal one to spend at home, using their OfficeLink home work stations to send and receive electronic mail. As Ramirez pointed out, this would actually improve their productivity if the elimination of commuting time were factored into the equation. Just then, unfortunately, his PortaPage pocket communicator beeped and its miniature screen displayed a message: "The Marketing VP needs to talk with you tonight."

Changes in Marketing Systems

The above scenario shows how I envision the practice of marketing ten to fifteen years in the future. While the scenario may seem exotic in some respects, it is actually quite conservative. All of the devices and systems mentioned in the story existed by 1983, at least in the form of prototypes or small-scale tests. No fundamental innovations in technology would be required to bring the scenario to life—only the widespread adoption of existing types of equipment and existing systems for recording, storing, communicating, and analyzing information. Moreover, the scenario is conservative in that the marketing institutions and tasks it depicts are basically similar to those of the 1980s. Jane Ferguson, Tom Fitzgerald, and the other participants in the story have essentially the same jobs as they would have in 1983. Universal Electronics still distributes its products primarily through independent retailers, and consumers like the Charles family still buy most products in retail stores. Some new types of marketing research suppliers are in operation, but these are clearly recognizable as extensions or improvements of research services available in the mid-1980s.

How, then, is marketing likely to change? Although my view may be too conservative, I think the main changes will be in the information-communications *capabilities* available to marketers and consumers—in the "tools of the trade." Just as television, jet airplanes, and computers have transformed the practice of marketing since the 1950s, further improvements in systems for recording, analyzing, and communicating data will lead to significant changes in marketing systems in the years ahead.

Needs and Opportunities

It has often been said that the computer and telecommunications industries are "technology driven." New products are often, perhaps usually, developed because technological advances make them possible, rather than in response to well-defined customer needs. If this is the case, it is useful to ask, "Within marketing, what needs and opportunities for improvement might be met by the new information-communications capabilities?"

In very broad terms, it seems clear that substantial improvements *are* possible in marketing effectiveness and efficiency. Marketing activities—including retail and wholesale trade, field selling, advertising, marketing administration, and marketing research—are both labor-intensive and information-intensive. Moreover, traditional approaches to planning and controlling marketing processes have always left much to be desired because of the inherent complexity and uncertainty that characterize customer behavior and because of the high cost of obtaining accurate, up-to-date information. New capabilities based on advances in information-communications technology are bound to offer the potential for improvement over current practice.

Applications of new "tools of the trade" will affect marketing most directly, and most rapidly, through automation of manual and semimanual systems for handling and recording transactions. Examples of transactional information systems include recording of sales and payment data in retail stores; distributors' and manufacturers' order entry systems; and specialized industrywide systems such as those now used by airlines and hotels. Considerable progress has already been made in automating retail point-of-sale systems, and to a lesser extent in order entry systems. By the mid-1990s it seems likely that automated systems will be in general use in the United States and other advanced economies. Direct benefits of automating transactional data systems include reduced labor requirements, improved accuracy, and faster availability of information. Indirectly, creative use of new systems may also provide other kinds of benefits. Companies or trade associations that pioneer in developing the systems may achieve overall competitive advantages; one example is American Hospital Supply Corporation, whose order entry system is described in Chapter 2.

Beyond the automation of transactional data systems, new electronic systems offer potential for improved marketing effectiveness through better and more selective modes of communication. For example, there has been widespread interest in the potential value of "narrowcasting." Cable TV networks, in particular, will provide opportunities to reach much more selective audiences than those reached by the major networks. To illustrate, in mid-1983 a program on the Cable Health Network included commercials for several prescription drug products, a category that has never been advertised on conventional television. The Health Network reaches a substantial number of physicians, and the same program was also transmitted through closed-circuit networks to hospitals.

New forms of communication may also, to some extent, supplant existing methods. Teleconferencing, for example, has been widely discussed as a possible substitute for much business travel. While few would claim that massive reductions in personal sales calls, meetings, or conferences are likely, *some* substitution seems very likely. Even a modest reduction in business travel expenditures would yield considerable savings. Another area open to "technological substitution" in communications is sales, which might change from reliance on personal contact to the use of videodiscs. Disc players, with high-quality pictures, random access, and large storage capacity, will be widely used for sales training and presentation and as catalogs.

A third area in which new information-communications capabilities offer the potential for significant improvements in marketing practice is that of measurement and analysis. Not only will information be recorded and transmitted at lower cost, but much more detailed, accurate, and timely information should be available to decision makers. Possible types of information could include sales force activity, customer service records, survey research results, and the results of controlled experiments. Moreover, improved software and greater user familiarity with decision support systems will surely lead to more extensive use of multivariate statistical techniques, and perhaps eventually to "expert systems," for data analysis.

To summarize, then, the development of improved information-communications capabilities seems likely to yield substantial benefits in terms of more effective and efficient marketing. Waste can be reduced, and customer satisfaction—the ultimate goal of marketing—will be enhanced. At the same time, the process of change in marketing methods will no doubt create both competitive risks and competitive opportunities for companies that succeed or fail in using the new capabilities.

The papers in this volume present the viewpoints of leading scholars and practitioners on how marketing will change as a result of the use of new electronic systems. These papers cover a wide variety of topics: order-entry systems, buyer-seller relationships, in-home shopping, cable TV advertising, decision support systems, and strategies for marketing the new electronic systems themselves. None of the authors claims to be clairvoyant, so the papers should be viewed as suggestions of *possible* changes and their implications. With this qualification, it is hoped that the papers will provide useful food for thought by academics and managers as they explore the rich possibilities of the latest generation of change in marketing.

CHAPTER 1

An Agenda for Teaching and Research: Some Suggestions

Robert D. Buzzell
Harvard Business School

The primary objective of the Harvard Business School colloquium summarized in this volume was to identify and explore the issues raised for the field of marketing by changing information-communication technology. As the information systems and methods of communications used in marketing change, so too must the courses, teaching materials, and research activities of business schools and other educational institutions. In this first chapter of the colloquium proceedings, I offer some suggestions for the agenda of marketing educators and scholars in the years ahead. I have not attempted to set forth a comprehensive game plan for academic work—only to highlight some of the needs and issues that were discussed at the colloquium. These include new kinds of teaching materials and methods, specific research issues, and general comments on research strategy.

As might be expected, my own interpretation of the issues posed by the new information-communication systems is oriented toward the Harvard Business School's particular educational philosophy, resources, and goals. But I believe that all educational institutions in the field will face similar challenges as marketing practice changes. Each will, of course, respond in its own way depending on its own needs and possibilities.

Teaching Materials and Methods

The scenario of "Marketing 1995" presented in the introduction to this volume depicts marketing managers using electronic work stations to retrieve and analyze data, to communicate with each other, to place and fulfill orders, and to carry out their duties in other ways. It also envisions a world in which vastly detailed information is collected, stored, and made available for analysis on virtually every aspect of a marketing system. An obvious question is, How should business schools prepare their students to function effectively as managers in this new environment? I believe that three kinds of changes will be needed, in the areas of instruction in research and analytical techniques; practice in the use of information systems; and incorporation of new theoretical knowledge into the marketing curriculum.

Research and Analytical Techniques

One of the capabilities that new information systems will provide to future managers is that of quickly and easily carrying out complex statistical analyses of marketing data. It will be as easy to use multivariate techniques such as regression, clustering, and multidimensional scaling as it is to calculate a square root on a hand-held calculator. But the availability of all this "instant statistical horsepower" carries with it some risks. The danger is that managers with limited training in statistical methods will use the techniques improperly. In the past, the solution to this problem in most organizations has been to require that complex analytical methods be used only by qualified technical specialists working as staff advisers to line managers. This kind of separation of responsibilities is natural and easy to maintain when the statistical analyses are done on mainframe computers, in a batch mode, as special projects supervised by staff specialists. The examples of present-day decision support systems described by Charles Lillis and Bonnie McIvor and by Rudolph Struse in Chapters 5 and 7, respectively, of this volume suggest that this "special project" approach was still the usual practice in 1983.

In the future, the situation is almost certain to change. Managers will be increasingly *able* to use even the most complex techniques, and apply them to even the largest data bases, by means of desk-top terminals. Just as managers now create their own simple tables and graphs without requesting staff assistance, they will want to create their own regression analyses, trade-off analyses, and so on. It seems unlikely that organizations will be able to limit access to particular techniques only to qualified technical specialists.

I believe that in order to prepare managers for the world of the 1990s, many business schools must provide more extensive instruction in research and analytical methods than they do at present. This should include both data collection methods and data analysis techniques, in sufficient depth to provide an understanding of the limitations and assumptions of the techniques. Some schools, no doubt, are already providing this kind of instruction; many are not. Even for those that do, I would suggest that there is another need—that of providing realistic practice in the use of modern information systems.

Practice in Using Information Systems

Not only should business school students understand in conceptual or theoretical terms the methods used in marketing information systems, they should be given some hands-on experience in using the systems. This will require access to terminals and data bases; more important, it will require the development of realistic exercises and "computerized case studies" to provide meaningful experience in the application of techniques to management problems.

A typical conventional business school case study includes, in addition to background information and a statement of a more or less specific issue, some financial or statistical data, or both, in the form of tables and graphs. In preparing a case, the student typically spends much of his or her time manipulating the data in the case—for example, in calculating financial ratios or calculating rates of change in key variables. Usually only limited kinds of analysis are possible, either because information is not provided or because of time restrictions.

An ideal marketing case in 1990 will enable—and require—the student to do much more quantitative analysis than is possible with present-day materials. Instead of a few exhibits summarizing key data, we should give students access to unsummarized data bases and let them construct their own exhibits. This will, of course, require that we obtain much more extensive and detailed statistical information on the company situations described in the case studies. But if practicing managers are convinced of the educational value of the process, it should be possible to get the needed cooperation.

Some efforts have already been made to develop case studies along the lines suggested here.[1] What I am suggesting, then, is not novel. But considerable work will be needed to develop the number and variety of materials that will be required for the marketing courses of the 1990s.

Incorporating New Theory into the Curriculum

In Chapter 20 of this volume, John Hauser forecasts a "revolution in marketing theory" in the not-too-distant future, as a result of greater availability of data and analytical techniques. It is by no means clear when or how such a revolution will occur, or how genuine breakthroughs can be distinguished from false alarms. But it does seem reasonable to expect that some new theoretical knowledge will be developed in marketing by the mid-1990s, even if it is limited to specific parts of the field such as consumer response to advertising and promotion.

As new marketing theory does emerge, business schools must find appropriate ways to incorporate it into their courses. For some, this will pose no problem; advanced courses are already strongly oriented toward theory, most of which at present is borrowed from other disciplines such as psychology. For others, especially those that are primarily oriented toward management practice, incorporating theory into the curriculum will be more difficult. Perhaps we can learn something about how to do this by studying how our colleagues in finance deal with the capital asset pricing model.

Research

Academic research in marketing has always reflected the current practices and concerns of practitioners in the field. This is not to say that there is no basic theory or that there are no pure theorists in marketing. But even a cursory review of the books, journals, and conference proceedings published in the field reveals a strong emphasis on practical topics, such as managing field sales forces, testing television commercials, evaluating new products, and setting prices. If these management concerns change, or if new methods of dealing with them are developed, based on the new "tools of the trade" discussed in this volume, it is inevitable that academic research will also change. Moreover, the kinds of research that are feasible in marketing have always depended in part on what kinds of data are available from companies and from syndicated research services. Since one by-product of the new information systems used in marketing will be a massive increase in available data, academic researchers can anticipate having many more opportunities for empirically testing their theories. In many instances, marketing academics (in their role as consultants) will no doubt also play major roles in designing new information systems and deciding what *should* be measured. They can therefore influence what kinds of data are collected as well as benefiting from them as a research resource.

In this section, I offer some comments and suggestions for future academic research in marketing. As noted earlier, the topics mentioned here are drawn largely from the discussions that took place at the colloquium.

Channels of Distribution

The development of new types of information and communications systems may lead to changes in channels of distribution in some industries. In Chapter 2 of this book, E. Raymond Corey describes five examples of wholesale distributors using automated order entry systems, and also providing new customer services based on computer systems, to improve their competitive positions in their respective markets. He also cites estimates by executives of the same companies that indicate more general trends favoring wholesalers versus direct distribution by manufacturers. The implication is that wholesalers are somehow better situated to develop and use electronic systems than manufacturers, retailers, or end users such as hospitals. A similar point of view is expressed in a recent study of trends in wholesale distribution conducted by Arthur Andersen and Company on behalf of the Distribution Research Education Foundation. Arthur Andersen staff members surveyed 250 persons, including executives of wholesaler firms as well as manufacturers, consultants, and others, to obtain opinions about likely future trends. Among the conclusions of the study were the following:

- Technology, particularly in the use of computer-based systems, will offer the wholesaler-distributor opportunities to achieve growth and profitability levels not previously possible.[2]
- Merchant wholesalers are predicted to increase their share of total wholesale sales from 51% in 1972 to 58% in 1990.[3]

If wholesalers are gaining in importance as a channel of distribution, why is this so? Are they, in fact, in an inherently better position to develop and maintain automated order entry systems than their suppliers and customers are? To what extent do systems such as those of McKesson Drug and American Hospital Supply represent simply more efficient handling of existing wholesaler functions versus a shifting of functions previously performed by customers or suppliers? Research by marketing scholars might help to shed light on these and related questions. One kind of research, suggested by Corey, would involve detailed comparisons of the costs of specific elements of the marketing task under alternative channel arrangements.[4] Depending on the product involved, these specific elements might include field selling, applications engineering, order entry and fulfillment, storage, inventory carrying, transportation, credit, and product service.

Another way in which new electronic systems may affect distribution channels is through in-home shopping via videotex systems. Will the volume of goods and services distributed through new in-home systems reach a significant level in the foreseeable future? If so, how will this development affect existing retailers? Walter Salmon, in Chapter 4, argues that in-home electronic systems will *not* be an important factor primarily because of limitations on the kinds of products consumers are willing to buy without personal inspection. But consumer attitudes toward shopping may change, especially when people become more accustomed to living and working in a world of ubiquitous electronic systems. Continuing research on the potential of in-home systems will be useful for monitoring changes in this area.

Economies of Scale in Distribution

There are some indications that the advent of computer-based information systems and new forms of telecommunication are leading to greater economies of scale in wholesale and retail distribution. On this point the consensus of the executives surveyed in the previously cited Arthur Andersen and Company study was that large distributors will account for a substantially greater percentage of total wholesale sales in 1990 than in 1981.[5] Corey cites additional evidence of the same trend in Chapter 2 of this volume and attributes it directly (in part, at least) to the adoption of computer-based systems.

In retailing, the advent of electronic information-communication systems may also be leading to greater economies of scale. The relatively new modes of organizing the merchandising function, which rely heavily on data from point-of-sale systems, are generally associated with large retail chains, not independent stores or local department store companies. Moreover, effective use of computer-based systems appears to have been a significant factor in the rapid growth of some large chains during the 1970s, including B. Dalton, Toys R Us, and The Limited.

How important are information and communications systems as a source of scale economies? Are the advantages of larger wholesalers and retailers the result of lower systems costs, or do the systems simply provide better information and thereby more effective decisions? To what extent does the growth of larger distribution firms reflect other factors, such as bargaining power vis-à-vis suppliers or preferential access to capital markets? Can smaller firms also benefit from computer-based systems, particularly as the costs of hardware and software continue to decline? If not, what are the implications of increasing concentration in wholesale and retail trade for manufacturers, consumers, and public policy?

Information Systems and Competitive Advantage

As discussed above, information and communication systems may be sources of economies of scale in distribution. To the extent that this is true, the systems may be sources of competitive advantage for larger firms. More generally, innovations in information processing and telecommunications may be used by firms to gain competitive advantages over their rivals to a degree not previously possible. This prospect was discussed in a colloquium on information systems held at the Harvard Business School in June 1983. At that meeting, F. Warren McFarlan suggested: "With dramatic speed, the sharp reduction in the cost of IS (Information Systems) technology (computers, remote devices, and telecommunications) has allowed it to move from applications which were more back-office support to those which offer major competitive advantage. Particularly crucial systems in this regard are those which develop interorganizational links between customer and supplier."[6]

A prime example of the use of information and communication systems as a competitive weapon is American Hospital Supply Company (AHS), described by E. R. Corey in Chapter 2 of this volume. AHS utilized remote order entry terminals and an effective inventory control system not only to preserve their middleman role from the threat of direct distribution, but also to gain market share from other distributors. The system was so effective, in fact, that the company's rivals initiated legal action, claiming that the order entry system constituted an unfair competitive advantage.[7] There can be no more convincing evidence of competitive success than that other firms in an industry are forced to sue for relief!

There are other examples of companies using information and communications systems as major elements of competitive strategy. American Airlines and United Airlines, for instance, operate the two most widely used order entry (reservations) systems for travel agencies. Both systems (Sabre and Apollo) list the flights of other air carriers as well as those of the "host" airline. But according to carriers that compete with American and United, the systems give the host airlines significant advantages in at least two ways:

- In displaying available flights from city A to city B, the systems are "biased" in favor of the host. For example, if there are four flights from New York to Chicago at 8:00 A.M., the Sabre display always shows American's flight at the top of the list.
- The systems give the host companies access to competitors' traffic data on specific flights, enabling American and United to identify competitive opportunities and take appropriate action.[8]

The increasing potential of information and communications systems as competitive weapons raises some interesting questions. In what kinds of industries are these systems most significant? On the face of it, the potential impact seems likely to be greatest for businesses in which transaction-processing activity accounts for a substantial proportion of total operating costs: retail banking, credit cards, insurance, travel, brokerage, and so on. But there are no doubt other possibilities, too. Wherever field salespeople must collect and analyze complex data to determine customer needs, or to prepare bids, information systems might be used to improve efficiency and effectiveness. Similarly, as Walter Salmon suggests in Chapter 4 of these proceedings, some retailers will undoubtedly find ways to use new systems for in-store sales presentations or other purposes and thus gain advantages over competitors.

Will information and communication systems act as "barriers to entry"? To what extent can creativity in the use of such systems offset other sources of competitive advantage, such as product differentiation? For that matter, can the systems act as a new kind of *source* of product differentiation? These are a few of the issues toward which research could usefully be directed.

Buyer-Seller Relationships

As interorganizational data links come to play a greater role in marketing, relationships between buyers and sellers will surely change. Traditionally, as described by Louis Stern and Patrick Kaufmann in Chapter 3 of this volume, these relationships have been based primarily on personal contacts. Sales representatives call on buyers, purchasing agents, store managers, or factory managers not only to get orders, but to provide customer services, obtain information, expedite deliveries, and so on. In the future, if many of the routine processes of placing and processing orders are handled via electronic systems, how will the other dimensions of the buyer-seller relationship be handled? Under whatever types of arrangements are worked out, will customer loyalty to particular suppliers be reduced or enhanced?

One aspect of the buyer-seller relationship has received quite a bit of attention in academic research—that of *conflict* in distribution channels.[9] Will the use of interorganizational data systems tend to reduce conflict, or lead to changes in the areas of conflict or in the ways conflict is resolved? It would be useful to study some of the industries, or individual buyer-seller relationships, in which the newer systems are most fully developed, in order to see how they compare with more traditional situations.

Market Segmentation

The concept of market segmentation plays an important role in marketing thought and practice. It is generally accepted that marketing programs are most effective when they are designed for particular groups of customers. In consumer markets, the groupings may be based on income, age, sex, location, or life styles. Industrial marketers, too, find it useful to vary their product offerings, prices, customer services, and communications for buyers on the basis of their size, manner of product usage, and so on. But the benefits of custom-tailoring market programs for segments must always be weighed against the economies inherent in standardization. In consumer product and service advertising, in particular, network television advertising has been an extremely efficient means of communicating with mass audiences and thus has worked against segmentation. The new communications systems of the 1990s, however, will greatly facilitate the use of different messages for various subgroups within a mass audience. Michael Drexler and David Braun describe examples of advertising directed to specific consumer market segments in Chapters 8 and 10, respectively, of this volume. In his introduction to the session at which the Drexler and Braun papers were presented, Stephen Greyser summed up the prospects as follows:

> For the traditional intensive (mass) advertiser, the emerging world of fragmentation offers special challenges. These focus on the balance between the continued pursuit of mass audiences and communicating with narrower segments, particularly with tailored messages. . . . I see a move toward *collecting* a broad audience through a series of more selective audiences. . . . *Accumulation rather than aggregation will be the key.*[10]

The mere technical ability to reach narrower segments more efficiently will not, however, guarantee *effective* communication. What kinds of messages will work best in advertising aimed at teenagers, Hispanic consumers, retired persons, or fitness enthusiasts? How can clear product "positioning" be maintained in a situation when many, varied advertising presentations are employed?

For companies that market industrial products and services, new telecommunications methods also offer opportunities for segmentation. Electronic order entry terminals or videodisc players might, for instance, serve as "catalogs," with the content and presentation being varied for different customers. Here, as in consumer advertising, questions might be resolved about the most effective ways of defining segments and tailoring messages to their needs and interests.

The Marketing Mix

The availability of new communications systems presents new alternatives to marketing managers for reaching customers and end users. These new forms of communication will, in some cases, be attractive alternatives to traditional methods of personal selling, advertising, and sales promotion, and significant shifts in budget allocations may occur. To some extent, modifications in communications programs will reflect increased market segmentation, as discussed above. In some cases, the new systems will enable advertisers to reach audiences previously accessible only through personal sales calls, telephone, and direct mail. The cable television advertising of investments described in Chapter 11 by William Waters is an example. More generally, cable TV will provide opportunities to use advertising for many products and services used by relatively small, specialized categories of customers. Prescription drugs and medical equipment will probably be advertised on "narrowcasts" to physicians; textbooks to educators; and so on. To what extent will electronic media supplant traditional personal selling efforts for these kinds of products? How will the role of the salesperson change?

The Communication Process

Efforts to understand how marketing communications affect people's attitudes and behavior have been a major topic of research since the early twentieth century. Researchers have sought to develop general models of response to communication and to measure relationships among audience characteristics, message types, and the communication medium employed.

People's responses to the new forms of communication may differ from their responses to existing forms. Of particular interest are the *interactive* systems such as videotex. When the consumer plays an active role in choosing, modifying, or responding to communication, will the relationships identified in past research still hold? What kinds of messages can be designed for selective or interactive viewing by the audience?

Michael Ray suggests, in Chapter 13, that the new systems will make consumers better informed and thus more powerful in the marketplace. The same prospect exists, presumably, for industrial buyers. But how much of the increased supply of information will customers actually want or use? Is there such a thing as too much information?

Marketing Organization

Another aspect of marketing practice that will be affected by the new information and communication systems is organization within companies. In retailing, the firms that are most efficient in merchandising, and that exploit computer-based information systems most fully, are centralized national or regional chains. These companies are generally organized differently from traditional department stores. Will department stores modify their organizations in response to the competitive challenge of the specialty chains? What other changes—in methods of compensation, selection and training of personnel, and so on—will reorganization imply?

As noted earlier, relationships between buyers and sellers are being altered by the spread of direct order entry systems. An indirect consequence may be organizational changes within the buying and selling firms, whether they are manufacturers, distributors, retailers, or service providers. An obvious possibility is that fewer people will be needed to perform buying and selling tasks. Will there be massive reductions in field sales forces, purchasing departments, branch banks, insurance agencies, travel agencies, and elsewhere? Or will people be reassigned to other tasks? Will new skills be required, and if so, how can people be trained for them?

The use of marketing decision support systems (DSS) such as those discussed in Chapters 5, 6, and 7 may also lead to organizational changes. Charles Lillis and Bonnie McIvor, in Chapter 5, cite an example in which a DSS was used to coordinate the marketing of systems involving products from several autonomous departments of the General Electric Company. The DSS acted, in effect, as a proxy for a centralized marketing unit. Will developments of this kind lead, eventually, to greater centralization of line authority? If so, how will this affect performance measurement and compensation systems?

Multinational Marketing

The prospect of reaching multinational audiences via satellite television transmission could provide an additional incentive for standardizing brand names, packaging, and advertising—at least within Europe. In Chapter 9, Boris Wilenkin points out the rather considerable obstacles that still remain in the way of such a development. But in spite of the obstacles, the possibilities are intriguing and some companies will no doubt experiment with new approaches. In some cases, the advent of the so-called new media may even be used as a pretext for persuading managers of autonomous subsidiaries to participate in uniform marketing programs.[11] Even in these cases, the longstanding issues of standardization versus country-specific marketing strategies in multinational firms must still be resolved. Managers must balance the economies of standardization against the "fine tuning" of localized approaches. In the 1990s, it seems likely that the widely discussed successes of Japanese companies in many industries, together with the capabilities offered by new information and communication technology, will stimulate greater standardization.

Marketing the New Systems

In addition to exploring the effects of new electronic systems on marketing in general, participants in the colloquium discussed issues related to the marketing of the systems themselves. Major innovations have always led to significant shifts in distribution systems, methods of selling and advertising, and other aspects of marketing. For example, the development of a mass market for automobiles in the 1920s entailed the creation of an entirely new form of retail distribution (the franchised dealer system), the first widespread use of installment credit, and the concept of annual model changes. What kinds of changes in marketing institutions and practices will evolve to accommodate the mass adoption of new electronic systems?

John Quelch and George Yip, in Chapter 16, explore the kinds of cooperative, multifirm marketing arrangements that they believe will be needed for videotex systems. Will other information and communications systems require similar "cooperative marketing"? What are the key elements of such cooperative arrangements? What can be learned about them by studying similar systems in other industries, such as construction and defense contracting?

The companies that market information and communications products and services are, for the most part, "high-tech" organizations. As such, they do not appear to conform very well to the principles of business strategy that have been developed during the 1970s for more traditional industries. Research might, therefore, be usefully directed to the nature of competitive strategies in high-technology industries. John Cady, in Chapter 15, suggests one approach to this subject: a typology of situations based on the two dimensions of technological maturity and user familiarity with an industry's products. This classification scheme is, however, untested. Does it, in fact, provide useful insights? One participant in the colloquium, Paul Strassman, was critical of Cady's approach and pointed to various other factors that he considered more important in particular situations. Can a better strategic classification scheme be developed, or must each situation be treated separately? Students of "strategic marketing" would do well to explore these questions in the years ahead.

Identifying Lead Users

Eric von Hippel, in Chapter 17, discusses the concept of lead users. He envisions the possibility of substantial improvements in developing new products or services, and in evaluating their market potential, by focusing marketing research on users whose needs and product uses emerge earlier than those of the market as a whole. Von Hippel cites examples of past industrial product innovations to demonstrate that many of them originated with users rather than with producers. In the same way, he suggests, the capabilities of new information and communication systems may be determined more by the creative efforts of users than by the product development activities of system producers.

If marketers can identify lead users accurately, there is no doubt that this approach holds great promise. But how can true lead users be distinguished from "false leaders"? For example, the mere fact that a small subset of personal computer owners uses them for electronic mail does not necessarily indicate that the majority of owners will eventually adopt this application. Further research on the characteristics of lead users would clearly be helpful.

The Economics of Information

Perhaps the most complex topic on which research is needed is one mentioned by Stephan Haeckel in Chapter 18. We need, he says, a new kind of economics to understand the value of information itself. Users of the new systems, Haeckel reminds us, do not buy computers, PABXs, LANs, or software for their own sake. They buy, instead, the *results* that these products and services enable them to achieve—and these results are expressed in terms of some-one having more or better information, more rapidly and perhaps at lower cost, than would otherwise be possible. How can we assess the value of various types of information in particular situations? Must each case be dealt with individually, or can a more general approach be developed?

The concept of a new economics of information may have some relevance for the issues raised by Mary Gardiner Jones in Chapter 12. She points out the difficulty of dealing with information as if it were just another product, like coal or plywood. Perhaps a new way of conceptualizing information would help to guide public policy makers, in addition to providing a needed framework for private decisions about the purchase and sale of information products, services, and systems.

Concluding Remarks

The issues posed by the adoption of new information and com-munication systems in marketing are numerous and far-reaching. Marketing practice will change in many ways. Probably the most important ones are those that we cannot foresee at all; creative combinations of technology with other elements will no doubt be used to transform some businesses completely.

As practice changes, so too will marketing theory. As John Hauser suggests in Chapter 20, we may be on the threshold of a revolution in theory. The mass of information that *can* be provided by the new electronic systems might provide scholars with re-sources comparable to the astronomical observations that Tycho Brahe so patiently compiled in the sixteenth century. But, as Hauser reminds us, it is not enough just to be able to make numer-ous, detailed, and accurate measurements. Theory is needed in order to determine *what* should be measured. As Frank Bass put it in the discussion at the colloquium: "The way science progresses is through the interaction of theory and data. . . . The new information and communication technologies have the potential for us to have data and theory interact to a much greater extent than in the past."[12]

There is a challenge, then, for students of marketing to deter-mine what information should be collected by the new systems and to use the information creatively to develop and test general propo-sitions. What kinds of propositions? Theodore Levitt, in Chapter 21, suggests one criterion for selecting areas of research: that of relevance to practitioners. He calls for a new beginning in the relationship between "the academy" and the "real world." On this point there was considerable agreement among the academics and the practitioners who attended the colloquium. The new technologies may make many things possible, but to use them effectively will require cooperation and mutual respect among marketing scholars and practicing managers. In this respect, the challenge and the opportunity presented by the new technologies are the same as those faced by business education in 1908, when the Harvard Business School was founded.

PART ONE

Sales and Distribution Systems

CHAPTER 2

The Role of Information and Communications Technology in Industrial Distribution

E. Raymond Corey
Harvard Business School

Typically, industrial products are distributed through a mix of manufacturer-direct-to-user systems and manufacturer-through-intermediaries-to-user channels. Intermediaries may include industrial distributors (wholesalers), jobbers, and agents. Usually, manufacturers have gone direct to user-customers for products in the early phase of market development that require technical selling, for "big ticket" capital equipment, and for large quantities of raw materials, component parts, and expendable items used in the production process. Furthermore, they tend to deal directly with large accounts and with medium-sized customers in geographically concentrated market areas.

Intermediaries have taken on the smaller accounts in less concentrated areas. They also serve usefully as conduits for a wide range of expendable supplies, components, materials, and lower-priced equipment items sold in small amounts. Their function, as Chandler has described it, has been to coordinate "the flow of . . . finished goods from a great number of individual producers to an even larger number of individual consumers."[1] Intermediaries typically buy in carload and truckload quantities and in large lots and sell in bags, drums, less-than-carload (LTL) amounts, or simply a few units. In today's parlance their primary function is to "break bulk." Their numerous product lines, far broader, typically, than any one of their supplier's lines, enable them to achieve scale economies in serving relatively small users that are not possible for most producers. Hence intermediaries are able to supply the vast and fragmented American industrial market at transaction costs significantly lower than the manufacturers who use their services. By buying frequently in small quantities from local distributors many user-customers can reduce their own inventories of materials, parts, and supplies. In addition they can simplify their buying routines by patronizing a limited number of sources. Finally, many industrial customers value their personal relationships with the local wholesaler and his or her representatives.

The vast majority of intermediaries operate locally; there has been no economic advantage in expanding operations beyond the boundaries of the county or the state. Typically, wholesalers, agents, and jobbers are small businesses. Data from the 1977 census on the number of establishments, average revenues, and average number of employees for merchant wholesalers, for example, in nine Standard Industrial Classification (SIC) categories are listed in Table 2.1.

As in so many areas of industrial activity, however, the tides of change in industrial distribution are gathering force. One can see in the making a significant reshaping in America of those systems that

TABLE 2.1 Merchant Wholesalers, Selected Types of Industrial Distribution Businesses, 1977

Sic Code	Type of Business	No. of Establishments	Average Sales per Establishment	Average No. of Employees per Establishment
503	Lumber	12,681	$2,175,132	11
505	Metals, minerals	6,584	4,988,920	16.21
506	Electrical goods	17,109	1,773,950	11.35
507	Hardware, plumbing, and heating equipment	15,221	1,307,550	10.86
5083	Farm and garden machinery equipment	13,567	1,113,670	9.26
5084	Industrial machinery and equipment	13,441	1,555,780	9.64
5085	Industrial supplies	9,896	1,331,060	11.17
511	Paper and paper products	8,995	1,669,330	12.70
516	Chemicals and allied products	5,987	1,661,380	8.84
	Total	103,481		

Source: U.S. Bureau of the Census, *Census of Business, 1967,* vol. 4; *Wholesale Trade-Area Statistics* (Washington, D.C.: Government Printing Office, 1970), Table 2; *1977 Census of Wholesale Trade,* vol. 2; *Geographic Area Statistics* (Washington, D.C.: Government Printing Office, 1979), Table 1.

take goods and services from producer to industrial user. Increasing shares of many markets for industrial products will be captured by intermediaries between the manufacturer and the consumer. Large national wholesaling organizations will grow dramatically to take substantially greater shares of distributor-served markets. Many will expand by offering value-added services not traditionally part of the distributive function. Some will grow by acquisitions, and some will grow by integrating backward into manufacturing.

In the process, new lines will be drawn, based primarily on transaction cost differences, between the marketing functions performed by distributors and manufacturers. It is likely, too, that small, local distributing organizations will decline in number and in relative importance. And, finally, changes in the systems for serving industrial customers will mean changes in the way those customers buy. These things are not difficult to see; they are happening now.

To further our understanding of the nature and extent of the change and of its underlying causes, let us examine five large industrial distribution businesses in four companies:

McKesson Corporation
McKesson Drug Company (MDC)
McKesson Chemical Company (MCC)

General Electric
General Electric Supply Company (GESCO)

Arrow Electronics
Arrow Electronics Distribution Division (AEDD)

American Hospital Supply Corporation
American Hospital Supply Division (AHSD)

Each of these distributors operates nationally. Three of them—the two McKesson businesses and American Hospital Supply Division—are the largest in their industries in sales revenues; the remaining two are the second largest in their respective fields. Each has used computerized data links effectively in its internal operations and in its interactions with both suppliers and customers. With one exception, each has gained significantly in market share in the last five years, and at the same time each has made significant gains in sales and earnings in a period of generally low economic activity. Each is a division of a larger corporate entity. Table 2.2 details essential facts about these five businesses.

In strict terms, one business, McKesson Drug Company, may not be classed as industrial but is engaged, rather, in consumer goods marketing. MDC is included here because certain important points

TABLE 2.2 Salient Data on Product Lines, Customer Bases, Supply Sources, and Stocking Locations for Five National Distributors ($ in millions)

	Product Lines	1982 Sales	Approx. No. of Items in Product Line	Customers	Approx. No. of Suppliers	No. of Distribution Centers
American Hospital Supply	Patient and surgical care products (e.g., intravenous solutions, surgical gowns, gloves, syringes, suction tubing, therapeutic devices)	na	50,000	Hospitals	2,000	57
Arrow Electronics	Commercial semiconductors, electromechanical and passive components, military semiconductors and connectors, computers and computer-related products	$348	230,000 items (130 product types)	OEMs	80	33
GESCO	Lighting, lamps, control and distribution equipment, motors, generators, transformers, wire and cable, renewal parts	$900 (approx.)	500,000 (80,000 product types)	Contractors, utilities, industrial and commercial firms	500	155
McKesson Chemical	Industrial chemicals (e.g., solvents, food and pharmaceutical chemicals)	$628	1,500	45,000 industrial firms	250	63
McKesson Drug	Pharmaceuticals, health and beauty aids and sundries	$1.9	50,000	14,000 retail drugstores and mass merchandisers, 2,000 hospitals	2,500	56

Source: Company data.

of distinction as well as similarities may be drawn between it and the other four businesses.

The purpose of this study is, first, to understand each company's strategy and the role of computerized data links in its implementation. A second objective is to understand the effects of computerization, in the context of other external factors, on (1) structure and competition in the distributor-served market segment and (2) distributor-manufacturer relationships. A third purpose is to relate the observed developments to current theories of distribution.

Elements of Strategy and Implementation

Although they represent five different industries, the five businesses in this study have been successful by pursuing similar strategies. First, each has achieved national market coverage, or close to it. Second, each offers broad product lines as well as value-added services to its customers. Third, all count as a key success factor their superior performance in product availability and rapid delivery. Their organization and control systems are oriented toward achieving efficiencies in operating costs and in the use of working capital. Fourth, each has stressed in its promotional programs the value-added services and their ability to minimize customer costs of ordering and carrying inventories. Individually, they spend little on advertising, and they do not promote individual brands except when their suppliers provide special incentives to do so. The execution of these strategies has depended crucially on data processing and communication systems that facilitate ordering and delivery and provide a steady flow of information internally, as well as between distributors and customers, which is useful for accounting, pricing, and inventory control. Let us consider each element more closely.

National market coverage has been a key strength in serving large customer accounts at which procurement is centralized and use is decentralized. In GESCO's case, for example, 70 percent of its industrial segment sales volume comes from the *Fortune* 1000 companies. Some of the largest of these accounts purchase under national agreements that cover corporatewide requirements for a specified list of products at prices that are negotiated annually. GESCO's ability to serve these accounts at multiple locations is a key element in its competitive strength in this large and important market segment.

A broad product line addresses the needs of those customers whose operations require a steady flow of large numbers of items of small unit value that, in total, amount to a high percentage of customers' costs of goods sold. Being able to supply the bulk of their requirements from a single source considerably simplifies purchasing, ordering, and delivery routines. The residential and nonresidential contractors who account for almost half of GESCO's business, for example, place orders almost daily for next-day, to-the-job delivery and typically maintain little or no inventories. Having full product lines is also important in serving intermittent needs. Often these requirements are satisfied through searching local suppliers and buying from the first source to have the item in stock. Thus to serve their markets, American Hospital Supply Division and McKesson Drug each include between fifty thousand and seventy thousand items in their lines (see Table 2.2). McKesson Drug's line covers an estimated 65 percent of what the retail druggist sells. Arrow Electronics Distribution Division lists 230,000 items, grouped into 130 product types.

By guaranteeing product availability and rapid delivery, especially for "flow stock," the intermediaries can minimize their and their customers' inventories. Being assured of supply of flow stock is of prime importance to buyers, who are measured first and foremost by whether or not they avoid work stoppages because of a lack of production materials. This concern is an important psychological element in buyer behavior. Thus, the distributor sells not only working capital savings but also peace of mind. To the extent that customers can rely on supplier inventories, distributors improve their own return on investment (ROI) by reducing their working stocks of parts, materials, and supplies. Hence, consistent performance in on-time, from-stock deliveries becomes a highly significant element of competitive advantage in the case of all five distribution businesses, because it increases the user-customer's comfort level in relying on local distributor stocks.

Caught between the need, on the one hand, to optimize delivery performance and, on the other, to optimize their own stock turnover, successful distributors have tended to provide large stocks of high-turnover items on a local basis and to provide on a regional level stocks of lower-turnover items. Orders that cannot be filled from the branch nearest to the customer are then supplied from regional stocking points. Of the fifty thousand items in the AHSD product line, the average branch stocked twenty-five hundred, another two thousand were carried at each of seven locations serving the regions, and the remainder were held at a single stocking point serving all regions. Items were classified into the three stocking categories according to the level of demand and the item's criticality for hospital operations. The AHSD system performed at a 95 percent fulfillment ratio: That is, 95 percent of line items ordered were delivered on the designated day of the week on which each hospital received its delivery from AHSD, provided the order was received by noon of the preceding day.

A second way of optimizing inventory investments is to rely on the distributor's suppliers to ship some items directly from their stocks. Usually these are items of relatively high unit value, such as capital equipment, or large quantities of low unit value goods for which the customer has placed an individual order. McKesson Chemical, on average, fills 80 percent of its orders from stock; 20 percent are shipped directly from manufacturers' stocks. In serving the contractor market, GESCO fills from stock about 95 percent of its orders from the residential construction market, but only 50 percent of orders received from nonresidential contractors. The remainder is shipped directly from GE product departments and GESCO's outside suppliers. The difference between the two segments is the size of the orders placed and the type of products purchased. Nonresidential contractors buy in significantly larger quantities, and often buy for installation large pieces of electrical equipment not used in residential construction.

The planned deployment of inventories at local and regional stocking points and in vendors' warehouses has achieved significant savings in working capital and inventory carrying costs. In addition, the large national distributors have reduced inventory-to-sales ratios without impairing on-time order fulfillment in two other ways. If an order is received for an out-of-stock item, a computerized data base provides immediate information on what items in stock are direct substitutes and may be used, if the customer wishes, to fill the order. Finally, some distributors—American Hospital Supply Division is one—are working actively with customers on standardization programs. By getting hospitals to reduce the number of different specifications they require, AHSD can meet their needs economically from a reduced list of stock-keeping units.

Promotional programs by the distributors seldom focus on individual brands except in connection with special campaigns sponsored and funded by the vendor. Instead, the five distributors covered in this study concentrate in their promotional efforts on the cost-saving advantages they can offer their customers and on improving customer cost containment programs. American Hospital Supply, for example, devoted extensive resources and considerable effort to conducting customer seminars emphasizing hospital supply management. It has sponsored five two-day conferences each year for the past eleven years to discuss such topics as logistics management, hospital productivity, legal aspects of purchasing, new developments in health care legislation, and quality assurance. With eighty-five to one hundred purchasing managers, department administrators, and hospital finance and control managers attending each seminar, total attendance has reached about three thousand representatives of AHSD accounts. A corporate publication, *Password,* also stressed hospital cost containment and provided testimonials on the benefits of using the AHSD automated order entry and fulfillment system.

The Use of Computerized Information Systems

The essential element in strategy implementation for these five businesses is the use of internal computerized information systems and external (distributor-customer) data links. The individual product lines, markets, and customers' buying behavior, however, significantly shape the way in which data systems can be integrated into buyer-seller relationships and the strategic opportunities that exist for using data links as a marketing tool.

All five businesses have developed internal data systems that give inside salespeople, buyers, and operating managers immediate access to the following information by item:

- in-stock availability by stock location;
- amounts on order from suppliers and scheduled shipment dates;
- items that can be substituted for those that are out of stock;
- prices by quantity levels (and in some systems the price at which the last sale was made); and
- sales volume, by branch, for each month in the preceding twelve months.

These systems may also be used to obtain the following information by customer:

- volume of purchases by item each month for the preceding twelve months;
- items on order and promised shipment dates; and
- accounts receivable and payment record in terms of average days outstanding.

The information provided internally by computer has made possible dramatic reductions in transaction costs. McKesson Drug reports an increase of more than 50 percent in stock turns. Through inventory networking, the company has reduced the number of its distribution centers (stocking points) from ninety-two in 1975 to fifty-six in 1983, without any deterioration in delivery performance. A cadre of 250 telephone sales clerks who took orders and typed up purchase forms eight years ago has virtually been eliminated. In addition 13 buyers at a central location have replaced the 160 located at the ninety-two distribution centers in 1975. Further, McKesson Drug's order fulfillment ratio stands at a remarkable 96 percent, that is, only 4 percent of the dollar value of orders received is out of stock. Finally, because of its ability to provide overnight delivery and thereby to reduce its customers' inventory levels, McKesson Drug has been able to reduce customer payment terms from the conventional thirty days to fifteen days. The result has been a marked reduction in its working capital requirements.

McKesson Drug provides the most dramatic example of the use of internal computerized information systems to reduce transaction costs. To lesser degrees, each of the other four businesses has achieved significant reductions in the same categories. Four of the five businesses (McKesson Chemical is the exception) have developed round-the-clock automatic order entry systems by which orders may be entered at the customer's location, received at a distribution data center, processed automatically, and invoiced without human intervention. The customer can determine the supplier's in-stock position on any item the latter has committed to stock for the customer, the prenegotiated price, as well as prices and locations of substitutable items.

The foundation of GESCO's Sentry program, for example, is a systems contract whereby GESCO is committed to stock, for a specified time, agreed-upon quantities of regularly purchased items at prenegotiated prices. When the buyer is ready to order, he or she can use different computer access devices ranging from a simple transaction telephone to a CRT terminal with an attached printer. After the buyer identifies himself or herself, the computer asks a series of questions such as billing and shipping addresses, customer and order references, and desired shipping mode and date. The buyer then itemizes the order and the computer then supplies the order's total value, if a video screen or printer is available. If the ordered quantity is not available from the local warehouse, XPD (Expedite), an internal computerized information system, is used to locate supplies in other warehouses in the area or to suggest substitutable products.

At McKesson Drug, the Economost and Econotone services use

an electronic device to enter bar code scan information from shelf labels for items that need to be restocked. The clerk in the retail store transmits an order automatically over telephone lines at a speed of six hundred items per minute. The order is received and processed in McKesson's Data Center, transmitted to the McKesson distribution center nearest the customer, filled, and delivered the following day. Economost order filling, billing, and packing in the distribution center are organized by merchandise category in order to conform to the store's shelf-stocking plan for easy check-in and stocking. Item price stickers using customer-supplier formulas are provided for prescription and over-the-counter products.

The number of customers linked by computer to their distributor sources varies considerably. At McKesson Drug about 95 percent in dollar value of all orders received are processed through its Economost system. GESCO has 250 of its larger accounts on its Sentry system; Arrow has several dozen. The variation in coverage reflects differences in the amount of sales volume per month per account. Each company has set a rough cutoff point for justifying the installation of CRT terminals and other access devices and for establishing and maintaining individual account data bases. McKesson's management estimates that it needs to realize, as a general rule of thumb, a minimum of $2,000 a month per account to support computerized selling and servicing costs. GESCO requires $4,000 a month. Arrow expects $1 million in annual sales volume, but its system requires that a full-time Arrow-employed operator be located on the customer's premises. If that were not the case, the minimum annual sales volume, according to Arrow management, might drop to $300,000.

Another consideration is the number of items the customer may potentially buy from the distributor. The greater the *number* of items, regardless of the dollar value per item, the greater the advantage of computerized order entry systems over telephone ordering. An additional factor to be considered is the customers' readiness to introduce computerized order entry routines into their own operations. The introduction of these routines changes operating and control procedures, significantly reduces the human relations element in the buyer-seller relationship, and overall creates a need for change in the culture of a customer's organization.

It was noted earlier that while McKesson Chemical, the largest distributor in its field, had developed effective internal data systems for managing its inventory and purchasing routines, it had not attempted to develop data links with individual customers comparable to those found at McKesson Drug, Arrow, GESCO, and American Hospital Supply. Simply stated, the strategic opportunities for doing so are not the same. McKesson Chemical's customers buy small amounts intermittently and order only one or a few items at a time. Further, their purchases of the kinds of chemicals McKesson sells typically represent only a minor part of their total cost of goods sold. These order and use patterns are easily handled through personal selling and telephone ordering. They would hardly justify extensive investments in computerized customer order entry systems.

Significant differences in strategic opportunities also exist among the five businesses with regard to the nature, extent, and usefulness of information services they can provide their customers. Again, McKesson Drug and American Hospital Supply are at one end of the spectrum; Arrow and McKesson Chemical are at the other end, with GESCO in the middle.

For McKesson Drug and American Hospital Supply, the volume of business they do with each customer may represent a very significant element of operating cost; orders are recurring and are placed for large numbers of items often in small quantities. Consequently periodic reports on an individual customer's purchases by item and on ordering patterns may be immensely useful to the customer for internal accounting purposes, for regulating inventory levels, and for improving purchasing efficiency.

Aggregated data on product demand levels by geographic area are useful to the customer also for planning purposes. Not surprisingly, these data services can be supplemented by others using information generated both from the distributor's data base and from his or her knowledge of the industry and of the customer's business. Thus McKesson Drug offers the following services on a fee basis:

- Econoprice—a newly introduced program that provides retail pharmacies with continually updated retail price labels for various dispensed quantities of prescription items based on the retailer's pricing formula.
- Econocharge—a computerized accounts receivable program that enables pharmacists to offer their preferred customers the convenience of a store charge account.
- Econoclaim—a computerized service, currently being tested, that enables retail pharmacists to process more rapidly third-party claims for prescription drugs.
- Econoplan—a guide to the retailer on shelf space management.
- Econofiche—a microfiche service that provides updates on price and product information, drug interaction, Medicaid numbers, product warranties, and more.

In addition to its ASAP (Analytical Systems Automated Purchasing) for order entry, American Hospital Supply offers other services.

- ADMIS (American Department Management Information System) is a microcomputer and software package for determining the hospital's actual cost of supplies, labor, and time for delivering a service or performing a medical or surgical procedure.
- ACLAIM provides comparable cost data for performing laboratory tests.
- STRAPCOE (Strategic Planning in a Competitive Environment) provides forecasts of the numbers of medical procedures that may be performed and medical conditions that may be diagnosed within a hospital's service area in selected future years.
- AHSECO is a hospital consulting service for outfitting laboratory operating rooms and other functional spaces and for installing equipment and built-in furniture.

Like McKesson Drug and American Hospital Supply, GESCO also provides customer-specific information. A Sentry customer receives monthly reports by item, showing quantities ordered, prices, number of times each item was ordered, and amounts delivered to each customer location or job site. Another report compares these data with year-ago purchases for use in performance reviews and forecasting.

McKesson Chemical, too, has moved to offer services to its customers based on its expertise in the transporting, use, and disposal of chemical substances. McKesson Environmental Services is a newly organized technical consulting organization that performs environmental audits and diagnostic and monitoring services, and assists clients in meeting their regulatory and compliance requirements. McKesson Envirosystems Company recycles solvent waste streams from industrial customers and then markets the refined products, primarily through McKesson Chemical.

These value-added services generate added revenues. But they are especially significant for (1) building account relationships for the sale of products and maximizing account share, (2) motivating a customer to maximize purchases from its leading wholesale supplier as a way of building a relevant, customer-specific operating data base, (3) preserving account stability by raising switching costs, the costs that would be incurred by throwing out one supplier's computerized system and replacing it with another, and (4) minimizing the importance of personal relationships in sales transactions, thus reducing the risk of losing an account if a field sales representative leaves to join a competing firm.

Effects of Computerization on the Distribution Industry

In the case of all but one of the five industries represented by the supply businesses discussed above, the distributor-served segment of the market has grown more rapidly than has the industry as a whole (see Table 2.3).[2]

The growth of the distributor-served market segment may be attributed to several factors. First, the escalating cost of personal selling has tended to limit manufacturers to serving directly only the large customers.[3] A manager at McKesson Chemical estimated that chemical manufacturers find it uneconomical to serve accounts that yield less than $100,000 in sales annually. McKesson Chemical has forty-five thousand accounts, many of which provide annual sales in the range of $1,000 to $2,000,000. An Arrow Electronics manager asserted:

> Carrying the lines of a large number of manufacturers, electronic distributors can economically serve the 100,000 small-to-medium size customers to whom credit, prompt delivery and assurance of supply are important. Sure those people, too, would like to have a direct relationship with the manufacturer but can't wait three months for delivery. And the manufacturers really aren't set up to do credit checks on small companies, to make calls for just a few units each of a short list of items, and provide technical service. In fact most electronics and computer manufacturers probably sell direct to no more than a thousand accounts.[4]

The growth in the distributor-served segment of the electronics market in the past decade is quite probably related partly to the

TABLE 2.3 Distributor-Served Market Segment as a Percent of Total Market

Electronics	15%	(1972)	22%	(1982)
Ethical drugs	45	(1973)	57	(1980)
Hospital supplies	62	(1972)	40	(1982)
Electrical components and equipment	30	(1972)	50	(1982)
Chemicals	15	(1972)	22	(1982)

Source: Estimates by executives of the firms interviewed by the author.

proliferation of small- and medium-sized users of these components and to the rising costs of reaching these customers directly. Distributors carrying the lines of many manufacturers and selling to large numbers of small customers are able to achieve inventory cost efficiencies that manufacturers could not realize in serving this market. This capability is significantly enhanced by the use of internal and distributor-customer computerized data systems.

Another factor limiting the relative growth of the direct-served market segment has been a growing concern in industry about the rising costs of carrying inventories. A prime cause is the significant increase in interest rates in the 1970s. This put pressure on industry to minimize inventory investments at all levels—manufacturer, distributor, and user-customers.

The wide publicity given to the Japanese *kanban*, or just-in-time, system of managing flows of materials and parts from suppliers to end product manufacturers has also heightened awareness of the competitive significance of managing product flows efficiently. Furthermore, the distribution businesses studied here have benefited by emphasizing the bottom-line profits to be gained by controlling inventories. This has been a central theme in their promotional programs. American Hospital Supply maintains that "for every dollar spent on the price of a supply, another dollar is spent by the hospital on the logistics management process—ordering, holding inventory, distribution, revenue collection and product consumption. Together these costs represent fully 40 percent of the total hospital nonlabor budget."

Hospitals are particularly sensitive to the issue of escalating costs. Health care costs have risen from less than 6 percent of the gross national product in 1965 to nearly 10 percent, or about $285 billion, in 1981. Hospital management sensitivities to rising costs have been further heightened by the enactment of federal legislation under which hospitals will be reimbursed under Medicare and Medicaid programs on a flat-fee basis for procedures in 467 "diagnostic-related groups" (DRGs). Until this change, reimbursements to the hospitals were made retrospectively in amounts based on their costs. AHSD's promotional programs, therefore, respond to an urgent need in the market it serves.

One may safely surmise that the growing importance of distributors' roles and their increasing participation in industrial markets is due to changes in the transaction cost structures of manufacturers compared to distributors. This has come about because of such external factors as rising personnel costs and rising interest rates. Further, the development of computerized customer-distributor data links and internal information systems has made possible transaction cost economies of wholesaling that have tended to increase the advantages to manufacturers and user-customers of selling through these channels of distribution.

At the same time that the distributor-served segments of industrial markets have been growing, the market shares of the largest distributors, in some instances, have also been growing. The ten largest electronic components distributors (Arrow is the second largest) increased their combined share of the distributor-served segment of that market from 37 percent in 1972 to 55 percent in 1982. Approximately 350 other electronics distributors share the remaining 45 percent. In the case of the hospital supply industry, the one national distributor (American Hospital Supply) and five large regional distributors have increased their combined share of the distributor-served segment of the market from 23 percent in 1972 to 55 percent in 1982. The remaining 45 percent is accounted for by 484 local distributors. The sales of American Hospital Supply, the leading company, grew fivefold from 1972 to 1983.

Acquisition has been an important element in the growth of the leading firms and has been a way to achieve economies of scale in inventory management, selling costs, purchasing, and providing value-added information services to customers. In addition, by "going national" the leaders are able to negotiate with and serve more effectively their large national accounts at multiple receiving locations.

The use of computerized information systems has in effect made it more difficult for small, local distributors to compete. According to a McKesson Drug manager:

> It takes as much for a one-warehouse wholesaler to load a price change into the system as it takes for us to put it into the computer for 56 distribution centers. We can do centralized purchasing; we can invest in computerization, in automated warehouses and we can use mathematical models for order filling and delivery. We can carry a wider range of products. Also over a period of time we have been able through computerization to accelerate the billing time, reduce inventories at the retail level and go from 30-day to 15-day terms for accounts receivable. The resulting ROI increase gets passed on to our customers through lower prices.

The Impact of Computerization on Distributor-Manufacturer Relations

The use of computerized information systems in industrial distribution, as well as the growth of the large nationals and superregionals, significantly affects the relative bargaining positions of distributors and manufacturers. The more a distributor can get his customers to standardize, the larger the percentage of his supplier's business he represents, the greater his geographic coverage, clearly the more bargaining power he has. On the other side, the more the manufacturer represents of any one distributor's total gross margin dollars, the more its products are differentiated, have high brand identity, and require highly technical selling, the more active it is in creating user demand, then the greater the power of the manufacturer. Another factor is the use of multiple, competing channels systems as opposed to exclusive representation in each geographic market area. To be completely dependent on one distributor in a market area is to allow that distributor to control the user accounts in the area and the volume of business they represent as a bargaining lever.

The steady growth of the large nationals, however, and their access to user market information of value to themselves and their suppliers tends to give them an advantage in negotiating with their manufacturing sources. Bargaining takes place on a range of subjects. First, while manufacturers seldom give exclusives and, by the same token, distributors typically carry competing lines, this may become an issue: "One of our major competitors," remarked an Arrow Electronics manager, "took on the TI [Texas Instruments] line, and the next day National Semiconductor and Motorola took their lines away from them."

Second, the distributors and manufacturers will negotiate territorial franchises. According to one manager, "Some suppliers franchise us every place we do business; some franchise area by area. One supplier with whom we do $9 million in business annually refuses to franchise us in a certain area; it's a running battle; we threaten to drop their line; they say they don't believe it." Third, the manufacturers will attempt to keep the distributor "price competitive" in the marketplace. While suppliers will typically lower prices in any geographic market to "meet the equally low price of a competitor," they tend to resist strongly the pressures to grant concessions to large distributors because of the sales they "control" in the customer market.

Fourth, distributors will seek the supplier's support in technical selling, salesperson training, product promotion, missionary support, and providing assistance in closing the order. Fifth, manufacturers and distributors will negotiate a definition of "adequate" amounts of back-up stock in the manufacturer's warehouses and at the distributor's stocking points; this is seldom an objective, mutually agreed-upon judgment. Sixth, distributors will be involved in vendor product quality problems in the field and in improving quality at the factory. Seventh, both sides will participate in evaluating the adequacy of the distributor's selling effort, service levels, and promotional support for the manufacturer's products. Eighth, they will also negotiate the question of the manufacturer's selling direct to accounts the distributor also serves and vice versa.

It is to be expected that the large nationals growing through acquisitions and their own superior management skills will increasingly force manufacturers to franchise them nationally, although not without resistance. The manufacturer fears declining sales volume in areas and accounts served by the smaller regional and local distributors as these intermediaries become competitively weaker. Similarly, through centralizing purchasing, commanding large market shares, and using their buying power as leverage, the nationals are likely to exert increasing pressure on the prices of suppliers.

It is unclear where the line will be drawn between distributor-served and manufacturer-direct-served market. That will clearly be a function of:

- the costs of personal selling;
- the fragmented or concentrated nature of the market;
- the value to customers of the information services that distributors may now provide;
- the technical maturity of the product;
- order size, dollar value per item, and order frequency;
- the extent to which distributors can supply the technical product-support and application services the manufacturer has traditionally provided; and
- the extent to which the large nationals can maneuver their suppliers into serving all but the very largest customers through distributors.

The Relevance of Theory

In understanding the dramatic growth of national industrial distribution organizations, including the underlying causes for this phenomenon and its impact on supplier and customer relations, it is helpful to refer to the relevant theory from the fields of economics, history, political science, and organizational behavior. A systematic survey of the theory and its relation to the empirical observations reported above is beyond the scope of this paper. Instead reference will be made here to four prominent theorists, to suggest that, in general, the empirical observations are consistent with their positions. In addition, I will note that the field studies suggest some extensions to current theory. My reference points are Alfred Chandler, business historian; Oliver Williamson, theoretical economist; Louis Stern, political economist; and Torger Reve, organizational behaviorist.

Alfred D. Chandler, Jr.

Describing the rise of mass distribution in the United States, Alfred Chandler attributes this important development to the speed and regularity of stock flows made possible by the coming of the railroads and telegraph. The new modes of transportation and communication reduced the costs of distribution and permitted marked improvements in stock turns, thus lowering inventory-to-sales ratios at all levels of manufacture, distribution, and use. "Economies of scale in distribution," Chandler notes, "were not those of size but of speed."[5] The role of the distributor, or mass merchandiser, was to coordinate the flow of products from a large number of individual producers to an even greater number of users.

The development of computer-based information systems for use in distribution simply permits the flow of goods to occur at even higher speeds, and with higher levels of efficiency in the deployment of inventories and improvements in inventory-to-sales ratios. A significant contribution to improved efficiencies in the coordination of product flows from producer to user has been the generation of unprecedented amounts of useful control information. Information feedback from users to wholesalers to manufacturers on the timing and level of product demand has made possible a degree of precision in adjusting production to use that could never before be achieved. Further, such information has revealed important opportunities for economizing on ordering behavior, again leading to transaction economies.

Chandler has recently noted:

> Thus, the economic advantage of a wholesaler or other marketing intermediary is that, by handling a number of related lines for a number of manufacturers, he can distribute the output of each at less expense than it would cost a single manufacturer to carry out the same function. Until the manufacturer's volume reaches a scale that would reduce unit costs of transporting, storing and distributing his products to the level of that achieved by the wholesaler through his economies of scope, the wholesaler has a cost advantage in the distribution of the product.[6]

On this point Scott Moss points out: "Provided that such a minimum efficient scale in transactions exists, the intermediary will have a cost advantage over his customers and suppliers only as long as the volume of transactions in which he engages comes closer to that scale than do the transactions volumes of his customers and suppliers."[7]

In this regard, the significance of the rise of the large national industrial distributors is that their use of computerized information systems and their national scope of operations permit scale economies never before possible. To the extent that these scale opportunities are more available to distributors than to manufacturers and customers, the distributor-served segment of the industrial goods market is likely to grow vis-à-vis the direct-served segment.

Furthermore, those intermediaries who move quickly to take advantage of new information technologies, and thereby to increase the scope of their geographic coverage and the range of their product lines and to achieve significant reductions in transactions costs, will significantly improve their competitive positions. Such gains are likely to depend on (1) the mastery of information system use in distributive operations, (2) the adaptation of organization structure to achieve greater centralization of decision making, and (3) the ability to attract or generate the capital to make the requisite investments.

Oliver Williamson

Oliver Williamson's thesis that "the modern corporation is mainly to be understood as the product of a series of organizational innovations that have had the purpose and effect of economizing on transaction costs" is also highly relevant.[8] Williamson has focused especially on transaction cost as the mediating variable in the choice between internalizing transactions within hierarchical organization structures or externalizing them through market mechanisms. Selling to user-customers through the firm's own field sales force and factory branches is an example of the former. Selling through such intermediaries as wholesalers, jobbers, and agents illustrates the latter. Thus, Williamson perceives firms and markets as alternative governance structures.

Williamson, like Chandler, sees transaction costs as being importantly affected by the transaction-specific investment that must be made in the sale of the product and in its movement to the market. Examples of transaction-specific investment would be (1) refrigerated cars and cold storage facilities for transporting and holding stocks of perishable products, (2) field repair facilities to provide after-sales service to buyers of electrical machinery, or office equipment, or trucks, and (3) technical expertise in selling the product, tailoring it to meet the buyer's needs, and assisting the buyer in its installation and use. Both Chandler and Williamson contend that the existence of the need for such transaction-specific investments leads to internalizing transactions, because market institutions typically do not find such investments attractive and do not make them.

Williamson identifies three types of asset specificity: *site specificity*, such as locating stocks for a particular customer near the point of use; *physical asset specificity*, such as production lines dedicated to making goods for a specific customer; and *human asset specificity*, such as the technical knowledge required to sell a product, adapt it to the customer's use, and train personnel.[9]

Clearly, current developments in industrial distribution are consistent with Williamson's constructs. Manufacturers have been limited in their ability to spread rising selling costs across broader product lines and rising sales volumes. At the same time there have been dramatic improvements in transaction cost efficiencies at the wholesale level. It is to be expected, therefore, that there will be a shift in the balance between market-mediated and firm-mediated transactions in favor of the former. And that in fact is what has happened. As noted earlier, in four of the five industries discussed, there has been a marked increase over the past decade in the distributor-served segment of the market.

The position taken by both Chandler and Williamson that transaction-specific investments tend to lead to forward integration (i.e., internalized or firm-mediated transactions) bears reexamination, however. In serving their markets, the large national distributors have, in fact, made transaction-specific investments, particularly in computers and terminals designed for and dedicated to individual accounts. Distributors have also reserved inventories for specific customers; nor is it uncommon for these intermediaries to place such stocks at the customer's use location. Further, there is evidence in the cases discussed here that distributors are finding it attractive to invest in the selling expertise required to market technical products.

What needs to be recognized is that certain kinds of transaction-specific investments may be made more usefully at the producer level, others at the wholesale level—and therefore will be relatively attractive to manufacturers or to distributors, as the case may be. Especially interesting is the situation, not uncommon, when some transaction-specific investments are more appropriate (and more attractive) at the distributor level and some at the manufacturer level for the same accounts or market segments. This might be the case when a manufacturer maintains the application engineering resources required to get industrial customers to adopt some highly technical product, while its distributors support the product in the field with specialized service facilities and spare parts availability. Such instances make it difficult to make clear distinctions between firm-mediated and market-mediated transactions and to claim that to the extent that asset-specific or transaction-specific investments are required, the tendency will be to internalize the transaction.

The above observations notwithstanding, the empirical evidence does, indeed, support the Williamson thesis that "where asset specificity is great, buyer and seller will make special efforts to design an exchange relationship that has good continuity properties."[10] This is exactly what is happening in distributor-user relationships in the case of those accounts in which there have been substantial investments in computerized data links.

Parenthetically, it may be observed that the importance of *information* as a transaction-specific asset suggests that it could usefully be identified as a separate category in the current three-part Williamson typology. He subsumes it now under "human assets." Information, however, is of such significance in achieving transaction cost economies, in buyer-seller relationships, and as an element of competitive strategy that to relegate it to the status of a subcategory is to deny its centrality in the explanation of modern distribution economics.

Finally, Williamson's focus on transaction cost as the mediating variable does not adequately recognize the complex interdependencies between producers and wholesalers. Here is where one must turn from economics to political science to understand how power relationships do in fact significantly affect which transactions the firm chooses to internalize within hierarchical organizations and which it leaves to market mechanisms.

Louis Stern and Torger Reve

Louis Stern and Torger Reve approach distribution theory from a political economy perspective. They view distribution channel relationships as interactive sets of major political and economic forces that affect the performance of the system collectively and the behavior of individual channel units. Two propositions put forth in their article "Distribution Channels as Political Economies: A Framework of Comparative Analysis" are of particular interest in connection with the present discussion. The first proposition is:

> The more centralized planning processes predominate, irrespective of the transactional form, the more efficient and effective the marketing channel for a product or service is likely to be.[11]

The second proposition is:

> In marketing channels in which market transactions are the predominant mode of exchange and in which power is centralized, centralized planning processes will emerge.[12]

These hypotheses are supported by the empirical evidence. Within the large national distributor organizations, one observes major centralization moves particularly in the scheduling of shipments, the management of inventories, and negotiations with suppliers. Such centralization is made possible through the existence and effective use of centralized data bases. Access to a centralized data base permits the maximum utilization of the firm's buying power in dealing with its suppliers. It facilitates the optimal deployment of inventory, and allows rapid response to sales trends in the marketplace. It makes possible precise measures of performance in such key areas as stock turns, inventory carrying and delivery costs, tactical pricing at the field level, and market shares by geographic area and, in some cases, by individual account. In brief, it permits centralized planning of strategy and operations.

One may also observe the efforts of distributors such as American Hospital Supply, McKesson Drug, and GESCO to extend and integrate their own planning with that of customers to optimize product flow efficiencies. Again, to the extent that large national distributors can provide meaningful and current market demand data to suppliers, they are likely, as well, to integrate suppliers in what may turn out to be planning systems directed from the distributor level and encompassing the flow of goods from production through distribution and into use.

Centralized planning managed at the distributor level is likely to emerge in particular in companies like GESCO and American Hospital Supply where increasing percentages of their sales are derived from self-manufactured products. By internalizing product flow transactions, these companies lay the groundwork for centralized planning. Further, they consolidate their positions as planners for the marketing system by working toward standardization of customers' requirements, maximizing their sales of generic as opposed to brand products, and buying from smaller producers. Each of these thrusts enhances a distributor's power to take over the system planning function vis-à-vis suppliers and customers.

If one combines the theoretical constructs of Williamson, Chandler, Stern, and Reve with empirical data, another hypothesis is suggested:

> The balance of power in the channel is likely to reside with those members making transaction-specific investments that yield benefits most valued by the customer.

The tremendous pressures on cost containment in hospitals, for example, lead to managements' placing a high value on procedures that will economize on the acquisition of supplies and on computerized information systems that contribute significantly to their ability to control costs. By making investments in computerized systems to serve these purposes, American Hospital Supply is able to increase its sales volume with each account, enhance its market share, and thereby gain in its strength to negotiate with its suppliers. It creates dependencies among its customers, which may be used to increase the extent to which AHSD's suppliers are dependent in turn on it. Further, the old adage "knowledge is power" applies: To the extent that AHSD obtains more information on hospital supply markets than its vendors have, it enjoys important negotiating advantages.

It may be further hypothesized:

> What elements of the transaction customers will value will change from one stage to another in the product life cycle and from one set of economic conditions to another.

In the early stages of product commercialization, especially for new products in such technical fields as electronics and drugs, customers are likely to place a high value on gaining product information. In these circumstances, investments in technically skilled sales forces are likely to pay high dividends for the manufacturer. In comparison, when the product reaches the maturity or "commodity" stage, customers will be inclined to value all those factors that are important for minimizing transaction costs—product availability, credit, efficient ordering, and fulfillment routines—as well as assurance of supply. The opportunities to make investments minimizing transaction costs are likely to be most available and most attractive to intermediaries—especially the larger ones—under the following three conditions:

- large product flows of small amounts of a large number of items from diverse manufacturing sources
- geographically dispersed markets
- high customer dependency—that is, when customers may rely on a limited number of sellers for their needs of purchased products.

These are the conditions under which investments in computerized systems linking buyer and seller may pay the highest dividends.

CHAPTER 3

Electronic Data Interchange in Selected Consumer Goods Industries: An Interorganizational Perspective

Louis W. Stern
Northwestern University

Patrick J. Kaufmann
Harvard Business School

For a marketing channel to achieve its performance potential, it must provide mechanisms whereby information can flow smoothly, rapidly, and accurately among its members. These mechanisms take a variety of forms. For example, in the communication processes associated with ordering, purchase orders may be mailed, sent by telex, telephoned, or picked up by salespeople. They may be written, oral, or electronic. Each type of transmission and medium of communication implies a different level of technology.

One of the most sophisticated means of interorganizational business communication currently in use is the electronic transmission of machine readable data. The term most commonly used to refer to this method is *electronic data interchange* (EDI).[1] This chapter will explore the reasons for EDI's development and its actual and potential effects on its users. Our concern is primarily with the nontechnical impact of EDI on the relationship between manufacturers and distributors in selected consumer goods industries. An interorganizational perspective is taken, focusing on the relationships between firms which utilize EDI communications systems.

There are two types of information transfer used with EDI. One is the terminal-to-computer link, which is found mostly in *intra*organizational networks and in the early stages of *inter*organizational networks. A much more sophisticated development, however, is the computer-to-computer link which requires the integration of two or more independent systems. Several industries have employed variations of this configuration; the systems range from the simplest record-keeping systems to the most advanced inventory control and replenishment programs, from microcomputers to the largest mainframes.

The multiplicity of possible hardware, software, and telecommunication combinations creates two major technical requirements for EDI. *Message standards* must be developed so that by organizing the data in a prespecified manner the message's content and meaning are clear. In addition to the message standards, *communication standards* must provide for the compatibility of sender's and receiver's communication discipline and protocol structures. These standards provide for coding consistency, connecting and disconnecting procedures, rates and types of data transmission, receipt acknowledgments, and addressing procedures.[2] Both of these required standards act as translating procedures by which data generated by one organization's internal system can be restructured and sent in a form which allows them to be received and understood by another organization's internal system.

It is possible for both organizations to adapt to an industrywide *message* standard or for one organization to adopt another organization's format as the standard so that only one firm's software needs to be altered. It is also possible for a third party—often called a service bureau—to receive communications under one firm's message format and to translate and forward the message in another firm's format. *Communication* standards, however, present a more difficult problem. While some aspects, such as when lines will be open for transmission, are easily accomplished by agreement of the concerned parties, other aspects of communication standards are restricted by hardware and telecommunications capabilities. The communication standards, like message standards, may be achieved through alterations to internal systems of one or both organizations or through the use of a third-party service bureau acting as a central switch. However, when the network is to contain more than two communicating organizations, the decisions about how to achieve compatibility become much more complex.

The Present Study

Preliminary background material for this paper was collected from a variety of sources. A search of general business, academic, and trade publications was conducted. Trade association spokespersons, service bureau executives, and organizations with varying degrees of interest and participation in EDI were contacted by telephone. An EDI convention, sponsored by the Transportation Data Coordinating Committee (TDCC), was attended, and informal discussions were held with a number of the participants.

During the preliminary phase, it became obvious to us that the major impact of EDI on interorganizational relationships could be best examined by focusing on the relevant dyads in those consumer goods industries with maximum variance in their approach to EDI. First, two industries with substantially different forms of EDI participation were chosen: the grocery industry and general merchandising. We chose to focus on the grocery industry because it has the most advanced industrywide EDI system—the Uniform Communication Standard (UCS)—which contains both message and communication standards and which is being implemented throughout the industry by manufacturers, brokers, and distributors. The UCS is the result of the joint efforts of six grocery industry trade associations. General merchandising, however, was chosen because it presents unique problems for EDI development due to the wide range of products and high variability of assortments carried by retail outlets. To some degree, these problems have led to individual efforts by large organizations to establish idiosyncratic EDI systems in contrast to the industrywide effort that produced UCS.

Second, we decided to concentrate our research on manufacturer-distributor as opposed to distributor-retailer dyads. We adopted this approach because the latter are often typified by vertical integration or by franchise arrangements while the former are generally comprised of independently owned and operated organizations without formal ties. Our interest was on how EDI might impact interorganizational relations in the absence of a hierarchically-imposed control system.

In-depth personal interviews were conducted with the respondents shown in Table 3.1. Conversations were also held with companies outside our sample which served to corroborate some of our major findings. Our interview guide is reproduced in Appendix 3.1.

We were seeking impressions and perceptions rather than hard data; the questions we posed were open ended. A more structured study was not attempted because most of our interviews were conducted with companies that considered themselves to be in the pilot stage of EDI implementation. At the time of our study, very few firms had had more than a year's experience with it. These companies were chiefly concerned with the effects of EDI on internal productivity. As the productivity aspects of EDI become man-

TABLE 3.1 Interview Conducted for EDI Study

	No. of Firms	President[a]	Marketing Personnel[b]	Sales Personnel[c]	Distribution Personnel	Data Processing Executives	Human Resource Personnel	Total Respondents
Manufacturers—Total	5							
Food	3			4	1			5
General Merchandising	2				1	1		2
Distributors—Total	7							
Food	3		1			3		4
General Merchandising	3		2			2	1	5
Drugs	1		1					1
Brokers—Food	1	1						1
Service Bureaus	3		3					3
Totals	16	1	7	4	2	6	1	21

[a] Does not include executives from three trade associations that were contacted for the study.
[b] Includes such personnel as vice president—marketing, marketing or merchandising manager, product manager.
[c] Includes such personnel as vice president—sales, sales manager, sales person.

ageable and managed, organizations will be forced to examine the effects of EDI on interorganizational relations.

Benefits of EDI

Certainly, no firm is going to make the investment in electronic data interchange systems unless there are some clear benefits. The firms we selected for personal interviewing were all committed to EDI; therefore, the responses we received were biased in EDI's favor.

Both manufacturers and distributors reported actual and potential benefits to be (1) reduced order lead time; (2) higher service levels; (3) fewer out-of-stock situations; (4) improved communication about deals, promotions, price changes, and product availability; (5) lower inventory costs; (6) better accuracy in ordering, shipping and receiving; and (7) a reduction in labor costs.

From a distributor's point of view, it would seem that the potential savings in inventory carrying costs ought to be the primary motivation for adopting EDI; however, in our interviews, this was not the dominant consideration. In fact, distributors felt that accuracy of data transmission and speed of communication concerning how and when merchandise was being shipped were equal in importance to inventory cost savings. Speed, accuracy, and completeness-of-information factors permit both the distributor and the vendor to be more fully informed about their relationship. This is a very positive aspect of EDI systems since, as the decision sciences postulate, the availability of complete and perfect information to all parties in a bargaining relationship may facilitate their achieving mutually satisfying outcomes. On the other hand, communication speed may generate conflicts, especially when distributors are informed instantaneously that a deal item they've ordered cannot be immediately shipped or that other backlog difficulties have occurred. It may also introduce some inflexibility. Changing an order is more difficult, since it is transmitted, processed, and shipped so quickly.

A benefit for distributors, which is being realized by very few to date but which has important implications for interorganizational relations, is that it is possible with EDI for a distributor to obtain reorder histories for products that are delivered directly to retail stores by vendors. For example, in some states, liquor cannot be handled through distributors' warehouses because of state law; liquor wholesalers must deliver the merchandise to individual retail stores. Orders are obtained from store managers, and records are maintained by the wholesalers. With the advent of EDI, the chain management is able to assemble purchase histories by item by store. The implications of the analysis that can be done with such data are profound.

From the vendor's (manufacturer's) perspective, EDI is viewed more as a service and productivity-enhancing tool than as a merchandising tool. In fact, some vendors insist that the service advantages (e.g., giving the distributor faster turnaround on orders by reducing lead time), not the cost savings, are the most important considerations. (The productivity gains will increase when more distributors have EDI. At present vendors maintain two systems—the paper and EDI—to accommodate the heterogeneous patterns of their customers.) In the food and general merchandising industries, where competition for distributors' time and attention is intense, slight differential advantages are considered extremely important. While these advantages are rapidly eroded by others offering similar services, the drive to be continuously innovative in logistical issues is strong. This is true even though vendors are aware that merchandising decisions, such as amount of shelf or floor space devoted to a product, are only remotely affected by improvements in physical distribution factors.

Despite claims by manufacturers that EDI's major advantages basically rebound to distributors, there are some real cost savings that manufacturers will enjoy as more distributors come on line. For example, order-processing costs will be greatly reduced; no longer will it be necessary for a salesperson to enter an order into the computer upon receipt from a distributor. The order will be transmitted to the computer directly. Furthermore, the salesperson's role in the entire order-taking process will be significantly reduced. This supposedly will free the salesperson for other tasks which are more closely related to selling than to order processing. Therefore, the salesperson should become more productive while at the same time order-processing costs will be significantly lowered.

The two major advantages of EDI in terms of reducing the time required for ordering and billing are (1) electronic data transmission (versus mail) and (2) the direct entry of data into the recipient organization's internal systems. If, prior to EDI, orders were telephoned to the vendor, the first advantage is lost. The elimination of key punching, however, is a major advantage no matter what system was previously employed. And the increased accuracy, coordinated invoicing, shipment confirmation and so forth available via

EDI provide clear advantages over telephone ordering systems. In fact, the entire receiving and reconciliation process should improve through EDI.

Despite the articulation of all of these perceived benefits by our respondents, almost every company we talked with indicated that their channel counterparts would benefit more from EDI than they would. In only two cases, in which distributors had developed their own proprietary systems, was there an outright acknowledgment by the distributors that the lead-time savings (and thus concomitant inventory holding cost savings) had driven them to *encourage* or *force* their major vendors to adopt the system. In other cases, especially among those companies associated with industrywide efforts at generating standard EDI formats, there was a hesitancy to make strong claims for cost savings or to indicate that they were the primary recipients of the rewards. As mentioned earlier, vendors felt they were servicing their accounts better, and distributors felt that vendor order entry savings and savings associated with scheduling order picking more efficiently gave vendors a major benefit. At this point, both parties seem more certain of the other's rewards than of their own.

Factors Affecting EDI Use

To take advantage of the cost savings available under EDI, the distributor must be confident that the vendor has the capability both to decrease shipment turnaround time and to maintain a continuous source of supply. As lead times are shortened, inventory levels can be fine tuned, thereby increasing the distributor's vulnerability to out-of-stock situations. Unless the distributor is assured that supplies will be maintained, inventory levels will not be lowered, and therefore, potential savings will not be realized. In other words, EDI places an additional strain on the supply relationship, and vendors must be prepared for this.

However, the grocery manufacturers we interviewed were skeptical about the data-processing capabilities of some of the distributors they could be directly linked with in the future. They felt that greater sophistication was required, especially with regard to software adjustments. The choice of the initial UCS pilot participants and their choice of subsequent partners were made very carefully; therefore, the data-processing expertise of channel members who were paired at the outset may have been atypical. In contrast, in the general merchandise industries we examined, distributors were more concerned about the data-processing skills of their suppliers than vice versa. But the largest impediment to the diffusion of EDI for general merchandise is the enormous variety of available sizes, styles, colors, and vendors (foreign and domestic). Arriving at a uniform EDI system, especially for apparel, may present insurmountable problems with message formatting and standardization of codes. Interorganizational data systems are being developed slowly and are a long way from widespread adoption among soft goods merchants and vendors.

For the vendors that sell to general merchandisers, the number of connections required per day is staggering. For example, one company told us that it has one million customers. If only 5 percent of its customers were to join its EDI system (the company manufactures high-turnover consumables), and if each ordered once a week, there could be ten thousand connections per workday. To assimilate this flow of communication into a computer system requires a considerable investment in hardware and software.

Other impediments to EDI's diffusion have been security and control issues. These are most prevalent when third parties like service bureaus are involved. The issues are rarely raised when parties are directly linked, because there is no way for one party to obtain information about competitors through the other party's computer. Nevertheless, we were told of one incident in which data waiting to be sent to a third party were inadvertently sent to a directly linked second party.

In order to overcome some of these barriers to widespread adoption, some general merchandise distributors have simply forced their vendors onto their idiosyncratic systems. If industrywide standards are not soon in coming, vendors may be required to communicate in multiple "languages" with their customers. The diseconomies associated with maintaining parallel systems may end up defeating the purposes for which the systems were first constructed.

Changes in Company-to-Company Relations

Although EDI systems heighten organizational interdependence and therefore increase the opportunity for conflict, most respondents indicated that, in fact, relations with linked companies had improved. Implementation of EDI has allowed both distributors and manufacturers to process data quickly, reduce lead time, and maintain appropriate inventory positions. Although more coordination is needed, EDI generally has lessened rather than increased conflict.

When major suppliers electronically connect to a distributor, it is an important step forward in the relationship between the parties. Generally, the vendors a distributor connects with are those with whom the distributor has had the closest relationships. This does not imply any cause and effect; it indicates that close relationships get closer as the two organizations confirm the relationship by establishing linkages such as EDI.

On the other hand, the increased speed of communication reduces "slack" time, such as the time the vendor might normally take to prepare for the receipt of an order. Vendors must react quickly and anticipate distributor requirements by holding increased levels of safety stock. For example, one general merchandise distributor has a policy of not permitting back orders. This means that if a vendor cannot ship the full amount of an order, the remainder of the order must be reordered in the next order cycle; the distributor does not allow carry-overs from one cycle to another. A major vendor of this distributor, in complying with the shorter lead times induced by the EDI system, has indicated that more inventory is kept on hand for this distributor because of the need for instantaneous response combined with the distributor's policy on back orders. Under the previous ordering system, there was more slack, which permitted the vendor to adjust its production and its inventories as necessary. Now it must anticipate needs more rigorously and favor the linked distributor when supplies are tight.

The impact of EDI on the internal systems of the organization must be anticipated. Substantial before-the-fact planning is required prior to any transmission of data. It may involve functional areas of each organization not normally included in interorganizational planning. Electronic data processing, legal, accounting, financial, buying, and sales personnel all become active at one point or another. Organization theorists point to such "multiplexity" in contact points as affecting the redundancy of an interorganizational relationship.[3] A redundant relationship will result in creative problem solving and cooperation between organizations. For example, for vendors, EDI projects are generally funded by the sales department and executed by the data processing department. Their implementation is in the hands of management information people, but interaction among other functional groups is usually required before the projects are completed. In one way or another, all of the various groups may interface, directly or indirectly, with the distributor's counterparts to complete the linkage. When technical people alone have been responsible for initiating a project and for monitoring its implementation, there has been less satisfaction with the projects than in cases where other departments have been more fully involved.

Finally, the legal implications of EDI implementation are still unclear. EDI systems eliminate paper purchase orders and invoices and, therefore, the legal terms of agreement found on the backs of these forms. However, grocery industry companies operate under the assumption that the language found on paper forms also applies to electronic transmissions. In the general merchandising industry, written blanket agreements are sometimes circulated to vendors, which the vendors must sign before orders are electronically transmitted. Another approach has been for distributors and vendors to exchange terms and conditions to keep on file. If third parties are involved, they are generally held "harmless" by agreement.

While the implications of EDI in relation to contract law are probably small, it should be remembered that EDI systems are relatively new and that most work with them to date has been more experimental than routine. Once EDI becomes commonplace, it is likely that many companies (as in the general merchandising industry) will negotiate blanket agreements to cover transactions conducted under EDI.

The Role of Third Parties

Numerous third parties have played a role in the development of EDI systems. For example, the American National Standards Committee formulated cross-industry standards for general merchandise, Touche Ross created the UCS standards, and a variety of trade associations have provided forums for discussion of EDI issues. But of all the third parties, service bureaus have been especially important in facilitating interorganizational linkages via EDI. A service bureau is an independent organization that can be used as a clearinghouse for data transmission within or between industries. A service bureau may translate messages sent in the format of the sender into a format recognizable by the addressee as well as provide a communications interface between two or more companies.

One of the major obstacles to the diffusion of EDI systems is the fact that most major companies want to use their own protocols and formats. They would prefer to have their customers or suppliers conform to what they have invested considerable resources in developing, rather than to adopt universal standards which may not fully satisfy their internal requirements. While this is understandable, it means that unless the firm has the power to dictate protocols and formats, it will be difficult for the innovation to spread. In fact, when there are firms of equal power, with strong vested interests in their own standards, there will be stalemates. Because installing EDI systems is not one of the most pressing needs of most firms, there are many large companies which will sit back and see what happens over time rather than conform to some other firm's method of transmitting purchase orders and receiving invoices (or vice versa).

Both in their role as central communication clearinghouses in cooperation with various industry groups and as agents for specific firms, service bureaus have assisted companies with modest data processing resources (as well as some firms with highly sophisticated DP operations) to participate in EDI. They accept electronic transmissions for their clients, store the message in an "electronic mailbox," and purge the file when the client "picks up the mail." The service bureau will also send messages for a client.

Service bureaus have tended to find particular niches in specific industries. This is due in part to the fact that when an industry group develops only a message format, it normally enters into an agreement with one service bureau to act as the central communication clearinghouse. When communication protocols such as the UCS are developed, any service bureau can act as an agent for an organization deciding to avoid direct communication. Service bureaus focus on either the clearinghouse or agent role.

A major benefit of using service bureaus for EDI is that they keep up with software requirements, thereby permitting their clients to maintain interfirm communication in the midst of a highly dynamic and fluid situation. Even with all the various industry efforts to agree on standards, any major consumer goods supplier that wishes to link up with distributors will face, at a minimum, six different standards in addition to the idiosyncratic formats of companies who insist on keeping their own. It is not surprising that service bureaus have served a useful purpose in this area. As one company official told us: "No matter how much time you put into developing standards, you'll never find out about them until you actually use them. This is why third parties are so helpful in these situations—they can make adjustments and they can absorb risk." When distributors employing their own standards begin to force EDI onto their customers, hiring a service bureau may be the only feasible way that less sophisticated data processing vendors can comply with the request. Forty percent of one major distributor's vendors have turned to service bureaus for help in this kind of situation, a reaction which the distributor finds preferable to dealing with literally hundreds of small vendors directly.

Clearly, there are strong advantages to using service bureaus, just as there are advantages to employing independent intermediaries generally. But there are also disadvantages. For instance, there is the cost. A major distributor has indicated that: "The third party rate structures that are being floated now do not fit with the way the chain does business." A second argument used against third parties is that they are perceived to complicate the relationship between buyers and sellers; disputes are more cumbersome to settle when third parties are involved. With all the communication required, it is difficult to locate the cause of problems. Adding another communication node is viewed as increasing the probability for error. This factor must, however, be balanced against the reduction in the overall number of linkages which the use of an information intermediary implies. A third argument is that there might be a differential advantage to keeping the EDI system in-house, because of a company's familiarity with its own system. A fourth argument against using service bureaus is concern over system privacy. Security and control are essential. Some companies fear the potential for service bureaus to summarize and distribute data to fourth parties without the companies' consent or knowledge. And finally, there is concern over the service bureaus' monopolizing data transmission in a given industry. The more that information is centralized, the more power such information potentially places in the critical node in the network.

The Role of the Sales Force

Perhaps the greatest anxiety about EDI has been articulated by salesforces. The electronic transmission of orders would appear to threaten their role, if not their existence. One quick answer to this concern is that, for many companies involved with EDI, the salesperson was not involved with routine orders prior to EDI and therefore would not be affected by the change in mode of transmission. The salespeople in these situations can focus their efforts on making presentations concerning new products and promotions for deals to the buyers or merchandisers.

This quick answer, however, would be misleading, since in many other companies, salespeople have also picked up orders on a weekly or more frequent basis, and have phoned them in to vendor distribution control centers. This is true even when the distributor has developed sophisticated models dictating economic order quantities. Only when computer to computer data transmission is combined with automatic inventory replenishment systems can salespeople be eliminated from the routine ordering process entirely.

When salespersons no longer pick up orders, they have additional time to call on various departments within a distributor's home organization, and to check on retail shelf space allocation, displays, and so forth at the local level. However, vendors have been known to refuse to participate in EDI systems because they believe that the contact time with the distributor's buyer would dissipate. To these vendors, the personal contact is important.

There are reasons why a company might want its salespeople to pick up and phone in orders, despite the seemingly unproductive nature of the task. First, phoning in an order may be quicker than using EDI. Second, and more important, when picking up orders, salespeople can make orders "ship-ready" by seeing that they contain the appropriate weight or number of pallets for a carload or truckload shipment. They can also verify that the right codes have been used and the correct sizes have been requested. Finally, they can check whether the specific requirements of deals have been met. When salespeople pick up orders, they can work with a distributor's buyer or assistant buyer to add items, if needed, for ship-ready purposes or to encourage a change in the order so that a particular deal can be fully complied with. Although distributors can program their computers so that all of the parameters associated with ship-ready orders and deals have been accounted for, there is no doubt that the personal "touch" may eliminate after-the-fact scrambling on the part of the vendor or the buyer. But whether the cost associated with a salesperson's scrutinizing routine orders would overcome the benefits to the distributor and vendor is not yet known.

Third, there is always the possibility that buyers, having once agreed on a promotional program or new product inventory level, will change their minds. If orders are transmitted electronically, the salesperson will not know about this change until after it has taken place. And in one experiment in the grocery industry, the distributor and vendor maintained a manual and an electronic system side-by-side for a period of time and noted that there were some differences in the orders.

Fourth, because picking up of orders has been removed, salespeople will not be calling as frequently on accounts as they previously had. While they will have more time to get involved in the administrative decisions (e.g., financial, shipping, and accounting questions) between companies, the number of contact hours may be reduced.

Fifth, prior to EDI, salespeople could, when reviewing routine orders with buyers and/or assistant buyers, get them to help in meeting their end-of-the-month sales quotas. Such help in "making their numbers" is no longer easily available under EDI. Again, distributor buy-outs at the end of deals may be missed, since salespeople will see orders after-the-fact and will therefore not be in a position to alert buyers of these opportunities as the orders go out.

Finally, in some companies, orders have been placed over the phone through "market coordinators." The coordinators are familiar with all the accounts in their territories and are responsible for following through on orders. These coordinators often "elevate" orders (i.e., encourage additional purchasing) when in direct phone contact with customers. If EDI is fully implemented, the coordinators' role may become obsolete, thus lessening the effectiveness of the integrated sales effort.

While the majority of companies with whom we talked downplayed the effect of EDI systems on the role of salespeople, it is our belief that the number of salespeople will decline as the need for salesperson contact with distributor organizations decreases. This, however, is more a function of combining automatic inventory replenishment systems with EDI than of EDI alone. The long-term consequences could be that even more discretion will be placed in distributors' hands. Indicative of this is the reaction of food brokers who simply stand-in for or replace a vendor's salesforce. Concerned from the outset that EDI systems might impact their functions as sales and promotion coordinators, brokers made certain that they were included in the grocery industry's UCS pilot study and have clearly spelled out the role they intend to play. Some brokers have been particularly aggressive and innovative. They have set up EDI systems with distributors for their clients, which are often smaller grocery manufacturers. The brokers participated in the UCS experiments and have developed sophisticated data processing skills so that, in addition to acting as an external salesforce, they can remain a communication link between distributors and vendors. There is no doubt that the brokers saw the potential effects of EDI and are now trying to solidify their positions within the marketing channel by adapting to these communication changes.

Another threat to the role of the salesperson is the potential use of EDI for transmitting information on promotions and deals to buyers, thus eliminating even more of the sales function. At present, grocery trade deals, for example, are announced through the mail by individual vendors in letters addressed to buyers. The salesperson presents the specifics of the deal and sells the "event" to the buyer. During the availability of the promotion, the salesperson attempts to ensure that the distributor follows through on its plans. But the system is highly imperfect in that when the actual orders are placed, distributors often neglect to take advantage of the deal. Evidence of this is the existence of a company which makes a considerable sum of money each year by pointing out to distributors deals with which they had complied but failed to reflect in their purchase orders, and then splitting the cost savings on a 50-50 basis. If promotions were announced electronically rather than by mail, deals could be programmed into the reorder systems and prices and quantities automatically adjusted. EDI has the potential for routinizing the entire process associated with such promotions.

The Role of Buyers

For many distributors, the performance of buyers depends on their ability to maintain high service levels (low out-of-stocks) and high turnover (low inventories). Buyers will gravitate to vendors that will facilitate their achieving these goals. Being linked with vendors in an EDI system is a mechanism toward accomplishing these goals. Therefore, buyers are expected to be enthusiastic about such systems. In truth, however, the systems seem to be mainly advocated by other departments in the distributors' organizations, and buyers, by and large, are largely impassive about electronic transmission of orders. This is probably because the major change in their order-placing functions was the computerization of economic order quantity models, which removed much of the routine ordering from their continuous surveillance. EDI is, for them, merely an extension of a process with which they are already familiar. In the grocery industry, the buyer or assistant buyer still screens orders before they are electronically transmitted. In certain general merchandise companies, however, where EDI ordering is done by tape, the buyer does not interact with the purchase order at all. In fact, the buyer generally sees the purchase order *after* the vendor does.

For the most part, distributors believe that EDI systems have not changed buyers' basic relationships with vendors. As one distributor explained to us, EDI systems have had an impact on vendor-buyer relations of 1 to 1½ on a 1 to 10 scale, where 1 equals no impact at all. Another distributor, however, was concerned that electronically sent orders cannot be manipulated by buyers. Like those vendors concerned about the role of the salesforce, this distributor believes that "merchandising input would disappear if the data processing people had their way." Its concerns are similar to the vendors' concerns, that is, the purchase order won't contain everything it ought to contain about deals and so forth before it is transmitted. In addition, the diminishing of salesperson and buyer contact concerns this distributor, especially with regard to the planning of promotions.

Intraorganizational Changes

There can be no doubt that the relationship between data processing, marketing, legal, accounting, and sales/buying departments has been intensified by the introduction of EDI systems. The advent of such systems has been especially significant for data processing personnel. In fact, as these individuals become increasingly important in maintaining and implementing such systems, their power will increase within their home corporations because of the boundary-spanning, troubleshooting role they will assume.

Another implication for the internal organization of companies is that the ability to receive orders immediately has highlighted a vendor's ability to service the orders. This factor places more stress on a company's internal response system. The absence of slack time forces a vendor to react much more quickly; when lead time changes from a week to a day, a great deal of attention is placed on how inventories are being managed to maintain service levels. On the other hand, as distributors' inventories are drawn down, they will face similar internal demands relative to out-of-stock. While this increases interorganizational dependency, it also brings with it increased intrafirm pressures.

EDI Developments in the Foreseeable Future

EDI is in its infancy. Therefore, our interviews basically reflected the interviewees' perceptions about the *potential* of EDI systems. The perceptions were not unrealistic, because, in a number of instances, the potential had already been achieved, for example, a substantial reduction in inventory levels. In this section, however, we are concerned with EDI developments which have rarely been realized, but appear to be feasible.

Until now, the focus in EDI application has been on the transmission of purchase orders and invoices. In the relatively short-term future, attention will turn to electronic shipment notification which will inform distributors as to quantities actually coming from the vendors. Strong consideration of the use of EDI systems for electronic funds transfers (EFT) will also begin. This issue is exceedingly sensitive, because distributors will not want to lose the float they receive on their money when they pay bills by mail. If EFT is to be coupled with EDI, then there will have to be some way in which distributors are compensated for the loss of the normal float.

Clearly, EDI makes available more data with which to make decisions as well as perform operational tasks. Eventually, firms will begin to use the data creatively. When distributors do this, it will bring about further consolidation of power at their level of the marketing channel. But the likelihood that they will look at the data analytically in the near future is very low; therefore, sophisticated vendors have adequate lead time in which to develop strategies that anticipate distributors' long-term needs.

At present, many EDI systems are batch systems, by which distributors send and vendors process orders at night or, at least, at specific times of the day. In the future, it is likely that many systems will be on-line and will operate on a real-time basis. This would speed up the order cycle even more. In fact, EDI systems would then be significantly faster than phoning in orders via code-a-phones and similar devices, thereby making the latter mechanisms obsolete in terms of productivity.

Another area of likely attention is promotion and deal information. In fact, price and deal notification could be handled efficiently via EDI systems. If this happens, the implications for the salesperson's role are that there will be less and less need for face-to-face contact with buyers. Even though the need will diminish, however, it is not certain that there will actually be a significant reduction in contact time. This is because many distributors and vendors believe that salesperson-buyer interaction is critical to effective merchandising and marketing. The discussions in which they engage are important for business strategy. Therefore, even though buyers could, through increasingly sophisticated analysis of readily available data, make excellent decisions on their own, they will continue to rely on the advice of salespeople based on the belief that deal decisions should always involve personal interchange of ideas between vendors and distributors.

At some point, scanning data from the front end of stores will be wedded with EDI systems. The linkage will be from retail cash register all the way to vendor via intermediary computers. At the present time there is not enough confidence in data collected from front-end scanners to rely on them for inventory replenishment purposes. The initial retail store/vendor linkage analysis will probably be accomplished for the testing of new products where a vendor will access purchase information from selected stores and thereby be able to monitor purchase rates and inventory levels and react accordingly. The data analysis implications of this are important, particularly if the vendor can also couple these purchase data with consumer panel information.

From a marketing research perspective, the major benefits of EDI—for example, forecasting, inventory analysis, promotional logistical effectiveness and efficiency—are yet to come. Once EDI becomes a two-way communication system, the interactive properties should significantly enhance interorganizational coordination efforts. At the present time, however, EDI systems are not high-priority issues for most distributors or vendors; therefore, these grandiose potentialities are far from being realized.

Interorganizational Research Issues

From the information we were able to gather about EDI systems, a number of researchable propositions regarding the future of interorganizational relations can be suggested. We only present a few of them here as a conclusion to this exploratory study. We have not spelled out in detail the reasoning underlying them, but there is a vast literature, particularly in the behavioral and social sciences, that would support the conceptual underpinning of each proposition. Our investigation to date—as represented by the discussion above—leads us to believe that there would be considerable empirical support for these propositions if they were tested via field research.

First, because EDI systems provide records in a form that permits ease of reconciliation and analysis, the information available to linked distributors and vendors will be more complete and accurate than previous information. The better the quality of information (defined in terms of completeness and accuracy) flowing between two parties in a bargaining situation, the more likely it is that they will come to highly satisfying (e.g., joint profit-maximizing) decisions.

Second, because EDI involves electronic data processing, sales, accounting, finance, legal, and merchandising personnel, it requires contact at various departments and levels between two (or more) organizations. The greater the redundancy of contact, the greater will be the commitment to the interorganizational relationship on the part of the parties, leading to effective and efficient modes of conflict management.

Third, computer-to-computer linkages between organizations require the development of formal rules and procedures to deal with the transmission and receipt of data. The more formalized the relationship becomes (defined in terms of specific rules and procedures), the less flexibility will be available to the parties in dealing with disputes or changes in the environment.

Fourth, EDI will lead to the amassing of more and more data available for analysis. But the trade-off is information overload. Therefore, until the parties assign to subunits the specific responsibility for data analysis, the data will not be utilized to its fullest potential. These subunits may have to be specially created. Existing subunits tend to be too myopic for the task; they may also lack the sophistication required to perform penetrating analyses and to draw meaningful inferences.

Fifth, when power is severely imbalanced between a vendor and a distributor, the more powerful party will dictate the type of EDI system and standards to be used. When power is more equally divided among the major vendors and distributors in a given industry, the industry as a whole is likely to become involved and to develop standards which will satisfy all members, even though the standards arrived at will not be optimal for any given member.

Sixth, the larger and more technologically sophisticated the company (in terms of its internal systems), the more likely it is to increase its cost advantages by developing EDI links with its suppliers or customers. Those cost advantages will be realized to the extent the company can integrate EDI and its internal systems.

Seventh, companies with EDI links are slow to recognize other significant aspects of the links beyond the routinization of mundane tasks (ordering, invoicing, shipping, receiving, etc.) when the systems have been initiated, developed, and maintained primarily by data processing personnel.

Finally, at this stage in its development, EDI can be likened to using computers for file and record-keeping purposes. The important relational effects between organizations will be felt when applications analogous to decision support systems are added to EDI systems.

APPENDIX 3.1 Electronic Data Interchange Systems Interview Guide

1. Describe the type or types of electronic data interchange systems that presently link your firm to supplier or customer firms. What is contemplated for the future?
   Probe
   - types of operations performed
   - master/master; master/slave
   - dedication to one supplier/customer
   - service bureau/direct ties into intraorganization information and control systems

2. How did your firm become involved in electronic data interchange initially? What factors were involved in determining whether and with whom linkages would be established? How do your relationships differ when comparing linked firms with nonlinked firms? How have the relationships changed over time?
   Probe
   - length of association with linked organizations
   - comparison of relationship with linked organization and with other organizations
   Obtain
   - permission to talk with suppliers/customers on system
   - get names of contacts; also, names of those not on system and contacts

3. Were any trade associations involved in the development of your data interchange system? What were the dynamics of that involvement? How were common standards achieved?

4. What organizational or person-to-person problems, as opposed to mechanical problems, are or were being encountered in implementing the system?
   Probe
   - resistance within the organization—where?

5. Compare and contrast the manner in which you purchase from or sell to the now-linked suppliers/customers with how you used to purchase from or sell to them. In other words, we would like to have a before-after comparison which focuses on changes in the roles of important actors in the relationship, such as purchasing agents, salespeople, credit managers, traffic managers, account managers, and so forth.
   Probe
   - boundary personnel role changes

6. Was a blanket term agreement negotiated to cover electronic orders and transactions and, if so, how does it differ from your previous purchase order or acknowledgment forms? How do you settle disputes now compared with when you did not have the system in place?
   Probe
   - changes in dispute settlement procedures
   - frequency of reference to agreement
   - who negotiated the agreement
   Obtain
   - copy of both blanket agreement and old purchase order or acknowledgment form

7. What fears or worries did you or your organization have about the data link system which were founded or unfounded?
   Probe
   - power shifts between organization
   - role of sales force, purchasing agent

8. Does the data linkage system restrict or constrain the strategic or tactical decisions of your organization? Of the organizations with which you are linked? What happens when you face a change in your environment? Can you adjust easily? How?
   Probe
   - Is the price of commitment to this system an inability to react quickly?

9. In what ways has the data linkage system changed your organization's relationship to those organizations with which it is linked?
   Probe
   - expected continuity
   - trust
   - conflict

10. What do you foresee for the future? How will future systems differ in design and effect?
    Probe
    - closer ties with more extensive links with existing linked organizations
    - more linkages of the same depth
    - change from master/slave to master/master

11. What are the likely competitive reactions you see to the systems you have developed with your suppliers/customers? What do you see in the future when these kinds of systems have proliferated, if they do proliferate?

Probe
- when everyone tries to link with common suppliers/customers, will this force going to master/master relationships?
- how will this change the power structure in the industry?

12. Some have argued that the new data interchange systems are simply a form of electronic mail that speed up communications rather than change the form and substance of the way in which firms actually communicate. How do you view these systems? Will they revolutionize interfirm relationships or are they basically rapid communication devices?

CHAPTER 4

Where Is Electronic In-Home Retailing Going?

Walter J. Salmon

Harvard Business School

If the recent avalanche of articles on electronic in-home retailing is an indication of its impending importance, then store retailers are an endangered species.[1] But the publicity and reality of this subject are incompatible. For the remainder of this decade, and perhaps this century, there is likely to be more froth than substance to electronic in-home retailing.[2]

Cited typically as the main advantage of electronic in-home shopping is the convenience of purchasing merchandise and services any time of the day or night without leaving home. While it is acknowledged that direct mail and telephone shopping already offer these advantages for certain merchandise and services, the popular press has promulgated the idea that electronic in-home shopping will provide more complete and timely information, and that the user can interactively select the information he or she particularly requires. This article disputes some of these alleged advantages, but more importantly it delineates a broader frame of reference for the assessment of the future of electronic in-home retailing. There are six aspects to this frame of reference:

1. the organization of an electronic in-home shopping system;
2. the quality of information provided by an electronic in-home shopping system;
3. the economics of an electronic in-home shopping information system;
4. the goods and services that can be economically distributed through such systems;
5. potential consumer interest in such systems; and
6. responses of store retailers to electronic in-home shopping.

I will discuss each aspect of this frame of reference and its implications separately.

The Organization of an Electronic In-Home Shopping System

Since other contributors discuss the organization of an electronic in-home shopping channel in depth, I will provide only a cursory discussion of this issue.[3] The probable components of an electronic in-home shopping channel are (1) a two-way communications channel between the system operator and individual homes; (2) a computer system that includes hardware and software at the system operator and user ends to activate the communications channel (the channel itself can be either telephone or cable with two-way capability); (3) a computer system that acts as a conduit between the system operator and individual providers of products and services; (4) and individual providers of products and services.

Owners of one or more of the components of such a system will have to integrate these components, ensure that hardware and software systems are compatible, abide by government regulations, market the system to the public, administer it on an everyday basis, and last but not least, earn a return on the funds required for capital expense and start-up costs. Accomplishing such packaging is not an insurmountable task, but it presents a far greater challenge than acting as channel commander for a less vertically intertwined channel of distribution. By itself, this perspective on the emergence of electronic in-home shopping suggests that such a channel is likely to have a prolonged gestation period.

Information Quality Provided by an Electronic In-Home Shopping System

A second reason for the expectation of a prolonged gestation period is the quality of information that such a system will provide. The phrase *quality of information* refers to the speed and clarity of such a system in providing text and color pictures with sound and motion. Currently, experimental in-home electronic shopping systems already provide, with adequate clarity, a quantity of letters and numbers that fill a television screen within ten seconds. Most experts believe that this capability will satisfy the needs of most consumers for clear and rapid transmission of letters and numbers.

Yet the expectation is that even in 1990 the capability of such systems to provide color pictures will be much more limited. Good color graphics without either sound or motion appears to be the prevailing 1990 forecast. Although some experts are more optimistic, the following discussion is based upon the transmission of only color graphics, without sound or motion, by electronic in-home shopping systems in 1990.

This limitation has different implications for selling services compared to selling merchandise. Good color reproduction with sound and motion is hardly required for engaging in routine service transactions such as paying bills or making airline or theater reservations. Technical considerations, therefore, should not hinder the growth in the availability of these services through electronic in-home shopping. As will be discussed later, however, there are questions about the value added of electronic in-home shopping systems in the sale of at least some of these services compared to existing touch tone telephone shopping systems.

Color graphics without sound or motion does, however, restrict the merchandise that can effectively be sold by means of electronic in-home shopping systems. If the appearance or demonstration of the merchandise is important to the consumer, and the consumer does not recall appearance or functional characteristics of the merchandise, then there may be a preference for catalog or store retailing to satisfy consumer information requirements. Thus, if an electronic in-home shopping system does not transmit pictures of a quality at least equal to those in a direct mail catalog, the system becomes an inferior channel of information for the sale of most items of apparel and home furnishings. Furthermore, this channel may be unable to compete with store retailing (or even door-to-door retailing) of products that require demonstration.

Despite its envisioned limitation in transmitting pictures, electronic in-home shopping systems could be successfully used to sell merchandise if the appearance of the merchandise was familiar or unimportant to the consumer. Branded grocery or health and beauty items, possibly well-known brands of men's shirts or underwear, or books, records, and tapes are illustrations of this type of merchandise. Later I will challenge the assumption of the feasibility of selling some of these items by means of electronic in-home shopping on economic grounds. Nevertheless, some of this merchandise does constitute a market for electronic in-home shopping, albeit a small one.

The Economics of an Electronic In-Home Shopping Information System

A much neglected perspective on electronic in-home shopping is its economics. Can it satisfy consumer interests more economically than other channels of distribution while concurrently earning an adequate return on investment for its sponsors? There are two separate aspects to the economics of electronic in-home shopping. They are the economics of the information system and the economics of the fulfillment system—the warehouse and delivery arrangements required to deliver the merchandise or services the customer orders. This section of the article discusses the economics of the information system.

Electronic in-home shopping, observers agree, will be only one of the services provided by a two-way interactive videotex system, and quite probably not the most important. To understand its economics, therefore, it is necessary to understand the economics of the overall information system. These economics consist of the capital and operating costs of the system and the expected revenue.

To assess these economics, let us consider a model of a current and a 1990 videotex information system. This model is based upon the assumption that in a city with 1,000,000 people, or 300,000 households, 150,000 households purchase a two-way cable-transmitted interactive videotex system with the capability of delivering the text and pictorial information cited in the previous section. Reviewed below are some of the critical assumptions incorporated into the model, the outcomes suggested by the model, and their implications.

Because videotex in 1990 is assumed to be capable of transmitting only rather primitive pictures, its 1990 sources of revenue are mainly those that do not require attractive illustrations. For example, it is assumed in the most likely case that electronic in-home retailing will capture 25 percent of the classified and Yellow Pages advertising aimed at videotex subscribers, but because display advertising is so "picture dependent," only 1 percent of the display advertising aimed at videotex subscribers will be diverted to electronic in-home retailing.

Estimates of the revenue to be derived from each of these sources in 1990 are presented in Table 4.1. Three sets of estimates are shown: a most likely case, a worst case, and a best case. These three differ only in terms of the *shares* of total consumer expenditures for each service that a videotex system is assumed to achieve by 1990. The shares of total consumer expenditures from which the revenues shown in Table 4.1 are derived are shown in Table 4.2.

Growth rates for total consumer outlays between 1983 and 1990 for classified advertising, *Yellow Pages* advertising, display advertising, intercity transportation, and home banking activity are assumed to be unaffected by the availability of videotex systems. For home security, it is assumed that 2 percent of households subscribe to a centrally monitored system at a cost of twelve dollars per

TABLE 4.1 Estimated Average Videotex System Revenues per Household, 1990 ($)

Revenue Source	Annual Revenue per Household		
	Most Likely Case	Worst Case	Best Case
Classified advertising	$ 13.00	$ 5.20	$ 26.00
Yellow Pages advertising	11.00	4.40	22.00
Display advertising	7.15	3.58	10.73
Home banking:			
bank processing costs[a]	32.26	32.26	32.26
postage costs[a]	35.84	35.84	35.84
Transportation services (ticket purchases)[b]	6.70	3.35	10.05
Home security	2.59	2.59	2.59
Direct mail retailing[c]	4.70	2.35	7.83
Total	$113.24	$89.57	$147.30

[a]Revenue figures for banking services represent displacement of banks' or households' costs for conventional systems, with savings shared 50-50 between consumers and videotex system operators.
[b]Transportation service revenues represent 10 percent commissions on ticket purchases.
[c]Retail revenue represents 18 percent communication costs on sales of those categories suitable for sale via videotex systems.

TABLE 4.2 Share of Consumer Expenditure Achieved by Videotex System, 1990 (%)

Revenue Source	Share of Consumer Expenditures		
	Most Likely Case	Worst Case	Best Case
Classified advertising	25%	10%	50%
Yellow Pages advertising	25	10	50
Display advertising	1	0.5	1.5
Home banking[a]	50	50	50
Transportation services	50	25	75
Home security[b]	90	90	90
Direct mail retailing[c]	30	15	50

[a]Fifty percent of checks assumed to be written at the point of purchase; videotex system is assumed to capture 100 percent of remaining activity (13 checks per month per household with a processing cost of $0.36 per check).
[b]Ninety percent share of total penetration, estimated at 2 percent of household.
[c]Videotex system shares of direct mail retail expenditures are based on only those categories suitable for sale via videotex systems: certain apparel, insurance, books, records, and tapes.

household per month; of these households, 90 percent are assumed to use the cable system (rather than telephone) because of lower cost.

By far the largest source of revenue envisioned for videotex in 1990 is home banking, which is expected to account for 60 percent of total revenue per household. That videotex will derive so much revenue from home banking is, perhaps, somewhat optimistic. This revenue stream assumes that convenience and cost effectiveness will lead to 100 percent conversion to home banking among videotex subscribers in 1990. Although videotex subscribers are likely to be disproportionately affluent and technologically sophisticated, the 100 percent conversion rate may assume, among even these subscribers, too swift a change in consumer behavior.

There is, in addition, another major question about the stream of revenue expected from home banking. Home banking and bill paying using a touch tone telephone as the communications channel between the consumer and bank computer is already a commercial reality. How much of an improvement over this technology videotex represents remains uncertain. Therefore, the largest source of revenue for videotex in 1990 could be partially preempted by existing technology.

The final source of expected videotex revenue is in-home shopping. This revenue stream will be limited by two factors. One is the above mentioned limitations in the picture-transmitting capability of videotex in 1990. A second is the expense encountered in gathering and delivering many items of small value to consumers. As a result of these factors, the system's penetration of the total retail market for merchandise of all kinds is expected to be very small. The expectation is that instead of expanding the market for non-store retailing, electronic in-home shopping will be confined to a share of that market. That share will consist of items currently sold by direct mail that do not require promotion through attractive illustration or photography. Books, records, tapes, and selected ready-to-wear items are examples of this merchandise. These items will account in 1990 for about 18 percent of all catalog sales, or $8.7 billion. Electronic in-home shopping is estimated, in the most likely case, to gain 30 percent of that market among videotex subscribers (see Table 4.2).

The entire 30 percent, however, is not available to defray the informational expense of an electronic in-home shopping system. What is available is that proportion of the sales dollar which catalog merchants are accustomed to spending on communication costs, a proportion that amounts to 18 percent of sales. The resulting stream of revenue, when divided among the number of anticipated house-

TABLE 4.3 Estimated Per-Household Capital Requirements and Start-up Promotion Costs for a Videotex System, 1990

	Amount per Household		
	Most Likely Case	*Worst Case*	*Best Case*
Central computer[a]	$200	$200	$200
Frame creation	8	8	8
In-home equipment[b]	200	300	150
Start-up promotion[c]	66	80	52
Working capital	15	18	12
Total	$489	$606	$422
Capital requirement for 150,000 home system (millions)	$73.4	$90.9	$63.6

[a]Assumed cost in 1990 = $1 million per 5,000 homes.
[b]Assumed cost in 1990 for best case = $1 million per 5,000 homes.
[c]Range of estimates depends on success rate of in-home sales representatives, ranging from 1 in 5 calls to 1 in 3.

holds in 1990, is only $4.70 annually per subscriber. Altogether, in 1990 a videotex system is expected to derive only $113.24 annually per subscriber from the sale of all goods and services. The questions surrounding the large proportion of this revenue expected from home banking may make even this estimate optimistic.

Uncertainty also surrounds capital requirements and start-up promotion costs for a videotex system (see Table 4.3). Among the major capital cost assumptions is that while the costs of the computer in the possession of the system operator and the equipment in the individual subscriber's household will decline by 75 percent and 80 percent, respectively, between 1983 and 1990, the necessary capital investment for these two items per household in 1990 will still total $400. Another sizable capital cost will be the initial marketing investment in convincing consumers to subscribe to the system. The expectation is that the marketing of a system will require advertising and door-to-door selling at a cost per acquired subscriber of $66. Working capital and initial frame creation costs will add another $23 per household, bringing the most likely case total capital requirements to $489 per household.

Annual operating expenses for a videotex system also include a number of costs (see Table 4.4). The largest is likely to be telecommunications. The connection between system operator and individual subscriber's home can be by either telephone or two-way cable. The model assumes a two-way cable connection and a "most

TABLE 4.4 Estimated Per-Household Annual Operating Costs for a Videotex System, 1990

	Amount per Household		
	Most Likely Case	Worst Case	Best Case
Computer maintenance[a]	$16.39	$ 16.39	$16.39
Telecommunications	24.00	48.00	12.00
Frame creation and revision[b]	13.12	13.12	13.12
General and administrative[c]	20.00	25.00	12.00
Total	$73.51	$102.51	$56.51
Total operating costs for 150,000 household system (millions)	$11.0	$15.4	$8.5

[a]Based on total annual costs of $2.46 million for a 150,000 household system.
[b]Based on total annual costs in the most likely case of $1.97 million.
[c]Based on total annual costs in the most likely case of $3.0 million.

likely" payment of $2 per month per subscriber to the cable operator for use of a channel. This estimate is half of the fee Home Box Office is paying a cable operator in one of the current experiments. It also represents significantly less than an increasingly "usage-oriented" telephone company might want for providing a comparable connection.

When revenues and capital and operating costs are compared, the result, without direct consumer payments above and beyond payments encompassed in the usage of specific services, is not enough to provide the system operator with an adequate return on investment (see Table 4.5). The system operator, it is expected, would have a weighted average after-tax cost of capital of at least 13.9 percent. This return assumes the system operator would have a capital structure consisting of 50 percent equity and 50 percent debt, and a 44 percent tax rate. Interest on debt, before tax, would be 14 percent. Because of the inherent risk, the assumption is that prospective stockholders would want at least a 20 percent after-tax return for their funds $(.50[.14(1 - .44)] + .50(.20) = .1392)$.

To provide the operator with a 13.9 percent return, each subscriber would have to pay, in the most likely case, an additional fee of approximately $11 per month. In view of the limitations of the envisioned system, it is by no means certain that in a city wired for two-way cable, half the available households, as assumed by the model, would subscribe. Obviously, failure to achieve a 50 percent

TABLE 4.5 Pro Forma Revenues, Costs, and Required Subscriber Fees for a Videotex System, 1990

	Per Subscriber		
	Most Likely Case	*Worst Case*	*Best Case*
Revenue before subscriber fees[a]	$113.24	$ 89.57	$147.30
Operating cost[b]	73.51	102.51	56.51
Contribution	39.73	(12.94)	90.79
After-tax cash flow[c]	21.45	negative	49.03
Net present value @ 13.9% capital cost[d]	($377)	($643)	($165)
Additional subscribers monthly fee for system operator to earn 13.9%	$11	$19	$5

[a]See Table 4.1.
[b]See Table 4.4.
[c]Based on a 44 percent tax rate.
[d]Based on a ten-year planning horizon.

penetration rate means either an unsatisfactory return for the sponsor or a still-higher monthly fee for subscribers. The latter would obviously make successful marketing of the proposed system even more difficult.

The Goods and Services Distributed through Electronic In-Home Shopping Systems

In addition to the debatable economics of the information system, there is another important reason for the pessimism about the future of electronic in-home shopping that pervades this article. Consumers, in all likelihood, would most value the system's convenience if it could economically relieve them of the highly repetitive and time-consuming task of purchasing food and other everyday necessities. For many of the busy and intelligent consumers expected to use electronic in-home shopping systems, the drudgery-to-pleasure ratio of this aspect of their shopping activities must be high. Unfortunately, it has been, and continues to be, difficult for any form of nonstore retailing to compete in this arena. There are several reasons for this situation, only one of which will be discussed here.

Because of the high proportion of the budget required for food and other necessities, most consumers are quite price conscious when purchasing them. Supermarket retailers, in response, have learned to operate successfully at low margins. By contrast, electronic in-home sellers of food and other necessities would find that the costs of gathering, packing, and shipping this merchandise to consumers would rival comparable costs for much higher-priced merchandise. For example, if United Parcel Service (UPS) delivery charges are used as a surrogate for retail delivery costs, then the delivery cost alone for a $10 order weighing five pounds would be $1.61. This sum would be approximately 75 percent of the gross margin normally available to retailers in the sale of such merchandise. While this example may exaggerate the cost problem for the "fulfillment function" in the sale of necessities by means of electronic in-home shopping (or any other form of nonstore retailing), it is indicative of the significance of the cost problem. The likelihood is that only the very rich would find electronic in-home shopping an economically satisfactory channel of distribution for the purchase of necessities. Unfortunately, by themselves they do not constitute a market segment of adequate size to sustain electronic in-home retailing.

For more expensive, nonnecessary items, however, fulfillment economics are far less of an obstacle to the success of electronic in-home shopping. Yet when surveyed about their interest in using two-way videotex for electronic in-home shopping, consumers are relatively unenthusiastic.

Potential Consumer Interest in Electronic In-Home Shopping Systems

Three of the more notable studies of potential consumer interest in electronic in-home shopping are known as Benton and Bowles, Ash and Quelch, and Blackwell and Offnut.[4] Descriptions of these studies and their findings are as follows.

Benton and Bowles Study This study involved four thousand households. The study was representative of U.S. demographics in terms of geography, income, and age. A total of 2,138 questionnaires were completed during November 1980. The study found that consumers ranked an in-home shopping service *lowest* of all services offered.

Ash and Quelch Study This study involved 239 households randomly chosen in London, Ontario. These households were representative of London demographics but with a higher income base. As in the Benton and Bowles study, questionnaires were delivered to the home (during May 1982). An in-home shopping service ranked twelfth among fourteen services offered in terms of consumer interest.

Blackwell and Offnut Study This study involved 360 households in Columbus, Ohio. Unlike the other studies, this study included users of QUBE, the interactive system operated by Warner-Amex. Of the 360 respondents, 238 (65 percent) were QUBE subscribers, and the remaining 122 were not. As with the Benton and Bowles and the Ash and Quelch studies, the researchers asked consumers to rank their interest in certain cable-delivered services. In-home shopping ranked last with both groups, the QUBE adopters and the nonadopters. Even individuals who have experience with marginally interactive cable for other services do not find any strong reason to shop by cable. Because of the limited technical capability of the QUBE system, however, it is possible that consumers were skeptical of the value of a two-way cable system.

Why consumers found electronic in-home shopping relatively unappealing is unclear. Considering the problems with other studies of potential consumer interest in revolutionary new products, we might conclude that the results are simply misleading. There are, nevertheless, some possibly legitimate reasons for consumer indifference to electronic in-home shopping. Consumers may recognize the inherent inability of electronic in-home shopping at its best to duplicate the sensory means such as touch and smell through which, in addition to sight, they receive information in a store environment. They might resent the delayed gratification arising from the time lapse between ordering and the delivery of the merchandise. They might fear loss of the social or entertainment component of in-store shopping. Conversely, they could fear the temptation, the perceived technological complexity, or the impact of electronic surveillance through electronic in-home shopping.

While the results of the research on potential consumer interest in electronic in-home shopping are not definitive, they are hardly a favorable omen for the success of this new channel of distribution.

The Responses of Store Retailing to Electronic In-Home Retailing

The final factor that will affect the success of electronic in-home retailing is the effectiveness of the counterattack from store retailing. Will it be hesitant or aggressive?

Although store retailers cannot achieve the ultimate convenience of electronic in-home retailing, they can enhance the convenience, speed, and satisfaction of the in-store experience. In effect, the management information systems of traditional retailers, spearheaded by increasingly powerful and versatile point-of-sale registers, have been the major component of these efforts. They have helped to improve the in-stock position or availability of wanted merchandise and the speed with which credit transactions can be approved; at the same time, they have helped to reduce the amount of time necessary at the cash register.

Morever, recently, retailers have begun to take advantage of new technology to add more speed, satisfaction, and convenience to the shopping experience. Consumer access to up-to-date, computer-controlled bridal registers and gift suggestion programs are manifestations of the partial automation of the in-store environment. The next step is the consumer-accessed in-store interactive information terminal. Because these are not dependent on cable or telephone, unlike electronic in-home shopping terminals, but instead rely on a videodisc or tape inserted into an individual store terminal, they can and do convey high-quality sound and motion pictures. Thus the pictorial quality of interactive devices available to the consumer for assistance in shopping in the store are better than at home. These terminals should enhance the merchandise information that store retailers can provide consumers while reducing selling costs.

Still ahead for store retailing is the introduction of point-of-sale terminals that allow consumers with credit or electronic funds transfer cards to consummate purchases without any personnel assistance. Some self-service gasoline stations are already equipped with early versions of these terminals.

Above and beyond the introduction of new technology to enhance the in-store shopping experience, store retailers increasingly recognize the preoccupation with value that characterizes contemporary consumers. Accordingly, on some merchandise they are endeavoring to reduce inventories and contain or decrease operating costs in order to maintain or lower prices. On other high-priced and more ego-intensive merchandise, they are endeavoring to enhance assortments and improve personal selling. These actions, together with the introduction of new technology to promote convenience and satisfaction, should make them formidable opposition for electronic in-home shopping.

Summary

I have endeavored to construct a broader frame of reference within which to assess the future of electronic in-home shopping. Most of the press concerning this development has tended to glamorize the consumer advantages of electronic in-home shopping while ignoring the difficulties in organizing this channel of distribution and the technological obstacles to good picture quality. Furthermore, the economics of both the electronic in-home shopping information system and the fulfillment system on which most nonstore retailing depends are often neglected in appraising the future of electronic in-home shopping. Scant attention is given also to the significance of the lukewarm consumer appraisal of this new shopping opportunity, and to the weapons available or likely to be available to store retailers to combat it. When these additional factors are considered, the inescapable conclusion is that electronic in-home shopping will not, in the foreseeable future, revolutionize consumer shopping. Instead it is likely to encroach slowly on existing nonstore retailing, and its ultimate significance remains uncertain.

PART TWO

Marketing Decision Support Systems

CHAPTER 5

MDSSs at General Electric: Implications for the 1990s from Experiences in the 1970s and 1980s

Charles M. Lillis
University of Colorado

Bonnie J. McIvor
General Electric Company

This article describes our experiences with marketing decision support systems (MDSSs) at General Electric. Both the topic and our corporate laboratory are so broad and complex that almost any discussion short of something like the influence of the electric lightbulb on modern Japanese culture could be included. In addition, we've taken the liberty of looking into the future to speculate on what it may hold for MDSSs. As one limitation on scope, however, the reader should note that we are not experts in either information theory or communications technology and we are not going to talk about them.

What we shall report are managerial and behavioral observations growing out of the attempts by ourselves and others to develop and use MDSSs at General Electric. We shall discuss primarily, though not exclusively, industrial rather than consumer applications, because that is what we know. The discussion identifies and describes a sample of systems now in use, ranging from simple retrieval to state-of-the-art models, and examines one case in some detail. Along the way we make observations and draw conclusions.

A major result of our experiences is one simple proposition: A broadened awareness of strategic alternatives with an implied opportunity for strategic change is driven either (1) by marketing information from customer groups flowing upward through the organization or (2) by the application of marketing models at the general management level flowing downward. The first mechanism is far more prevalent than the second. We shall discuss industrial examples of both.

Why an MDSS?

More so than ever before, managers find themselves operating in a competitive environment. For better or worse, this incubates MDSSs. By necessity we make more decisions more quickly. They are often "bigger" decisions. More and more data exist. Increasingly sophisticated judgments must be applied. Multiple managers are involved. The competitive environment is constantly shifting.

In this setting, a common frustration is knowing that data exist somewhere in the organization, but they are not easily found, assimilated, formatted, or readily manipulated. If we impose on this classic environment an appropriate MDSS, we theoretically can deliver to key managers both relevant information and the capability to work with it, in order to produce more effective short- and long-term decisions.

Little describes an MDSS as "a coordinated collection of data, systems, tools, and techniques with supporting software and hardware by which an organization gathers and interprets relevant information from business and environment and turns it into a basis for marketing action."[1] Many of our systems fail to possess all the features found in some of Little's examples and we find with Keen and Scott Morton that systems can "provide a variety of levels of [decision] support," ranging from information storage and retrieval through statistical analyses to interactive modeling.[2] The emphasis should be on support for decision making rather than on completeness of the system.

These MDSSs, in nearly every form, have a powerful potential for impact on a business's procedures, strategies, and organization. As our thesis has suggested, this generally occurs from the bottom up by aggregating, analyzing, and modeling primary market data, but can also occur at the strategic level, from the top down, with the use of general models that capture key structural relationships in the market. We call these generic models.

GE's Experience: The 1970s and 1980s

At least one of almost every "type" of MDSS exists somewhere within GE businesses. We shall review a few specific examples, selected to demonstrate a perspective rather than a representative sample of the complete list. And the discussion will focus on strategy and organization issues rather than the user, technology, theory, or other issues. The examples of marketing decision support systems are perhaps best illustrated by locating those systems in a conceptual capability "field" (see Figure 5.1). One dimension of this field is a continuum that reflects the sophistication evolution of the systems. The other dimension depicts the ability of the system to support tactical versus strategic decision making. There is nothing sacred about this classification scheme; it simply provides a useful framework for discussion and the exact location of each MDSS is a complex judgment in itself. Without attempting to resolve the exact difference between tactics and strategy, let us say that generally tactical decisions concern objective-specific resource allocations, while strategic decisions concern objective formulation or change.

Returning to our capability field, the dimension of sophistication ranges from simple data bases of sales transactions, which are sometimes manipulated manually, to statistical analyses of these data such as demand forecasting, to alternative scenario analyses and interactive modeling of strategy alternatives. Several points relative to this continuum are worth mentioning. Each of these types of systems is in use today. This suggests that the more primitive systems are certainly capable of technological upgrading. The obstacles to upgrading are many and complex and will be discussed later. In some cases the most sophisticated systems have been developed by consultants rather than by the business. This may be a result of the organizational focus within GE on product departments, which may create obstacles to systems that focus on markets. Furthermore, the existence of advanced market decision support systems is not necessarily positively correlated with business success, which suggests a startling hypothesis about the motivation to develop MDSSs. In particular, is an MDSS a source of differential advantage that produces superior market position, or an attempt to save a weakened business? Finally, automated marketing information systems are recent creations at GE, where information systems have historically been under the aegis of financial operations. Other companies may have experienced the frustrations of trying to build, or extract, marketing information from financial information

Figure 5.1 Range of MDSS Capability in GE

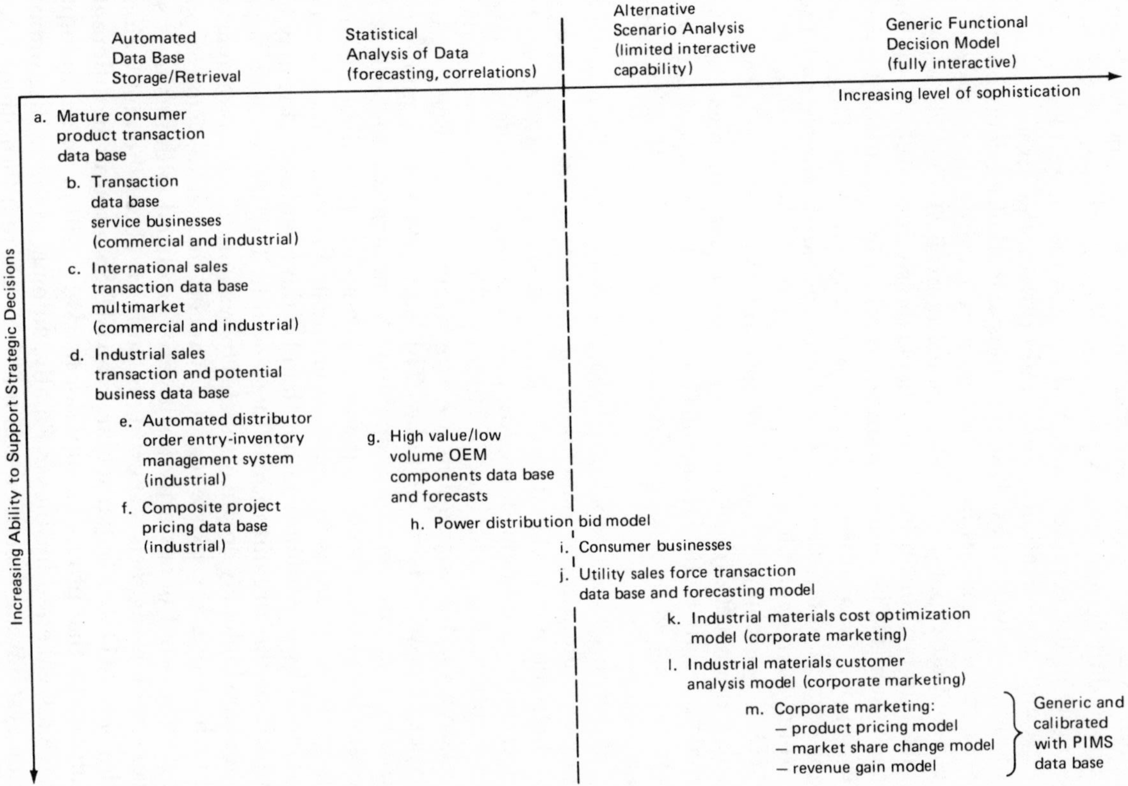

Automated Data Base Storage/Retrieval	Statistical Analysis of Data (forecasting, correlations)	Alternative Scenario Analysis (limited interactive capability)	Generic Functional Decision Model (fully interactive)

Increasing level of sophistication →

a. Mature consumer product transaction data base

b. Transaction data base service businesses (commercial and industrial)

c. International sales transaction data base multimarket (commercial and industrial)

d. Industrial sales transaction and potential business data base

e. Automated distributor order entry-inventory management system (industrial)

f. Composite project pricing data base (industrial)

g. High value/low volume OEM components data base and forecasts

h. Power distribution bid model

i. Consumer businesses

j. Utility sales force transaction data base and forecasting model

k. Industrial materials cost optimization model (corporate marketing)

l. Industrial materials customer analysis model (corporate marketing)

m. Corporate marketing:
  — product pricing model
  — market share change model
  — revenue gain model

Generic and calibrated with PIMS data base

Increasing Ability to Support Strategic Decisions →

systems. Information on orders, sales, and margins, as well as on competitive actions and the external environment more generally, are of maximum value when tied to legitimate and meaningful market segments. And segment-based data are of limited use to finance, hence the common misalignment problem between finance and marketing. The source of the problem is that the detail of market information required to meet the mission of the finance function is different from the level required to guide market decisions. Specifically, the finance function can meet its charge without information such as data on segment share and cost per customer.

On the vertical dimension of our capability field, we attempt to locate each MDSS in terms of its ability to support decisions of a strategic versus a tactical nature. We pose a simple hypothesis that those systems that are predominantly directed to data management support predominantly tactical decisions (e.g., items A, B, C, D). Those that are directed to data management and analysis are often designed to support tactical decisions, but may be very useful in making strategic decisions (e.g., items E, F, G, H). Those systems that are directed to devising alternative scenarios (simulators) and based on generic models are of use only for strategic decision support (e.g., items I, J, K, L, M). Simply stated, the present mixed development status of MDSSs within GE is the product of the commercially successful decentralized product organization structure of the company, combined with the historical dominance of the finance function in information system management. Nonetheless, each of these systems brings an important act to the development drama and deserves a brief review.

The following are brief descriptions of systems listed in Figure 5.1:

A. *Mature Consumer Product Transaction Data Base*
   This business, which deals with both consumer and industrial markets, has until recently not felt the need for marketing decision support systems. Much of the forecasting and budgeting has been done by clerks using financial data bases of past sales. Little was known regarding local or regional market share or competitive efforts. But with a more dynamic, competitive, and technological marketplace today, they are in the process of developing marketing-oriented data bases and information systems.

B. *Transaction Data Base—Service Businesses*
   These systems involve extensive data bases for prospects and customer tracking and activity reporting. They have on-line revenue tracking in their headquarters' central system. The his-

torical data bases are used as an input to forecasting on a national level. One of these businesses may soon implement an on-line system at the regional level to provide this input to the forecasting-budgeting effort.

C. *International Sales Transaction Data Base—Multimarket*
With the organization still being formed, this business has seen the wisdom of developing marketing-oriented data bases and systems along with financial systems. At the start they will consist mostly of order and customer tracking by geographical region, product, and market segment. It is hoped in the future to establish a worldwide on-line network that would include competitive and pricing information.

D. *Industrial Sales Transaction and Potential Business Data Base*
This industrial sales organization has three major order data base systems. Two use direct field input. These are used to track and forecast pending (available) business, based on monthly or quarterly entries by each sales representative as to business pending in his or her territory. Although at first it met with field resistance, it has proved beneficial to both management and the field as a good summary of sales activity. The third system is an actual order-tracking data base, in which the input is part of the order process. The data can be retrieved by customer, by product, by sales engineer, or by area and is available to product departments, sales management, and the field sales force.

E. *Automated Distributor Order Entry—Inventory Management System*
Participating distributors have "dial-up" terminals through which they can place orders, check on product availability and price, and determine the status of orders based on the product department's daily inputs on inventory availability. The system has also helped supplying departments detect and improve inventory control problems, within their departments as well as among distributors.

F. *Composite Project Pricing Data Base*
This data base develops price quotations for large multiproduct industrial projects. It consists of multiple product department cost data and historical files of current job information such as size, location, equipment, competition, and activity levels. It was developed to support a central organization established with responsibility and authority to set bid prices and manage delivery. The projects involve several product departments whose strategies, cost factors, and margins may be quite differ-

ent. It also enables the customer to have a single point for negotiation.

G. *High Value/Low Volume OEM Component Business*

The business has developed market data bases and analytic programs to forecast parts and service needs of all existing components in use by customers. The data base is worldwide and continually updated through field sales and sales management input. They also have some capability for forecasting component sales.

H. *Power Distribution Bid Model*

This model takes as input a given customer's bill of materials for a specific project, that customer's economic evaluation equation (from customer knowledge), and GE's own production economics, and then determines the bid on those products. The program also determines production needs, initiates necessary raw material orders, and has a tie-in to computer-aided manufacturing with necessary product design.

I. *Consumer Businesses*

Our consumer businesses tend to be more sophisticated in their systems capability because of the highly competitive and more homogeneous nature of their markets. One of these businesses has an integrated MDSS with econometric forecasting in interactive mode, sales data bases for on-line analysis, key market research data for analysis and retrieval, as well as alternative scenario models of physical distribution systems. Another business has complex models using product preference research information for product feature planning.

J. *Utility Sales Force Transaction Data Base and Forecasting Model*

This organization has built up an extensive data base on worldwide power-generating capacity from field input, along with an interactive model to forecast long-term generating needs by country. It allows managers to change assumptions on growth rates of population, electricity usage, and GNP to develop various scenarios of future demand for power facilities.

K. *Industrial Materials Cost Optimization Model*

Based on extensive cost data and market information, this model enables the product department manager to forecast future business, perform dynamic analysis, and develop alternative scenarios. Though developed for a specific project, it has ongoing capability.

L. *Industrial Materials Customer Analysis Model*

Customer-distributor audits covering sales record, share, perceptions of GE, buying policies, and so on, were loaded into microcomputer files, using packaged file software. Programs were developed to translate the files to interactive packaged software for in-depth strategic analysis of product department strengths and weaknesses. The program has capability through periodic file updates to be a continuing field-sales-driven MDSS.

M. *Corporate Marketing*

Product-Pricing Model   This model based on the PIMS data base allows managers to make assumptions on various factors that affect price, then input price points and estimate the impact on market share. It is not intended as a routine for setting price, but rather a guide for making pricing decisions.

Market Share Change Model   For three nonconsumer market structure types, the market share change impact of changes in six tactical independent variables has been modeled, tested widely, and utilized by a number of businesses to test alternative market segment share goal feasibility as a basis for segment target strategy. The model is market structure generic and calibrated with PIMS data.

Revenue Gain Model   This model is used to link the marketing mix and market situation with changes in price and market share, coupled with changes in market demand that yield expected change in revenue. The model has been programmed for microcomputers to allow the manager to experiment and test various mix factors and market assumptions.

As mentioned earlier, the development of these marketing-oriented data bases was the first step in building nonfinancial information systems. We possess a tremendous wealth of financial information, much of it on-line and ready to use, some of which is important to marketing. But the ability of marketing operations to access this information in a form useful for their analyses and decision making has been limited. In addition, little has been done to gather appropriate competitive and environmental information, especially in commercial and industrial businesses. The situation is improving as marketing personnel realize the benefits of supplementing existing systems or developing systems of their own.

Many of our MDSSs are primarily data bases of sales transactions. But many of these bases contain organizational, economic, and marketing correlates for these transactions. While these data have proved useful as they are, statistical analysis of the data has followed closely upon the developing of the marketing data bases. The primary need has been demand forecasting and the ability to analyze it according to such parameters as specific product lines, market segments, and geographic areas. Marketing systems have also given sales management a tool for measuring performance according to significant criteria such as market share, profitability, and business development.

Unfortunately, most business units that possess MDSSs, or have access to them, have not progressed beyond this point in using the marketing systems. In particular, there are very few systems developed by nonconsumer product departments that go beyond this point of statistical analysis. A number of problems contribute to the situation: lack of expertise in the product and sales departments, economic constraints, lack of awareness on the part of managers, or particularly dynamic high-growth or high-tech marketing environments. (We will go into impediments to the MDSS in more detail later.)

Nevertheless, a few product departments have taken the next step toward marketing-forecast models that create alternative scenarios of best case or worst case situations. These systems are generally on-line, time-shared systems, with some limited interactive capabilities. A case in point is our utility sales force model for forecasting future capacity requirements for utility customers worldwide. Various economic, generating capacity, and usage data on each country are collected from information from the field. Assumptions of growth rates and price elasticities are made and forecasts of each country's generating needs are developed. By changing the assumptions, market planners can get an idea of the range of future potential business. This type of scenario analysis is particularly suited to the long-range planning needed for the extended lead times in the power generation industry.

A Case Example: Two Tactical MDSSs in Concert

Keeping in mind the central thesis of this paper, that the existence of market information (in this case primary market data) will allow for strategic and then organizational change, let us look at a more or less typical case involving two of the MDSSs discussed earlier, which were developed for tactical decision support. Envision an industrial market consisting of two rather distinct segments (Figure 5.2). Segment A requires basically a distribution-intensive approach. The product is regarded by customers in this segment as undifferentiated. Success with distribution is based on coverage, service, ease of doing business, and price or terms. Segment B is a direct selling situation in which bundling of products and competi-

Figure 5.2 Two Tactical MDSSs in Concert

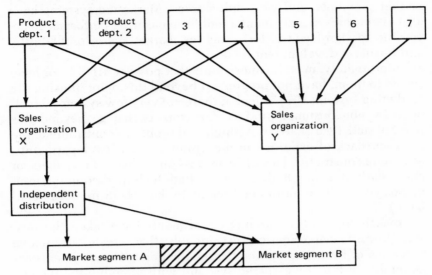

tive bidding on price, combined with long-established personal sales relationships and some user brand specifications, are important factors. Both segments are served with essentially the same products—at least, products of common technology, manufactured by the same product departments. A different MDSS was developed for each channel to market. They were developed, in fact, for different reasons, at different times, and by different people to be operated independently.

The MDSS for segment A, initiated in 1980, is an automated order entry system aimed at optimal inventory loading for the distributor and reduced transaction support cost for GE. Additionally, the A system provides information that is of assistance in production scheduling. This system is fully automated: Orders entered by distributors are "processed" by integrated warehouse and work-in-process computerized inventory control systems, which are linked to the computerized production scheduling models. The system parameters can be adjusted only by general management.

The MDSS supporting segment B is designed primarily to provide centralized bidding and packaging for large transactions involving products from a number of departments. This bidding responsibility includes accommodating non-GE product add-ons, and differing and dynamic product departments' goals, immediate and long-term. The MDSS is driven by a large, computerized, experiential data base that integrates past quotation and realization experience with buyer and situational information into a data bank. A standard format of environmental, influencer, product, economic, and geographic data is completed for each transaction bid upon. Individuals constructing the composite quotation consult the data bank for indications of past success in similar conditions and then produce the quote *without the benefit of statistical modeling help.* This MDSS has been in operation since 1978 and in that period of time the share of available business has increased by more than 32 percent, while the GE sales to the segment grew from $40 million to more than $100 million. It is perhaps understandable that further modeling is not a high priority, though the evidence suggests that an even more dramatic gain is possible by modeling the bid decision itself.

In combination these two MDSSs provide powerful benefits to these industrial businesses and their customers. Both maintain a computerized file of market-customer-transaction information; both provide a quicker information flow from market to seller; both augment inventory management and production scheduling; and both simplify customer dealings with GE. But neither is *modeled* in a form that allows simulation capabilities or use, and therefore each may seem to fall short of a rigorous academic definition of an MDSS. Yet between them, they can have profound strategic and organizational impacts on the elements of the company involved. Why? Tactically, they provide data on a transaction according to the specific market segment, which can, aggregated on multiple criteria, provide an on-line basis for perfecting the market mix. Strategically, analyses of the data allow for enhanced understanding of segments and their differential attractiveness, and thereby facilitate decisions about potential markets and manufacturing strategy. Thus, the reason for partial system development must lie elsewhere.

Despite their partial development, these MDSSs can have an organizational impact in two ways. First, and most simply, the use of the quotation development system is a direct proxy for a central marketing organization representing several independent product-based departments, each with responsibility for its own financial performance. Second, when a major strategic change is articulated, the organization required to implement must follow. In this situation, the availability of market data allowed the cognizant product departments to determine that margins were lower in segment B than in A, and that multiple product packaging in segment A would provide improved manufacturing scheduling and not reduce overall margins on the transaction. Faced with the composite quotation experiences and these data, the product departments formed a marketing organization to integrate their activities and direct the primary sales organization.

In this case, and in others in the company, the availability of market information broadened the range of strategic alternatives considered, which in turn led to strategic and then organizational change. The result is a market-based management, which is common in consumer businesses but far less so in industrial businesses. This naturally leads to the question: Will strategic and organizational change flow from MDSSs where primary market data are not available? We think it possible under some circumstances. Let us look at an example.

Generic MDSSs

Generic MDSSs have the ability to provide broadened strategic and organizational response to a market. This potential is, of course, most attractive when used in conjunction with primary market data and, unlike our previous case example, useful *only* in strategic decisions. There is not a single example within GE of a generic MDSS having sufficient capability or management confidence to be used directly in tactical decisions, although they are used in testing the feasibility of some tactical decisions.

The most sophisticated level of MDSS is the fully interactive decision model that a few GE departments are in the process of developing. Although academicians have been developing and working with this type of decision support system for several years now, industry has been slow to adopt or develop the models. Now, with the advent of the personal computer, more and more managers are discovering their advantages. Several of this class of MDSS have been developed by our Corporate Marketing Operations personnel for use in various businesses. Some are very straightforward such as the product-pricing model, which enables managers to test the impact of pricing strategies on market share, while others deal with the interrelationships of multiple mix and environment factors. Members of our staff have recently developed a revenue gain model to aid managers in more effective development of marketing mix plans that will achieve desired revenue performance (see Figure 5.3). In using the model, the manager is forced to make certain assumptions about how the elements of the marketing mix will affect price and share as well as how the external environment will affect share and demand and their ultimate impact on sales revenues. The model was programmed for personal computers using manager-friendly software, to enable the manager to test and compare marketing strategies.

Figure 5.3   Revenue Gain Model

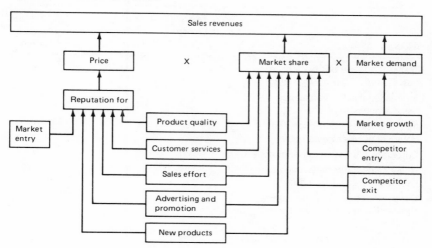

One application of the model involved looking at twenty-one industrial product lines and comparing their planned share growth to the model-predicted growth, given their planned efforts in field selling, media, and product quality, and their existing business situations. The model, calibrated with the Strategic Planning Institute's data base, was able to demonstrate where tactical efforts were out of line with environmental realities and to show their ultimate impact on long-term strategies.

Do All MDSSs Hold Strategic and Organizational Impact?

We have seen that some MDSSs have the potential for strategic and ultimately organizational impact; we now need to consider the potential of the other systems listed at the beginning. The service businesses and international and industrial sales transaction data bases that serve multiple markets, often with multiple products, seem to have the desired potential (see Table 5.1). Although their systems are still primarily used for information storage and retrieval, they provide the opportunity for statistical analysis and model development, which could enable management to look at the markets from differing strategic perspectives. The industrial sales force, for example, is an area in which systems development has the potential for major impact, by helping both product departments and sales managers to find better ways to bundle products and services. Some of these product departments have already

TABLE 5.1 MDSS Potential for Change

MDSS	Tactical Change Potential	Strategic Change Potential	Organizational Change Potential
Transaction data base—service businesses	Yes	Yes	Yes
International sales transaction data base—multimarket	Yes	Yes	Yes
Industrial sales transaction and potential business data base	Yes	Yes	Yes
Corporate marketing generic models	Yes	Yes	Yes
Utility sales force transaction data base and forecasting model	Yes	Yes	Probably
Consumer businesses data base, forecasting and product planning models	Yes	Yes	Probably not
Mature consumer product transaction data base	Yes	Yes	?
High value/low volume OEM component data base and forecasting model	Yes	Yes	?
Industrial materials model	Yes	Yes	?

been affected by the composite quotation system. This sales information should be useful for other systems development within and across product departments to better serve markets common to several more effectively.

By contrast, there are some systems in which the potential for major organizational impact may be less, although there may be opportunity for strategic impact. Our consumer departments are businesses whose products serve broad homogeneous markets, though they may have two distinct distribution channels—contract sales and dealers. This does not mean that an MDSS would not be beneficial, but rather that the impact may be more tactical.

Generally speaking, organizational impact will occur when there is a lack of market focus in the selling organization. Strategic impact will occur when the MDSS provides broad market segment coverage. Tactical impact will occur when there are data on the response to a marketing mix for a specific market segment. The majority of GE businesses are still in the tactical impact stage, with further development coming slowly.

MDSS Evolution: Equipment and Strategy

It is not surprising that MDSSs, at least at CE, have developed on the tactical more than the strategic level. A theoretical view of this

Figure 5.4 Evolution of MDSS by Capability and User — A Theoretical Perspective

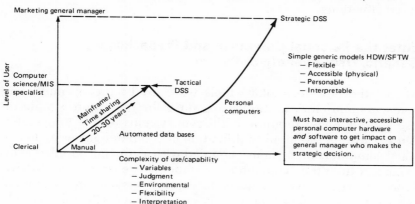

evolution is presented in Figure 5.4. The horizontal axis depicts the increasing complexity of the systems. Complexity here includes a number of variables: the number of judgments or assumptions incorporated, the degree to which the external environment can be reproduced, and the degree of flexibility. While the internal makeup of the system increases in complexity, the simplicity of use or "user-friendliness" should also increase, making the system accessible to general management as opposed to only computer specialists or marketing scientists. The vertical axis depicts the level of the system's users within an organization, from the lower-level clerks who handle the manual data systems, to the programmer, through the systems specialist, to marketing and general management.

Marketing data and decision support systems have tended to evolve from the lower left, with clerical workers logging sales, figuring margins, and computing budgets, up and to the right, with higher-level systems people incorporating complex computer systems with more variables and increasing analytic capability. Until very recently, this evolution has taken place within the realm of computer scientists or information system specialists, who were more or less remote from the decision makers of the organization. The hardware and software involved demanded considerable technical expertise. In fact, the mystique of the systems world was perpetuated by the perceived complexity of the systems and the general aloofness of the experts. Not surprisingly, the real strategic benefits were only rarely possible because of the general manager's inability to communicate problems to the systems people and their inability to respond with a solution based on information available. Therefore, the MDSSs reached a plateau where they only provided tactical support to middle management on fairly routine, semistructured situations.

Enter the Personal Computer and Prepackaged, Generic, User-Friendly Software

At first the new technology tools were used more by mid-level managers and clerical employees, since the tools were simple to use and no longer required high-level systems people to operate. But because of the rapid proliferation of computer games and personal computers in the home, coupled with a growing population of managers from the "computer generation," executives are discovering the real power of decision support systems in their own offices. These systems typically use generic models flexible enough to be customized to the manager's own specific problems. Most are designed to force the manager to make judgments about internal and external conditions, giving him or her the opportunity to test and study the impact of varying assumptions. They give a nearly real-world experience without the risks. They allow examination of strategy alternatives without creating large complex information handling and statistical systems.

The extent of actual utilization of generic models in industrial markets will depend primarily upon the data used in calibrating the models. To the degree this calibration is done with market- or business-specific data, the models will be used. This is essentially what the consumer market models have as an advantage, because the relevant marketing response functions are relatively stable across product markets and segments. These consumer market models are truly generic. The dilemma, while not entirely clear to these writers, seems to be that in industrial markets this response stability is found only in smaller segment aggregations, thereby driving up the system cost per market transaction. In an attempt to deal with the dilemma, we at GE developed a series of "generic" market management models (some are listed in Figure 5.1), which we calibrated by using structurally positioned data from the PIMS research data base. These have had generally weak acceptance in the company to date, though they have received favorable press and academic review. It does not appear that widespread industrial market application is imminent.

Conclusions and Observations

If a rigorous definition of an MDSS is applied—it includes data banks, statistics, models, optimization, and Q/A capabilities—then there have been no industrial MDSSs in GE until very recently.[3] Furthermore, those systems that most closely fit the strict definition are rarely fully used even where they do exist. For example, the market share change model, which has been shown to be quite effective, now has only one user. Why this is so is not clear, but the following factors are certainly partly responsible.

- Many GE businesses that serve industrial markets are organized for strategic management at product department rather than market level.
- The performance gain produced by data and statistics alone has been so pronounced that the *perceived* incremental gain to be derived from modeling and simulation is low.
- Marketing, as a function, is not always viewed as a source of significant competitive differential advantage.
- On-line computing system development is expensive and subsequent access is awkward.
- The industrial markets are "made" more directly with different mix elements than are consumer markets.
- Experimentation is very risky in industrial markets.

In a capsule form, uncertainty about product and market boundaries and marketing mix response functions are perhaps the strongest inhibitors to MDSS development and use.

MDSSs: Where Are We Headed in the 1990s?

There seems to be, at least in the business literature, little disagreement that MDSSs will become more prevalent and more powerful. But inhibitors, particularly in industrial businesses, are pervasive and often as powerful as the systems themselves. Any discussion of where MDSSs are likely to go in either development or use is limited by the specific situation and company. Nonetheless, several "thrusts" appear inevitable.

- Emphasis should, and probably will, continue on developing market data and statistics rather than models and simulators (market status rather than market response).
- Generic models will get infrequent use in industrial markets.
- Personal computers will be used primarily for data storage and flexible format reporting more than for model-assisted decision making, though the frustration of attempting to use them at general management level will intensify.

- Centralized, time-sharing MDSSs will continue to grow in popularity and use over personal-computer-based systems for tactical applications involving many users and multiple management level use.
- Development of MDSSs will only accelerate when their value can be accurately demonstrated at the bottom line.

CHAPTER 6

Steel Axes for Stone Age Men

Vincent P. Barabba
Eastman Kodak Company

There once was a tribe of Australian aborigines called the Yir Yoront. The central item in the Yir Yoront culture was the stone ax,
which tribe members found indispensable in every activity—from
producing food to constructing shelter. For the elders, the stone ax
was a symbol of masculinity and respect. The men owned the stone
axes, but the women and children were the principal users. Thus,
according to a prescribed social system, the tools were borrowed
from fathers, husbands, or uncles.

Enter some well-intentioned missionaries. They distributed
steel axes to the Yir Yoront to help them improve their living conditions. There was no important resistance to the shift to the new tool;
the aborigines were accustomed to obtaining their tools via trade
with others. Moreover, the steel axes were more efficient for most
tasks, and as a result the stone axes rapidly disappeared among the
Yir Yoront.

The missionaries had distributed the steel axes to men, women,
and children, old and young alike. In fact, the younger men were
quicker to adopt the new tool than were their elders, who maintained a certain distrust. The result was a major disruption of sex
and age roles among the Yir Yoront. Elders, once highly respected,
now became dependent upon women and younger men and often
were forced to borrow steel axes. In addition, the trading rituals of
the tribe were undermined, because stone axes had previously
formed the basis of trade. Ties of friendship among traders broke
down. Overall, the religious system and social structure of the Yir
Yoront became disorganized as a result of an inability to adjust to
the innovation.

Naturally, the steel ax alone did not cause all these changes
among the Yir Yoront. But researchers concluded that it was central
to most of the cultural disorders.

In retelling this story, I have drawn on the seminal work of

Everett Rogers of Stanford University on the adoption of innovation.[1] He contends that innovation, as part of a complex innovation-
decision process, must pass through four stages of activity before it
is successfully adopted:[2]

1. Introduction (the *knowledge* stage)
2. Successful testing (the *persuasion* stage)
3. Acceptance for adoption (the *decision* stage)
4. Reexamination (the *confirmation* stage)

Indeed, we do not have to look very far into the literature surrounding the adoption of decision support systems (DSSs) to see that
even when a system is actually operative and beneficial, we can
expect its adoption to be a long and tedious process, its introduction
to be far more complicated than we might at first have supposed,
and its effects on the existing system to be both positive and
negative.

From my viewpoint as a practitioner, the key issue today is *not*
the coming breakthroughs in hardware and software for sophisticated marketing decision support systems (MDSSs). Indeed, by
choosing the analogy of steel axes for Stone Age men, I have revealed my own perspective on the critical area that must be addressed next—namely, preparing *people* to use the tools already at
hand. Otherwise, as Nigel Piercy points out: "We should have
learned enough from other innovations to see that there is a *quicksand* between potential and realized gains, into which opportunities may be lost, and even worse, penalties may be incurred."[3]

Thus, in this discussion I want to call your attention to the ways
in which the introduction of a *significant change*—such as an
MDSS—can affect the people within an organization. I will present
a two-part methodology, still being developed, that I have found
extremely useful in managing the implementation of such a change.

The First Step: Six Significant Questions about Change

Let me begin by describing the first of two steps I have utilized
when asked to "come in and help implement a change so that the
organization can use information better." I call this step the Six
Significant Questions. To set the context for these questions, let me
return briefly to the work of Everett Rogers. He points out that
before introducing an innovation into an organization, we must
understand not only the issues but also the people involved, both as
individuals and as a group.[4]

To understand the people involved as individuals, we need to know several things. What is their ability to handle sophisticated tools? Do they basically understand what is involved? How secure are they in their positions? What are their values? Can they influence others? To understand the people involved as a group, we need to know how they interact. How traditional is the group? Do they do something in a certain way because they have always done it that way? Or, are they willing to try new ideas?

It is equally important to remind ourselves that acceptance of an innovation does not necessarily ensure its use. Therefore, it is essential to take a good look at the organizational environment as well. I have found that a set of six questions can bring to the surface the human and organizational barriers that can stand between innovation and its adoption. The first question is the megaquestion. If you cannot answer yes to both parts of this question, then you should *not* proceed to the other questions on the list.

1. Have those who manage the organization agreed that there is a need that will utilize the change being proposed?

    Have they designated a "champion"—that is, a person or a group of people—to make sure the change comes about?

2. Who has participated in planning for the change? Who has not?

3. What, if anything, does the change modify or replace? Are there significant alternatives, with potential for success, that may continue to divert energy and confuse the issue?

4. Who within the organization will benefit immediately as a result of the change? Who will benefit over the longer term?

5. Who will suffer immediately? Who will suffer over the longer term?

6. How will the change affect the major relationships within the organization:

    individual job relationships?

    organizational relationships?

    social and other informal relationships?

A Case History from the Census Bureau: The Impact of Potential Change

A case history from my first term as director of the U.S. Census Bureau (1973–1976) will illustrate the insights that can be drawn from asking the six significant questions. Not only is it a useful example, but it also allows us to examine the process in some detail without being concerned with the proprietary issues that would arise in discussing an MDSS from the private sector. The experience was also an important benchmark in my own search for better ways to address the various elements of a "complex" problem such as the development of an MDSS.

Background

Because of the enormous volume of data involved at the Census Bureau, tabulation had always been a primary factor in overall efficiency—specifically in completion of various tables and surveys. Over the years, because of the bureau's early involvement with computers, a core group of applications programmers had evolved. They were expert both as mathematicians *and* as programmers. They were the specialists, the people who listened to your problem and said, "Here's how I'll solve your problem, using a computer." These applications programmers were an extremely useful resource within the agency. For example, in the early days of computer technology, generalized software was either unavailable or inefficient in terms of computer utilization. But a smart programmer-mathematician could get inside the machine and make it as efficient as some of the systems not available until the 1980s.

As generalized software became more available and more efficient, however, the applications programmers did not want to change how they were doing things. They felt that others in the bureau should continue to come to them to articulate any significant problem. They remained convinced that they were still the best resource for solutions; their high-powered skills would make the newer breed of computers even more efficient. From the perspective of bureau management, the situation created a larger problem: First, we were still dependent on this one expert group for computerized solutions to significant problems. Further, the solution software written for a particular machine would have to be completely rewritten if the bureau ever changed machines.

The first innovation that caused some disruption was the introduction of the new computer language—a basic executive system that was portable from machine to machine. This meant that the bureau could make modifications in the hardware without making major modifications in the programs. Although each program was not as efficient, the total system was *more* efficient because we could modify the machine without changing the software.

Unfortunately, from the perspective of the applications programmers, the scenario went like this: "I am a high-powered programmer-mathematician. Until now, if you wanted to get anything processed in the bureau, you had to come and talk to me. Now, however, the bureau can hire anybody who understands how computers use generalized systems. This new person doesn't have to be both a programmer and a mathematician, like me, capable of writing complex machine language. Suddenly, this new person is as valuable as I am!"

Then, something else began to happen within the bureau: With more powerful machines and generalized software, we found that an analyst and a clerk (without a skilled programmer) could use these tools to make tables. As the mathematician-programmers were quick to point out, this was actually an *inefficient* use of the computer, relative to its total capability. Yet from the perspective of bureau management, we saw two advantages: first, less powerful people could work on the computers to make tables; second, we could make and adjust more tables, more frequently.

The Generalized Tabulating System

The next innovation occurred when several of these "new breed" of computer specialists within the bureau developed an original approach to the design for a generalized tabulating system (GTS). The assignment actually originated outside the bureau with a request from the U.S. Agency for International Development (AID). They asked, in effect, "Can you give us a simple computer program for tabulating the census results in the countries where we provide services?" In response, this group of bureau specialists came up with a new approach for a GTS. It worked for those countries supported by AID—primarily because it was much better than what they had been using. In addition, the system provided users a flexible, rather easy-to-use language that could be learned by programmers as well as trained nonprogrammers.

Following widespread acceptance of this system and various refinements, the bureau specialists (or the GTS group) said, "We think we've got a pretty good solution here. Why don't we see if we can use some variation of this within the Census Bureau?" In a subsequent report, they described their efforts this way:

> Using our AID experience, we were convinced that a very powerful, easy-to-use Generalized Tabulating System (GTS) could be built for the Bureau. We discussed the possibility with anyone in the Bureau who would listen . . . and the almost universal answer was that the Bureau is unique and the idea would not work here. . . . The widespread perception within the Bureau was that we were individuals who had worked in an obscure corner of the agency, but had never participated in projects affecting the main mission of the Bureau.

Subsequently, the work of the GTS project came to my attention, as director of the bureau. At my request, the GTS group prepared a major proposal for the development of GTS for the bureau. But as this particular *change* was contemplated, I became increasingly aware of growing tensions among various factions within the bureau. It was at this point, in my role as manager of the organization, that I sought to address the issues surrounding the change represented by the GTS and to involve the various factions in seeking solutions.

As a first step, I arranged for a survey to be distributed to more than a dozen bureau divisions that were likely to be affected. A written response was required. The actual survey contained nineteen questions that I have since condensed to the six significant questions listed above. One procedural note may be interesting: I allowed the bureau's associate directors—each of whom headed several divisions—to summarize the responses from their divisional directors. But I insisted that the replies from the individual divisions be submitted for review along with the summary statements.

A Sampler of Answers to the Six Significant Questions

I have already characterized the first question as a megaquestion:

1. Have those who manage the organization agreed that there is a need that will utilize the GTS being proposed?

   Have they designated a "champion"—that is, a person or a group of people—to make sure the GTS comes about?

Along with other senior management in the Census Bureau, I recognized that a GTS could streamline the bureau's production of statistical tables. While I was extremely interested in the potential of the system proposed by the GTS group, I had not yet designated a "champion" for it within the Census Bureau. Rather, I viewed the survey as a crucial first step in addressing the change that a GTS represented—by bringing to the surface issues and involving participants from throughout the bureau.

I have selected replies from the answers given to the other five questions in the bureau survey.[5] They have been grouped to reflect the three predominant viewpoints among the many factions within the bureau. The pro group comprises those who were generally in favor of the proposed change; the con group includes those who were primarily against the proposed change; and the neutral group designates those who saw both sides of the issue.

2. Who has participated in planning for the GTS? Who has not?

Pro Group: We understand that the success of the GTS project largely depends on the commitment of the executive staff and the cooperation and acceptance of the programming groups. To explain the research and planning involved, those proposing a GTS have given several presentations to the executive staff. The proponents have also offered several workshops on the GTS, but because of the limited size of the sessions, the proponents were able to communicate with only a small number of programmers and managers.

The current plan is to offer assistance and advice on table generation techniques to any branch in the bureau. It is hoped that these workshops and system modifications will convince a larger portion of the bureau's programmers that generalized software is the trend of the future.

One of the most difficult problems to overcome in introducing a GTS is that subject-area individuals and managers, who are the people to benefit the most, do not really understand the nature and purpose of the change. . . . The primary planning has taken place within another division. . . . Thus, a decision is needed from top bureau management that the project has enough merit to warrant a serious planning, development, and evaluation effort, with the necessary involvement of all bureau divisions.

Con Group: We are not aware that there is a plan for a GTS. This has truly been a well-kept secret!

Neutral Group: There has been limited internal input. But to be a viable system, both user division programmers and subject-matter analysts will have to participate more actively in the development of a GTS for the bureau.

3. What, if anything, does the GTS modify or replace? Are there significant alternatives, with potential for success, that may continue to divert energy and confuse the issue?

Pro Group: In our view, a GTS, when completed, will replace most custom-written tabulation programs at the Census Bureau. The GTS should be thought of as a tool to simplify the communication process between people and the computer in one specific area—producing statistical tables.

The GTS will allow subject-matter managers and analysts to communicate more directly with the computer through a tabulation oriented, high-level language. In fact, the actual computer coding for most tables may be performed directly by nonprogrammer subject-matter persons, freeing up the programming staff to solve other pressing computing problems.

In terms of modification, the introduction of a GTS will mean each subject area must use the same package, so their input files will have to be standardized to fit the GTS. Output tables produced by the GTS will also be standardized. This will allow the publication process to be more readily automated.

Con Group: If you buy the rosy definition of a GTS (put forth by the proponents), then you have very little contact with the reality of computer software . . . and the types of problems that must be solved in publication of statistical data as practiced at the Census Bureau.

Neutral Group: A GTS will more likely supplement existing packages, rather than replace them. We see it as an aid to producing timely, smaller packages of tables for use by nonprogrammers, but not readily able to replace the wide variations of tabulations currently required on almost all surveys and censuses.

We see a GTS as having the potential for expanding the ability of analysts to explore data by means of tabulations and cross-tabulations . . . and [the capability] to serve as a production tool within the bureau as well as other statistical organizations. We see a GTS as having less potential for replacing specialized procedures for individual high-volume applications.

In terms of modifications occurring with the introduction of a GTS, the programmer-analyst work environment would be modified.

Programmers, it would seem, would be responsible for structuring and maintaining data files and performing specified data manipulations. But at this point, the data analyst would interpose himself to generate the required tabular output. This, of course, would be an invasion of the programmer's current province, which may or may not be significant. Of significance is that the system adds a new dimension of responsibility to the analyst.

4. Who within the organization will benefit immediately as a result of the GTS? Who will benefit over the longer term?

Pro Group: Almost everyone should benefit from a really good GTS. If tabulations can be produced more quickly and at lower cost, sponsors both in and out of the bureau benefit, as well as the bureau itself. . . . Even programmers could benefit: Tabulations are exceedingly boring to do month after month, and many programmers would be quite relieved not to have to do so many of them.

Con Group: We see no immediate benefits.

Neutral Group: The data users, both within and outside the bureau, would benefit immediately in that more data would be available on a more timely basis. Since fewer custom-coded programs would be required, there would be economic benefits also. Nevertheless the overhead costs associated with writing, implementing, and utilizing a generalized system—which necessarily is less efficient to run than systems written for specific tasks—may offset the savings.

5. Who will suffer immediately? Who will suffer over the longer term?

Pro Group: Introduction of a GTS, although not immediately producing massive personnel changes, will be a threat to certain individuals. Eventually, it should reduce the size of applications-programming staffs. At the same time, it would diminish the bureaucratic status of applications-programming managers. It can also be construed as a threat to applications programmers whose only skills are writing custom tabulation programs.

Con Group: Data producers and users will suffer immediately if the system is imposed roughshod on the bureau without an opportunity to appreciate its strengths and deal with its weaknesses; is not supported by good training and maintenance; or is used as a tool to attempt to control all access to the computer or to achieve "power" over bureau operations.

In any event, computer systems and tabulation needs are becoming ever more complex, and any hope of nonprogrammers ever taking over programming functions with magic buttons is fast fading.

Neutral Group: We had differing opinions about who would be likely to suffer immediately. Some said no one would suffer, while others seemed to think the bureau's programmers would be affected. . . . Theoretically, a GTS would free programmers to tackle more complex projects. But those who would be immediately affected are those who specialize in tasks that might be accomplished by nonprogrammers. A good number of these people could become superfluous. Since it would take some time to adapt to the GTS, programmer cuts could be achieved through attrition rather than through a reduction in force or other extreme measures. In any case, programmers may perceive a GTS as a threat to their prestige and economic security, and thus it would produce a lot of anxiety within this group.

6. How will the GTS affect the major relationships within the organization:

● individual job relationships?
● organizational relationships?
● social and other informal relationships?

Pro Group: Certain informal organizations at the bureau will be affected in power and position by the GTS and other new generalized software. The most directly affected will be the computer user community—namely, programmers and computer analysts.

Con Group: We do not know the special and informal organizations in which those affected by a GTS participate, and we have no opinion on how they might be affected. What is the meaning of the question?

Neutral Group: Shifts in occupation will affect the division of labor in that greater cooperation will be required between statistician and programmer—which we need. . . . The distinction between these two groups will undoubtedly be lessened if a GTS is implemented. Statisticians will be able to perform many programmer functions. But the reverse is not necessarily true: Programmers may not assume any additional functions. On the other hand, it may also be true that low-level programmers will become GTS coders and stop traditional "programming" completely, thus creating a new position.

The GTS experience is probably a good example of what happens when the megaquestion is not answered satisfactorily, and when there is no closure on the fundamental issues underlying the innovation. In the intervening years, bureau management did not establish a stated value for the GTS, nor did they designate an enduring "champion." As a result, though the system was implemented initially, its use has lessened over time. Interestingly, the set of proponents and opponents did not change. Some proponents are fully committed to the system and swear by it. Opponents still deride and ignore it. And the "fence sitters" have drifted away from it because no one actively tried to convince them to use it.

The GTS experience is also a good example of the need to monitor the continual process of change. As the situation and problems have changed, the GTS "issue"—as originally stated in the mid-1970s—has seen its day. While the tabulation bottleneck problem was important then, current issues are broader and include the need for improvement in the quality and speed of the whole process—from data collection to eventual publication. Given new computer and system concepts, the tabulation phase is now a smaller part of the whole. Further, the contention between the programmers and analysts has lessened, since analysts now have an accepted and larger part to play.

The important point is that events outside the control of the Census Bureau have forced this change. As an example, the bureau has had difficulty in hiring programmers, while at the same time the need for programmers has been reduced because much of today's and tomorrow's computer software is geared to the analyst.

The Second Step: Overview on a Design Process for Answering the Six Significant Questions

I earlier described this experience as an important benchmark in my own search for ways to deal with the various elements of a "complex" problem. From the GTS Census Bureau survey, I learned that it was useful to ask the six significant questions. The answers allowed me to understand the complexity and depth of the barriers that stood between the proposed innovation and its adoption. But those same answers did not provide me, as a manager, with sufficient understanding to develop a solution that would not only be implemented but also be accepted by the various interest groups in the bureau.

In the terms of Everett Rogers, I had the tools to deal with the *knowledge* and *persuasion* stages (as Rogers describes the innovation-adoption process), but I did not yet have a useful approach to the *decision* stage.[6] During this phase the individual undertakes activities that will lead ultimately to adoption or rejection of the innovation. Rogers points out that most people do not accept an innovation without first using it on a probationary basis to determine its utility. Innovations available for a trial period are generally adopted more rapidly. (The fourth and final stage in the innovation-adoption cycle is further testing by direct application, or *confirmation*.)

I realized that the critical next step was to devise a process that could better address the various elements of a "complex" problem *and* point the direction for implementation of change through pilot projects. It was this experience that led me to explore further the ideas being developed by Ian Mitroff and Richard Mason, both former students of C. West Churchman. I first met with them in relation to work we were doing on the census for the year 2000.[7] This effort, plus useful insights from others, led to a process called strategic assumption surfacing and testing, or SAST. (See Appendix 6.1 for further explanation.)

From the practitioner's perspective, the SAST process offers a number of advantages. For example, it incorporates a design approach that both supports creative thinking and facilitates assumption-based planning. In addition, SAST takes into account the need to address the special problems associated with the actual introduction of an innovation. Thus, the "champions for change" can utilize the SAST process to design a direction for implementing the critical decision stage. A manager can emerge from the SAST process with a plan for putting into place a variety of mechanisms for implementing the activities needed to cause the change (e.g., pilot projects, prototypes, and action teams).[8]

There was another key element as well: It is generally accepted that managers must ensure that the ultimate choice to adopt an innovation is *not* limited to the nominal head or to relatively few leaders of an organization. Participants in any position of influence, as well as those who would use the innovation, should be alerted to the impending decision and encouraged to express their opinion. I saw that the SAST approach took this into account with its powerful formation of differing groups and subsequent debate and synthesis techniques.[9] Furthermore, if effectively used, the SAST process can provide a manager with a framework for answering the six significant questions. In particular, the SAST process can elicit valuable insights from participants about what must be true for an innovation to work. In other words, what are the underlying assumptions held by the key people and groups involved that can facilitate or hamper adoption of an innovation?

In my second term as director of the Census Bureau (1979–1981), I used the SAST process in dealing with a number of complex problems. One of the most important issues concerned the constitutional question of differential undercount—the fact that blacks and other minorities are missed more often than whites in the count of the United States population. My successors at the bureau have used the SAST process to address several complex questions concerning the 1990 census as well as issues of public affairs policy and agency organization.

A Marketing Decision Support System: One Practitioner's Perspective

I have used the SAST process as the initial step in designing the introduction of an MDSS in two major corporations.[10]

Let me set the framework for this discussion by presenting a practitioner's definition for a marketing decision support system.[11] An MDSS may be many things, but one set of characteristics that seems to provide real benefits, in terms of better information for better decisions, is the following:

- An organization of people who understand and know how to use both the computerized system and the marketing information;

this organization must be competent in several key disciplines, including:

Analytical data processing
Data base design
Statistics
Model building
Marketing analysis

- A computerized system for storing information about selected markets
- Software that allows the organization to retrieve relevant information and to manipulate the information into reports and models

The system elements under the term *MDSS technology* include the following:

Data acquisition system
Data base management system
Retrieval/report writing/query processor
Model bank
Statistical analysis tools
Graphics
Directories between specific data elements and higher-level information-classification schemes

Designing an MDSS: Using the SAST Process to Answer the Six Significant Questions

Let us reconsider the six significant questions. In this context, we will see how these questions can be applied to gain insights into the *implementation* phase of an MDSS—after the SAST process.

Again, Everett Rogers offers useful insights.[12] The likelihood and rate of adoption are directly related to the organization's, or the individual's, demonstrated ability in the following five situations: (1) the ability to see easily the relative advantages of having such a system over not having it; (2) the ability to illustrate the manner in which such an information system is compatible with present organizational procedures; (3) the ability to absorb the technical jargon of a vast and complex tool quickly; (4) the ability to divide the concept and test it so that no person or organization feels threatened; and (5) the ability to communicate the results of such an innovation's effects.

The *interplay* of these abilities or attributes can influence the effective implementation of change. For example, if an innovation has the potential for a large payoff, but there is no way to "try it out" through a pilot program, then the innovation is likely to face an uncertain future.

A Case History from Eastman Kodak: Using the Design Process for Developing an MDSS

Let us keep the above attributes in mind as we tackle the six significant questions in greater detail.

Background

We can enlarge our frame of reference for an MDSS if we consider also a concept developed at Kodak called the MArket INtelligence—or MAIN—system. The MAIN system has five functions, designed to do the following:[13]

1. *Assess market information needs*: Develop for the company a priority list of operationally defined market information needs.
2. *Measure the market*: Gather required market information in a cost effective manner.
3. *Store, retrieve, and display information*: Store market information in a way that facilitates further analysis and linking with other planning information.
4. *Prepare descriptive analysis*: Analyze and interpret market information through descriptive analyses to be utilized by decision makers in developing subsequent policy analyses and business plans.
5. *Evaluate*: Assess the application of market intelligence information to the decision-making process.[14]

The third function—to store, retrieve, and display information—relates to the MDSS. At Kodak we happen to call it MIDSS (pronounced MIDAS—an acronym for *Market Intelligence Decision Support System*). At Kodak, an MDSS is called MIDSS, and it is part of a five-function system called MAIN.

New Insights into the Six Significant Questions

Let us now consider the answers to the six significant questions about our development of MIDSS at Kodak, within the context of the MAIN system.

1. *Have those who manage the organization agreed that there is a need that will utilize the change being proposed?*

Have they designated a "champion"—that is, a person or a group of people—to make sure the change comes about?

In my experience, one of the best examples of a response to this question is the opening statement by one of Kodak's top managers—J. Phillip Samper, executive vice president and general manager, Photographic Division—at the first corporatewide MAIN System Planning Conference, held in May 1982. We brought together thirty participants, with widely differing backgrounds and perspectives, from throughout the Eastman Kodak Company. Our objective was to develop a plan for implementing the Kodak MAIN system. We utilized the SAST process to address key issues, especially those surrounding the development of MIDSS. Here is Mr. Samper's statement:

> Our job is to insure, on a worldwide basis, that the information about the marketplace, about technology, about competition, about our performance—that all these are joined together to develop a scenario which allows us to position ourselves in the marketplace.
>
> I am convinced that the Kodak MArket INtelligence System (the MAIN System) can enhance these functions greatly with the availability of a worldwide data bank—retrievable on demand—that utilizes information to tie business objectives to critical issues.[15]

2. Who has participated in planning for the change? Who has not?

One of the most obvious insights I can offer about this second question is that *all* those who have a stake in the change should participate. There are two useful guidelines on who should be included: (1) those with content or knowledge who can aid in the solution process, and (2) those with "ownership" who need to understand the reason for change in order to aid acceptance and eventual implementation. In other words, whoever is affected by, or will affect, the manager's ability to put this change (i.e., the MDSS) into place should be involved in the planning.

Participants in the Kodak MAIN Planning Conference, for example, were drawn from the three key areas involved with marketing information: the suppliers (that is, the technical people), the information managers, and some of the ultimate users. In retrospect, this third group was not adequately represented. The ultimate decision maker (Phillip Samper) supported the conference effort by his opening statement and his presence during several sessions. But many of the people who function as the *intermediaries* between top management and the information managers—the middle-management personnel who must constantly solve business problems—simply did not have the time to attend the planning conference.

At this point it is natural to ask, Why isn't the planning community more involved? The answer becomes obvious when we understand that these are probably the most pressured people in any business organization that has to deal with crises. Thus, a good many of the ultimate users of the MDSS—the middle managers who are in a response mode all the time—are likely to feel they do not have time for the SAST process. The result is that the more you need an MDSS, the more likely key information users will feel they don't have time to deal with it.

Nevertheless, as these users start to see the value of the MDSS in operation, managers can find effective ways of involving them. For example, the MDSS "champions" can decide to go ahead *without* the full participation of the users. It's wise to recognize the likelihood that the initial design—and subsequent implementation—of a prototype or pilot project will suffer from some limitations. The next time around, however, the "champions" of the change are likely to have higher priority for the users' time and attention.

There is another advantage in using the SAST process in this situation. This approach makes the underlying assumptions more explicit. If a user who did *not* have time to participate does not like some aspect of the design, the MDSS "champion" can say, "We're doing it this way because we assumed such and such. Which of these assumptions don't you agree with?" In essence, with SAST, we have an "audit trail" of how we arrived at the system design. A person who wants to criticize the results must *first* go through the audit trail to criticize the assumptions.

Let me describe a concrete example: In the design of the MAIN system, we assumed we would be able to bring to the surface *every* critical underlying assumption of *every* plan. If we had had four or five top planners at the conference, they would have challenged us on this by saying, "Why do all that? You'll never have time. Why don't you focus on only the *most* critical assumptions?"

In retrospect, we could see that the group members were not challenged sufficiently on that point. In contrast, the conference brought forth very effective challenges concerning the technology because of our strong and diverse representation in that area. The strength of the SAST process is that it provides an opportunity to raise all the issues. But the quality of the assumptions raised and debated depends on the diversity of the participants.

3. What, if anything, does the change modify or replace?

In simplest terms, the implementation of an MDSS replaces the old way of doing things. In my experience, "the old way" was often an ad hoc series of interrelationships that tried to function as a decision support system. I can also say that an MDSS replaces an earlier system that focused on reacting to current problems. In large measure, that was true because there was no way to foresee or understand a potential problem *before* it occurred. By contrast, an effective MDSS—which *is* an assumption-based system—requires us to look at our assumptions about the future.

I want to underscore another point from my perspective as a practitioner: It takes a long time to get the data in place for an effective MDSS. Within Kodak, for example, we are still putting the pieces into place. At the same time, I have discovered that the *anticipation* of the MDSS is already causing changes. For example, at the conclusion of a major series of research studies on an important facet of consumer attitudes about photography, the information managers took time to examine longer-term issues relating to the effective implementation of an MDSS. They asked essential questions, such as, "How do we organize these data so that the next time we need to answer related questions *anyone* can go to the computer and pull out the data?" That insight grew from the recognition that questions are going to be asked and the data should be there, even if the information managers who originally translated the data are not still there. Thus, I can ask the rhetorical question, Do we have an MDSS? I would answer no, not yet. But to the question "Are we thinking like an MDSS?" the answer would be yes.

I would like to share one more comment, this one from a colleague at Kodak who read an earlier draft of this paper:

> In your paper, you ask: Are we thinking like an MDSS? I agree with the yes response. Further, I would say that many people within the company do not even realize that this has happened even though they are doing it. For instance, following the major benchmark study for our division, management committed the time and resources to carefully analyze the results. Then, they combined these data with a process for developing recommendations for further actions and future plans. . . . This process will be utilized with each of the subsequent studies for this division. Knowing this in advance of the study makes it possible for managers to devote the time required to fully identify their information needs.

It is also important to recall that at Kodak the MDSS concept is fully integrated into a total market intelligence system of five interrelated functions:

1. Assess market information needs
2. Measure the market
3. Store, retrieve, and display information
4. Prepare descriptive analysis
5. Evaluate

That leads to a related point in answer to the question on what does an MDSS modify or replace? In my experience, an MDSS replaces a less systematic way of thinking. But for an MDSS to accomplish this objective successfully, it requires a more disciplined approach within the context of a concept like the MAIN system.

As I have just recounted, the prospect of an MDSS is already causing people within Kodak to identify and relate to the components of the MAIN concept—to generate better information resources for better decision making. In addition, this more disciplined, holistic approach is replacing the notion of one-time special-purpose market research projects. That not only cuts down on some expenditures, but it also encourages the use of information in multiple ways. In addition, the design process that we have developed within Kodak for an MDSS—using SAST—is a way to link the underlying assumptions to the final plan. We are providing a process that makes formal the surfacing and testing of critical, underlying assumptions. And, of course, this approach can be—and is being—applied to product and market planning activities as well.

A final key element in an MDSS design is the fact that the use and applications of an MDSS will constantly change. This year we ought to be thinking about how we are going to change the MDSS next year, because some of the things that are *replacements* this year are going to be modified through our working experience with the MDSS itself.

And even the manner in which we use the SAST process for MDSS and other forms of planning will probably change dramatically. It will be less time-consuming and much more abbreviated in terms of how many assumptions we look at. We are also working on techniques for true one-person SASTs, in which someone can, in essence, use a computer to conduct an SAST, because the computer, based on historical and future assumptions, will provide the challenges to the individual planner.

4. Who within the organization will benefit immediately as a result of the MDSS? Who will benefit over the longer term?

Those who are likely to benefit immediately from an MDSS or a similar innovation are the people who want to see a more systematic way of approaching problems within the organization. The real beneficiaries are the people who look at the world in a certain way—regardless of where they work or for whom.

It is important to note that the initial expenditure for MDSS design is being influenced by the increasing complexity of the environment and the lines of business that the company produces. The planning procedures that existed before will simply not be effective any lon₋er. In effect, we are saying, "Let's systematize the way we do our business." We need a framework that allows us to look at today's fast-changing environment in a highly organized way. Furthermore, an assumption-based MDSS means that we have anticipated and thought about potential changes, and, therefore, we will be better able to deal with them. There *is* a cost involved, just as there are cost implications in the decision to make any capital expenditure to increase capacity before we are actually out of capacity.

Another group to benefit are people still in school today—those who are going to be trained in complex DSS approaches. When they enter the corporate world a few years from now, there will be resources for them to use. In contrast, those entering corporations today have skills that far surpass our available tools and information.

In summary, we can all benefit if we meet out next challenge— namely, to get the right people in place to use the tools we already have. This includes new employees, who are able to use the "tools" but do not yet understand the business, as well as seasoned employees, who understand the business but need to be taught to make better use of the tools. Our objective three to four years hence, when the MDSS concept is really rolling, must be to have the right people in place to utilize it.

5. *Who will suffer immediately? Who will suffer over the longer term?*

The person who is likely to suffer from a new MDSS or similar innovation is anyone who has learned a skill *and* does not want it to change. In my opinion, the person who says "I've learned this job and I'm set" is going to suffer most. And in all likelihood, that kind of person will be among the technical community. In a similar vein, the information managers will face constant change—and will suffer if they cannot cope with it. Generally, people who like stability are likely to suffer, because we must assume that change will always be taking place.

Another group that could be affected are those individuals whose organizational influence is based on either a real or perceived control over information. A basic premise of an MDSS is that a company's decision making can be improved by making explicit the basic assumptions that underlie a plan. The MDSS achieves this by helping managers gain improved understanding of the strengths and weaknesses of the information that supports those underlying assumptions. If an MDSS makes this understanding more readily available, and if it does so through processes that circumvent those controllers of information, then their role will be reduced—if organizational control is the sole basis for their position.

6. *How will the change affect the major relationships within the organization:*
   - *individual job relationships?*
   - *organizational relationships?*
   - *social and other informal relationships?*

First, the MDSS is likely to blur the reward criteria within the organization. For example, it will be more difficult to measure an individual's contribution to the total marketing plan, because people will no longer have specific responsibilities. That can have some long-term benefits; for instance, everyone is more likely to feel a part of the plan. Further, accountability could be strengthened at the point where it belongs: the decision maker who finally approves the plan.

Second, this innovation is likely to blur organizational boundaries. The trends in that direction were highlighted by John Rockart and Michael Treacy in an article entitled "The CEO Goes On-Line."[16] Their central point is that two major factors are starting to change the ways a company can funnel information to the CEO's office: (1) today's improved computer technology and (2) the increasing analytic orientation of top managers. In fact, as they point out, "in some companies the responsibility for using such data-based support has moved into the executive office itself. Perhaps more important, the top managers of these companies have become active participants in the process, not just final consumers of its output." I especially like two of the quotations from CEOs involved in this "blurring" of the traditional organizational structure:

> There is a huge advantage to the CEO to get his hands dirty in the data. The answers to so many significant questions are found in the detail. *The system provides me with an improved ability to ask the right questions and to know the wrong answers.*
>
> I bring a lot of knowledge to the party. Just scanning the current status of our operations enables me to see some things that those with less time in the company would not see as important. Although the resulting telephone calls undoubtedly shake up some of my subordinates, I think in the long run this is helpful to them, too.[17]

The CEOs' comments point out some interesting trends in the field of information services that have long-term implications for those of us who are managing the development of the DSS concept in our organizations. For example, when we examine the relative

Figure 6.1 Levels of Activity in Information Services in Early Stages (yesterday)

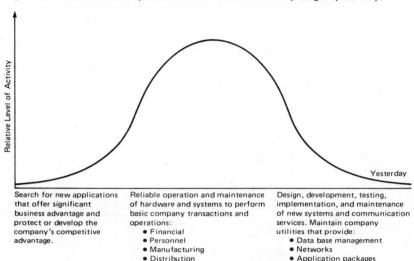

| Search for new applications that offer significant business advantage and protect or develop the company's competitive advantage. | Reliable operation and maintenance of hardware and systems to perform basic company transactions and operations:
• Financial
• Personnel
• Manufacturing
• Distribution | Design, development, testing, implementation, and maintenance of new systems and communication services. Maintain company utilities that provide:
• Data base management
• Networks
• Application packages |

Three Basic Types of Information Services

level of activity that was taking place "yesterday" in the information services area, we see that the primary focus was on people skilled in handling the reliable operation and maintenance of hardware and systems to perform basic company transactions (see Figure 6.1). Then, as we approach "tomorrow" in the information services field (represented by the dotted line in Figure 6.2), the relative levels of activity will probably shift dramatically. There will be a greater need for more skilled people (1) to handle the search for new applications and (2) to design, develop, and test new systems.

The dramatic shifts in the activities of information services will have major, long-term implications for those of us who are responsible for DSS development. In fact, let me use the Census Bureau example to illustrate this point. Let me add to the distribution curves three quotations as stated by each group when faced with the six significant questions about change (see Figure 6.3). In the future, we're likely to see a surplus of people in the information services field who can handle the activity surrounding the reliable operation and maintenance of hardware and systems. Further, it will be important for us, as DSS managers, to understand the motivations and assumptions of this group—*and* their likely reactions to initiatives for innovation and change.

At the same time, we in DSS management are going to find our-

Figure 6.2 Levels of Activity in Information Services in Future (tomorrow)

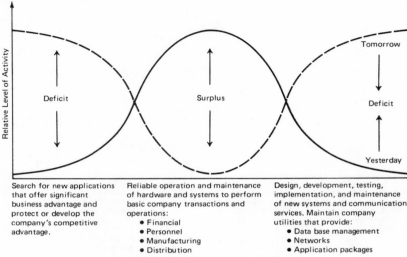

Three Basic Types of Information Services

| Search for new applications that offer significant business advantage and protect or develop the company's competitive advantage. | Reliable operation and maintenance of hardware and systems to perform basic company transactions and operations:
• Financial
• Personnel
• Manufacturing
• Distribution | Design, development, testing, implementation, and maintenance of new systems and communication services. Maintain company utilities that provide:
• Data base management
• Networks
• Application packages |

selves facing an increasingly short supply of other skilled people in information services, namely, those who can lead the way in the successful search for new applications and in the design of new systems. For those of us responsible for DSS development in the public or private sectors, the problem is *not* going to be the technology: The hardware and systems are going to be available. Our problem will be finding the skilled people to handle the activities that will enhance—or limit—the speed at which we can develop the information systems we need. These are problems we must solve if we are going to realize the potential and value of the DSS concept.

Conclusion: Understanding Innovation and Human Nature

In terms of human nature, we are clearly not so far removed in our environment today from the people in the opening story about steel axes for Stone Age men: We too need to deal with the impact of change on people. Indeed, that note was sounded most eloquently for the 1980s by G. R. Wagner:

> Surrounding all the techniques, methods, and tools in a Decision Support System (DSS) are people. They are an integral part and important foundation in any successful DSS—all the more so when a group begins digging into its members' assumptions.

Figure 6.3 Relation between Modes of Activity and Attitudes toward MDSS

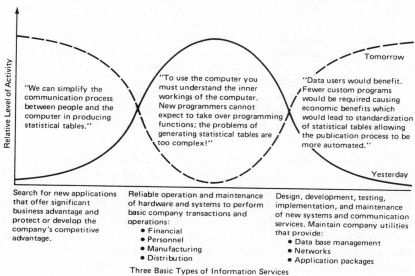

"We can simplify the communication process between people and the computer in producing statistical tables."

"To use the computer you must understand the inner workings of the computer. New programmers cannot expect to take over programming functions; the problems of generating statistical tables are too complex!"

"Data users would benefit. Fewer custom programs would be required causing economic benefits which would lead to standardization of statistical tables allowing the publication process to be more automated."

Search for new applications that offer significant business advantage and protect or develop the company's competitive advantage.	Reliable operation and maintenance of hardware and systems to perform basic company transactions and operations: ● Financial ● Personnel ● Manufacturing ● Distribution	Design, development, testing, implementation, and maintenance of new systems and communication services. Maintain company utilities that provide: ● Data base management ● Networks ● Application packages

Three Basic Types of Information Services

The computer itself is a valuable support tool, one which will extend and support us with integrity . . . *to the degree that we understand ourselves as extensions and support systems for each other.*[18]

In today's increasingly complex world, innovation is an area that demands our best, whether our purview is the public or the private sector, large organizations or small. I am drawn, once again, to the fascinating arena provided by the 1980 census—in particular, the controversy surrounding the differential undercount of blacks and other minorities, which I mentioned earlier.

In the book that evolved from that experience, we set the framework that relates not only to the specific Census Bureau decision but, more importantly, to the large issues of handling innovation and "complex" problems in a variety of organizational settings.[19] That, of course, includes the introduction of an MDSS within the corporate setting.

Above all, the book is a report of a more adequate way of managing increasingly complex issues. These complex issues are characterized by their synergism. Whereas once the scientific and technical aspects of issues could be clearly separated from the ethical, legal, moral, and political issues, this is no longer so. To attempt to wrench the scientific from the other issues is not only to distort the true meaning of the issue as a whole—since the various aspects do not exist in isolation or separately from one another—but also to render proper management of the entire issue inoperable. *The main theses of this book are (1) that complex issues of this type are growing, seemingly without bound, and (2) that new methods are needed to cope with all the so-called separate dimensions simultaneously.*

[It seems clear that] what is true of the Census Bureau is becoming true of all institutions . . . public and private. In many ways, the Census Bureau is merely a convenient example of what is happening in general. *We hope that those who are charged with managing complex institutions or are affected by them will read this book in the spirit of learning what they can do to understand better the complexities involved in managing their own institutions* [emphasis added].[20]

The message of this paper is to emphasize that the introduction of the DSS concept is a positive step forward in the continuing development of management decision making, and not a step backward like the introduction of the steel axes to the Yir Yoront people. At the time of the introduction of the steel axes, neither the well-meaning missionaries, who brought the innovation, nor the tradition-bound Yir Yoront elders, who resisted accepting its increased value over the traditional way of doing things, understood the process or the impact of their respective actions. In retrospect, we are not surprised by their ignorance of the crucial nature of their roles.

Today's DSS missionaries and management decision makers cannot hide behind a veil of ignorance. The evidence drawn from the successes and failures of the past is clear. If both the promise and the value of the DSS concept are to become a reality, each of us—developer and adopter—must understand, in more meaningful and productive ways, each other's motivations and basic underlying assumptions.

APPENDIX 6.1 Strategic Assumption Surfacing and Testing

This brief introductory overview has been developed by Kodak's Market Intelligence group.

Strategic Assumption Surfacing and Testing (SAST), as a procedure, is designed to reveal the underlying assumptions of an existing or proposed policy or plan and to help create a map for exploring the reality of the surfaced assumptions. SAST has been designed to deal with complex problems. The process is not intended to replace the exercise of creative managerial judgment. Rather, it is intended to complement the exercise of such judgment. SAST was designed on the premise that in today's business decision environment, any position worth promoting will have significant uncertainties associated with it.

It is usually the inability to deal with these uncertainties that either stops or delays the implementation of creative (different) managerial initiatives. SAST does not ignore uncertainty: Indeed, it also aggressively challenges what appears to be certain. It does so to ensure that, prior to implementation, the assumptions upon which our initiative has been based are likely to stand the test of reality in the marketplace. SAST attempts to provide a path to reducing the risk of dealing with uncertainty by identifying meaningful approaches to increasing our understanding in the most critical areas of uncertainty.

With these objectives in perspective, SAST has been designed to be

- adversarial, because underlying assumptions need to be explored and their strengths and weaknesses determined. These judgments, particularly when dealing with complex issues, are best made in the context of a systematic critical review.
- participative, because the involvement of both the users and providers of information is required to determine our current and potential understanding of complex issues. Additionally, the level of management responsible for implementing the solution must be involved in its development.
- integrative, because criticizing an initiative is not enough. Strong points from various perspectives need to be combined to form a strategy that has the support of key individuals and organizations.

In terms of design criteria for an MDSS, the SAST procedure has proved to be extremely valuable in generating

1. some answers (usually at the strategic level).
2. some assumptions that are generally accepted by key persons,

ranging from technical aspects (such as hardware and software solutions) to environmental and interpersonal considerations within the organization.

3. other assumptions that require more research to ascertain their certainty or uncertainty (typically, these are the critical planning questions at the operational level).

4. design criteria for a prototype or pilot project, to demonstrate the immediate value of the MDSS to top management.

By our definition:

- A *prototype project* is designed to meet the functional criteria, but is *not* expected to hold up over time.

- A *pilot project*, designed to function on a smaller scale, is expected to meet all the criteria, including long-term performance and the possibility for expansion.

An important result of this process is that the outcome generally requires fewer resources (time and money) to eventually receive management approval, and, we hope, minimizes the probability that ideas leading to a market advantage are lost to the company.

There are five basic steps to the SAST process:

1. group formation
2. assumption surfacing and rating
3. debate
4. information requirements analysis
5. synthesis

For more in-depth reading on strategic assumption surfacing and testing (SAST), I would direct the reader to Richard O. Mason, Ian I. Mitroff, and Vincent P. Barabba, "Creating the Manager's Plan Book: A New Route to Effective Planning," *Planning Review*, July 1980, pp. 11–16; Richard Mason and Ian Mitroff, *Challenging Strategic Planning Assumptions: Theory, Cases, and Techniques* (New York: John Wiley, 1981); Ian Mitroff, Richard Mason, and Vincent Barabba, *The 1980 Census: Policymaking amid Turbulence* (Lexington, Mass.: Lexington Books, D. C. Heath, 1983); Vincent Barabba, Richard Mason, and Ian Mitroff, "Federal Statistics in a Complex Environment: The Case of the 1980 Census," *The American Statistician*, August 1983; and Ralph H. Kilmann, K. Thomas, D. P. Slevin, R. Nath, and S. L. Jerrell, eds., *Producing Useful Knowledge for Organizations* (New York: Praeger, 1983).

APPENDIX 6.2 Do's and Don't's of Introducing an Organization to an MDSS

DO	Ask the six significant questions, number one first.
DO	Get the right answer to number one.
DO	Use the SAST procedures, streamlining them to the most important, least certain, and most relevant issues in your *current plan.*
DO	Create a pilot MDSS, and use the pilot to demonstrate feasibility and benefits.
DO	Provide facilitators, information managers, for each key group.
DO	Survey those with a stake in the key organizations. Identify the extent to which each • wants change • thinks he or she has effective tools • wants to use the system directly or through an intermediary • wants to participate in the design
DO	Use results of the survey to segment the potential users of the MDSS.
DO	Design the MDSS to address each significant segment.
DO	Let the new capability sell itself by example.
DO	Give the organization time to evolve into its own use pattern.
DON'T	Attempt to force or mandate use of new tools.
DON'T	Take away old tools.

Note: I am indebted to George Nix for this useful—and amusing—checklist.

CHAPTER 7

The Four P's of Marketing Decision Support Systems: Promises, Payoffs, Paradoxes, and Prognostications

Rudolph W. Struse III

Carnation Company

My professional persona is that of a practitioner; thus, I shall focus on actual experiences and on practical considerations in using this new information technology. Theoretical and philosophical issues have been left for others better qualified to address them. I have not summarized or reviewed the literature on marketing decision support systems (MDSSs) on the assumption that the reader will be familiar with the concept as outlined by J. D. C. Little, Peter Keen, or Michael Scott-Morton.

I will summarize my involvement with this new technology so that the reader will be aware of the experiences underlying my observations and opinion. In the last six years, I have

- introduced an MDSS into two different *Fortune* 500 companies;
- examined a number of commercial products claiming to embody the MDSS concept;
- used the three major MDSS products—INF*ACT, EXPRESS, and ACUSTAR;
- installed an MDSS in different types of computing environments ranging from time-shared mainframes to a dedicated super-minicomputer;
- worked on MDSS applications hands-on as well as through internal staff and outside consultants;
- incorporated external marketing data such as those obtained from

Nielsen, SAMI, MAJERS, purchase diary panels, distribution checks, and consumer tracking studies with internal data such as factory shipments, pricing, promotional allowances, and other marketing expenses;

- used MDSSs in approximately ten different product categories representing over $8 billion in annual sales for brands accounting for over $2.5 billion in annual sales; and
- spent over $2.5 million for MDSS software, hardware, and services.

Neither company was among the first to use marketing decision support systems. Neither was one of the largest, most sophisticated, or most extensive users of MDSS technology. What differentiates my experiences is variety and range in terms of companies, categories, and MDSS products.

In reviewing these last six years, I have cataloged my experiences and observations around four broad concepts:

- the promises of MDSS and their relevance to a company;
- the practical payoffs that can be realized;
- the paradoxes and problems inherent in implementing a real MDSS; and
- prognostications of the future development of MDSS.

Since the practical value of MDSS at this point is still controversial, I have cited specific cases and vignettes to provide some documentation of the technology's "payoff."

Promises

The MDSS concept is more humanistic than other technological movements such as management information systems (MIS) or management science (MS). MIS projected the computer as the solution to management's problems; MS asserted experts in "scientific" methods to be the solution. Marketing decision support systems position the "manager" as the solution—albeit appropriately equipped with decision support technology. By amplifying the capabilities of the manager and by eliminating impediments to the rational functioning of the manager, MDSS improves the chances that a company will achieve its goals of increased sales, share, profits, and so on. Proponents of the concept have ascribed a variety of specific benefits to it. Those frequently cited include:

- increased staff efficiency (more work done in less time);

- increased managerial effectiveness (managers focus on key issues);
- faster response to change;
- more complete use of available data;
- more understanding of market dynamics;
- development of models to better control businesses;
- more alternatives evaluated;
- heuristics replaced by analytics;
- establishment of a common information base; and
- uniform analysis.

Given just this partial list, one might wonder why every corporation is not using an MDSS. Since not all corporations are using the technology, and since some have explicitly declined to even try it, let alone adopt it, there are some barriers that MDSS must overcome.

One barrier is skepticism. The claims made for the MDSS bear an uncanny and unfortunate likeness to those made by the proponents of MIS and MS. After having been once or twice burned, managements are wary of accepting at face value claims made for decision support systems. Another barrier is the differential relevance of benefits. Not every manager will be interested in every benefit: The appeal of specific benefits varies with the level of management. In general, one might use the following paradigm to classify the appeal of various benefits: Senior management is more interested in the benefits that increase the effectiveness of their subordinates, while junior and middle managers are more interested in features helping them do their jobs more easily and quickly. Given a healthy degree of skepticism within a company and the lack of unanimity among levels of management over what MDSS should deliver, it is not surprising the technology has not been universally adopted.

Unlike some colleagues, I have yet to have a management ask for a decision support system. In each instance, the Marketing Research Department initiated the discussion and negotiation process that led to the development of an MDSS. Consequently, in each case it has been necessary to match the possible benefits of an MDSS with the needs of the various levels of management. While management's specific needs will vary with each organization, I observed some recurrent themes.

- All managers need to cope with an explosion of information.
- Line managers feel that change is accelerating.

- Senior managers perceive increases in the extent and intensity of competition.
- Shifts are occurring in the balance of power between manufacturers and retailers.
- For many companies, rates of growth in primary product markets have declined.

Payoffs

Underlying management's skepticism over the promises of a marketing decision support system are the questions of which are real and which are ephemeral. Specific attributes or features of a given MDSS are easily verifiable, but the benefits are not so easily ascertained. In fact, some may require several years of expense before any verification is available.

The cases and vignettes below illustrate applications and actual business results produced by MDSSs. Following these vignettes are some observations concerning the factors influencing the adoption of decision support systems within a company.

Cases and Vignettes

Case 1 In proposing an MDSS to business unit M of Ace Manufacturing, we claimed that it would increase the efficiency of the existing staff—that is, the existing staff could do more work in the same time or the same volume of work in less time. After unit M authorized an MDSS, its senior manager requested that we monitor staff efficiency to verify this claim. Though we did not conduct a controlled experiment, we developed an objective measure of the staff output for the year before and for the year following the MDSS. The implementation of the MDSS was the primary difference between the two time periods: Little else changed in terms of the market or the staff's "clients." The staff did fifty projects in the pre-MDSS period. This grew to 505 projects in the post-MDSS period. Was this typical? Was it really due to MDSS? Was it simply an experimental effect like the Hawthorne experience? While definitive proof is still to be compiled, I would answer these questions by saying "probably," "yes," and "only to a small extent," based on having directly observed and worked with this staff over several years.

Case 2 Another aspect of staff efficiency is that of scale. There are some projects that are simply not feasible without "power tools." A group reporting to me at Ace Manufacturing was asked to develop a summary showing the extent to which major retail food chains were utilizing the company's trade deals across all product lines. The required data were being collected, but had not been integrated into a single summary. (Actually, MIS had been the first choice for producing this summary, but was in the midst of a major system conversion and could not begin working on the group's request for twelve months.) When the Marketing Division initially asked for help, there was no MDSS: The summary had to be done manually. Ignoring the time and effort required to locate and move the sixty-six cubic feet of paper (which were the "man readable" records for a *single* retail customer), we still found that constructing this summary for one account required about fifty-five hours. Needless to say, we stopped after the first account. About a year and a half later, when an MDSS was available, we found this summary report could be set up with about fifteen hours of work. And it could be produced for the 250 largest accounts in about one hour of total time thereafter. Was this use of people's time unique to an MDSS? Was this an efficient use of an MDSS? This case does not illustrate a unique benefit of an MDSS per se as much as one of computer systems in general. It probably was not an efficient use of the MDSS. Nevertheless, an explicit need of the Marketing Division was answered and answered quickly with the MDSS: Neither the manual "system" nor MIS had ever responded to the need, while the MDSS did. Though conceptually inefficient and inelegant, the MDSS was vastly more efficient than the alternative systems because it got the job done.

Case 3 While all work needs to be done sooner rather than later, there are situations where timeliness is essential. This vignette is a personal favorite because the situation was dramatic and seemed impossible. At 11:15 A.M., Ace's vice president of marketing called: He excitedly yelled something about our second largest customer dropping part of the product line. This sounded serious, but not critical. Unfortunately, as he expanded, the picture became clearer and more serious. The executive vice president of our customer was in the board room for what had been expected to be the start of a routine "plant tour." But shortly after arrival, he announced that Zenith Supermarkets were planning to drop twenty-three of our items (or about 25 percent of the total items Zenith was buying from Ace at that time). The reason was an analysis of the sales of these items: Zenith had found the turnover rate for these items was below the threshold required for distribution in their stores. Zenith's executive vice president had also announced he was leaving promptly at noon. We had forty-five minutes to develop ammunition for the marketing team to use in persuading him to reconsider. We first tried to imagine and reconstruct the analysis that Zenith must have done. Converting our factory shipments to Zenith into per outlet "turns," we found the twenty-three items in question did appear to move slowly. Rather than stop at that point, as Zenith had, we needed, and were able, to go deeper in understanding these findings. We next observed that Zenith's "turns" for the twenty-three items were low compared to other comparable large accounts. This led to calculating item turn rates for Zenith's direct competitors—that is, the other retail chains in Zenith's marketing territories. Our customer's competitors were getting much higher turn rates on these same items in the same markets. Since geography, time periods, and market position had been taken into account, it appeared that the explanation for the different turn rates might be differences between Zenith and its competitors. A hypothesis was formulated that differences in pricing or merchandising practices would be most likely to produce the differing sales rates. Zenith's competitors were found to have featured these items more frequently and with larger discounts than it had. At this point, we made a rough estimate of sales and gross income Zenith could realize if it changed merchandising practices to match its competitors and if it got comparable turn rates on the items. All of this work was delivered neatly formatted and summarized to the board room by 11:57 A.M.

The immediate result was that Zenith's executive vice president reconsidered his decision. Zenith later ran a test in a sample of stores to see if the turn rates of the items could be improved by a shift in merchandising practice. None of the twenty-three items was dropped by Zenith. This responsiveness was only possible because the MDSS for this business had been previously set up and because the problem happened to correspond well with the data in the MDSS.

Case 4 While efficiency and responsiveness are desirable, increased "effectiveness" is usually seen as a more important benefit of an MDSS. Effectiveness may be increased by getting managers to focus on more important issues or by improving managers' understanding of a market and its response to their actions. This was demonstrated when one of Beta Company's major products began experiencing increasing competitive promotional activity— primarily in the form of trade deals. Management could simply match competitive deal levels for each of its three brands, but felt this would be expensive and, possibly, counterproductive. These managers asked how allowances could be allocated to blunt the effect of competitive deals, but at a lower total cost. Though not elegant and certainly not optimal, the approach consisted of an approximation of relationships between sales and dealing activity in each market for each brand. The premise was that areas with higher responsiveness to dealing were areas where higher marginal returns could be realized. Trade promotion funds could be allocated across markets, within and across brands, based on the expected marginal returns. While more elegant analysis and modeling was possible, we rationalized staying with a simple approach, because (a) we could do the simple one in time; (b) the quality of the data available did not justify a higher level of analytic sophistication; and (c) the more complex approaches might have less credibility with the managers who actually had to allocate the money.

Case 5 Some months later, another of Beta's line managers questioned how consumers responded to pricing. Each brand in the category came in several sizes. Although packages might be viewed as small, medium, and large, there were variations between brands in the actual weights within size groupings. The question posed by the manager was the extent to which consumers reacted to price per unit or price per pound. This knowledge might allow Beta to change its sizing and pricing simultaneously to increase sales and operating profits. Using the MDSS in analysis of the elasticity of sales with respect to unit price and per pound price indicated that both factors were at work, but to different degrees. The net result was a possibility of a 30 percent profit increase by simply changing package size and price points. (Beta has yet to achieve the 30 percent gain, though changes in the competitive situation make it difficult to determine if the analysis was correct or not.)

Case 6 The manager of a major division of Beta believed price was the key determinant of market share for her brand. Most of the analytic work done with the decision support system focused on trying to untangle the cross-brand price elasticities. Although a long series of consistent internal and external data was available, the original questions concerning price elasticity were never answered (due to technical problems with the data). Nevertheless, some surprising results did emerge. Beta's promotional activity for this product simply shifted sales from one size to another rather than attracting sales from competitors. This observation led to overhauling the promotional plan, which led to increasing gross operating profits by $1.5 million per year.

Case 7 While an MDSS typically includes time-series data such as sales, prices, and market share, the technology can be applied wherever there is a consistent set of data. A simple illustration is a data base containing the results of ten years' worth of new product concept testing. One of the serendipitous results of this analysis was learning there was little practical difference among different schemes for weighing purchase intent scales. Almost any set of ordered weights could be used and one would reach the same conclusions about which ideas were more or less appealing to consumers. This and other "surprising" findings have not changed the overall effectiveness of Beta's new product development process. But the costs of new product concept tests and the agonizing over how to best summarize the purchase intent data have been reduced.

Case 8 As noted, some of the results yielded by an MDSS have appeared serendipitous, but I believe this has not been so much luck as bright people using tools that magnify their personal characteristics and initiative. Ace Manufacturing found itself watching a competitor's new product perform better than anticipated. Fortunately, this was a regional competitor, so Ace was able to launch its version of the product nationally. In the rush to bring this product to market, the marketing team was unable to develop a package up to Ace's standards. Though there was no negative consumer response to the package, Ace was dissatisfied with it and eventually decided to upgrade it. The improved package would also allow some special merchandising of the product. The new package required several million dollars in capital investment, since new machinery was needed for both the existing and new production lines. The Sales and Marketing Divisions were forecasting a 30 percent to 50 percent increase in sales because of the new package and its merchandising feature, so management felt secure in moving forward. In fact, within marketing and management circles this project was soon viewed as a "no risk" investment. Consequently, neither the marketing group nor management felt any research was necessary.

Initially, only two existing production lines could be converted to the new package. Additional lines would be converted at quarterly intervals as the machinery became available. Sales results for the first few months the new package was in distribution were somewhat disappointing, but since this was a "no risk" project, the next production line was converted on schedule. A junior clerk used Ace's MDSS to pursue some patterns she saw in these sales results. What this person turned up did not solve any problems, but rather found one previously unimagined. She noted that wherever the new package displaced the old one, sales of certain other products sold by Ace quickly fell. This was puzzling, since there wasn't any apparent relationship between the new package and these items. Further examination indicated these products shared only three characteristics: (a) all were sold in the same section of the store; (b) all were moderate-volume items; and (c) all were high-margin items. The unexpected side effect of Ace's "no risk" investment was a multimillion-dollar reduction in operating profits. Ultimately, it turned out the feature of the new package allowing better merchandising was resulting in a reduction of shelf space for Ace's other products. This affected the lower-volume (and higher-margin) items more than others. Marketing and engineering teams later modified the package to eliminate the merchandising feature in question, and this stopped the erosion in Ace's other items. Just as significant as the financial results were the changes in attitude that took place in Ace. The concept of "no risk" investments was recognized as invalid and management gained new respect for the complex interactions and dependencies among Ace's products (as well as for the capability of a bright young woman).

Case 9 One of Beta's young turks assigned to brand H observed that the flavor of the brand that performed best in taste tests had only 40 percent of the commodity distribution. He believed that if he could increase the distribution of this flavor, brand H's share would increase proportionately. His plan was to provide Beta's sales representatives with customized sales materials for each retail account, showing the merits of stocking this flavor. With nearly a thousand sales representatives, the magnitude of this task and the short time available led to Beta using a commercially available MDSS package. During the implementation, the manager's underlying concept was significantly modified and expanded. In fact, several flavors and varieties of brand H had distribution gaps. This manager was able to identify, *for each retail account in the United States*, every item in the brand H line not stocked by it, representing an increased profit opportunity for that retailer. Rather than simply asserting that these items were profit opportunities, he showed this by taking the actual aggregate sales experience of each retailer's competitors and projecting the retailer's sales, using these competitive sales rates. Additionally, he identified competing flavors and varieties that were turning over more slowly than the projections for the missing brand H items. Thus, the retailer faced a relatively easy and credible decision, with Beta's interests aligned with rather than independent of his.

This approach produced additional distribution for the featured items and the largest quarterly share gains in the history of brand

H—despite one major competitor launching a new product and another restaging its brand.

Case 10   In the months following the implementation of an MDSS for brand L at Beta, there was a dramatic increase in the number of complaints over the quality of its external marketing data. Neither the data nor their quality had actually changed, but their use by the brand's managers had. With the MDSS, managers were for the first time able to test some pet hypotheses. But they overlooked the fact that the external data were based on samples and, thus, subject to statistical error. By treating the data as error free, considerable time and money were wasted "analyzing" a lot of random noise and only a little bit of information. Not surprisingly, most of the pet theories were not confirmed. Since this string of negative results contradicted what the managers "knew," they concluded the data were incorrect. Later the MDSS was used to purge the "noisy" observations: Among the remaining reliable observations, they did find distinct relationships among various marketing measures. After this, complaints over data quality dropped dramatically (and the more technically oriented groups found a noticeable increase in the requests for analysis from the marketing managers).

Case 11   Ace invested in new technology that would increase the convenience of a popular product. Initially, a small-scale controlled distribution market test was run. While results were extremely favorable, management discounted them because of the artificiality of the test. Later, an expanded test was run with dramatically different results. This led to a third and fourth round of test marketing, with each producing somewhat different outcomes. Although Ace tried to keep the major marketing variables constant, there were differences in each case. Prior to the fifth round of test marketing, management asked if the existing results could be somehow reconciled. A new product "flow" model—SPRINTER—was employed and considerable progress was made in reconciling the four sets of test market data. Nevertheless, there were points where estimates of market elasticities were needed. Because this new product was an entry into a category where an MDSS was installed, it was used to estimate the missing elasticities. These additional data were the key to linking the test results together. Based on this new understanding of the product's behavior, management concluded a fifth round of test marketing was not needed, since the product could not be sold in sufficient quantities to justify the capital investment.

Case 12   In one of Ace's product segments, price changes were an everyday occurrence. The factory price of individual items literally changed on a weekly basis. But in a study of actual shelf prices, a distinctive pattern was noted—nearly all retailers priced on the "9's." Since factory price increases were only a fraction of the increments used by retailers, Ace's price changes were not simply being passed on by retailers as assumed by management. Rather, these price changes were being distorted or amplified as well as shifted in time. After tracking the weekly pricing behavior of Ace's fifty largest accounts for nearly a year, some regularities were found and these provided an opportunity for Ace to increase its margin without adversely affecting its average shelf price and, hence, its sales volume. The trick was in managing the size and timing of price changes. Retailers' pricing behavior indicated that they had a target range of profitability for the Ace brand rather than a single figure. Knowing this, Ace could estimate the highest price it could get at any point without going outside the range. In effect, some of the retailers' margins were shifted back to Ace. The best estimate of the program's effect was that it added a couple of percentage points to operating profits while costing only a few thousand dollars per year.

Case 13 Beta's senior management was concerned that a major product was being "backdoored" into international markets (i.e., wholesalers based in the United States were buying large quantities only on deal and then exporting the product). If not controlled, "backdoor" exports could undermine the company's pricing and market position overseas. Management needed a rough assessment of the frequency and magnitude of this problem prior to its annual review meetings with its international managers. The MDSS team took various criteria suggested by the sales group and scanned the historical customer shipment records for the previous several years. Large, infrequent orders coinciding with promotional allowances by accounts located in port cities were the most effective screening criteria. While the *exact* extent of the problem was not completely determined, sales and management teams judged the analysis sufficient to identify the magnitude of the problem. The analysis identified all the accounts known to be involved and almost all of those suspected by the sales team. In addition, some probable or high-risk accounts were spotted. Knowing the approximate extent and locale of the problems, management developed plans to minimize the impact of exports by these accounts in the future.

Case 14 While preparing to introduce a major new consumer product, the Marketing and Sales Divisions found that a competitor was about to launch its new entry into the same category. Knowing that the battle for shelf space and warehouse slots would be fiercer than ever, the sales group requested that special reports be prepared analyzing competitive brand performance at the uniform product code level for the top fifty geographic markets. Since this division of Beta did not have an MDSS or comparable information management technology, the request could not be accommodated in time for the product launch. A year later, a nearly identical situation arose. This time Beta had a partially implemented MDSS, which delivered the needed materials within three days at a cost of about $1,000.

Case 15 For years, Ace Manufacturing advertised brand C in a consistent pattern. Partial sponsorships of popular prime time network TV shows were purchased throughout the entire year. Brand C had one or more prime time spots, averaging about twenty to twenty-five gross rating points, every week during the year. When Ace began buying external marketing data to track competitive performance and marketing activity, the managers of brand C found that it consistently lost share during its category's peak seasonal period. Further, C's share of advertising was considerably higher than its share of market in the off-season, but dropped below its share of market during the peak season. The brand's media buying and scheduling pattern had originated in the days when nearly all prime time shows were sponsored by individual companies, and at a time when C was growing at a rate that masked the effect of seasonality. Within a year, the managers had adjusted C's media plan to take better advantage of seasonality and the efficiencies possible with "scatter" buying.

Case 16 After increasing the effectiveness of brand C's media schedule, the marketing managers decided that a substantial increase in C's total advertising budget was in order. The additional money was split between more prime time TV and "spot" TV in key geographical markets. (*Key markets* were defined as those in which C had a higher share of the market.) The MDSS for C was used to track the expanded advertising program and estimate its incremental effect so that the next year's plan could take advantage of the current experience. What was learned was a bit different from what had been hoped for. There did not appear to be any overall effect related to the increased advertising. But a bright analyst working with the advertising agency and marketing group found effects at the local market level that were correlated with C's share in those markets. Where C had a high market share, there was little incremental response to the increased advertising. Where C's share was lower, there was a large proportional response to the incremental advertising. There were exceptions to the pattern, such as where C had unusually low distribution or unusually high pricing. The results led to a more extensive series of controlled experiments investigating the relationships among advertising, market share, and pricing. The experiments generally confirmed and refined the analysis done with the MDSS. The result for C has been a continuing evolution in the efficiency of its advertising.

Case 17 One of Ace's senior officers who had been asked to improve the company's corporate planning process called upon Ace's MDSS to help him find a problem. This officer had reviewed the five-year plan developed by the corporate planning department: He knew there was something fundamentally wrong with the plan, but could not put his finger on the problem. In relating this plan to the available market data, this manager found that for the company to meet the forecast profits, capital expenditures, and so on, it would have to both expand its primary markets and increase its share faster than it ever had in the past fifteen years.

Case 18 Ace's incentive compensation for sales had been developed before chain grocery warehouses became dominant in distributing consumer packaged goods. The program depended on tying sales to the stores each representative called upon. When direct store delivery was the dominant mode of distribution, there was no problem. But with the elimination of this method for most product categories, the company's internal records were no longer adequate. Rather than abandon the incentive system that had worked so well for many years, the company made arrangements with the large warehouses to get weekly withdrawal data for its items for each of the individual stores serviced by the warehouse. These data were then processed to calculate salesmen's incentive compensation. Two bright sales managers realized that this was a tremendous data base for sales and marketing if they could only tap into it. Since they did not know just what they wanted to do, MIS refused to work on anything until they could define exactly what they wanted and how they would use it. Eventually Ace's MDSS was tried on a pilot basis to see if anything useful could actually be done and if it could handle the sheer volume of data involved. A prototype "field sales support system" emerged from the pilot test, through which sales representatives could access their accounts' store level sales patterns by using portable terminals and run about a dozen types of simple analyses. Where it was initially used, there was an improvement in out-of-stock situations and a subsequent increase of several percent in the total sales. Nevertheless the volume of information did pose a problem that was not fully resolved; this has prevented expansion of the system.

Factors Affecting Adoption

Both Ace Manufacturing and Beta Company realized substantial business improvements as a direct result of developing and using marketing decision support systems. In fact, there has been little difference in the type or magnitude of the contributions to each company. Yet each responded differently. Ace embraced and adopted MDSS technology. Beta has been reluctant to adopt MDSS as a regular part of its management practices: Beta uses the MDSS technology on a project basis, much like its other "research" tools.

These disparate reactions by Ace and Beta suggest that whether a company fully adopts MDSS depends on far more than the technology's objective performance. It is my opinion (influenced no doubt by my education at the hands of sociologists) that the nature of a company, as a *social organization* rather than as an economic organization, shapes its response to an innovation, such as an MDSS, far more than the productive benefits of the innovation. Having worked as a "participant observer" in two organizations using an MDSS, I will outline my observations about the salient differences between the two milieus. These observations cover four areas: structure, functioning, corporate culture, and players.

Organizational Structure   Ace was organized functionally and was a steep pyramid, whereas Beta was decentralized with a nearly rectangular, shallow structure. All managers at Ace had specific, well-defined jobs and knew exactly where they fit into the hierarchy. Beta had few job definitions and no organizational chart. Both firms attempted to develop their managers internally whenever possible. Ace had low rates of turnover among its managers, resulting in a large cadre of experienced, long-tenured professionals. In contrast, Beta had rather high rates of turnover among its junior and middle-level managers, though the ranks of its senior executives were stable.

Functional Variables   Ace delegated authority extensively, with top management exercising oversight on major decisions. Teamwork was valued and was essential in order to accomplish anything: No significant action could take place if the functional groups did not cooperate. Consensus was the goal among middle and senior managers (though obedience was more valued among the rank and file). All significant actions at Beta were authorized by its senior management. Senior management treated middle and junior managers as staff rather than line. With the short lines of communications due to its shallow, rectangular structure, the senior management could be quite responsive to changing circumstances when this organizational structure first evolved. But as the scale and complexity of the company grew, this responsiveness could be maintained only at the expense of depth in the review and analysis of various courses of action. To balance this, senior management decreased the level of risk it would accept (giving an appearance of being adverse to risk). Ace Manufacturing was highly "proceduralized"—committees abounded as did task forces, study teams, and so on. The interactions between levels in the organization were ritualized to a large extent. Beta represented the opposite pole—procedures were noticeable by their absence. The nature of the interactions between levels of management was largely left to the discretion of the players involved.

Corporate Culture   By culture, I refer to the prevailing norms, beliefs, and myths of each organization. Ace's management took the position that it would compete with any company entering what it considered its markets. It promoted the idea that markets were to be developed and expanded. Beta was built around the ideal of a flexible, opportunistic style of running a business whereby the company would react to changes in the market. Aggressive competitors were to be avoided, as were heavy investments that might create exit barriers. Innovation and market development were less desirable than exploitation of existing markets.

The mythology of the companies was generally consistent with the business norms inculcated among the management teams. Ace's mythology glorified the toughness and competitiveness of its marketing and salespeople; the heroic salesmen who helped Ace become a national company; the wisdom of its research and development manager in anticipating the technologies needed to become a national leader; the courage of the owners who "bet" the company on new markets, new technologies, and new products; and the notion that teamwork and willpower were sufficient to overcome all obstacles. Beta's mythology was centered on an altogether different set of themes—cleverness, timeliness, and insight. Its myths portrayed its managers as outwitting Beta's competitors. Managers were described as able to make decisions on the spur of the moment without time for preparation or advance warning. These myths emphasized that the race goes, not to the swift or the strong, but to the clever.

Ace, at the time of the MDSS work, was trying to change its "knowledge" system. Ace's business strategy was shifting from a purely expansive one to one emphasizing market share and profitability. Consequently, new external data sources were added to provide appropriate feedback to managers. Ace needed its managers to learn quickly how to use the new information to address its new goals. With the shift, managers could not rely on their historic rules of thumb and heuristics: Most of their "intuitive" knowledge had been devalued.

Players Ace hired college graduates, but not MBAs or doctoral graduates. The personal values emphasized were hard work, teamwork, loyalty, discipline, willpower, and so on. Beta recruited its management trainees from the "better" graduate business schools. The characteristics valued were intelligence, insight, initiative, accomplishment, and so on. At Ace, people were harnessed together and nothing could be accomplished without teamwork. Individual roles were well defined and did not significantly overlap. Power was distributed in accordance with formal position rather than on any personal or informal basis. At Beta, power was distributed more informally, since management did not explicitly delegate any authority. Access to senior management, foreknowledge of senior management's point of view, and information or support that could be used to elicit a favorable decision by senior management were the common currency whereby individuals accrued some measure of informal power. Socializing outside of work occurred in both companies, but in different styles. Beta's junior and middle managers socialized informally. At Ace, social activities were organized, with all functions and all levels of management participating. The lack of definition in jobs and responsibilities at Beta was a source of concern for most managers. Most felt they did not know the rules for being successful or for "getting ahead." Consequently, few were inclined, or in a position, to take the initiative in changing how they ran their business.

With limited data, I can't prove that these differences in the organizations caused their different reactions to their MDSS applications. But after experiencing both environments and applications, I am convinced the organizational differences were the causal factors—albeit compounded by mistakes in applying the technology and by the problems inherent in the technology.

Few would debate that the implementation of an MDSS should be tailored to and couched in terms of the "social" organization as well as the "economic" organization. But none of us has much practical knowledge of just how an MDSS should be "adjusted" to differing corporate cultures. Although I am tempted to conclude that we should not have introduced MDSS technology to Beta, I'm not sure this is the right answer, since the company has, in fact, received considerable financial benefit.

Paradoxes

Typical of an immature and evolving technology, marketing decision support systems pose a series of problems and contradictions for the implementer. Some are purely mechanical, while others revolve around the very underpinnings of the field. I have skipped over the mechanical problems, since many are likely to be solved in the near future and most are specific to the software and data used. Instead I have focused on conceptual and strategic problems, which pose a more serious challenge.

A central goal of an MDSS is to assist managers in performing better analysis, which will replace their simplistic rules of thumb. Although MDSS facilitates improved analysis, it does not guarantee it. Paradoxically, an MDSS may produce the opposite effect to that intended: By providing managers with a high-powered data management and manipulation capability, an MDSS may expand their ability to do erroneous and faulty analysis. This possibility creates a real and significant problem for management. How can they "audit" or assure the quality of the results being produced? Certainly senior managers do not have the time or expertise to trace through the volume of complex analysis that could be churned out. Most likely, their response will be to apply some rough heuristics or rules of thumb as tests of reasonableness, which is the very situation MDSS promises to remedy.

An underlying premise of the MDSS concept is that of one "economically rational man." Through better analysis and greater understanding, a company will make better business decisions. Curiously, the decision to use MDSS technology rarely can be made on a strictly rational basis. It isn't easy to test drive an MDSS. While one may consider starting with a pilot test, the costs to implement a nontrivial MDSS are substantial. This expense, coupled with the long time before any verification will be available, means that management makes the decision on faith or hope. (Given the exaggerated claims made by specialists in data processing, management information systems, and marketing science, and their generally modest accomplishments, it is amazing that management has any faith left.) Marketing decision support systems were explicitly created to enhance managers' performance by providing better data and information. In an economically rational world, this is a valid premise. But it ignores the fact that decisions are made on the basis of knowledge (i.e., that which is believed to be true) rather than information or data.

Another premise of the MDSS concept is that a firm's internal and external marketing data contain significant insights into the dynamics of its businesses. There is a potential trap in this premise. If there has been little competition in an industry, or if most firms have simply emulated the market leader, the historical data represent only a fraction of the *possible* marketing actions and market responses. Since this problem is not detectable from the data themselves or from within a decision support system per se, the users may incur large opportunity costs while enjoying a false sense of security from having used the latest technology.

The rapid progression of the computer technology on which MDSS is based may be inadvertently leading managers to emphasize the short term at the expense of the longer term. An MDSS makes it feasible to analyze large volumes of data, such as a long time-series of marketing data for a brand. But it also can be used to analyze the most recent week's or month's results for a business "instantly." Since this latter use is dramatic and visible, it can quickly push out the more significant applications if not controlled.

MDSS technology was created to overcome some of the inadequacies of traditional management information systems. The red tape, delays, and inflexibility associated with MIS departments have left marketing and sales managers gnashing their teeth in frustration for years. To respond to the first paradox cited—that of how to ensure "good" analysis—some MDSS implementations have used intermediaries. Intermediaries are highly trained in the use of the MDSS and analytic methods: They help identify and translate the manager's concerns and needs into objective analysis. The danger inherent in this solution is that the intermediaries can quickly become a bottleneck (with many of the same characteristics of an MIS department).

Each of the above paradoxes can pose a threat to the momentum and credibility of an MDSS within a firm. For the most part, definitive resolution is unlikely in the immediate future. In the interim, triers and adopters of MDSS technology will have to struggle with each on an ad hoc basis, though perhaps with a greater awareness than those who have gone before.

Prognostications

The safest bet for the future is that decision support system products and implementations will change. A major question for end users is whether this change will be evolutionary or rapid and discontinuous. The pace of change in computer technology has increased the odds of discontinuous change by making new approaches by new vendors feasible. Holding aside the possibility of dramatic, unexpected change, there are some predictable directions in which MDSSs are likely, and need, to evolve.

MDSS computer software is user friendly compared to programming from scratch with languages such as FORTRAN, COBOL, LISP, or PL/1. But these systems are not user friendly in a more modern sense. The microcomputer revolution has fundamentally changed users' expectations, which, in turn, will force MDSS vendors to improve the "user interfaces" of their products. The microcomputer revolution will fundamentally change MDSS in other ways as well, though the major MDSS vendors have been slow to take advantage of the momentum created by IBM's entry into the personal computer market. True mainframe capabilities packaged in a desk-top machine have been developed in prototypes; it is only a matter of time until a desk-top MDSS is a reality. MDSS vendors are currently integrating micros into their systems, and one vendor will offer a desk-top MDSS by 1985.

The revolution in micro technology may make MDSS affordable and practical for nearly all types of companies, but it also might kill off MDSSs inadvertently. If an MDSS is to displace bad analysis with good analysis, it has to make the incremental cost and effort of good analysis attractive. Microcomputers may shift the marginal costs and effort back in favor of bad analysis.

A question that has attracted relatively little attention to date is how to make the MDSS more proactive. At present, the technology sits mute unless instructed to do something. In effect, the manager is to be the scout or problem spotter who calls in the MDSS. Some managers have exception reports run on regular cycles in order to identify areas where a business is not performing as expected. This is a step forward, but one of low generality and power. This division of labor between the manager and the MDSS may not be optimal: The computer, while very poor at "thinking associatively," can handle vast amounts of data quickly. A possible approach would be to give the MDSS some basic rules for recognizing relationships within a data set that it could then use to search a data base on its "own" initiative. These rules might even be modified in light of its experience. Some of the work done in artificial intelligence may have application here. Short of full-blown application of artificial intelligence constructs, there is considerable room for the development of "expert" systems—that is, those with "stored intelligence." By studying what experts do in analyzing a set of marketing data, one can program an MDSS to mimic aspects of the expert's performance. Though not a replacement for a true expert, these approaches will extend some expertise to applications and firms where none is available or affordable.

Yet to be resolved is the extent to which the contributions of an MDSS are strategic or tactical. If strategy involves allocation of resources, choices about where and whether to compete, determination of the minimum viable size for a business, and deciding what value to add to a product, an MDSS is likely to provide guidance for allocating resources, since it may estimate the market's responses to a firm's marketing actions. This would be typically done at the individual brand level, but in principle could be done across product categories or business units. In the other three areas, an MDSS per se is less capable: The typical implementations of an MDSS are not optimally configured for these tasks. Even though improved analysis could improve the strategic planning process of most firms, MDSSs are better suited for questions about resource allocation at the brand or division level and marketing operations.

Given the diversity of problems and practices in marketing, there is a question whether a single package or program is sufficient and efficient for implementing an MDSS: It may be necessary to use multiple packages in combination to deliver the total range of capabilities implied by the MDSS concept. For example, one package might support line managers; another might support model building; and another might be for financial and planning groups. The uses of multiple packages could be segmented by function. Or there could be a standard user interface or shell insulating users from the different packages making up the total system. Several companies are known to be trying the first path, and at least one vendor is working on the second.

Summary

The costs and mechanical limitations of MDSS technology will be rapidly reduced in the next few years. Business will have access to more sophisticated and capable implementations. But all of the significant technological progress made to date may be for naught if attention isn't given to understanding the interaction between decision support systems and the firm as a social system. Unfortunately, these social interactions will be much more difficult to study and resolve than the technical problems.

PART THREE

Impact of the New Technologies on Advertising

CHAPTER 8

The Changed U.S. Media Environment

Michael Drexler
Doyle Dane Bernbach

My purposes in this discussion of the changed U.S. media environment are three.[1] First, I want to review some facts about the changes in that environment, focusing on the new electronic media, but not forgetting the impacts of technology on the print media. Second, I want to offer some projections of further change, emphasizing what I consider to be realistic estimates of the household penetration of the new electronic media, and an assessment of the effects of the new media on network TV audiences. Third, I want to comment on the implications of these changes for advertisers, and offer recommendations that I think advertisers should be taking into account in light of the changes.

Review of the New Media

In this section, I shall summarize the current state of the various new electronic media. Let me state at the outset that I believe the new technologies will not exist in a vacuum. Instead, the new electronic media will be part of the total communications spectrum; they will augment traditional media forms, and will provide many more options to both the consumer and the advertiser.

Basic Cable

Cable, although it has been around since 1948, is nonetheless a new electronic medium for advertisers. Only for the last few years has it offered a substantial amount of programming generally not available on traditional broadcast television. This ability to offer many more channels of programming dates from 1975, when Home

Box Office innovatively began to distribute its pay-TV programming by satellite. Communications satellites can carry up to twenty-four television channels simultaneously, so once a cable system buys a satellite-receiving dish in order to receive one channel, the distribution mechanism is in place for twenty-three additional channels. Today, there are about forty satellite-delivered program services available only to people who have cable.

Cable subscribers now represent 37 percent of all television homes. They pay an average of $8 per month for basic service. This gives them better reception of broadcast stations, plus access to many advertising-supported cable channels like Cable News Network, ESPN, MTV, and USA Network. For the last few years, the level of cable penetration has grown to the point where advertisers are interested in it as an avenue for commercial messages.

Pay-Cable

In addition, 62 percent of these cable subscribers, or 23 percent of the total population, pay about $9 per month extra for at least one *premium* channel such as Home Box Office. These at present are commercial-free. And more than 50 percent of all cable subscribers today have the opportunity to take more than one premium channel, for example, HBO and Cinemax. Thus, while there are about nineteen million pay-cable subscribers, among them they account for twenty-four million pay subscription units.

Two-Way Cable

In addition to new and different kinds of programming, two-way or interactive cable, as exemplified by Warner-Amex's QUBE system, allows passive viewers to become active *users* of their television sets. They can participate in programs from their homes—whether these be game shows or a soap opera in which the viewers can decide which of several alternative plots will be followed. They can also order merchandise without even having to pick up the phone. There are now about 250,000 two-way cable homes, but almost all the major market cable franchises awarded since 1980 call for the construction of two-way facilities. The additional cost to the subscriber for this interactive capability is about $5 per month.

Pay-Per-View

Two-way cable offers many other possibilities, such as pay-per-view. Pay-per-view allows people to pay for what they want to watch on a program-by-program basis. It started at the QUBE system in Columbus, Ohio, where viewers could pay a separate charge to see certain movies or take guitar lessons or other courses. More recently, certain promoters have used pay-per-view to generate sizable revenues for boxing events, rock concerts, and major movies. There are about two million homes that have pay-per-view capability, through an addressable converter—a box on the TV set that can scramble or unscramble a particular channel by electronic command from the operator.

Analysis of the national pay-per-view events that have been promoted so far indicates a consumer acceptance or penetration rate that varies from less than 10 percent to as much as 33 percent of the audience potential, at prices ranging from $8 to $25 per program.

Subscription Television

Subscription television (STV) is one of the alternatives to cable in delivering pay-TV programming such as movies, sports, and specials. STV uses conventional broadcast stations, mostly UHF channels, to deliver a scrambled signal to subscribers who pay a monthly fee for a decoder that enables them to unscramble the picture. The typical STV subscriber pays about $20 per month to receive just one channel of additional commercial-free programming. There are now about twenty-five STV stations serving about 1.5 million subscribers. About 500,000 subscribers also take what is called an adult tier, a late-night offering of adult programming for which they pay an extra $5 per month. The STV industry was heavily regulated by the FCC until this year, when it became possible for the first time to offer STV programming twenty-four hours a day, and in markets with fewer than four conventional broadcast stations. Multichannel STV, where one operator offers several STV channels, is now also likely.

Multipoint Distribution Service

Multipoint distribution service (MDS) is a method of distributing pay-TV by microwaves. The subscriber requires a special antenna, which must be within the line of sight of the MDS transmitter. The transmission coverage area is limited to a maximum of twenty-five miles, and microwave signals are even more problematic for consumers than the UHF signals used by STV operators. They can be adversely affected even by the leaves on trees. There are now more than 300 MDS operators serving about 750,000 subscribers, most of whom are in multifamily dwellings. MDS programming is similar to that offered by STV operators—movies, sports, and specials. The cost to the subscriber is also similar to STV, about $20 per month for one channel.

At the moment, MDS systems are allowed to operate only a single channel in any one market. But two companies, Microband Corporation and CBS, in a joint venture with Contemporary Communications, have petitioned the FCC to allow as many as eight channels of MDS multichannel service in the same market. It is expected that the FCC will approve these petitions. Eight-channel service is now, in fact, being tested in Salt Lake City. Microband has estimated that it could build multichannel MDS facilities in each of the top fifty markets within two years for a total cost of only $35 million. If so, multichannel MDS would be a lot cheaper than cable from a cost-of-construction standpoint—although cable, of course, could offer more than eight channels.

Direct Broadcast Satellites

It is estimated that there are now thirty thousand communications-satellite-receiving dishes owned by individuals, mostly in rural areas or areas without cable service. With one of these dishes, it is possible to receive all twenty-four channels on any given satellite. Since these dishes cost up to $5,000, it is unlikely that a mass market will develop for them at any time soon. If the diameter of the dish could be reduced from ten feet to eighteen inches, with a corresponding reduction in price, to about $300, there might very well be a mass market for this concept. At least, that's the thinking behind direct broadcast satellites (DBS).

DBS satellites differ from the present communications satellites in that they operate with a great deal more transmitting power, and at higher frequencies. Since there is an inverse relationship between the amount of transmitting power and the size of the dish needed to receive it, it is possible to have DBS dishes as small as eighteen inches in diameter. But there is also a correlation between the power of the satellite and the *number* of channels it can transmit; thus, unlike communications satellites, which can transmit up to forty channels, DBS will more likely send out three to six. Like MDS, DBS requires line-of-sight transmission between the satellite and the dish. DBS signals are also subject to microwave interference.

Comsat and seven other companies have now been authorized by the FCC to begin construction of DBS satellites. Launch and operating approval is expected this year, when DBS transmission frequency allocations will be established. The earliest we are likely to see DBS in full operation would be in the latter half of 1984.

Of the eight companies now authorized to build DBS satellites, some intend to provide only pay-TV commercial-free programming, while others also plan to offer advertising-supported programming. Comsat plans to charge $32 per month for its three-channel service, as well as to offer certain pay-per-view programs for additional charges. The cost of constructing and operating a full-scale DBS service is expected to exceed $500 million.

Videocassette Recorders

There are now more than five million homes with videocassette recorders. These enable VCR owners to tape programs from television, play back prerecorded cassettes, or, with a camera, make "home movies" on tape. The "time-shifting" capability of a VCR allows owners to record one channel while watching another, or to tape a program while away or asleep for viewing at another time. VCRs truly enable people to watch *what* they want, *when* they want.

The first consumer VCRs were introduced in 1975 at a price of about $1,300. Today, there are two different *in*compatible VCR formats. The price has come down to under $400 for the least expensive models. Blank cassettes, with a recording time of up to six hours, can be bought for as little as $12. *Prerecorded* cassettes, offering movies or informational programming, typically cost about $60. Many of these can be rented, instead of purchased, for as little as $2 to $5. Movies usually appear in cassette form several months after their distribution in theaters, but still some time before they would be seen on a subscription or pay-cable channel.

One further key point regarding VCR use is the issue of whether VCR owners should be allowed to tape TV programs off the air. Producers say this is an infringement of their copyright protection, and a U.S. appeals court declared off-air taping illegal in 1981. This decision is still being studied by the U.S. Supreme Court.

From an *advertising* perspective, there is another consideration. There is evidence that many VCR owners delete some commercials (48 percent, according to a Nielsen study, "usually" or "frequently" do so) in programs they tape off the air. Further, when playing back programs recorded with commercials, about half skip past the commercials. Although VCR penetration is now only 6 percent of the population, and a considerably smaller percentage is likely to delete commercials in any one program, the implications of this phenomenon for advertisers are certainly quite serious.

Videodisc Players

Videodisc players were first introduced nationally to the consumer market in 1981. There are now about five hundred thousand of them in several different, *incompatible* formats. The least expensive player is priced today at about $250. Prerecorded discs are also less expensive than prerecorded cassettes, with discs selling for $15 to $30, versus $60 or more for the comparable cassette. This price differential is narrowing, however.

Although the average VCR owner buys approximately one and a half prerecorded cassettes per year, there is evidence that the average owner of a videodisc player purchases about twenty prerecorded discs each year. This highlights the primary difference between these two technologies: The VCR is bought mainly for its *recording* capability, while the videodisc machine now offers only *playback* capability. This may change in the future. Discs with the ability to record *once*, but without the ability to be erased, are expected to be available in 1984. Until discs are able to be erased and used *again*, however, VCRs should continue to hold a competitive edge over videodisc players.

If a consumer is interested only in the playback function, videodiscs offer several advantages over cassettes. One of these advantages is price, as already noted. Other advantages are better sound and picture quality, although with rapidly advancing VCR technology, it is possible that these particular advantages may be eliminated in the future. The laser disc, one of the formats now available, offers certain additional features that cannot be matched by VCR machines. A laser disc can provide random access to any one of fifty-four thousand separate frames or pictures, meaning that any one of them can be called up instantly. This is a truly "interactive" capability. Tied to a home computer, the laser disc can be a powerful educational tool, or it might provide movielike video games. Its possibilities are just beginning to be explored.

Videotex and Teletext

Videotex and teletext can transform the TV screen into a catalog of alphanumeric and graphic pages of information, offering such options as news, sports, weather reports, stock market quotations, entertainment listings, airline schedules, and shopping information. While most of these data bases are now available to personal computer users, they require a knowledge of computer language in order to gain access. Videotex and teletext can be accessed by untrained users with a hand-held keypad. These technologies are now available on a limited basis and are being tested in many markets. We will see them more widely available in 1984, but with only limited national penetration until at least 1985.

There are many companies competing for this market, and several different technologies by which they can be distributed. *Broadcast* teletext will use existing TV stations to send out up to two hundred pages of information at any one time. Cable teletext can send out five thousand pages, but its potential market consists of cable subscribers only. Videotex has virtually unlimited page capacity, and, in addition, it is two-way transactional. Thus, the videotex subscriber could bank or shop at home. Videotex would utilize either two-way cable or telephone lines, or a combination of one-way cable for incoming information and a telephone line for outgoing requests. There are other technological variations offered by each of these different media. In addition, synthesized sound is expected to be added to what is now a silent medium.

Once manufacturers build decoders directly into their TV sets, it is likely that broadcast teletext will be available free to viewers. Advertising would be expected to cover the cost of this service. Cable Teletext, with its much greater page capacity, is expected to be offered for a subscriber fee of about $10 per month. Videotex, with its more costly two-way home terminal, is expected to cost between $20 and $30 a month. Additional revenue for all of these services will come from advertising, which could take the form of sponsorship billboards on particular editorial sections, or full pages of information about a given product or service.

Other Technologies

There are many other technologies that will affect television in the years ahead. Satellite master antenna television (SMATV) can compete directly with cable. The SMATV operator places an antenna, including a satellite dish, on the top of a multiunit dwelling, usually a large apartment building or complex. The operator then connects individual apartments by means of wire. As long as no wires cross public property, no local government approval is needed, nor does the operator need to pay a franchise fee. In order to preempt this kind of competition, many cable operators are providing SMATV service to large buildings before they begin to wire the rest of the community.

Low-power television stations are now authorized to provide a single channel of satellite-delivered programming over the air, but with a transmitting power of no more than one kilowatt (versus several hundred kilowatts for a regular TV station). The power restriction limits their effective coverage area to no more than fifteen miles. The FCC has such a backlog of applications that it will not be until mid-1984 at the earliest that all of them can be considered. From an economic standpoint, it probably makes most sense for low-power stations to become STV operators, transmitting scrambled programming for a fee.

Video games are already having an impact on television viewing, as are home computers. The Cable Shop allows viewers to see long-length infomercials of their choice. High-definition television will greatly improve the TV picture. Large projection systems and flat-screen TVs will be commonplace in the latter part of this decade, and a 3-D television is likely in the 1990s. With technology advancing as rapidly as it is, virtually anything we can imagine will be possible. Whether there is a market for all of these technologies is something else again. Consumers do not really care how impressive the technology is. Rather, they ask, What's the benefit to me? What does it cost?

Some Predictions and Projections

With those questions in mind, let's look at some predictions about the relative success these technologies might achieve by 1990. In order to do this, it is helpful to analyze them in terms of certain consumer benefits, such as picture quality, program choice and local programs, two-way interactivity, and cost to the consumer.

Picture Quality

Cable TV offers the highest-quality picture. While not every cable system does, cable does have that potential. Broadcasting and DBS can offer good picture quality. In some markets, the broadcast picture is perfect, but on average it must be rated only good. While some DBS subscribers may get excellent reception, others may be affected by microwave interference. On balance, these two technologies must be rated good. A rating of fair goes to STV and MDS. Again, some subscribers will get better reception than others but, on average, picture quality can be said to be only fair.

Program Choice and Local Programs

In terms of program choice—the ability of these technologies to offer multiple channels—cable offers a potentially unlimited number of programs. Broadcasting offers a limited number. STV, MDS, and DBS offer a very limited number. All except one of these technologies can offer local programs that many viewers may want to see. Only DBS cannot, since all of the programming is transmitted by satellite to a very large geographic area.

Two-Way Interactivity

Which of these technologies is inherently capable of offering two-way interactivity? I say "inherently" because any of them could be accessed by going to the phone and dialing an 800 number. But which ones do not require the use of a telephone? The only one that doesn't is two-way cable.

Cost to the Consumer

What is the cost to the consumer of these different video technologies? Traditional broadcast is free (in out-of-pocket terms), since it is supported by advertising. The average home can receive five channels. Cable, including one premium channel like Home Box Office, costs an average of $17 per month, with a minimum of twelve channels. STV and MDS cost $20 per month for one channel of commercial-free programming. DBS would cost $32 per month for three to six channels of commercial-free programming.

Looking Ahead

In addition to the obvious importance of government regulation, we also have to recognize the importance of market timing. For example, cable is now available to over 60 percent of all television homes, and about 60 percent of them (about 37 percent of all TV homes) have decided to subscribe to it. DBS, were it available today, would have no competitive edge over cable in attracting the 40 percent who have chosen not to subscribe, unless DBS could offer new and different programming. I think that is unlikely. Programming costs money, and I suspect that an established pay service like Home Box Office, with over eleven million subscribers, would be more likely to afford better programming than a new DBS service with no subscriber base at all.

Let's look ahead to 1990. By 1990 there will probably be 95.5 million TV homes. Of these, 78 percent will be passed by cable (i.e., could subscribe), and 52 percent of all TV homes will be subscribing to cable; further, 75 percent of these 52 percent (or 39 percent of all TV homes) will be paying extra for at least one premium channel. Let me note that pay-cable seems to be the factor driving the increase in the percentage of cable subscribers among homes passed. Until 1980, that figure was under 50 percent; it is now 59 percent, and projected to be 63 percent in 1985 and 67 percent in 1990. Although slowly due to urban wiring cost and marketing expense, most cable growth in the remainder of this decade will occur in the top fifty markets. As major market penetration grows, "more programming variety" will replace "better reception" as the most important reason for people to subscribe to cable.

Today there are twenty-four advertiser-supported cable networks, a number I foresee declining to twelve to fifteen by 1990. At that time, we predict pay-cable revenues will provide over $10 billion to cable television's coffers, with basic cable delivering about $6 billion in annual subscriber fees. Advertising will represent about $2.4 billion of that total, and several advertising-supported networks will unfortunately go the way of the Edsel and of CBS Cable.

It is also my opinion that some of the pay-cable services will begin to accept advertising in order to reduce prices to subscribers and obtain additional revenues. Moreover, many cable operators are looking for other income sources. I believe that pay-per-view and videocassettes in addition to nonprogram services such as home security, shopping, and energy management, as well as videotex and teletext, will also contribute toward cable revenues. This, in part, will result from the development and installation of new hardware, and from an increasingly sophisticated use of marketing techniques among local system operators.

Assuming that STV and MDS beome multichannel media, together they will probably attract 8 percent of the population. DBS could attract 6 percent, mostly in rural areas. Two-way cable will probably be taken by 10 to 15 percent. Pay-per-view could be available to between 25 and 35 percent. Videotex and teletext would be likely to achieve a 14 percent penetration. VCRs could be in almost 30 percent of all homes and videodisc players in about 5 percent. Although many observers expect the primary use of videodisc technology to be in education and industry, the advent of "music video" recordings could spur videodisc growth well beyond the 5 percent estimate (see Table 8.1). I believe that most realistic observers of the media scene agree, within one or two percentage points, with these projections.

Impacts on Traditional Television

How will traditional television, particularly the networks, be affected? Although I believe that substantial portions of the popula-

TABLE 8.1 Doyle Dane Bernbach, Inc., New Electronic Media Estimates (000s)

	1970	1980	1983	1985	1990
Television households (TVHH)	58,500	76,300	83,300	86,500	95,500
Total cable households	4,700	16,800	30,800	38,000	49,660
% TVHH	8%	22%	37%	44%	52%
Pay-cable households	—	7,600	19,200	24,220	37,245
% TVHH	—	10%	23%	28%	39%
Videocassette recorders	—	1,500	5,300	15,570	29,605
% TVHH	—	2%	6%	18%	31%
Videodisc players	—	—	500	1,200	4,800
% TVHH	—	—	1%	1.4%	5%
Videotex/teletext	—	—	—	3,460	13,370
% TVHH	—	—	—	4%	14%
Subscription television	—	800	1,800	4,300	7,600
% TVHH	—	1%	2%	5%	8%
Direct broadcast satellite	—	—	—	80	5,700
% TVHH	—	—	—	—	6%

tion will embrace these new electronic media, by no means am I predicting the downfall of traditional television. Broadcast television will adapt, and will continue to be a very successful medium. Nevertheless, network shares will probably continue to decline (see Table 8.2).

But neither do I subscribe to the belief of certain doomsayers who predict that many of these new electronic media will not survive. We all know about the demise of CBS Cable and the Entertainment Channel, and I expect certain other cable networks will go out of business. In 1982, it was estimated that cable network

TABLE 8.2 Prime Time Network Audience Projections

	1970	1980	1983	1985	1990
U.S. TV homes (000s)	58,500	76,300	83,300	86,500	95,500
% Homes using television	56.5%	60.0%	60.0%	62.5%	64.0%
3-network share of audience	90.0%	86.0%	74.0%	68.0%	60.0%
3-network rating	51.0%	51.6%	44.1%	42.3%	38.4%
Average network rating	17.0%	17.2%	14.7%	14.1%	12.8%
Average net household audience (000s)	9,950	13,125	12,245	12,195	12,220

Source: Estimates by Doyle Dane Bernbach, Inc.

advertising revenues fell short of operating costs by about $150 million. Some of the reasons for this are that we have been suffering through a major recession; cable is a *new* medium for advertisers (and understandably quite often the last one to be added to a media plan and the first one to be dropped); and, unquestionably, we are lacking good audience measurement. Attractive programming with high appeal is also a problem.

But to put all of this into perspective, we must remember that Home Box Office lost money for five straight years and the ABC Television Network lost $113 million from 1963 to 1971, yet both are today highly profitable enterprises. I predict the same kind of scenario for many of the cable channels supported by advertising. Their 1982 advertising revenue was more than twice what it was in 1981, and in 1983 it is expected to grow by at least another 50 percent. Cable TV's share of television-advertising expenditures should grow to 7 percent by 1990.

Overall, I have no doubt that these new electronic media will develop and they will affect our lives enormously. Furthermore, their benefits will be synergistic: the combined impact of all of them acting together will be greater than the sum of their individual contributions.

Broadcast Programming

The consequences of the new electronic technologies will also affect the content of TV programming. I expect to see certain key features in the future. Network broadcasting will continue to provide mass appeal situation comedies, adventure-drama, variety shows, news, sports, and made-for-TV movies. Basic cable will offer special and general interest programming for entertainment and education. Pay-cable networks will provide first-run movies, major sports events, show spectaculars, theater productions, concerts, and series. Local broadcast TV stations will increase their appeal in individual markets (with local news, personality talk shows, regional magazine formats). Local cable TV systems will also offer programs for communities and neighborhoods. Commercials will be distributed via satellites to local TV stations. Cable TV will continue to siphon audiences away from over-the-air broadcasting. (Networks are expected to lose approximately twenty-six share points between 1980 and 1989, equivalent to eleven rating points in prime time.) Prime time network TV audiences will not diminish substantially in actual size due to additional growth of TV homes and TV usage. Public broadcasting stations (PBS) will carry commercials. Broadcast programming and print editorial will become integrated; for example, editorial material done in one form will reappear in another form, extending the use of a single creative product.

Print Media and Technology

Because of the relative importance of TV to advertisers, and because much of the "technological action" is in the new electronic media, I have concentrated my review and projections on the electronic side. But print media also are being affected by technological advances. More specifically, magazines are being affected by technology in very specific ways. Through the use of satellites, multiple printing facilities decentralized throughout the country will cut cost increases of distribution. Satellites will also provide shorter closings for advertisements and faster distribution. Computers will provide customized editorial options for the reader; first, by region or market; second, by ZIP code; and, third, by subscriber.

As a consequence, the character of magazines will change. For example, media integration will be likely, in order to amortize creative talent and costs. For example, we have seen magazine articles turned into a cable TV series. In addition, I expect we shall see more "magalogs," combined magazines and catalogs. This form is already emerging in the retailing field, with department stores issuing their own magazines.

There will be similar changes among newspapers. Tabular information such as stock quotes, sports results, movie listings, and classifieds will be supplied by videotex and teletext TV technology. Wire service use of satellites is currently available, and satellite services will expand. In reverse, newspaper publishers will become major suppliers of information for new video technology. Some newspapers will adopt satellite transmission to local printing plants, as the *Wall Street Journal* has done, to become national newspapers. Satellites will enable advertisers to order and "ship" advertising schedules to newspapers more quickly. Finally, advertising production will be simplified by computer systems using optical laser technology.

Summary of Implications about Major Media

Technological developments, of course, are not the only factors affecting the media environment. Time does not permit exploration of media cost considerations, government regulatory changes, and the like. Instead, let me offer, in summary form, my expectations for the four major media. First, television will have continued fragmentation of mass coverage, segmented audiences, costs that increase but not as rapidly among specific customer groups, personalized programming to suit special interests and life styles, more local and regional advertising opportunities, more and better audience measurements, new opportunities for graphic display on TV screens and two-way interactive communication, and integrated product messages on prerecorded video cassettes and discs. Second, radio will have efficient although more expensive advertising per unit, an influx of new stations, and SAT networks, and programming choices that will provide more precise media targeting, greater reliance on merchandising opportunities, more opportunities for program development and syndication, and better and easier coverage of ethnic and minority markets. Third, magazines will have greater audience selectivity through circulation breakouts of general magazines and special interest publications, more volatile circulation patterns, editorial options by consumers extending to geographic segmentation and advertiser tie-ins, shorter closing dates, improved reproduction fidelity, more regional, local, and demographic editions as audience target editions, magazine editorial and advertising integrated with television, and more special issues. Fourth, newspapers will have more equitable, although not cheaper, pricing between national and local advertisers, ordering of space through computerization, greater choices of positions and sections to provide increased flexibility; editions targeted to the suburbs through geographic editions of metro papers and improved availability and quality of suburban papers, and improved (including color) reproduction and use of videotex and teletext in place of traditional sections of the paper.

Overall, I see the traditional media structure surviving in tandem with the new media technologies. The new technologies will fragment mass media audiences and create a more personal media environment.

Implications for Advertisers

What does all this mean for advertisers in the U.S. market? Many people are addressing this central question directly, and I shall only offer some observations about three areas I consider significant: media fragmentation and the effects of demassification, the nature of the effects of commercials, and the need for more customized research.

Media Fragmentation

Media fragmentation will continue to increase. Already, the three major TV broadcast networks have lost a total of sixteen prime time share points since 1970; it is expected that network shares will decline to about 60 percent by 1990. But in pay-cable households, some prime time network ratings are down as much as 35 percent. True, this represents only about 23 percent of the country, but pay cable is growing, and it is growing much faster as it enters the major cities.

An optimist will look at increasing fragmentation and see the new decade as the era of marketing segmentation, with infinite opportunities. Media audiences will be smaller, and we will have a better perspective on our media and marketing targets. Nevertheless, this "demassification" will require more of advertisers. For example, target audiences must be defined more precisely, not only by demographics, but also by life styles and behavior. Media rate structures must be examined from a different viewpoint—combinations of media, long-term commitments, franchise positions, new volume and frequency discounts, and so on. Research must examine more diversified attitudes and opinions in greater depth—new media forms, purchasing and behavior, life styles, commercial measurements, and media uses. Creative treatments must become more varied to meet the needs of new, more specific audiences—longer length commercials, infomercials, multiple-page treatments, unusual space units, integration with program and editorial material. "Demassification" will require more time, more effort, more creativity, but there will be more media opportunities to produce better results.

The Nature of Commercial Impact

With the advent of the new technologies, we also have to take another look at commercial impact. Long characterized largely as a product of dominant units in print or heavy frequency of TV exposure in a limited time frame, commercial impact may be even greater when multiple commercials are scheduled in programs uniquely designed to suit the specific needs or benefits of the advertiser's product. It now costs about $85,000 for one thirty-second nighttime network commercial. The same budget can buy 160 spots on the cable television networks. The reach is limited, but if impact is also frequency, cable television will offer more frequent exposure for an advertiser's dollars. In the past, television has not been considered a medium for reaching only a few hundred thousand people.

Different measurements that challenge some traditional notions will be needed. For example, let us consider audience accumulation patterns. These patterns may be different for audiences viewing commercials on cable television and video recorders. Moreover, with an increase in overall viewing, particularly among light or nonviewers of traditional television, exposure patterns may also change. Again, media evaluation standards will change. We now make intermedia comparisons quantifying the numbers with effectiveness factors to place relative values on a commercial or advertisement within the various media. But what happens when a daytime soap opera is recorded and played back at night? Or "The Tonight Show" is viewed by some audiences in the morning? Will we give these shows different values according to the different viewing environments?

What is the incremental value of a commercial scheduled in a program environment that is tailored to the specific needs and interests of the advertiser? What are the relative values of a two-minute or five-minute commercial versus a page or a spread in a magazine? How do we evaluate a program schedule when, through VCRs, different members of a household watch the same show at different times? Right now, the audience for a program is predictable and is all reached at a given time. But video recorders will change all that, and will generate a "follow-on" audience as well.

More Customized Research

With individual viewing patterns changing as a result of multiset ownership and more outlets to the video terminal, and with the advent of video recorders and a new freedom in the time chosen for viewing, customized research, including attitudinal and behavior measurements, will become more important. We will have to measure not only audience viewing but also audience reactions to programs and attitudes toward advertising with the new media technologies. But even these data may not go far enough. Interactive television systems may be the ultimate measure of television research in the future, providing instantaneous and continuous information through terminals attached to the television set. And they may also allow viewers to comment on programming or commercials spontaneously and register their enjoyment and interest in programs, as well as their receptivity to commercials. These possibilities, still not fully developed, indicate some of the problems we shall have to confront.

Applications and Recommendations for Advertisers

Based on what we do know, let us examine some of the ways advertisers have begun to use the new technologies. As noted, media segmentation permits advertisers to develop their own programs specifically for the special interests and life styles of key prospects. Further, the growth of cable television programming for selective audiences also allows us to personalize copy for special appeals. Let us look at some examples:

For a manager of home improvement products with company-owned retail outlets, Doyle Dane Bernbach, Inc., worked with a leading magazine to develop a low-cost program on home decorating that used the editorial material of the publication. We did not expect big ratings, but we did expect to reach a uniquely interested segment of viewers in the how-to home-decorating market. We then could take the concept a step further. Utilizing this how-to program on home decorating, we could transfer the program to videocassette for utilization on VCR equipment in local retail stores—extending the media concept to the point of purchase. We had the ultimate form of a program commercial with an integrated product message. For Atari, we created special commercials designed specifically for the hard-to-reach teenage audience. The commercials were placed on Music Television (MTV), the twenty-four hour rock video cable network. In 1982, Bulova became the official timepiece of the Cable News Network; eight times every day, the Bulova logo is superimposed over CNN's programming, with a digital reading of the exact time.

In the future, we shall see more advertising techniques used to reach various market segments. Here are some of the principal actions we are recommending to advertisers.

1. Use cable to supplement the already deficient audience delivery of networks to cable and (especially) pay-cable households.
2. Use cable to achieve greater focus on key audience target segments—for example, special interest programming to suit specific consumer interests and life styles.
3. Develop special commercials, in length and in style, for the new technologies, commercials more integrated with the program environment.

4. Undertake, or participate in, experimental copy and media testing use of videotex and teletext to learn more about the products and services appropriate to these media, and about the kinds of audiences most effectively reached by them.
5. Consider production of prerecorded video tapes and discs of special program material with integrated product demonstrations or mentions.
6. Explore generic commercials in recognition of delayed playback and repeat viewing of videotaped TV programs.

CHAPTER 9

A European Perspective on Media Changes and Their Implications

Boris C. G. Wilenkin
Unilever, Plc.

Before I embark on the hazardous task of forecasting the future, it is necessary to understand the present. This is particularly the case in the area of European media, since in many respects it differs significantly from the situation in the United States. I make no apologies, therefore, for describing the main features of the European media scene and the problems these pose for a manufacturer-advertiser of fast-moving consumer goods. Since the new technologies in communication are concerned with the video screen and, where advertising space is relatively readily available, video is the most popular medium for the above advertisers, I will concentrate here on the television scene.

Viewing

The first fact is that television viewing is far less of a way of life in Europe than it is in the United States. The United Kingdom has always prided itself on its standard of programming and it is perhaps for this reason that viewing is higher there than in any other European country, but it is still well below that of the United States. In France and Germany, neither country being particularly noted for the quality of its TV offering, viewing is at about half the American level, and the Dutch barely reach a third (Table 9.1). It can be argued that in Europe, quality rather than quantity is the determining factor in attracting viewers.

It must also be admitted that there are far fewer channels avail-

TABLE 9.1 Levels of Television Viewing

Countries[a]	Average Adult Viewing per Day		Channels
	Hours	Minutes	
United Kingdom	3	10	4
Spain	3	0	2
Italy	2	40	· 2
West Germany	2	13	3
France	2	9	3
Netherlands	1	27 (per evening)	5–13
United States	4	12	

Source: Unilever estimates, based on commercial research data.
[a]With populations exceeding ten million.

able to European viewers than is the case in the United States. There are today only national channels or networks; with the exception of the Benelux countries, which are predominantly cabled and can, therefore, receive neighboring national networks, European countries can receive only two to four channels.

Advertising

The amount of air time made available for advertising is controlled by government. In half of Europe air time is limited to about four hours or less per week, ranging from none at all in Norway, Sweden, and Denmark to four hours and twelve minutes in France. This means that demand vastly outstrips supply, as can be seen by the relationship between availability and proportion of advertising spent on television in countries where air time is relatively abundant compared to those where it is relatively restricted (Table 9.2). TV advertising is predominantly national. Only in the United Kingdom is regional advertising fully developed. Germany has the possibility of limited regional variation, as has France (from January of this year) and Italy through the non-government-controlled private network.

The inflexibility of television as an advertising medium extends both to booking arrangements and price. In five countries— Austria, France, Italy (the national channel), the Netherlands, and West Germany—bookings have to be made two to four months before the *year* of transmission. Prices are constant. This means that, for all intents and purposes, bookings are made on the basis of obtaining the maximum ration and bear little relation to potential

TABLE 9.2 Relationship between Available Air Time and Advertising

	Proportion of Advertising Expenditure Spent on TV	Maximum Advertising Minutes Allowed per Week (1982)
Portugal	57%	945
Greece	56	770
United Kingdom	41	980
Ireland	35	580
Spain	34	693
Austria	32	120
Italy	31	392 + 14% of private TV (from July 1983)
Total population: 178.9 million		
France	18	252[a]
Netherlands	17	180
Finland	13	175
West Germany	12	240
Belgium	9	231[b]
Switzerland	5	360[c]
Total population: 168.2 million (including Norway, Sweden, and Denmark)		

[a]Extended to 378 in 1983.
[b]Sold (in French only from Luxembourg).
[c]120 minutes per channel (French, German, Italian).

audience. Indeed program details are probably not known at the time of booking, although since the advertising breaks are few and are usually concentrated around the main news program, there is less scope for good buying than under a freer system. Even in Spain and Belgium, bookings have to be made six and four months in advance, respectively.

A new phenomenon that is beginning to have an effect on the use of TV advertising is the rapid growth of VCR penetration in the major European countries. From a low base in 1981, penetration doubled the following year and forecasts suggest that this growth will continue (Table 9.3). The use of VCRs and the remote control switch for changing channels combined with a system whereby commercials are shown in a few lengthy blocks at specific times mean that even when people are watching television, live or recorded, they are easily able to avoid the commercial breaks if they wish to do so.

It can be seen that the situation in Europe differs considerably from that of the United States in several ways.

TABLE 9.3 VCR Penetration of Households (%)

	End 1981	End 1982	Forecast End 1985
Belgium	3%	6%	11%
France	2	4	17
Netherlands	4	8	15
United Kingdom	6.5	16	40
West Germany	4	10	15

Source: Estimates by J. Walter Thompson.

- There is less TV viewing.
- There is less air time, both for programs and for advertising.
- This translates into less audience fragmentation, which from the viewpoint of the advertiser seeking mass audiences is a positive thing.
- There is more government control, leading to less flexibility in use.

The European advertiser is thus faced with the following problems:

- There is a lack of air time in most countries, with some still forbidding any advertising.
- There is inflexibility in terms of coverage, bookings, and price.
- There has been a decline in viewership, particularly for commercial breaks.
- There is less accurate audience measurement than hitherto.
- Air time costs increase at a faster rate than the costs of other media.
- There has been an escalation in the cost of making commercials.

Nonetheless, television is still regarded as an extremely effective advertising medium for fast-moving consumer goods.

One can conclude from this brief summary that there is ample scope, if not need, in Europe for more advertising air time, with greater flexibility through new channels competing with existing ones. Transmission could be either by direct broadcasting via satellite, which could allow the same commercial to be used on a Pan-European basis, or by cable. The latter would also provide the geographic flexibility that is lacking. From the point of view of communication the only drawback to new channels would be a further fragmentation of the audience.

What Might Happen

If it is accepted that there is a need for more commercial air time for advertisers, what are the various possibilities and considerations? Although direct broadcasting via satellite is technically possible, one should bear in mind that national satellites (private satellites are not allowed) were allotted orbital positions in order to minimize, even in Europe, multinational reception. This was done by varying not only their geographical position but also their place in the band, upper or lower megacycle, their polarization, left hand or right hand, and finally whether the Pal or Secam system was used. All these problems can be sorted out on the ground, given sufficient equipment. This leads to a consideration of cable reception, since it is obvious that a cable operator can make the necessary adjustments easily and economically. Today, however, only Belgium, Denmark, the Netherlands, Norway, and Switzerland are even adequately cabled (Table 9.4). None of the major countries approaches double figures, and despite the situation in the countries named above, on a cumulative basis less than 10 percent of European households are cabled.

Since today European governments control television, directly or indirectly, and are extremely unlikely to give up their powers, it is vital to understand their motivations. On the one hand they see television as having far greater social than economic importance. A number of them apply restrictions not only to advertising but also to programs to the extent of rationing strictly the quantity of imported material. Protecting the people from the threat of wall-to-wall "Dal-

TABLE 9.4 Cable TV Penetration of Households (%)

	Estimate for End 1981
Belgium	75%
Denmark	51
Netherlands	60
Norway	21
Switzerland	29–34

Source: Estimates by J. Walter Thompson.
Note: These figures are for Community Antenna networks.

las" is a position that goes down well with the intellectual fringe in most countries and is well supported by journalists. On the other hand one or two of the larger countries, in particular France and the United Kingdom, are anxious to develop cable or direct broadcasting systems, not so much for the benefit of their people, but for the export possibilities this policy might bring. A recent brief review by the *Financial Times* of London illustrates the complex political situation. Articles on the cable issue in Belgium, Finland, France, the Netherlands, and West Germany revolved around the political issues in each country.[1]

Commercial considerations follow closely upon the political considerations. Although some countries hope to be able to use their experience to sell both systems and programs on the export market, as mentioned above, this does not mean that they will finance them centrally. Notably, Mrs. Thatcher's Conservative government expects any new systems to be run privately and, therefore, to be financially viable without recourse to state support.

Even in those countries where television is entirely state financed, the money for new channels has to come from somewhere. This can mean from the viewer in the form of an extra licensing fee, from taxation, or from advertising. The question currently being asked, now that the technology-led euphoria is dying down and the commercial issues are beginning to be discussed, is whether there is an adequate consumer demand for more channels. Inevitably, and perhaps more particularly in Europe, the answer must lie in the quality rather than in the quantity to be offered.

American experience suggests that even in a country with a voracious appetite for television, commercial success is difficult to achieve. In the United Kingdom three new television ventures have been launched recently: First, a new national commercial channel, which has had a struggle to make its mark, and earlier this year, two breakfast programs, one commercial, the other not. In the latter case the noncommercial channel appears to be drawing the lion's share of the audience, leaving the future of the commercial company in serious doubt. The lesson here is that although there is perhaps little difference in the quality offered by the two competitors, viewers at that hour of the day prefer their television without commercial breaks. Their time is limited and they are probably much less receptive to advertising then than in the evening; research has found that advertising is popular and not considered obtrusive at the later hour.

Governments and companies seeking licenses will have to consider very carefully whether they can attract enough viewers to make an investment in new channels and in hardware worthwhile.

The Advertiser

The advertiser, we have already noted, is frustrated. In most countries he or she has too little television time and pays too much for it. So in principle more seems better. Further, from this side of the Atlantic, the possibility of Pan-European media must seem very attractive. Let us examine this last concept, even if we know that there are technical and political obstacles to be overcome before European channels can be truly operative. One major assumption that has to be made is that there will be a worthwhile audience. If we accept that, although it is far from certain, are there obvious international brands for whom this medium is attractive?

We find a lot of national tastes, and thus markets, in Europe coming closer together as both the legislators of the community and the traveling habits of the people encourage greater interchange in consumption. It can be argued that there is more similarity in taste and in purchasing behavior among the youth of Paris, London, and Copenhagen in the area of soft drinks and records than there is among their parents within the same country for day-to-day food items. Will the similarities of the youth of today be translated into greater uniformity of taste and habit when they become the parents of tomorrow? Advertising is an important motor that could give a positive answer, but today it must be admitted that with a few notable exceptions such as Coca-Cola and Pepsi-Cola there are few products in the European foods and drinks markets that have international application. The markets for cleaning products, whether personal or household, show greater similarities as habits are common. All those with washing machines use them in the same way and have similar motivations. The same thing holds for dental hygiene and hair care, even if the models, human rather than mechanical, vary in their looks, depending on their country of origin.

To return to food, a number of our product fields show very different patterns of purchasing and usage across Europe. In France annual margarine consumption is only two kilograms per head. In the Netherlands the figure is over six times as great. Germans get through nearly eleven liters of dried soup in a year, compared with a British consumption of under three, with the Italians hardly drinking any at all. In the frozen food area not only do consumption figures vary enormously, the market is highly developed in the United Kingdom but still in its infancy in France, and tastes are very different. Peas may be a lead product in the United Kingdom, but in Germany it is spinach. This implies both different messages and different media weighting.

In the large countries, France and Germany, these differences can occur within the same country, as they do in the United Kingdom, giving rise to another problem. The size of a country can require varying both the message and the rate of advertising spending by area. But as has been mentioned earlier, television throughout most of Europe is a national medium and local flexibility hardly exists. Even if we have a product with general international appeal, or one that will develop these appeals over time, do any other barriers confront the Pan-European marketer? Currently there are several that can influence our product offering or market approach. These are legislation, price, control, and accountability.

Legislation

Despite the efforts of product harmonization within Europe, and in particular within the EEC, there are still differences governed by national legislation that hinder cross-border trade. Some products have to have varying formulations, ranging from preservative content to coloring. Others have to vary their presentation. In France and Belgium, for example, founding members of the EEC, margarine can only be sold in cubic form, even though there are no limitations of shape in other EEC countries.

Problems regarding products pale when compared with those surrounding advertising. Today the rules governing advertising content differ from country to country. To illustrate the point, J. Walter Thompson's London office recently showed how a Kellogg commercial used extensively in the United Kingdom was unacceptable legally in most of the other European countries. What was worse was that each country had its own reason for not being able to use the film. In one country, endorsement by children is not allowed, in another no mention of vitamin content can be made, in a third even mild comparative claims are forbidden, and so on. Advertisers are trying to promote a common code but so far little progress has been made. The danger of harmonization of current legislation is that this will be based on the most restrictive elements from each country.

Price

A further problem confronting a prospective Pan-European marketer, particularly of fast-moving consumer goods, concerns price. Not only do costs still vary across Europe, leading to differences in price for the same brand, but the inflationary conditions of the last few years have induced a number of governments to control prices, which creates artificial differences between the price of a brand in country A and country B. This in turn leads to cross-border trade to the detriment of the manufacturer of the international brand, perhaps to the point of discouraging him from using the same brand name throughout Europe.

Control and Accountability

Today many multinational operations in Europe are run with profit responsibility and control of day-to-day operations vested in the hands of the local national operator. If his brand mix includes an international brand, he may have to accept a common name, a common presentation, and, unless he can show that for one reason or another these are not acceptable in his country, common formulation and advertising. If television became international, where would the decision be made on advertising content, on campaign booking, and on how the costs are to be allocated? A strong case could be made for using a satellite to give additional advertising support for brand X in Germany. But the cost would be based on total coverage. If only 40 percent could be attributed to Germany, it is likely that the German company would only buy the much needed air time if it was charged only 40 percent of the cost. But the French, Belgian, and Dutch companies, which account for the other 60 percent of coverage, might for tactical or profit reasons not want this additional air time and would certainly not want to pay their share. Either they will be obliged to do so by the corporate headquarters, which negates the concept of profit responsibility at the local level, or the German company will pay vastly over the odds for their campaign or drop the idea and risk an under advertised product.

The many local problems listed above suggest that direct broadcasting via satellite is too blunt an instrument for the majority of Pan-European marketers. The message has to be diluted to be acceptable legally and its targeting capability is more that of a shotgun while the sophisticated advertiser requires a riflelike precision. Cable must be the solution as the basic carrier, although, here again, not only are cable systems lacking in the major countries, but also under current legislation in certain countries no changes can be made by the cable operator either to programming or to advertising. The operator is licensed merely to transmit existing and authorized channels. The advertiser needs a local cable operator who is allowed to vary output as he thinks fit. Indeed one can foresee a situation like that in the United States, where a license is only granted, as with commercial radio in the United Kingdom, if adequate local programming is carried. Given local programming, local advertising follows naturally. Here is a medium that can attract both the local and the multinational advertiser.

Where We Stand

Despite the long list of problems that any Pan-European advertiser faces, we welcome the new technological developments that will hopefully provide more means of reaching the target audience and in a more efficient manner. But what of the actual brand and advertising content implications? Do we envision more Pan-European brands supported by international campaigns? The easy answer is that we, in Unilever, will endeavor to do what is best in the circumstances, and these can vary case by case. Two major factors must be kept in mind. First, we must do the best possible job for each product and each brand we market. We must provide the right product for the Belgian housewife if the market warrants it, even if her French or Dutch cousins want a variation. We must also provide the communication appropriate to the audience. Our starting point is the target consumer and not a search for a possible common denominator that will enable us to use Pan-European media.

Second, our philosophy has always been based on giving the responsibility of annual and longer-term profit targets to the management of individual companies throughout the Unilever world. One cannot on the one hand give this responsibility and on the other impose either product or advertising on an unwilling local management. After all, who should know better what is right for their countrymen and women than they?

Having said this, it is equally obvious that where it is appropriate, we will sell the same product, under the same brand name supported by the same advertising to as wide a target as possible. But this is not different from the position today, where Pan-European advertising hardly exists. Personal washing habits are pretty much the same throughout Europe and it is not surprising that Lux Toilet Soap conforms to the above description. We want to provide the consumer with the best toilet soap at the price, presented and advertised in the best manner.

Thus, *one formula*, *one brand* name, and *one advertising* campaign is not only the most appropriate answer, it is also the most efficient. We are obviously in favor of internationalization where it makes sense. Already habits in the washing, tooth cleaning, hair care, and cosmetic areas are fairly universal across much of Europe and we have brands bearing the same brand name, positioned similarly and supported by the same advertising campaign. In addition to Lux, brands such as Denim and Impulse are further examples.

We are already organized for internationalization, and have been for many years. This applies not only to our own management but also to the advertising agencies with whom we work. Our four main agencies are aligned by product group, so that the best advertising ideas can be, and are already being, developed and used internationally even if media opportunities do not yet exist and brand names are different. Internationalization of habits and thus needs will continue to grow, promoted by travel as much as by media. Nevertheless, we foresee a much slower development in the food area. Our thrust will continue to be to provide what the consumer wants and this will dictate our product and brand strategy rather than the international media opportunities that technology may provide.

The Future

Let me take a last rub at the crystal ball and look at what it shows for the European media scene in the late eighties and nineties. There will clearly be a search for alternative means of communication as audience fragmentation reduces the cost effectiveness of traditional television spot advertising. A possible scenario might include satellite advertising for international brands in the form of "electronic posters," advertising by local cable to reflect both better consumer targeting and the concentration of the retail trade, and sponsored programs and infomercials aimed at specific target groups. A further result of fragmentation of the television audience might be a swing back to the print medium, since readership can be more easily estimated than viewing, leading to a better evaluation of media schedules based on print. As a result of ever-increasing competition both from other manufacturers and from retailers with their own brands, the winners will be those who make the best use of their marketing dollar, pound, or franc. Sorting out the media jungle satisfactorily provides that opportunity in the years to come.

CHAPTER 10

The New Electronic Media: How Advertisers Are Adapting

David K. Braun

General Foods Corporation

Marketing adaptation is a way of life for successful advertisers. These days, the growth of the new electronic media is testing the ingenuity of many advertisers, including General Foods.

In this paper I will try to assess the need for adapting to the new electronic media—or NEM as it is called in the trade—from the standpoint of the packaged goods advertiser. I will discuss some of the market trends at General Foods that have helped us cope with the complex advertising implications of the NEM. To do this, I will draw on a number of case histories to illustrate different approaches used by different brands. The concluding section will identify several management issues that I believe are derived from the NEM phenomenon, and deserve management attention throughout the advertising industry.

The new electronic media—and comments about it—will be easier to understand if they are viewed in the broader context of socioeconomic trends in the United States today. The key observation is that our society is no longer homogeneous—in its behavior, in its attitudes, or in its aspirations. As recently as the 1950s and 1960s, the "other-directed society" aspired to own that suburban house with the white picket fence. If we didn't already live there (with two children, a dog, and a station wagon), we were at least headed in that direction. That was a time when husbands worked and wives stayed home, a time when advertisers could address a monolithic body of average U.S. consumers. We could use broad, general language delivered through mass magazines and the living room television set. Marketing was relatively simple. But times have changed. That prototypical target family of working husband, housewife at home, two kids, a dog, and a suburban house now represents only 7 percent of U.S. households. America has evolved from a farm and foundry economy to one dominated by service and information. This change, combined with the women's movement and economic inflation, has produced a work force that includes fully half of all women over eighteen. Nearly four of every ten adult women work at least thirty hours a week.[1]

Our former homogeneous goals and values have been replaced by an extremely diverse set of aspirations and life styles. As far back as 1977, Larry Light aptly referred to this cultural shift as "The Age of Me."[2] This trend toward individualization has both led and been enhanced by the tremendous growth in "life style" magazines and in the number of homes with more than one television set. Half of all homes now have two or more TV sets. Why is this important? It means that television watching in America—like Sunday afternoons and the evening meal—is no longer considered a family experience. It is now an individual experience.

It is hard to imagine a more receptive climate for the emergence of the new electronic media. Technologically, of course, NEM is an independent development that might have proceeded without the socioeconomic individualization I have been describing. But, in reality, the two go hand in hand. Growth trends exhibited by the new electronic media during the past few years could not have occurred without the individualization of United States society, and NEM has itself validated the emergence of the individual as a force to be reckoned with.

The recent growth of the new electronic media, especially cable, is impressive. Cable household penetration has risen from 17 percent in 1978 to 37 percent in May 1982.[3] Most current projections indicate a household penetration approaching 60 percent by 1990. The average household is now able to receive eleven separate television channels. New systems are being installed with channel capacity as high as sixty channels. Old systems are being upgraded to carry twenty to thirty channels. The result is that viewing behavior, especially in the new larger-capacity systems, is being dramatically altered. Of necessity, the three broadcast networks are the big losers: The networks' prime time viewing share has declined from 90 percent in noncable homes to a more modest 56 percent in homes with pay movie channels.[4] Added diversity is changing viewer attitudes toward network programming and the presence of commercials. Interactive television and service programming on cable is creating a more active viewer attitude, replacing the total passivity of the average viewer of the 1960s. Upscale, urban, younger demographic groups are being attracted to cable, which makes them less available to broadcast advertisers.

Although the household penetration of videotape recorders and videodisc players is much lower than cable to date, the growth and development patterns of these NEM forms are similar to those for cable. They will become major forces to be considered by advertisers in the late 1980s and beyond.

Marketing Implications

General Foods (like most other large packaged goods advertisers) has believed for a long time in the principle that successful advertising must address a perceived consumer need, and position the product to satisfy that need. We believe this principle will continue to be valid, even in our individualistic society. But faced with cable television and the fragmented marketplace it serves, advertisers will have to devise and adopt new approaches to advertising. What this means, of course, is that brand positionings will be targeted more directly to the needs of individual—and smaller—market segments. Tighter targeting will allow us to use more effective selling messages, which we hope will offset the reduced reach and frequency of individual commercials.

For years, packaged goods advertisers have relied primarily on demographic data to define target audiences. To be sure, life style, attitudes, and brand usage descriptions were also employed. But the fact that media audiences were not quantified along similar lines made it difficult for advertisers to use such qualitative classifications for media selection. The reliance on broad-scale demographics has become more troublesome with the individualization of our society. Just think how much the two key demographic discriminators—age and sex—have lost as surrogate measures of behavior and attitude differences. Health and fitness are of great interest to many senior citizens as well as younger people. Women work, exercise, buy life insurance, and regard themselves as equally important as male prospects for many products and services positioned exclusively for men ten years ago. As a result, general demographics, used in the traditional way, have lost some of their edge as a marketing tool.

A new development called PRIZM makes it possible to combine demographic and geographic data in a more effective way. PRIZM clusters the population by individual ZIP codes according to several characteristics. Group S1, for example, comprises "educated, affluent, elite, white families located in owner-occupied greenbelt suburbs." This cluster contains four smaller groups that are individually more homogeneous demographically than S1 and, at the same time, different from each other. The four S1 subgroups are labeled in a way that connotes psychographic dimensions: "Blue Blood Estates," "Furs and Station Wagons," "Two More Rungs," and "Pools and Patios."[5] Despite its *demographic* homogeneity, each group includes ZIP codes from diverse sections of the United States.

This approach has the potential of helping advertisers select media more effectively. Radio and television markets and individual stations and programs can be assessed in terms of their audiences, grouped by PRIZM clusters. As individual cable operators develop a greater capability to handle advertising, their uniquely local franchises will offer television advertisers a new dimension of selectivity. And the "life style" characteristics add conceptual understanding that will help in selecting segmented print vehicles and in developing the advertising message itself.

Media Planning in the 1980s

The individualization of society and the recent availability of qualitative targeting data have permanently altered our approach to media planning. Traditionally, we have used a "top down" process: National media (network television and consumer magazines) were evaluated and budgeted first. Local media such as spot TV, spot radio, and newspapers were used to fill in delivery shortfalls from the national plan and to increase weight in areas of higher assessed opportunity. In a budget sense, most of our plans have been very heavily skewed to national media types.

Although this process still prevails in many cases, there is a growing tendency to plan "from the bottom up." Several different target audience segments may be identified as deserving advertising attention; these are then ranked in order of importance. An "optimum plan" is then developed for each segment in turn, utilizing the various unique opportunities for reaching each target group. The planning process can continue this way until the budget is exhausted; or it can set aside a residual amount for coverage in forms of national media. The latter approach is generally preferred, and media planning is rapidly becoming an iterative process, with conscious trade-offs being made to achieve the right balance.

The "information age" approaches to media planning have made the process more logical. Nonetheless, tradition dies hard. One reason for this is that in many cases the old way of doing things was simpler. Planning cost targets, which once were relatively accurate for a homogeneous "corporate" target group, are now less accurate and more diffuse. This makes it more difficult to track year-to-year changes in cost efficiency for the corporation as a whole. It also makes it more difficult to compare the cost efficiencies of alternate media plans.

The marketplace buying leverage of large packaged goods advertisers, once maximized by the luxury of only a single target group and cost structure, is now fragmented across a variety of target groups and the media that serve them. Because we believe it is right for the business, our solution at General Foods has been to proceed in the new direction; but the inevitable transition is requiring us to communicate more frequently with management both up and down the line. It is essential that management becomes familiar not only with the new concepts of media planning but with their implications for quantified performance analysis as well.

Understanding the new media will not be easy. Advertisers will need to create new media models to reflect the environment of the 1980s. The viewing diary, the key to understanding television audience behavior since the beginning, significantly distorts viewing patterns for independent stations and cable. Measuring audience delivery by the average TV household is inadequate in a world where 37 percent of homes with cable have radically different television environments and viewing behaviors.[6] In large-capacity systems with remote channel tuners, average program ratings may no longer be an acceptable indicator of commercial audience ratings. And tracking the audiences of cable network advertising schedules by geographic area really requires finer geographic breaks than traditional broadcast "areas of dominant influence" (ADIs).

Advertisers are addressing these needs by pressing for different kinds of syndicated research, fielding proprietary studies of their own, and developing new computerized methods of processing a growing body of data. They are also relying much more on judgment in making media decisions than was the case in recent years. Fundamental issues—how advertising affects sales, and how much is the "right" amount under a particular set of marketplace conditions—continue to be as important as ever. The good news is that facilities now exist to combine store scanners with "split cable" media delivery capability. This affords advertisers the opportunity to probe the advertising and sales relationship within a more controlled environment.

Cable Advertising: New Challenges

The emergence of the many new cable channels raises the question of whether existing broadcast commercials for a given brand are satisfactory for cable programming. The most prevalent form of broadcast commercial today is the thirty-second unit, which is designed to call attention to itself and deliver a couple of fairly general copy points to a diverse audience whose characteristics are not well defined. We currently believe that broadcast commercials are probably quite acceptable for general interest cable programming, such as the superstations and mass cable networks. But we strongly suspect that there are more effective copy approaches for highly segmented programs with a more active viewer involvement. The ability of cable advertisers to preselect an audience with in-depth interest in a particular subject frees the advertiser from past constraints, allowing an opportunity to talk about the product in a more focused way.

In order to assess whether the opportunity warrants the additional cost of making separate commercials for cable, we need to know a lot more about the size of the additional advertising impact gained from such commercials. General Foods is involved in a test of advertising effectiveness now involving nine brands and several different cable networks. The answers we get from this test will help us decide how much segmented cable programming to purchase and how much special cable advertising to produce.

To illustrate how some advertisers are exploring this area of opportunity, I would like to discuss several recent examples of advertising produced especially for cable. Although I have stayed with mass consumer products, I have chosen examples from General Foods as well as other companies. The first example is a campaign for Tang targeted at the Hispanic community. It is no coincidence that we are talking about Hispanic advertising and the new electronic media in the same sentences. Although the Hispanic market segment has existed for some time, the emergence of the NEM has only recently produced a change in thinking about segments versus national averages. For several of our brands, the Hispanic market represents a very major business opportunity. Tang is one of those brands.

The secret to any successful advertising is understanding how the product is perceived within the target community. Benefits ascribed to a product by Hispanics may be different from those perceived by the general population. The advertising must recognize these differences. Another important consideration is the Spanish dialect to be used in the commercial. The Pacific Southwest, Miami, and New York all have heavy concentrations of Spanish-speaking people. But the Southwest is Mexican-American, Miami is largely Cuban, and New York is primarily Puerto Rican. The approach to Spanish advertising would be different for each of these areas. In this particular case, the Tang commercial was developed for the Southwestern United States, where the bulk of the U.S. Hispanic population lives. (See Appendix 10.1.)

My second example is a commercial for Post® Grape-Nuts cereal. It was made specifically for programs dealing with health and fitness: broadcast programs like "Morning Stretch" and cable programming like "Alive and Well" or the Cable Health Network. This commercial is very different from Post® Grape-Nuts' traditional advertising. (See Appendix 10.2.)

The third example is a long-form infomercial developed for our Oscar Mayer subsidiary. This commercial was used in the Cable Shop experiment conducted in Peabody, Massachusetts, by J. Walter Thompson and the Adams-Russell cable organization. Although this family of commercials was used in a program made up exclusively of long-form commercials, it could just as easily have been scheduled for one of the several women's service programs on cable. (See Appendix 10.3.)

We now have three commercials that have run on Warner-Amex's Music Television channel. The MTV channel presents audiovisuals of popular current rock groups. The first one, for Maxwell House coffee, is designed to talk to young adults between the ages of fifteen and twenty-five. The purpose of this commercial is to increase coffee drinking among this group, which has not entered the market in recent years. (See Appendix 10.4.) The second commercial, for Kraft, is an innovative attempt to make the Kraft line of products more relevant to youth and their impulse budgets. Regardless of how you feel about this commercial, Kraft was clearly committed to the need for a different approach for use on MTV.[7] (See Appendix 10.5.) The last commercial is one for the Camaro Z28, a car designed for those sixteen to thirty years old.[8] This is a good example of the New Wave graphics approach, and the commercial is a very effective piece of communication to the Camaro's target audience. (See Appendix 10.6.)

Last is a Kodak commercial used on the Weather Channel.[9] At certain times each day, the Weather Channel has a segment called "Event Weather," which forecasts the weather expected for a few major events scheduled to take place around the country. Events like these are traditionally captured on film by many people who attend. Kodak uses this natural connection to make a memorable statement about Kodak quality. In this case, the commercial itself is from Kodak's broadcast campaign. It is the Kodak logo on "Event Weather" that makes this more than an everyday advertising buy. (See Appendix 10.7.)

Direct response advertising has certainly found a home in cable television. Whether it's the return of the famous "juicer-squeezer-slicer," or advertising for those records that "are not sold in any store," or offers using 800 or 900 numbers, cable seems to have rediscovered direct response advertising. Kraft sponsored a movie on Ted Turner's WTBS superstation, using every commercial position to present a different recipe, in the traditional Kraft fashion. At the end of the program there was a mail-in offer for a recipe book containing all of the recipes shown on the program and many more.

Bristol-Myers runs the Bristol-Myers WTBS Theatre on Turner's superstation once a month. Early in the program, a commercial position is used to offer viewers four titles from which to select next month's Bristol-Myers Theatre presentation. A 900 number is given for telephone voting by the viewing audience. At the end of the program, the winning title is announced and the audience then knows they have helped to select next month's feature presentation. Bristol-Myers seems pleased with the prospect that this programming courtesy will rub off on consumer attitudes toward their products.

Challenges for Management

The emergence of the new electronic media has created several management issues for advertisers.

Greater Risk

The traditional quantification measures for media audiences are proving to be inadequate in the world of cable television. Diaries dramatically distort viewing behavior, tending to favor channels with larger audience shares at the expense of programs with smaller shares on cable and independent stations. Statistical reliability of measures erodes quickly as the syndicated services attempt to measure very small audiences in somewhat haphazard distribution patterns. Most of the cable networks are not large enough thus far to be reported by the ratings services. As such, advertising purchases on them must be based on judgment or on ad hoc research. Most people in the field believe that the attrition rate among the current cable networks will put several of them out of business in the next few years. But since no one knows which ones, long-term buys must be made with care to reduce the risk to the advertiser.

Concern about the "Unfamiliar"

The new electronic media are having a dramatic effect on the viewing behavior of consumers. The assumptions and media principles that previously served advertisers well are becoming unreliable. Unfortunately, the majority of people in product management and corporate marketing either do not yet have cable in their homes or have only recently acquired it. The trade and consumer press distort and exaggerate the picture by focusing on the news of the moment. And ad hoc research provides only a small piece of the puzzle at a time, often raising many new questions in the process.

Reliance on Judgment

The result of the two issues just described is the need for a culture shift from an information-logic-data mode to a greater reliance on the advertiser's judgment. The analytical MBA mind, so long sought by packaged goods advertisers for product management positions, needs to be tempered ever more by qualitative experience and intuition. A volatile, uncharted environment does not lend itself as well to the formulas and calculations of the past. While research may eventually bring greater quantification to the NEM world, until then, decisions must be made more on qualitative assumptions.

Higher Costs

Possibly the most obvious issues raised by the new electronic media concern costs. The emergence of NEM has tended to drive up advertising costs, at least in the short term. Fledgling cable networks must invest in expensive programming to attract audiences. As dozens of new channels succeed in attracting an audience, the networks' costs per thousand viewers (CPMs) escalate. At least for now, we are faced with the old truism of economies of scale operating in reverse. Some advertisers, General Foods among them, seek a partial solution in reassessing the value of advertising exposure on cable. We are asking whether segmented, special-interest cable programs offer significantly greater advertising value than their broadcast counterparts. Even if they do, we must also determine the optimum mix of specialized and broad-scale exposure.

Another cost issue concerns commercial production. Our judgment tells us that our standard thirty-second broadcast commercial is probably not our optimum vehicle for segmented cable programs. The need to assess the impact of commercials specially designed for cable programs prompted us to start the testing mentioned earlier. Assuming the results do show an incremental value, we must be able to produce and use these commercials for far less than the cost of their broadcast counterparts. We are finding that making the ad agencies and our product groups aware of this need—and getting them committed to the cost structure within which they must work—is a challenging task.

Marketing research costs are another major problem. It is expensive just doing recall tests for special commercials running on cable programs with low ratings. We are using some special techniques to increase program audiences to help reduce the cost of finding legitimate commercial viewers. If recall becomes the required approach to measuring commercial effectiveness in the new electronic media environment, it will take us quite a while to build up the kind of benchmarks we have enjoyed in broadcast recall testing.

Last but not least on the cost agenda is administrative overhead. The basic ingredients in a fragmented medium all seem to be inflationary. Measuring audiences for the five thousand individual cable operators represents a tenfold increase over the data demands of a broadcast environment, and the data are much less reliable. More individual operators, more commercials, smaller audiences, and more data all create either computer or human overhead pressures on the corporation. With the economy growing annually at 4 to 5 percent and many corporations growing less than that in real terms, the tolerance for incremental overhead is very low these days.

New Business Opportunities

In learning how to deal with this new media environment, we are seeking opportunities to increase our control over the cost and effectiveness of advertising by doing business in different ways. If we conclude that there is significant benefit in producing our own programs or commercials, we will investigate alternative ways to get into the production business. Coca-Cola must have already arrived at such a conclusion when they acquired Columbia Pictures Television last year.

Only time will tell if General Foods is successful in meeting the challenges of the new electronic media. But the attitude with which a corporation confronts new problems and new opportunities has an important bearing on how they are assessed and how they are solved. I'd like to close by quoting the chairman of General Foods, Jim Ferguson.

Building the business comes as much from the gut as from the head, from the heart as well as the mind. Once we've made our judgments, brought a reasonable amount of planning to a project and decided we've got a good shot at success—then let's take action. It means some risk taking. It means to trust our best judgments, to trust the competence of our people, to trust our gut and then to get on with it.[10]

We think this attitude is perfectly attuned to the needs of the NEM environment. As we face the new uncertainties posed by that environment, our personal judgment and our willingness to assume reasoned risks will determine whether we succeed or fail.

APPENDIX

CHAPTER 10
CABLE ADVERTISING

APPENDIX 10.1

Tang Commercial: "Let's Go to School"

Jingle: ¡Vamos a la escuela con Tang!
¡Con Tang!
Let's go to school with Tang! With Tang!

¡Vamos a la escuela con Tang!
Let's go to school with Tang!

Mujer: Un estudio universitario comprobó
Woman: A university study proved

que desayunar bien
that to have a good breakfast

ayuda a que a los niños les vaya mejor en la escuela.
helps children do better at school.

Por eso todas las mañanas tome Tang con su desayuno.
So every morning drink Tang with your breakfast.

Porque un vaso de Tang, con su delicioso sabor a naranjas,
Because a glass of Tang, with its delicious orange flavor,

contiene toda la vitamina
has all the Vitamin C

que los niños necesitan diariamente.
that children need daily.

Jingle: ¡Vamos a la escuela con Tang!
¡Con Tang!
Let's go to school with Tang! With Tang!

¡Vamos a la escuela con Tang!
Let's go to school with Tang!

¡Con Tang!
With Tang!

APPENDIX 10.2

Post Grape-Nuts Cereals Commercial: "Pool/Swimmer"

DATE: 6/2/83
LENGTH: 60 SECONDS

1. (MUSIC UNDER)
ANNCR: (VO) The chain
of good health

2. brought to you by
Grape-Nuts.

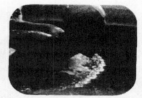
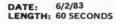

3. Swimming, a simple way
to stay in shape. But what's
really taking place is an
incredible chain of events.

4. Your brain sends a message
to your lungs demanding
more oxygen.

5. You breathe deeper, inhaling
three times as much air.

6. Your heart rate increases
to more than 150 beats a
minute,

7. pumping that oxygen to
your muscles. Where
combined with fuel from
food, energy is produced,

8. driving 600 muscles from
the tip of your toes

9. to your fingertips.

10. To keep the whole chain strong,

11. you must keep the food link strong.

12. Begin with a healthy Grape-Nuts breakfast

13. 'cause only Grape-Nuts is a natural cereal with nuggets of toasted wheat and barley.

14. With no sugar or artificial preservatives added.

15. WOMAN: And its nutty, crunchy taste is a stroke of genius. (SFX: CRUNCH)

16. ANNCR: (VO) Post Grape-Nuts,

17. Raisin Grape-Nuts

18. and Grape-Nuts Flakes Cereal.

19. Each

20. a strong link in the chain of good health.

Used with permission

APPENDIX 10.3

Oscar Mayer Commercial: "Calorie Counters/Brunch"

DATE: 6/2/83
LENGTH: 90 SECONDS

1. WOMAN: Calorie counters -- have you ever wondered what Oscar Mayer has in store for you?

2. Calorie counters, like these 90% fat-free cold cuts that can help you cut calories.

3. And a book full of recipes to help you create delicious low-calorie meals.

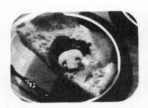

4. Today, we'll show you how to make this Canadian Fratada.

5. Fratada is an Italian term that means "open face omelet".

6. With the meat flavor from North of the border

7. and the egg flavor from the Italian border, this dish borders on the sublime.

8. And by using Oscar Mayer 93% fat-free Canadian Style Bacon,

9. this terrific brunch or late night snack dish is only 290 calories per serving.

10. You'll need one package of Oscar Mayer Canadian Style Bacon,

11. three eggs, two tablespoons of chopped fresh vegetables

12. like onion, green pepper, tomatoes, mushroom, broccoli or zucchini,

13. two tablespoons of grated parmesan cheese and a little oregano.

14. Use a small non-stick skillet, a bowl and a fork or a whisk.

15. First, arrange your 93% fat-free Canadian bacon slices around the edge of your skillet.

16. Each slice is only 40 calories. And by using a non-stick skillet,

17. you save 100 calories per tablespoon of butter you would've used.

18. Chop up your vegetables. Here we've got a touch of onions for flavor and tomato and green pepper for color.

19. Now break three eggs into your bowl and add three tablespoons of water.

20. Whip them up. The water will give you a nice light omelet.

APPENDIX 10.4

Maxwell House Commercial: "Jerry 1"

DATE: 6/2/83
LENGTH: 60 SECONDS

1. JERRY: I'll tell you when you know you're not a kid anymore.

2. When you start making changes in your own face.

3. You know what I mean? You start getting rid of your glasses, you get contact lenses.

4. When I first had glasses, though, I mean, I was like 13,

5. I didn't even understand it. I thought the reason I had to get glasses is

6. my parents didn't think I knew what they looked like. (LAUGHTER)

7. 'Cause every time I would ask my mother to buy me something,

8. she'd always say, what do I look like, a bank?

9. Well, especially when you're a kid. Your parents are the bank.

10. Where are you gonna get money? If you need money, you're gonna walk into a bank?

11. The teller's just gonna say to you what do I look like, your mother. (LAUGHTER)

12. Another way I knew I wasn't a kid anymore was with drinking coffee.

13. Very special drink. The only drink you can get in a restaurant they will automatically give you a refill.

14. You could be halfway through, you could be at the bottom--they'll fill it right up.

15. They won't do that with a hamburger. (LAUGHTER)

16. You're halfway through your hamburger,

17. they never come up with a big pot of chopmeat

18. and go let me make that a whole one for you.

19. (SFX: LAUGHTER)

20. (APPLAUSE)

Used with permission

APPENDIX 10.5

Kraft Commercial: "Kraft MTV"

DATE: 6/2/83
LENGTH: 30 SECONDS

1. (MUSIC UNDER)

2. MAN RECITES: Dip, whip, slip it to your lip,

3. we're gonna tune, tune, tune, into Kraft.

4. WOMAN: And make it right.

5. MAN RECITES: Flash, splash, dab a dash,

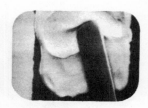

6. super spread,

7. spread, spread,

8. make it double delicious

9. with Kraft.

10. WOMEN: And make it right.

11. MAN RECITES: 'Cause the "K" in Kraft

12. makes the bite taste light,

13. it's the shinin' light

14. to your appetite.

15. Give it what you got,

16. make it hot, hot, hot.

17. Fill it sweet,

18. such a treat --

19. K-R-A-F-T's the beat. Come on and tune, tune,

20. tune into Kraft. WOMAN: And make it right.

APPENDIX 10.6

Chevy Camaro Commercial: "Camaro MTV"

DATE: 6/2/83
LENGTH: 90 SECONDS

1. (MUSIC)

2. (MUSIC)

3. (MUSIC)

4. (MUSIC)

5. (MUSIC)

6. (MUSIC)

7. MEN: Feel the beat...

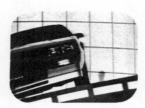

8. (MUSIC)

9. (MUSIC)

10. (MUSIC)

11. CHORUS SINGS:
Shadows...

12. (MUSIC)

13. CHORUS SINGS:
Shadows...

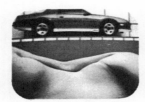

14. MEN: Ultra sleek...

15. CHORUS SINGS: Sha-
sha-shadows...

16. (MUSIC)

17. CHORUS SINGS:
Shadows...

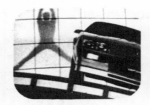

18. (MUSIC)

19. (MUSIC)

20. (MUSIC)

21. MEN: Sassy...

APPENDIX 10.6 (continued)

22. CHORUS SINGS: sha-

23. sha-sha-

24. shadows...

25. Sha-sha-sha-shadows.

26. MEN: Feel the heat.

27. (MUSIC)

28. (MUSIC)

29. CHORUS SINGS:
Shadows...

30. (MUSIC)

31. CHORUS SINGS:
Sha-sha-sha-shadows...

32. (MUSIC)

33. MEN: On the street...

34. (MUSIC)

35. (MUSIC)

36. (MUSIC)

37. ANNCR: (VO) Chevy Camaro. It'll have the competition

38. chasin'...

40. CHORUS SINGS: Shadows! (MUSIC OUT)

39. (MUSIC)

APPENDIX 10.7

Kodak Film Commercial: "America's Storyteller"

DATE: 6/2/83
LENGTH: 30 SECONDS

 1. (MUSIC)

 2. (MUSIC UNDER) ANNCR: (VO) To some,

 3. this is the ultimate test of a color film's sharpness.

 4. (MUSIC)

 5. A color enlargement stretching over 60 feet

 6. across New York's Grand Central Terminal.

 7. Yet enlarged, believe it or not,

 8. from this little 35 millimeter slide on Kodachrome film

 9. by Kodak.

 10. It's the sharpest color slide film you can buy.

Used with permission

CHAPTER 11

Bringing Wall Street to Main Street: The Search for Links in New Electronic Media

William F. Waters
Merrill Lynch

As far as I know, undergraduate philosophy courses still require students to contend with the problem of the three-legged chair. In his introduction to phenomenology, Edmund Husserl illustrated the limits of perception by pointing out that it is impossible to see more than three legs of an upholstered chair at one glance. (Remember that this was in the days before Breuer and Eames, and Husserl's own perceptions were limited to stuffed furniture.) The problem, of course, is that the fourth leg must be inferred. The observer cannot know for certain that it's there. But experience suggests that it is.

Undergraduate philosophy students—unless they've changed radically—tend to be blissfully unaware that phenomenology is superb training for business, or that they'll ever find themselves in a position to require it. But the problem of the three-legged chair is a useful analogy to the process by which an advertiser must adapt to the volatile and uncertain impact of new communications technologies. Three of the legs of the phenomenon can be known: The first—and nearest—is the nature of one's own business. A packaged goods company has different needs and priorities from those of a financial services company. And as a result, emerging communications technologies present a different spectrum of problems and possibilities, depending upon your vantage point. Second, the range of new communications technologies must be interpreted in terms of their capability to link a business with its specific target markets, and to do so cost effectively. Third, each emerging communications technology requires a response in terms of an invest-ment decision. A company has to judge whether it can afford to participate in experimental developments, and whether the poten-tial yield of a successful new medium will make the investment feasible. These are the three legs that can be seen. The fourth—the one that must be inferred—is the probability of successful innova-tions by both providers of new technologies and other users, specifically one's competitors.

In the Land of the Blind, the One-Eyed Man Is King

Perhaps the most critical challenge in the financial services indus-try is to determine who you are and what your business will be. Merrill Lynch only a decade ago was a securities dealer whose brokerage fees were fixed by federal regulation, competing in a business to which entree was strictly limited. Today we must com-pete—and must choose where to compete—in an industry in which the distinctions among traditional providers of products and ser-vices are increasingly blurred. Merrill Lynch today must compete in the marketplace with banks, insurance companies, and mass market retailers. And before too many years, we may have to com-pete with supermarket chains, packaged goods marketers, and oil companies. There's no reason why not: The General Electric Com-pany is already one of the leading providers of commercial and consumer credit in the United States.

Volatile as it is, the financial services industry is also highly frag-mented. Merrill Lynch is by far the largest securities dealer in the country. Yet our share of the total financial services market is quite small. The same is true of such giants as Citibank and American Express. No one institution accounts for more than a small fraction of the total market. In such a shifting and uncertain environment, a careful marketing strategy is imperative, and must define the tasks that our advertising must support. For the present, that strategy is, in the first place, to position Merrill Lynch in the marketplace, vis-à-vis a growing spectrum of competitors and products. This means using advertising to ensure that our actual and potential customers know precisely where to find us in the marketplace. Our strategy also demands that we use advertising as a vehicle for educating our customers. This serves two vital purposes: First, it offers an anti-dote to the confusion many—if not most—people feel in a financial market overloaded with information and investment alternatives; and, second, it underscores the distinct value Merrill Lynch brings to the market in serving as a source not merely of products but of knowledge and judgment.

To meet a varied and changing mix of financial needs, we must offer a profusion of products and services. To market these effectively, each must be presented as part of a package of information, advice, and judgment tailored to each investor's specific needs and goals. It is perfectly logical for a discount broker, for example, or a commercial bank brokerage service to market financial products as though they were packaged goods. The advertisement is the salesman for a packaged shelf product: There is no intervening sales agent. And there is unquestionably a market that wants to purchase one hundred shares of General Foods off the shelf—just as it purchases Maxwell House.

Merrill Lynch does not intend to be in that segment of the marketplace for financial products. We have determined that profitability and growth are clearly weighted on the side of higher-income consumers and more complex financial services, while at the same time continuing to offer mass market services through intensive automation. This judgment is rooted, first, in the fact that roughly 15 percent of our customers generate 90 percent of our revenues, and, second, in an awareness that we possess an invaluable asset in our network of highly skilled account executives. In their capacity as financial advisers, these people add incalculable value to what would otherwise be commodity transactions. Against this background, advertising is aimed, not at selling the consumer, but at motivating him to contact Merrill Lynch.

We use advertising to educate and to motivate not only consumers but also our own employees. This dual objective seems to be generic to all financial institutions, wherein the ultimate transaction with a customer hinges upon an employee's performance. But at the same time, our advertising has to strike a delicate balance: It cannot give away so much information that it undermines our account executives, and makes their customer feel comfortable in going to a discount broker and selecting an investment off the shelf.

It's Just Possible That Marshall McLuhan Was Right

More and more, the new communications technologies suggest that the medium is, in fact, the message. The ability of a medium to deliver the message—to the right people, and in a timely and useful fashion—may actually be more critical than the message itself. Nowhere is this more apparent than in the financial services industry: What Merrill Lynch or any competitor conveys to the market-place via advertising is, in the first place, irrelevant to all but a small segment of the audience. Most of the people most of the time do not have disposable income to invest with Merrill Lynch.

Second, what we communicate is marginally valuable information. We are prevented by law and market reality from providing investment information that is dramatically more insightful than that offered by our main competitors. We used to use television, for example, simply to advertise our image. And we still use network and local spots to do so. But the new advertising technologies have begun to provide us with opportunities to "narrowcast" our advertising—in other words, to target our messages to the particular segments of the market that are most likely to be productive for us, and to do so with that added value of acute timeliness.

Videotex

For Merrill Lynch, information is a vital component of advertising, because financial products and services are complicated. And unlike most consumer advertising, informational advertising depends heavily on timing and targeting. If you're selling life insurance, for example, you not only want to find young males who have established households, you want to find them shortly after the birth of their first child. So the impact of new technologies on our advertising is concentrated on these two dimensions: Those technologies that may enable us to target our potential market more precisely, and those that enable us to deliver more timely and valuable information. Furthermore, not all the new technologies for advertising are electronic wonders. One often overlooked development, for example, is the growing capability of direct mail advertising. A second is the use of private communications networks via satellite. A third is the extraordinary information that can be generated via computer-based point-of-purchase systems—whether credit cards or optical scanner-recorders at supermarket checkout counters.

Despite the endless assault with clichés, the information age is literally just beginning. We don't know yet whether people who buy Crest toothpaste also purchase fresh asparagus more often than other supermarket shoppers, but we will. And we'll know what kind of person buys term life insurance through a credit card bill promotion, and how likely that person is to own mutual fund shares. And as a result of the explosion in information, three things will most probably happen: First, a steady stream of magazine articles will appear to engage us in thinking about totalitarianism and free will, as though predictability in human behavior were a surprise. Second, advertisers' ability to segment and target their audiences will be greatly enhanced. Third, advertisements will become predominantly informational in content.

If Merrill Lynch transmits a videotex market letter on the Dow-Jones information system to personal computer owners—who can retrieve it at a charge—is that advertising? Perhaps not. But if a certain number of every thousand curiosity seekers who pay a dollar or so a page for our market letter subsequently call their local Merrill Lynch office, it'll do. And if the provider costs are amortized to any large degree among the retrievers, a rethinking of just what constitutes advertising might be indicated.

The Secret to Success in Business, According to the Late Charles Revson, Is to Always Come in Second

At present, there is relatively little to be gained from alternative advertising. There are too few decoders and home terminals to provide any real reach. And no single existing cable system can deliver an audience for Merrill Lynch products and services. But we are witnessing a revolution in communications, and to stand on the sidelines would be shortsighted. A process is unfolding, and it is the experimenters who will shape that process. This process would appear to embrace three distinct elements:

1. the development of appropriate technology;
2. the development of user familiarity through communications systems that are convenient and easily accessed; and
3. the development of content for the new communications channels.

Our products are ideal for computer-network communication: They are quantitative, complex, and time sensitive. Consequently, we are eager to explore new ways to transmit and display complex information for viewer analysis and, ideally, interactive response.

Merrill Lynch is participating in several videotex experiments. Prestel, the British Post Office viewdata system, offers our market letter to a limited number of terminals in the United States, Australia, and Western Europe. The Merrill Lynch market letter can be accessed and displayed, and the viewer is charged per page. We have been involved in a similar experiment with the Knight-Ridder Viewtron system in Coral Gables, Florida. In that system no charges are assessed for accessing Merrill Lynch research data. In

Park Cities, Texas, we are experimenting with a two-way cable system that allows access to Merrill Lynch information through the Dow-Jones News/Retrieval Service.

We are particularly interested in the potential of the Dow-Jones Service. It is designed to provide a vast array of continuously updated financial news and information, and to allow users to retrieve historical information. It is possible, for example, to retrieve all information published on a company listed on the New York Stock Exchange that has appeared in the *Wall Street Journal* during the previous three months. From this base, a computer program that would scan all Dow-Jones items and retrieve those related to companies in a Merrill Lynch client's stock portfolio is certainly feasible. Is this kind of communication advertising? I think it is, at least as far as Merrill Lynch is concerned. We are not interested primarily in either selling information or giving it away free of charge. What we want to accomplish through new communications technologies is to offer information so valuable to investors that they'll want to become Merrill Lynch customers in order to gain access to that information. At no time do we envision using interactive video systems to automate investment transactions completely. We do not plan to sell securities through a home terminal equivalent of the automated teller machine.

Our account executives—whose knowledge and judgment are vital to our customer relationships—will always remain in the loop. Transactions may eventually become electronic: Shares may be bought or sold via home terminal and electronic account transfer. But they will never be impersonal transactions. Impersonal financial transactions will be characteristics of the low end of the investor market. The vital components in serving upscale investors—Merrill Lynch's market—are advice, counsel, planning, and information.

Infomercials

Infomercials are another experimental development in which Merrill Lynch has played an active part. The Cable Shop—a Massachusetts joint venture between J. Walter Thompson and Adams-Russell—wanted to test a thesis. There is abundant evidence that people subscribe to a cable system to avoid advertising. The Cable Shop's thesis is that it is not the advertisements that people resent, but rather the program interruptions. They set out to test an all-commercial cable channel—a channel that actually offered nothing but advertisements. The expectation was that people would voluntarily tune in to watch advertisements. And, in fact, people did tune in. The key to attracting them was the infomercial—not a thirty-second spot, but a five or six minute informational piece that offered knowledge value.

Merrill Lynch produced twelve infomercials, each one focusing on a particular financial or investment subject such as mutual funds, bonds, or precious metals. We used an 800 number during the infomercial tests, and got a poor response. We have since repackaged six of the infomercials with a long shelf life for use on the QUBE system in Columbus, Ohio. Because we are convinced that for Merrill Lynch—and no doubt for other marketers of conceptual and complex products and services—providing valuable information will evolve into a very effective form of advertising. And we have discovered through experimentation that cable technology can be immensely useful to us, by affording us the opportunity to target audiences for product advertising and to create our own ad hoc networks.

We are currently running a schedule of sixty-second direct response commercials for Merrill Lynch products on the Cable News Network and the Financial News Network. There are currently four spots, each featuring an 800 number. The first—a commercial for Merrill Lynch Ginnie Mae Funds—was the subject of an experiment that won an EFFIE Award for effective marketing from the New York chapter of the American Marketing Association. We ran this commercial, called "The Rubber Man," on ABC Monday Night Football. The commercial featured a 900 number: Since no 800 number could handle the anticipated response, and since 99 percent of the calls come within five minutes of such a commercial, the Bell System provided a 900 number. This was not interactive. Callers simply heard a recorded message that quoted the day's interest rates on Ginnie Mae bonds and advised them that their local Merrill Lynch office was open that evening and waiting to take their calls. Each Merrill Lynch office remained open through the evening, and some had promotions with footballs, cheerleaders, and other stunts that were intended, not for the public, but for our own sales force. The morning after the commercial ran, small advertisements appeared in local newspapers in forty markets. Each ad repeated the main visual of the commercial, and carried the phone number and address of the local Merrill Lynch office.

The net result was that the commercial drew few calls as a network spot, but was the catalyst for a marvelously successful total merchandising package. A substantial volume of new business—not only for Ginnie Mae Funds, but also for other Merrill Lynch products—resulted from the total promotion. But if the commercial had run on network television without merchandising support, the indications are that it would have been ineffective.

Merrill Lynch has not run any other product commercials on network television since, but continues to look for timely and appropriate opportunities to do so. Nonetheless, the product commercials are proving quite successful as direct response advertisements to the more targeted markets reached by selected cable broadcasts.

Satellite Networks

Private satellite network events—subsequently packaged for cable costs—are now a regular feature of our marketing program. Our first experiment took place in 1981. As a result of the confusion surrounding changes in the federal tax laws, we saw an opportunity to provide a valuable service to our investor market. We scheduled a teleconference that would emanate from New York to thirty-four cities around the country. The conference provided analysis and interpretation of the effects of new tax laws for investors, and featured several of Merrill Lynch's top experts.

The teleconference was staged in a major hotel in each city and announced through newspaper advertisements in each market. Nationwide, twenty thousand people attended. A live feed to various cable systems reached another potential four to five million people. The video presentation was followed by a question and answer session orchestrated by local Merrill Lynch representatives in each city. The success of the venture—in terms of audience impact—was immense.

(As it happened, this event was scheduled on a night when President Reagan subsequently chose to make a nationwide television address covering, in part, the same subject of the tax law changes. Faced with the costly prospect of cancellation, we discovered that CBS was operating the pool feed for other networks. We contacted CBS and requested a feed to the Merill Lynch network. CBS demurred until we persuaded them that this ad hoc network met the definition of *network*. And for a modest fee, we carried the president's broadcast on our satellite and cable network—with a Merrill Lynch commentator in lieu of Dan Rather. The president's address appeared fortuitously within the Merrill Lynch program, with post-address commentary delivered by Merrill Lynch economists and experts. This phenomenon was in turn covered by a number of local independent stations and network affiliates, as well as newspapers in the thirty-four cities. From lemons came wonderful lemonade.)

We learned from this experiment that the private cable network system was a useful format. And by the timeliness of the subject addressed—and the exposure of the audience to some of our top Wall Street "stars"—we were able to offer our market a new value dimension. Yet, however successful in terms of good will and good press, that first satellite network trial produced little response in terms of new business.

Response to or interaction with information is a very delicate consideration for Merrill Lynch. It is self-defeating simply to give away so much information that the audience is motivated to circumvent Merrill Lynch and go to a bank or discount broker. In the same vein, we seek a measured response from communications through interactive video systems; we do not want to sell products electronically, or encourage investors to bypass their account executives. We conjectured that the initial satellite experiment failed to yield a measurable response because while the topic—the change in the tax laws—provided useful information to valued customers, it did not present a problem that Merrill Lynch could solve immediately and directly. In other words, our advertisement did not give the audience any means of response.

As a result, our second satellite network experiment was structured differently. The title was "Strategies for High Yields." And invitations were issued only to individuals who had $10,000 or more in a Merrill Lynch Money Market Fund. The ad hoc network consisted of twenty-six cities throughout the country, and it drew an audience of seventeen thousand. The format was identical: a presentation by top Merrill Lynch experts in this specialized investment area via videotape, followed by direct question and answer sessions with local Merrill Lynch representatives at each location. The result, however, was quite different. More than 35 percent of those who attended bought an investment product from Merrill Lynch as an immediate and direct result of the satellite presentation.

The QUBE System

Our first experiment in adapting the private satellite network program format for use with public audiences took place in 1982 via the QUBE system in Columbus, Ohio. Merrill Lynch presented a fifteen-minute tape on investing in gold, as part of a one-hour broadcast in which two local Merrill Lynch representatives answered questions over the telephone from viewers. The interactive nature of this type of programming meets the essential criterion—

for Merrill Lynch—of contact. It does not simply broadcast information impersonally, but provides a concurrent introduction to people who embody Merrill Lynch's market values of expertise and advice.

We are now airing infomercials on the QUBE system in Columbus, which allows viewers a direct interactive response by pushing a "yes" button for further information.

Information as Advertising

We have learned several lessons from our experience with satellite network systems to date, and they serve to reinforce our commitment to this medium. First, no existing system can deliver these audiences for us. At this point, no cable or interactive system has a demographic profile that could be even remotely as productive. This does not preclude its eventual emergence through the expansion of services like the Dow-Jones News/Retrieval Service. And this could make possible the subsequent distribution on a wide scale of initial private satellite network programs. Second, satellite network programs are not just direct response vehicles. They carry an important image value, and in consequence must be first-rate, professional productions.

We continue to use television to sell our image. And we have begun to use cable to sell products. We do this, not by advertising in the traditional sense, but by communicating a package of information. And from our early experiments with interactive videotex systems and home terminal networks, we know that—in the future—the provision of timely information and analysis will become a prerequisite to selling our products.

CHAPTER 12

Deindustrialization of the American Economy: The Impact of Antitrust Law and Policy

Mary Gardiner Jones
Consumer Interest Research Institute

The United States economy is in the midst of a powerful shift from smokestack industries to an information- or knowledge-based industrial structure. In 1983, 75 percent of American workers were engaged in service industries, with 50 percent of these workers in what is called the information or knowledge industries. Perhaps the most significant feature of these emerging information industries is their fused and integrative character. "Compunications" was an early label devised for the industry, followed more recently by such descriptive names as "telematics" and "informatics." But regardless of the names ascribed to them, the main characteristics of the new information-communications technologies are their lack of traditional structure and function (both organizational and legal) and the consequent openness of at least some members of the industry to new roles and approaches.

A great deal of research and analysis has been directed to predicting future markets for these new information technologies. Much less attention has been directed to the emerging marketing issues and policy implications flowing from the nature, scope, and products of the new electronic telecommunications service industries. This paper will review the nature of information as both a resource and an item of commerce, discuss the information industry marketing strategies, and comment on the antitrust implications of the marketing issues likely to be generated by these new information industries.

The Nature of the Information "Product"

Let me make a few observations about the characteristics of information and of the emerging information industries and their important role in society before discussing specifically the implications of this information world for antitrust regulation.

The Unique Characteristics of Information

First, information is an essential resource, not simply a commodity to be developed and marketed to meet public demand.[1] Information is critical to action and decision making. It is an important source of power and its availability in society is a critical dimension of the effectiveness of our political and economic system. Changes in and access to the flow of information can form the basis for new relationships and power balances between citizens and their government, between citizens, and among interest groups. It has been estimated by agricultural economists, for example, that the vast increase in agricultural output between 1920 and 1970 was the result of increases in productivity based on information rather than increases in capital stock. The burgeoning "electronic office" and the explosion of domestic and international communications and transmission networks attest to business's recognition of the importance of information to their decision making.

Consumers literally cannot cope today with our complex world without access to information. Just as business has learned, access to print information is no longer sufficient for consumers to meet their needs, in part because of the sheer volume of information available and in part because of the need to sort through and update information quickly or to discard information no longer relevant.

Second, the commercialization of information is raising new questions about how to "value" information to users. In the past, substantial amounts of "free" or "low cost" information were widely available to users. Companies provided information about their products and services directly to consumers as well as to schools and other sources. Telephone companies provided directories free in order to encourage use of their services. Government information programs and pamphlets of all kinds have been widespread. The U.S. Weather Service, the Department of Agriculture, through its nationwide extension services to rural America, and the Government Printing Office, through its publication programs, are just a few of the government agencies providing information to business and consumers. At the National Institutes of Health, "Medlar's" database of medical abstracts has been an important source of information on medical scholarship for hospitals and research centers.

As information becomes commercially valuable, problems are arising on how to treat formerly "free" information. Protests are being voiced from the private sector that government is competing unfairly with their information services and companies are reexamining their own information policies to determine their most profitable options. The federal government has responded to these protests by sharply reducing its output of information to the public. These cutbacks have been met with equally intense protests from user groups who depend on "free" information for their effective functioning and delivery of services to the public.

Third, information is diffusive, intangible, and infinitely leakable and expandable. Unlike a material product such as steel, information is not consumed or depleted, nor is its shelf life necessarily predictable. When the possessor of information shares it with another party, dominion over it is not given up and both parties continue to possess it. Moreover, time may make information obsolete in seconds, or information may retain its usefulness indefinitely. As a result of the new reproducing, tape, and communications technologies, information in its pure form, separated from its transmission mechanism, can be instantaneously and infinitely reproduced and possessed in whole or in part by every reader, hearer, or viewer, and can be equally easily passed on by them in the same format. These characteristics raise serious questions of how to value this "vanishing" product, what incentives exist to create or generate it, and what imperatives it creates for constant innovation in order to capture the one-time first—"viewer"—market, not to mention the energy and efforts expended to "protect" from leakage what some have described as the ultimate "prohibition" product of the twenty-first century.

Fourth, information may take many forms. It is raw data about an individual or a company known obviously to that individual and company, but also knowable by others through observation. For example, information about the financial status, administration, staff-to-patient ratios, quality of care, and so on of nursing homes can be known to proprietors, investors, staff, patients, patients' families, and others. Information may also be a byproduct of some other activity such as medical or education records, charitable donations, charge accounts, telephone or other directories, travel reservations, magazine subscriptions, and library users, information with no commercial or operational value to its original generator or possessor, but with great value to an information system manager.

Information is statistical data or organized compilations of facts, such as weather data, census data, directories (telephone, medical, legal, financial), that are typically publicly available or available to be known by somebody at any given moment, but were not originally assembled or generated for commercial purposes, or are a byproduct of some other function. Information is also ideas, editorials, and analyses, the product of "someone applying the refiner's" fire to the mass of facts and ideas, selecting and organizing what is useful to somebody.[2]

Fifth, information has an infinite number of uses, and the creators, processors, disseminators, and users of information may be in both the public and private sectors. A scholar, a business school student, or a commercial information provider may research the properties of solid metals, or gather data on nursing home quality or on the efficacy of an educational curriculum, and present those data, as well as the research findings and report, in electronic readable tape format or offer the information for sale for profit. An information system manager may see commercial value in offering the nursing home or education data base information to consumers, nurses, doctors, social workers, or regulators, while high school guidance counselors, social workers, or consumer organizations may wish to offer that same information free to their constituents. Scholars, professional associations, or government regulators may be interested in the solid metal data or the nursing home instructional data base for their own academic, professional, or regulatory purposes without any interest in transmitting it to others. Individual consumers, investors, or workers may have an interest in the data as a guide to individual decisions they need to make in connection with the use of these educational or nursing home services. Each of these various potential users would look at the same information somewhat differently and would probably use different search questions and key words in order to obtain the data for their particular purposes.

Sixth, information is universal and global. Language is no barrier to its use or to a demand for it. It has no real geographic locus and is essentially worldwide in its reach and availability. A data bank containing a full catalog of information on such things as stress reactions of solids is susceptible to comprehension and use throughout the world for a myriad of applications. Indeed, in some instances, for example, in cable systems, the identity of its users may or may not be known or knowable.

The Nature and Structure of the Information Industry

The crux of the information revolution lies in the merger of the computing and communications technologies, which have made possible the assembly of a total home-based information system comprising computer information banks, indexing structures, software programs, communications transmission systems, and receiver hardware.

Technologically, we are seeing a total merger of voice and data communication, one on one, broadcast one to many, on-line or store-and-forward via telephone, over-the-air TV and radio, satellite, microwave, cable and cellular radio, with computers, copying machines, and word processors, providing a broad variety of direct on-line and store-and-forward record communications. Entrepreneurially, we are seeing a similar mix of new and old industries and public sector nonprofit organizations participating in the generation and dissemination of a broad spectrum of new electronic services involving education, information retrieval, entertainment, messaging, computing, and transaction services such as teleshopping, banking, travel, home security, and energy-monitoring services. Boundaries between industries are rapidly disappearing. Electronic messaging systems are now competing with the U.S. Postal Service; cable TV is competing with broadcasters; and newspaper and computer-based information systems are performing many of the functions traditionally assigned to libraries. The videotex industry, defined as the providers of services that transmit digital data to the home, is now treated as a separate category in the *U.S. Industrial Outlook*, and its market in the United States alone is expected to rise to $12 billion by 1985.

These home-based information systems are capable of delivery of information and transactional services to the home user.[3] They may be either cable based or telephone based, and they may be either one way (teletext) or two way (videotex). Teletext systems can be received over the air on a specially adapted TV screen or via cable; some cable systems can offer two-way transmissions, and two-way systems are also available on telephone-based home computers.

Cable penetration of households by the end of the century is expected to reach 60 percent of American households (for one way) and 20 percent (for two way).[4] Industry spokespeople estimate that by 1990, 30.5 million personal computers will be in homes, and forty-five million homes will have videotex services.[5] By 1983, sales of paging devices, which can also be information terminals, will have increased from 400,000 in 1976 to 1.5 million.[6] Cellular radio, another emerging information source, is just on the threshold of explosive growth nationally.

Just as information is an infinitely diverse set of intangible concepts, so the companies engaging in its generation, dissemination, and use span a diverse set of established industries with distinct regulatory and commercial histories and traditions. The industries most deeply involved in the information business include the following:[7]

- Publishers such as Times Mirror and Knight-Ridder newspaper chains, Field Enterprises, World Book, Time, Inc., New York Times, Dow Jones, Reader's Digest, and a host of miscellaneous directory and other publishers.
- Broadcast networks and entertainment companies such as NBC, CBS, Westinghouse, Universal Pictures, Walt Disney Productions, and United Artists.
- Computer manufacturers such as IBM, Tandy, Texas Instruments, Atari, Timex, and Sony.
- Transmission and communications companies such as Western Union, AT&T, ITT, RCA, and Graphic Scanning.
- Cable systems such as ACS, Westinghouse's Teleprompter, Cox Cable Communications, and Warner-Amex.
- Major financial and retail institutions such as Citibank, Bank One, Merrill Lynch, Chemical Bank, Sears, Roebuck, J. C. Penney, B. Dalton Booksellers, and Federated Department Stores.
- Miscellaneous companies such as Lockheed and H & R Block's CompuServe.

Information Industry Marketing Strategies

Whether the hardware and transmission companies will dominate the industry or whether the software companies will ultimately control the market is not yet clear. One Japanese industrialist has forecast that "he who controls software, controls the world."[8] Yet the results are by no means in. There are some who see the computer (hardware) industry following the marketing models of the telephone and camera industries, minimizing the cost of the hardware and seeking its profits from the software. This is the direction in which Japanese industry is heading and may be the future of American development as well. For the videotex markets of the future, no firm patterns have yet emerged. There are several independent (nontransmission, nonhardware-oriented) producers of information: New York Times, Dow Jones, Lockheed, H & R Block's CompuServe, and Reader's Digest's Source. AT&T has made clear its intention to enter the information content business on its own, but a consent decree delays their entry until 1990. Strategies adopted by information industry members to participate in the information economy have embraced a wide variety of structural and tactical maneuvers. A substantial number of companies, notably cable and network broadcasters, have sought to enter or develop the new information market through mergers or acquisitions.[9] Some publishers, like Time, Inc., are proceeding to develop their own vertically integrated cable-based information systems, and major software-producing companies are countering with their own vertically integrated cable systems. Others have sought to test the market by a series of ad hoc informal joint ventures, frequently between and among commercial, governmental, and academic institutions.[10] Some joint ventures have been of a more long-range nature among established companies such as the recent agreement among RCA, American Express, Viacom International, Paramount Pictures, and Warner Brothers to develop a cable network to compete with the largest pay-TV network owned by Time, Inc., itself a joint venture among HBO, CBS, and Columbia Pictures.[11]

Other companies have focused on litigation and legislation as both offensive and defensive tactics to maintain existing positions in the information markets. Thus, Universal Studios, Inc., brought suit against Sony Corporation of America, charging copyright infringement through the home taping on Sony's Betamax VCRs of Universal movies shown on TV. Universal sought an order requiring the imposition of a tax on each Betamax sale, to be used to compensate the copyright holders. Similar copyright issues have also arisen as a result of cable companies' carrying of network programs for distant commercial markets into local markets.

New York textbook publishers recently settled a similar copyright infringement suit against New York University and eight NYU professors for photocopying printed materials for classroom use. The suit was settled after the university agreed to issue guidelines limiting the multiple use of copyright materials to abstracts and short text items (e.g., poems under 250 words or articles or stories under 2,500 words).[12]

Publishers of weeklies and specialized newsletters have recently registered similar protests against data bank information systems for unfairly reproducing their works in their data banks for electronic access. The New York Times Information Service, one of the targets of these protests, claimed that it was simply engaging in the traditional abstracting and bibliographical reference function and was not infringing the copyright of the protesting specialized newsletter and weekly publishers.

Litigation has also been used to bar particular industry members from certain information activities. Thus, the Newspaper Publishers Association filed a monopoly and unfair competition complaint against AT&T seeking to restrain an avowedly experimental market test by AT&T of the commercial viability of its *Yellow Pages*. Refusal of cable companies to accept a product is similarly under challenge as illegal conspiracies and price discrimination.[13] And finally, suit has been reportedly brought by competitors against a Southwestern cable company offering a security alarm system, alleging unfair competition with their noncable security system.

Not all information industry members resort to litigation to protest their asserted property rights in their information products. Some of the information systems carrying full text and abstracts of periodicals and journals, such as Nexis and Management Content, have sought to avoid the copyright issue by entering into agreements with their participating publishers to pay them royalties on any full text offered on their services and sent for by their customers. Others have sought legislative relief, in the form of legislative prohibitions backed by civil or criminal penalties for "piracy" or mandating the blacking-out of certain programs from local viewing. Efforts have also been made to get congressional relief from municipally imposed restrictions on the right of cable companies to have total control over the use of their program channels.

A novel effort to protect information from publications was presented by the recent action of supermarket chains in California to evict consumer price shoppers from their stores; the chains objected that their publication of comparative supermarket pricing was not fairly representative of their patrons' market basket and hence was unfair. After Federal Trade Commission (FTC) intervention, the supermarkets agreed to permit the price reporting to continue.

A few industry members have elected not to fight the inevitable problem of information being leaked. Their strategies are to treat their information products as rapidly obsolescing resources and to focus their efforts, not on protection, but on the continual development of new software programs and products.[14]

Antitrust Implications of the New Technologies

Both the United States and Europe have adopted competition as their goal for the development of their economies. Yet while pursuing competition as their goal, European policy makers will not necessarily invalidate an activity found to be anticompetitive if its net impact is deemed to serve the public interest. American policy makers have not yet formally adopted this approach, although concepts of public interest undoubtedly influence enforcement policy and perhaps even judicial interpretation in given cases.

With the new environment of adverse foreign trade balances and increased foreign competition confronting the United States, American antitrust policy is coming under renewed scrutiny. The emergence of the information industries poses a new and perhaps even more demanding challenge to traditional antitrust concepts. Antitrust policy makers must analyze these challenges carefully, not because competition is no longer relevant as an important force in our economy, but because information as a "product" may demand wholly different concepts of protection in order to maintain the force of competition.

Before taking up the analysis of the antitrust implications of the new technologies, it is useful to review the basic advantages traditionally attributed to competition, which include:

- Elimination of excess profits and the weeding-out of inefficient firms.
- Efficient allocation of resources among alternative uses.
- Stimulation of both the generation and adoption of technological innovations.
- Availability to consumers of higher quality and more varied choices to maximize consumer satisfaction.[15]

Of these four advantages, the last two pose the most significant challenges to antitrust officials in view of the nature of information as both a commercial product and a public necessity and the vital importance of the free flow of information to the social, political, and economic fabric of this country. Consequently, I will first consider information as a "product," then examine its commercial and noncommercial aspects, and, finally, analyze the various "markets" in which information products will be generated and used.

Information as a "Product"

The evolution of the new information society forces antitrust lawyers to confront the central issue of what information is and whether it can or should be treated as an ordinary "product" subject to proprietary and alienation rights. The efforts of supermarkets to prevent in-store copying of information about their prices, information that is publicly available to all by mere observation, illustrates the present reality and, in this case, apparent absurdity of too liberal an answer to this question. It will not be long before an information provider seeking to develop a data base on nursing homes or on medical or educational offerings will attempt to acquire exclusive rights to the information that the possessor (nursing home owner, hospital administrator, or college data-processing office) may be only too happy to grant in return for an unexpected and much needed new source of revenue. A government or academic researcher may be restricted from disseminating her or his research results because to do so might compete with a similar offering by a commercial entrepreneur. We have seen the efforts already being made by publishers and other information-entertainment software providers to invoke copyright to accomplish this end. While the publisher and other commercial generators of information are dealing in their own value-added products, other possessors of information for whom the information "product" is an unexpected byproduct of some other activity cannot be said to be dealing in a similarly value-added product. Nevertheless, the problems of what constitutes an information "product" subject to legal protection and alienation are involved in both situations.

Antitrust policymakers must resolve the question of whether information, at least in its most basic form of raw data, can be owned, alienated, restricted in any way, or monopolized because of its lack of economic scarcity and the difficulty, if not impossibility, ultimately of effectively excluding people from its use. They must determine whether possessors of original unprocessed information (e.g., nursing home operators, educational institutions, hospital record owners) have an absolute right of ownership over the information they possess. Similar questions will arise from noncommercial researchers over their dissemination of their research or of the facts underlying it. Concepts of privacy will tend to protect information possessors from mandated disclosure. But assuming information possessors wish to sell information in their possession, antitrust officials will have to decide how to deal with that "sale." Since each possessor knows the information in a unique form, each could be said in antitrust taxonomy to possess a "natural monopoly" of the information, and hence each could be subject to antitrust prohibitions on refusals to deal or on discriminating among persons to whom they provide the information. By the same token, it could also be argued that the very fact that the same information can be known, however differently in detail or reliability, to varying entities would dictate a conclusion that information could never be monopolized. How antitrust officials decide this question will determine the extent to which "sellers" or "purchasers" of information will be permitted to engage in exclusive arrangements or to agree to restrictions on its use or resale.

The essential "public" nature of information once disseminated into the marketplace is not limited to original possessors and non-commercial researchers. It is also the feature of the new information technologies that plagues commercial information and program developers and generators (so-called value-added information producers) in their efforts to protect their product from unauthorized copying, taping, and so on. Even when traditional legal rights are violated, the question of how to contain information that the technology seems to make virtually infinitely expandable forces antitrust officials to question the extent to which they can or should assist in the protection of what may be an inherently unprotectable commodity. Antitrust officials must also ask themselves whether society's goals to encourage the widest dissemination of information and the antitrust goals of maximum innovation and quality may not be better served by a policy of refraining from assisting efforts to protect against "reuse" or resale of information products. This is the area that will demand of antitrust policymakers a maximum of creative and risk-taking initiatives. History may offer some guidance. It has been recognized, for example, that the sale of books was ultimately helped rather than hindered by book collectors (who, it was originally feared, would assemble and then lend these books to their friends) and libraries (which, it turned out, reached other markets not tapped by the commercial sale of books). Questions will also arise about whether the recent embryonic emergence of writers' unions will impede or promote the development of non-royalty-based compensation packages.

If restraints on use and distribution of information product are not permitted, the private sector could be forced to follow the lead of its more advanced, freethinking members and place primary value and emphasis on innovation and new products. Undoubtedly some information products of value to the public will not be produced as too easily copyable or closed to constant innovation. But one of the major roles of the noncommercial sectors in the society (e.g., government, educational institutions, nonprofit entities, and libraries) has always been to fill the gaps in information product that cannot be profitably produced by the marketplace. There is no reason for this role not to continue for essential information products that are not produced by the private sector.

Thus, in essence, the new information society will create new mandates for public sector activity, generated by such factors as the ease of "leakability" of the information product, the value that can be ascribed to first use, and other similar features. When the information serves a clear public purpose and has not been generated by the private sector, the public sector, as is traditional, will fill the void in public need left by the marketplace.

Information as a Mixed Commercial and Noncommercial Resource

Ordinarily, antitrust does not deal with noncommercial forms of activity, for example, government, academic, or quasi-public-service organizations. Yet today, information technology and information generation and dissemination activities extend to the compilation, storage, and retrieval of information that can have both commercial and noncommercial origins and applications. Charges have already been leveled at the Medlar's program of the National Institutes of Health because it is said to "compete" unfairly with comparable commercial applications. More recently, the United States government created a storm of protest with its announced proposal to sell the United States weather satellites to private interests. The protests emanated not only from farmers but also from other commercial users who had come to depend on the reliability and impartiality of the government's weather and climate "products." It will not be long before similar situations arise with academic-generated research. If the researchers have unique skills or laboratory facilities or unique access to a particular data base, questions will arise about the extent to which the "information" generated can or should be monopolized or provided on an exclusive basis. While the policy issues involved are much broader than competition policy, it is, nevertheless, likely that the first lines of offense or defense may be private or government antitrust litigation charging restraint of trade or unfair competition. Hence, antitrust policy makers must reexamine the previously useful concepts of state action and noncommercial exclusions and begin to think through how they will regard the stream of information as it proceeds through its many diverse formats and packages. Government and academic handling of information can have serious effects on the free flow of information, on the availability of competition, and on quality standards. Any discriminatory conduct by government and academics can have serious anticompetitive effects. On the other hand, their public policy missions provide important options to an information-hungry society that must not be unreasonably excluded by the mere fact that the private sector is engaged in similar information activities.

Market Definitions of Information Products for Antitrust Purposes

Basic to determining competitive impact in antitrust enforcement is the definition of the market in which the product is deemed to compete. Again, in dealing with information, many traditional indicia of competitive markets and viability will lose their relevance and others may demand new interpretations in the light of the importance to society of the free flow of information. Geographic sites have traditionally been one important element in the definition of markets because of transportation and other barriers.

Yet information has no fixed geographical location and its reach may be either global or essentially local.[16]

Markets for antitrust purposes are also typically defined in terms of interchangeability of use, cross-elasticity of demand, substitutability, differences in production, transmission cost, technology, or physical characteristics. Translating these concepts into the information industry, with all of the variables and permutations in technology, use, skill, and availability, will not be an easy task. Home computers, videodiscs, TV, cable, and cellular radio are, or will be, capable of delivering information in a variety of forms to householders. Yet the technology and costs of each, the required user equipment and skills, and the comparative interactivity of the different technologies vary substantially. How these particular markets will be defined will have enormous impact on both users and information providers. For example, questions will arise about whether information providers must be permitted access to each of these media in order to be competitive, or whether the owners of the media can be permitted to exercise sole control over which information providers and which transactional service providers they will deal with. Could Mobil, as an information provider, insist on access to Warner-Amex's cable system to present its film on minitravel tips on the grounds of competitive necessity or fairness, or could Warnex-Amex successfully assert its right to present only American Express or Texaco travel documentaries on its cable system? And again, if Consumers Union or the publishers of *Road and Track* wish to present their automobile information packages on a given cable system, can they be excluded if GM has already been permitted to put its data base into that cable system computer? If cable owners can prevail in asserting sole right to control access to their channels, will antitrust then be confronted with the necessity of permitting Universal or Warner Brothers or other service providers to integrate vertically with a cable system in order to ensure themselves of product outlets?

It is obvious that the answers to these questions will depend in part on whether cable is regarded as substitutable, in whole or in particular applications, for DBS, telephone-based computer information systems, videodiscs, low-power TV, or MDS cable systems. These are questions that lend themselves to traditional antitrust analysis, assuming that the peculiarities of user skill, information provider access, and media suitability for the offering are carefully considered in the analysis.

A third aspect of understanding the market dynamics of information products is presented by the importance ascribed to the "package" or media by which the information is communicated. We have to ask ourselves whether the printed version of the encyclopedia competes with the encyclopedia available electronically through the Source or CompuServe. Does CompuServe's electronic offering of articles, movie reviews, and program listings from the *Washington Post*, the *Los Angeles Times*, or the *New Yorker* compete with the local dealer or newsstand selling the printed versions?

Does a two-way interactive videotex data base on nursing homes, accessible to users by key words or tree structure menus, compete with a one-way teletext data base on nursing homes containing fewer frames (e.g., more limited in content and detail) and accessible only by the user's selection of predetermined frames? Do these electronic and print media compete with voice information services? Considering these output products from the other point of view, do identical nursing home data offerings that are available on both cable and home computer compete with each other, or are they in totally separate markets because of the different costs and user skills required to access these systems, assuming they are both available to the user in the community?

And, finally, do the CompuServe or Source offerings of an amalgam of services, such as messaging, transactional services, and information retrieval, compete with other home computer information services, cable services, or single information networks that offer a narrower or different mix of information and services?

There is no doubt that in some respects the unique features of cable ("narrowcasting" and per-program capability) provide it with distinct economic and marketing advantages that tend to overshadow other potentially competitive media.[17] On the other hand, from the user point of view, for certain applications, such as information retrieval, information systems accessible by home computers currently offer a distinctly different product from cable-based information systems. The relative advantages of cable versus home computer telephone-based systems will differ enormously for different users and different types of services offered. In the future, whether a system is accessed by telephone, cable, or air-waves may, because of rate structures, be the determining factor in a user's mind about which system to use.

In short, the marketing implications of the new information technologies for antitrust officials and for users and ultimately for society are enormous. The ephemeral nature of information suggests the need for cooperation and sharing because of the difficulties of containing information and proving ownership. Yet clearly cooperation is not an antitrust principle, and indeed, in some instances, is regarded as the antithesis of the antitrust goal of competition. We have to recognize that in many respects, information in our society, like the air we breathe and the water we drink, is a basic resource and cannot and should not be subject to monopolization or restriction. Yet what policies will be most likely to promote its dissemination and prevent its restriction have not yet been determined. How we resolve these various issues will determine the extent to which we can, in fact, enjoy the maximum quality and diversity of information that could be potentially available to meet the needs and demands of all members of our society.

CHAPTER 13

An Even More Powerful Consumer?

Michael L. Ray
*Stanford University Graduate School
of Business*

Those of us in the field of marketing have long known that it is the consumer who gives marketing its life and its purpose. Yet as marketers and as marketing scholars, we have been woefully inadequate in considering the one external factor that should truly be our forte: the consumer. The question I believe we should ponder is the one that constitutes my title. That is, if the new technologies are completely implemented, what will be the consumer reaction? And how will the balance of power shift between marketing organizations and the public they serve?

My simple response to those questions is twofold. First, the new technologies allow a wider variety of choice of information and more consumer control over the "when" and "where" of information. This means that there will be a shift in the balance of power from the marketer to the consumer, from the sender to the receiver of information. Second, the most important characteristic of the new technologies is the possibility of consumer interaction with data bases of commercial information, all the way up to making choices and demanding service. The information may be presented in forms similar to advertising, but the flow of information and choice with instant feedback will be more like personal selling. Because of this, the distinctions now made between advertising, promotion, personal selling, and distribution will not be clear in the new technology.

These two fundamental changes—the shift in the balance of power to the consumer and the blurring of distinctions between the tools of marketing communication—have enormous implications. Advertising will have to "grab" the consumer but also, like personal selling, will have to "qualify" him or her and present a flow of convincing information that will fit a myriad of sequences of possible consumer concerns. Sales will be made and promotions will be offered; a whole new distribution system is possible.

Of course, the shift to this kind of marketing will not happen overnight. And the kind of media we have today will not totally disappear. The slow changes and creative marketer responses are illustrated by some of the other articles in this volume. But consider the possibility of just one technological innovation: interactive videodisc technology (IVT). The basis of this technology is the laser disc, which is capable of storing fifty-four thousand photos or documents, or thirty minutes of video or motion picture sequences as well as sound. Six thousand floppy discs would be required to store the same amount of information stored on one laser disc. And laser discs can be randomly accessed. The combination of a laser disc player (or several, thus magnifying the capacity), a microprocessor, operating software, a video monitor, and an input device (keyboard or touch screen) can produce a combined information center, advertising medium, and retail megastore, operating twenty-four hours a day in a kiosk or in the side of a building.

Consider this. You walk up to a display positioned in the outside wall of a shopping center. It is early on a Monday morning and you are on your way to work, but you want to buy a particular gardening tool now so that you will have it for the weekend. By merely touching the display in response to a series of questions, you are able to see a *Consumer Reports* type of review of the whole category and then commercials for the brands you are most seriously considering. Finally, you order the item, pay for it by inserting your credit card, and arrange for a delivery time on Saturday morning.

This, as anyone who has used an automatic teller machine at the bank knows, is not science fiction. In fact, ten touch screen IVT information units were installed at the Disney EPCOT Center and used by over two million people up to mid-1983. Other units installed at the World Trade Center also found that people enjoy using interactive technology. These successes, combined with the widespread acceptance of automated teller machines, the common use of videogames in public places of all sorts, and the rapid growth of direct marketing, indicate that here is finally a technology that will be *used* by consumers.

Perhaps the reason I am personally so enthusiastic about the information and retailing potential of interactive videodisc technology is that I have observed over and over again that seemingly exciting new sources of information have been virtually ignored by consumers. This seems to be something more than just the normal slow growth for the introduction of new technologies. For instance, in responding to a description of "home shopping of the future" in seven separate advertising studies, the majority of our respondents claimed they would use such systems, excitingly and graphically described in our cover story, for only *less than 10 percent* of their shopping. They preferred going to stores to shop.[1]

A project, supported by the National Science Foundation, on consumer information systems for local services (e.g., medical, legal, real estate, financial, auto repair, community, appliance repair services) looked for the existence and acceptance of such systems in any form. Only three or four real ones were found in the whole country in the late 1970s. Also in the course of that search we found many bits of evidence that there was a tendency toward "information avoidance" in the purchase of major services. That is, consumers did not seem to want to think about these services, much less gather detailed information about them.

Another indicator of a lack of consumer interest in the extra information from the new technology was the Times Mirror Shopping Channel, a noninteractive television program with consumer information that allowed viewers to purchase products through the Comp-U-Card telephone shopping service. Although it was heading slowly toward the break-even point in a five-market test that followed adequate developmental research, the project was dropped by Times Mirror. One factor in this decision must have been a lack of consumer interest.

There are literally dozens of indications that consumers are *not* hungering for the new information sources that might be provided by the new technology. Even in our research with standard advertising, we find that consumers seem to develop a sixth sense that allows them to avoid advertising messages. And when they do get the message, it is only up to a limited point; they tend to avoid further information.

But the picture isn't completely hopeless. Far from it. Research at Stanford University and elsewhere has shown that with the right combination of information need, segment characteristics, and information services, people can be drawn to enthusiastically use the new technology. That is, if there is a *real* need for consumer information, for example, for an important purchase with many detailed attributes, and if the service can provide information on the product category as a whole as well as on alternatives—as opposed to just allowing a purchase—consumers seem to use the technology. If there is a large enough segment of innovators, early adopters, information seekers, and people who have used similar methods in the past (for instance, we found in one study that people who had spent at least $100 per year for items through at-home shopping were very comfortable in using a new information service), the new technology can be profitable.[2] And if an information service is easy to use, has clear benefits, is interactive, and has complete nonbiased information, our research has shown that it can be a success.

In summary, the answer to the question in the title is that there could and probably will be an even more powerful consumer with the new technologies. The consumer can become more of a partner with the marketer, using communication tools that are amalgams of present marketing communication methods. But even with the potential and early success of interactive videodisc technology, for instance, there is substantial indication that consumers may not want this role of partner.

The broad implication for marketing is that the field should not forget its roots in a knowledge of the consumer. Instead of becoming more powerful by using the new technology, consumers may simply exert their present power to reject it. The future depends on the quality of our innovation, entrepreneurship, product champions, and marketing. Our success will depend on solid consumer analysis to fit together the information need, the segment, and the information technology characteristics that will lead to response. The potential result is not just a more powerful consumer but a more complete implementation of the marketing concept.

CHAPTER 14

Impacts of the New Technologies on Advertising and Advertising Research

Michael J. Naples
Advertising Research Foundation

It is now widely accepted that the new technologies will have an enormous impact on consumers and also on the ways in which most firms do business and conduct research. In research applications thus far, laser scanners, microprocessors, and computers have had a great positive impact on advertising and marketing research in the United States. Cable television had a major impact, even before it was considered one of the new electronic media. I believe that satellites, videocassette recorders, videodisc players, and other forms of new electronic media including two-way or interactive television and videotex are likely to have sizable impacts as well. It is one thing to state that the impact has been sizable; it is another to show clearly where and in what ways there have been demonstrable effects on advertising research and, by implication, on advertising itself. Let me offer a specific example.

One new research company (Information Resources, Inc.) recently took a great step forward with the application of the new technologies to research.[1] The company's achievements were described in detail by Jack Honomichl, columnist for *Advertising Age*, in a paper entitled "The Industrial Revolution Catches Up to Research."

> What Information Resource's Behavior Scan did in 1979 was take two relatively small test markets and automate data collection. The key to the system was to raise the capital and spend the money necessary to install UPC scanning equipment in the towns' grocery and drug stores.
> To get at who was doing the buying, Behavior Scan recruited a

large panel of households, each equipped with a plastic identification card. The customer making the purchase gives the check-out clerk this card, and now the purchase data collected via scanners can be traced to the individual household.

The final element of the Behavior Scan system is a targetable cable television system which permits controlled exposure of TV commercials to panel households.

The end result simply is that Behavior Scan shouldered the expense—i.e., capital investment—of wiring up these small markets, and, in the process, made possible exquisitely detailed analysis of consumer purchase behavior as related to specific promotion and advertising stimuli.[2]

To date, the advent of the Behavior Scan system is the most dramatic application of the new technologies to advertising research, but it is not an isolated case. It is simply the latest in a steady stream of breakthroughs that includes the original (and still going after ten years) AdTel "split cable" television laboratory test markets, computer-assisted telephone interviewing, and automated warehouse withdrawal volume tracking. In short, advertising research is clearly in harmony with the new technologies, and in fact represents an area of advanced application, clearly bringing new capabilities and benefits. Penetration of the new technologies is quite high in the research area, and they are thus having a real impact on the marketing of consumer products and services.

Let us consider the specific effects that I think are leading to new capabilities in advertising research, and thus affect the type of advertising consumers are exposed to and its delivery by various media both old and new. First, the new technologies have greatly increased the pure test marketing of advertising. It is not only possible to carry out effectively single variable tests, but major advertisers now seem unable to live without them. Tests of two advertising campaigns within one market, read for a year with equal spending behind both, and all other factors held equal, are now being run in controlled test markets by numerous companies. The escalating media prices of the late 1970s have meant new emphasis placed on advertising productivity, and with the help of the new technologies advertising research has matured enough to meet the challenge.

Second, the new technologies, starting with the "split cable" methodology (which was developed by ARF), are responsible for a major breakthrough—convincing a skeptical and frustrated advertising community that measuring the sales results of advertising is possible. For many years a book called *DAGMAR* (Defining Advertising Goals for Measured Advertising Results), published by the Association of National Advertisers, argued that influences on sales were too complex to allow us to isolate the role of advertising, and the industry should therefore settle for measurement of awareness and attitudes and give up trying to measure sales effects. The first crack in the dam came with AdTel's "split cable," and measurements of advertising's effect on sales are now more or less routine.

Third, the capabilities brought about by the new technologies have raised our sights regarding both the accountability and validity of our research measurement tools. In other words, the predictive validity of our research techniques, for example, those that measure one commercial alternative versus another before the marketplace, can now be assessed. In this regard, the Advertising Research Foundation is preparing to launch a major copy research validity project whereby ten pairs of commercials for which sales results are known through controlled or automated test markets will be subjected to six different pretesting methodologies to determine where the initial predictive power is strongest.

Fourth, these laboratories are now on the verge of yet another research breakthrough by producing what I have termed single source data (a term that has now caught on in the industry). They are about to capture both buying and media exposures from the same individuals. This development will help researchers answer some of their toughest questions, such as frequency effects and the differences in effectiveness of various media. At present, both Ad-Tel and Behavior Scan are busy installing electronic meters with the capability of reporting television exposure, even on a person-by-person basis. Work is also being carried on to capture magazine, newspaper, and other media consumption as well.

Fifth, the new technologies have thus brought the power of the microscope to advertising research, along with enhanced experimental design capabilities, and have thereby increased productivity and analytic power. In many cases this means that data are available faster, within shorter time intervals, and in more detail, and experimental design is enhanced by single variable control, single source data, and unobtrusive behavioral data measurement. Sixth, the new technologies are also producing improved data bases and data banks, and the networking of research services. Examples here are Behavior Scan's Fact Book and the PRIZM linkup with other data bases. Seventh, the new technologies, particularly the new electronic media, have brought the worlds of media and advertising research closer together. The advancing growth of the new technologies has forced media and research people to start talking to each other. The Advertising Research Foundation has even created a special council—the Media Communications Council—for this. Some examples here are the fact that cable areas do not correspond to television areas (ADIs, DMAs). Further, the ZIP code geodemographics are making precise targeting possible for both media planning and research. Eighth, the increased penetration of other new technologies could have similarly dramatic impacts on advertising research as well. Here, interactive TV (such as QUBE) and videotex could bring about significant and prospectively "for the better" changes in advertising research. Whole new capabilities for research are likely to arise in the next decade, and they will almost uniformly result from the various manifestations of the new technologies.

In sum, the impacts of the new technologies on advertising research have been revolutionary, and I am convinced that we are entering into nothing less than a renaissance era of discovery, learning, and application as a result.

PART FOUR

Strategies for Marketing the New Technologies

CHAPTER 15

Marketing Strategies in the Information Industry

John F. Cady
Harvard Business School

The information industry comprises numerous products and markets linked together by the converging technologies of deregulated telecommunications and word and data processing. Studies by Harvard University's Program on Information Resources (HUPIR) have suggested broad dimensions to the industry, including products and services that provide content or information to users, and those that provide the conduit over which information is carried. The principal vendor segments of this diverse industry are

a. data-processing companies;

b. common carriers that transmit information;

c. media companies that collect, own, or distribute information; and

d. equipment manufacturers that supply each of the other segments.

The matrix in Figure 15.1 was developed by HUPIR as a method for displaying the various segments of the emerging information industry, the array of participants, and the potential product and service strategies available to various participants.

This discussion deals primarily with the selection of marketing strategies for vendors in the information industry. It aims to show how the twin forces of technological maturity and customer experience provide a basic framework for the selection of marketing strategies for competitive advantage at the product-market level. I begin by discussing the need for a strategic framework for marketing and by examining some of the basic problems facing information industry marketers. I then identify technological maturity and customer experience as two key elements influencing the formulation

Figure 15.1 The "Information Business"

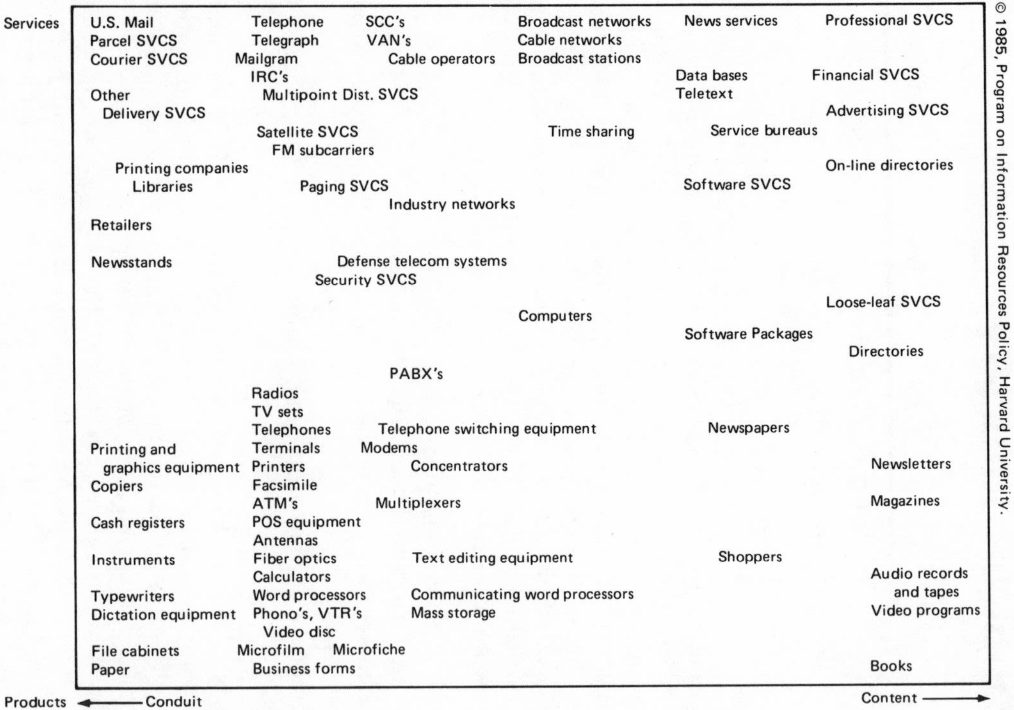

Services

Products ——— Conduit						Content ——→

Services

U.S. Mail	Telephone	SCC's	Broadcast networks	News services		Professional SVCS
Parcel SVCS	Telegraph	VAN's	Cable networks			
Courier SVCS	Mailgram	Cable operators	Broadcast stations		Financial SVCS	
	IRC's			Data bases		Advertising SVCS
Other	Multipoint Dist. SVCS			Teletext		
Delivery SVCS			Time sharing	Service bureaus		On-line directories
	Satellite SVCS					
	FM subcarriers					
Printing companies				Software SVCS		
Libraries	Paging SVCS					
	Industry networks					Loose-leaf SVCS
Retailers						
	Defense telecom systems					Directories
Newsstands	Security SVCS					
			Computers	Software Packages		
	PABX's				Newspapers	Newsletters
Printing and	Radios	Telephone switching equipment				
graphics equipment	TV sets	Modems	Concentrators			Magazines
Copiers	Telephones	Printers				
	Terminals	Facsimile	Multiplexers			
Cash registers	ATM's	POS equipment				
	Antennas					
Instruments	Fiber optics	Text editing equipment			Shoppers	Audio records and tapes
	Calculators					Video programs
Typewriters	Word processors	Communicating word processors				
Dictation equipment	Phono's, VTR's	Mass storage				
	Video disc					
File cabinets	Microfilm Microfiche					
Paper	Business forms					Books

Products

ATM	– Automated Teller Machines
IRC	– International Record Carrier
PABX	– Private Automatic Branch Exchange
POS	– Point-of-Sale

SCC	– Specialized Common Carrier
VAN	– Value-Added Network
VTR	– Video Tape Recorder

Source: "Mapping the Information Business," by John F. McLaughlin with Anne E. Birinyi, by the Program on Information Resources Policy, Harvard University, 1980.

of marketing strategy and discuss these elements in more depth. The heart of the paper then posits marketing tasks appropriate to various stages of technological maturity and customer experience. I then deal with the potential benefits and risks of participation in various segments of the information industry. Finally, I outline some of the principal marketing issues that information industry participants can address using the proposed framework.

An Elemental Framework for Marketing Strategy

The excitement that surrounds the information industry is loud and contagious. The technological ability to "put the world's information at everyone's finger tips" has generated a great interest in the business potential of the industry's products and services. An article in *Forbes* magazine underscores this enthusiasm for information technology by noting that "companies are offering the technology simply because it's exciting."[1] Unfortunately in some industry sectors, such as data base publishing, few firms are currently profitable. Despite the investment of millions by many large corporations, basic questions remain unanswered and issues unresolved. The questions include whether or not there is a demand for the product; the issues include pricing and stimulating usage among initial purchasers. These are marketing issues. And although marketing seems to take a back seat to technology in excitement, good marketing frequently distinguishes the profitable participants from the also-rans in the information industry.

The problems of marketing in the information industry are unique in several ways. Frequently marketers must attempt to estimate potential demand for products and services that are unfamiliar to customers, and because users are unclear about a potential benefit, they are unable to accurately predict their purchase intentions. An executive of the Source, a data base vendor parented by Control Data and *Reader's Digest*, recalled, "We asked our users if they would like an electronic encyclopedia. In each survey they said, 'Yes, yes, yes.' But when you get down to a simple unchanging file, it's a lot cheaper in print . . . [people] won't pay for it."[2] Just as frequently marketers find it necessary to undertake substantial efforts in customer education in order to ensure that purchasers and users obtain the maximum benefits from product attributes. Or marketers try to minimize the possibilities of customer misuse of unfamiliar products that might result in dissatisfaction with the brand or even the product category. Recent articles in the popular press have indicated that perhaps half of the microcomputers purchased by individual users are being substantially underutilized as electronic checkbooks and video game machines. A principal reason suggested for this phenomenon is that users underestimated or misunderstood the degree of sophistication needed to exploit fully the microcomputer's capabilities. One implication of this finding may well be that current purchasers of the microcomputer will neither favorably influence subsequent potential purchasers nor purchase the same amount of incremental hardware, software, and upgrade features as more sophisticated users might have.

There are other types of marketing problems as well. These result from the difficulties inherent in dealing with new and "exciting" technologies. One type of problem involves marketing products that embody an emerging technology. Such products occasionally do not meet expected performance standards or do so only at prohibitive costs. Outside the information industry, one may point to the Concorde—an exciting technological achievement and an obvious commercial disaster—as an example of an unacceptably high cost-benefit ratio. Within the information industry, the laser videodisc may provide an analogous situation in the consumer market.

Even as these technologies mature, moreover, they frequently present unique problems. The introduction of 16K random access memories (RAMs) was heralded loudly by the information industry and vendors of these products quickly rang up orders among their customers. The development of the product was, however, basically a step within the parameters of an existing and well-understood technology (integrated circuits). Customers were well aware of performance standards from previous 4K RAMs and thus critically evaluated what appeared to be unusually large numbers of defective 16K pieces. The high rate of defects increased customers' costs sufficiently that Hewlett-Packard, for one, broke its established buying patterns in order to obtain greater reliability: It had bought its 4K RAMs from U.S. vendors, but changed to Japanese vendors, who lagged in product technology development but led in manufacturing technology investment. This investment led to fewer incoming inspection failures, fewer failures in the production cycle, and fewer failures in customer hands.

The examples cited above suggest that two basic dimensions—the degree of customer experience and the extent of technological maturity—are useful in assessing market needs and potential marketing problems. Furthermore, these dimensions also provide a basis for the development, audit, and reformulation of marketing strategies and programs.

Technological Maturity

Successful strategies for the marketing of information industry products and services depend upon the technological maturity of those products and services. In order to understand the relationship between successful marketing strategy and technological maturity, four issues should be clarified.[3]

Base Technologies and Key Technologies A central notion concerning information industry products and services is that *every product is composed of a number of distinct and identifiable technologies*. These technologies may be manifest as product features and product performance characteristics (product technologies), or they may be implicitly present as performance levels or cost levels that derive from some aspect of manufacturing operations (process technologies).

This notion of product and process technologies has been labeled a design concept that determines the performance parameters of a product.[4] The point is that each component of the industry's products involves one or more identifiable technologies. Data terminals, for example, may embody the product technologies of flat screen display, VLSI processors, and videodisc storage as well as the process technologies of integrated circuits, keyboards, and large volume assembly.

Because products embody a number of distinct and identifiable technologies, and these technologies vary in terms of their competitive significance, it becomes useful to identify the technological characteristics of a product in terms of the technology's competitive impact. Researchers at Arthur D. Little have identified technology as a "base" technology when it is an essential foundation for a product and is widely available to all competitors. Base technologies correspond roughly to the "core concept" illustrated in *Industrial Renaissance*. The core, or base technology, "establishes the agenda for a product's technical development . . . and assumes a distinctive priority in the product's overall evolution."[5] By contrast "key" technologies are those having the greatest actual impact on competitive performance. Key technologies may be product technologies that affect performance characteristics or they may be process technologies that affect manufacturing costs. To return to the data terminal example, the base technologies of data terminals in the 1980s are the technologies of integrated circuits and keyboards. These technologies are widely understood, inherent to basic data terminal function, and broadly available to industry participants. Further, these technologies are "basic" regardless of whether the data terminals in question are dumb CRTs, portable terminals, or intelligent terminals. The "key" data terminal technologies, however, vary across the three types of data terminals. For intelligent terminals, applications engineering and 8-bit microprocessor technologies are key in the early 1980s, whereas large volume assembly, necessary for manufacturing economies, is key for dumb CRTs and portable terminals.[6]

Note that the significance of a technology as "base" or "key" is determined not so much by the nature of the technology as by the response of the market to that technology's cost and performance potential over available alternatives.

Competitive Impact A second premise concerning information industry product and process technologies is that these *technologies have widely differing potentials for competitive impact*. There are, as noted above, two general ways in which technology can have competitive impact. The first is through improvements in product performance; the second is through improvements in product costs arising from manufacturing operations. As an example of how the various technologies embedded in a product can have differing potentials for competitive impact, consider again data terminals. The development of improved flat screen displays for data terminals might have a much greater competitive impact than improving the performance of the terminal's integrated circuits. On the other hand, a significant manufacturing advantage in integrated circuits, if one could be attained, might initially have a much greater competitive impact than an improved flat screen manufacturing advantage.

Technology Life Cycles A third premise is that *technologies have life cycles* and can be classified according to their state of maturity. Numerous studies on technological innovation have affirmed the familiar S-shaped technology curve that describes the applications potential for a new technology. Although the duration of the curve can vary considerably (compare, for example, the relatively slow development of solar technology to the explosive development of integrated circuits), numerous empirical studies confirm that assessing the degree of technological maturity is useful in determining the future product applications potential for that technology. Researchers at Arthur D. Little, among others, have developed guidelines for assessing the degree of maturity of a technology.[7]

The degree of technological uncertainty: Highest for emerging technologies, and lowest for fully mature technologies, this measure suggests uncertainty concerning the technology's ability to meet latent or apparent market needs. An example might be videodisc technology in a laser versus conventional format, or videodisc versus VCR technology.

The level of interest in and business activity surrounding a technology: Interest, measured by investment and product development, will tend to be highest in the growth stage of a technology, where the basic uncertainties have been resolved and new applications are being developed. A current example might be the computer-aided design (CAD) arena.

The breadth of potential new applications: The vista for potential applications will tend to be the greatest for emerging technologies. Not until the technological and market uncertainties of a breakthrough have been resolved will the marketable range of applications be known. The potential range of application for biotechnology, for example, has attracted substantial speculative capital, but few actual products have emerged to test the potential against the market and against alternative technological solutions.

The technical nature of the work needed to develop the technology further: For an emerging technology, "uncertainty" tends to refer to technical performance characteristics. Thus investment and development efforts focus on improving and extending technical capabilities. Investment in the newly discovered genetic engineering technology is heavily focused on basic cloning techniques. In contrast, investments made in more mature technologies tend to be product development and applications oriented—extending the range of the base technology. Thus microprocessor technology today seems focused relatively more on extending the range of applications to such areas as General Electric's intelligent kitchen of the future and relatively less on basic microprocessor development.

The technical prerequisites for having access to the technology: In general, technical prerequisites such as specialized technical human resources, testing and development facilities, and expertise will be higher in a less mature technology. This is primarily because more work is needed to develop the technology early in the technology cycle. As the shift from technical to applications development takes place, the technical prerequisites for further development diminish and, in general, the technology can be developed by a broader base of industry participants. Intel's pioneering work in the development of the 64K dynamic RAM initially positioned the firm among the very few firms capable of perfecting the technology. After the design factors were successfully tackled, numerous American and Japanese firms entered the business and successfully extended the range of applications through improvements in manufacturing yields (and reduced costs) and in reliability.

The technology's general availability: As the technical requirements for further technological development decline, the base of potential and actual developers expands, and supply expands. Eventually users and commercial developers will have a choice of either making the basic products for which the technology was developed or purchasing those products in the market. When this stage is reached and availability is widespread, the technology is generally fully mature. An example might be the microprocessor chips that provide the technological base for the microcomputer. By 1982 most of the major microcomputer manufacturers purchased rather than produced their own microprocessor chips (a notable exception being Texas Instruments). Further, the industry had established a standard microprocessor in the Intel 8086/8088. The 8086/8088 microprocessor was widely available by 1982 and supported 70 percent of the new 16-bit microcomputers introduced at the 1982 Hanover Fair.

Technological Significance A fourth premise is that since products incorporate various technologies of differing competitive impact and at different stages in an observable life cycle, *the competitive significance of the distinct technologies embedded in a product will change over time.*

Key technologies mature, frequently become base technologies, and give way to new key technologies. In the general purpose computer market, a key technology of the 1950s was vacuum tubes, which gave way to transistors in the 1960s. By the 1970s solid logic technology was widely available and an industry base technology. In the 1980s very dense logic packaging appears to be a key technology. As our previous example of the microcomputer market shows, the key technology in that business in the 1970s was the microprocessor. By the 1980s, microprocessor technology had evolved to become the industry's base technology. Software technology and the technologies of large-scale manufacturing emerged as key by 1983. As new key technologies emerge and mature they replace old key technologies and are, in turn, replaced. With these transitions, the basis for competition and for marketing efforts is fundamentally changed.

One general observation about the life cycle of key technologies is that product technologies have a tendency to mature and give way to process as the critical competitive technologies. Researchers have noted a persistent correlation between technological maturity in products and relatively high levels of capital spending because of purchases of large quantities of specialized production equipment. Some observers of the development of very large scale integration (VLSI), which is frequently viewed as a major technological development, argue that VLSI technology is actually a mature technology: "While VLSI represents a dramatic step forward in chip complexity, it is fundamentally a step within the parameters of the existing IC (integrated-circuit) industry; this new technology is governed by a similar set of parameters and cost factors . . . . The primary factor responsible for [the dramatic] changes in cost and performance has been the process technology underlying IC production."[8]

Customer Experience

Successful marketing strategies in the information industry also require an understanding of how the extent of customer experience with products or services affects marketing requirements. The purpose of this discussion is simply to propose that the extent of customer experience with a product provides insight into the market requirements that marketing strategies must meet.

Customer experience refers to the extent of personal and organizational participation in the various technologies of the information industry. It is a summary measure of the amount of training and observation gained through personal and organizational exposure to those technologies. Experience includes the exposure gained through product purchasing and subsequent use, but is not limited to such purchase exposures. The reason for not limiting experience to purchase exposure is, as Everett Rogers has reminded us, because "in the case of technological innovation, it is the *idea* about the material product that is diffused as well as the object itself."[9]

Warren McFarlan and James McKenney, in their recent book *Corporate Information Systems Management,* describe customer experience with information systems (IS) in terms of four phases of technological assimilation.[10] (See Table 15.1.) In their model these phases describe the path through which corporations gain experience with IS technologies.

A recent study of the purchase behavior of customers of computer-integrated manufacturing (CIM) also indicates the existence of distinctive differences in behavior based on the level of experience with the concept of CIM and experience with the products that are included within the concept.[11]

Since experience, as I have defined it, seems to have such a direct impact on customer behavior in the information industry, it is of particular interest to identify and develop some generalizations concerning customer experience levels and the corresponding factors that may affect the selection of marketing strategy. Specifically, four factors appear to be important: product features, product usage, acquisition, practices, and information usage. The relationship between high customer experience levels and these factors is expressed in Table 15.2.

TABLE 15.1 Customer Experience with Information Systems (IS)

Phases	Level of Experience	Characteristics
I Technology identification assessment	Low	• Customers identify technologies of potential interest • Pilot projects used to explore technology • Develop technical skills through training, education, and specialized human resources
II Technological learning and adaption	Low–Moderate	• Identify problems technology can solve • Follow-on projects • Development of end-user insights and potential applications • Selling awareness of application to users
III Rationalization	Moderate–High	• Technology reasonably understood (IS and end-user) • Standards and cost-benefit studies • Development of procedures and standards • Management control
IV Maturity	High	• Technological skills, user awareness, and management controls in place • Widespread adaptation • Technology assimilated appropriately in company

Source: Warren McFarlan and James L. McKenney, *Corporate Information Systems Management* (Homewood, Ill.: Richard D. Irwin, 1983).

Product Features When customer experience with a product is high, there is a thorough understanding of the product concept, the benefits and costs of various product features, and a studied ability to discriminate among the brands of competing vendors. As customer experience grows, specific performance standards emerge and customers use such standards to assess performance.

Integrated circuits provide an example of products with which customers have extensive experience, and as a result, customers are able to undertake or require extensive product testing to meet specifications of performance and reliability. Computer-integrated manufacturing, on the other hand, is an emerging concept and there is very little agreement on the definition of the concept parameters by customers or vendors. This lack of agreement is a direct reflection of the low level of customer experience with CIM in the market.

TABLE 15.2 Correlates of High Levels of Customer Experience

Product Features	Product Usage	Acquisition Practices	Information Usage
• Good understanding of product concept	• Ability to assess and minimize performance risks	• Specific criteria for performance and financial evaluation	• Knowledge of product and vendor information sources
• High awareness of product features	• Ability to assess and minimize organizational risks	• Hierarchy of performance and financial criteria	• Knowledge of product and vendor alternatives
• Good understanding of product benefits	• High degree of confidence in product usage	• Systematized product evaluation procedures	• Access to sources of personal and impersonal product information
• Ability to discriminate among brands	• Relatively low levels of friction with old technologies	• Routinized decision-making process	• Routinized use of specific information sources in evaluation and purchase
• Specific product performance requirements	• Widespread product adoption		

Product Usage Relatively high levels of customer experience are associated with extensive and sophisticated product usage. Customers assess and minimize performance risks and organizational risks by routinely integrating products into their operating environment. Products with which customers are experienced will be adopted in a widespread fashion and users will frequently experiment with products and even modify or customize them after purchase.

Low levels of customer experience, on the other hand, are marked by a tentative use of the product. It may be frequently underutilized or used only by the product "experts," who may, or may not, share their experience with the rest of the household or organization. In the early years of consumer microwave ovens it was not uncommon to find these products used for warming coffee, making popcorn, and heating leftovers. The low levels of consumer experience with microwaves led to a significant underutilization of performance capabilities until industry vendors supplied microwave cookbooks, microwave cooking schools, and microwave foods to be prepared in specially designed microwave cookware.

Acquisition Practices Low levels of customer experience are marked by experimental purchases, pilot tests, and fundamentally ad hoc evaluation procedures. There are a number of reasons for these pratices. Decision makers may be dispersed throughout an organization and have little contact with each other. The products may have numerous applications and there is no dominant or logical organizational entity to take responsibility for procurement. There may be intraorganizational rivalries over control of a new technological product. In the commercial market for microcomputers and microcomputer software, for example, contention among data-processing, word-processing, and communications departments and end users over who should control microcomputer acquisitions, installations, and usage has led to a crazy quilt of buying patterns. The microcomputer's potential applications are currently not fully realized; individual and departmental purchasing have led to problems of compatibility in hardware and software. Such varieties of acquisition practices pose serious problems for marketers, who require some focus for promotional efforts, product development, and pricing decisions.

Information Usage Low levels of customer experience are generally associated with a paucity of information sources and content. Aside from the requisite technical papers, there is frequently a shortage of vendor and product information. Even advertising, sales promotion, and salesperson information will not provide comparative performance and operating statistics, since vendors and customers have not yet required (or determined) product standards. At low levels of customer experience, industry reports have yet to emerge, securities analysts' reports are highly speculative, and trade articles are of the "Assessing Your Need for . . ." variety. Interestingly, trade and technical articles frequently gauge the extent of customer experience as they proceed from titles such as "Planning for Your . . ." to "Using Your . . ." to "Improving . . . Practices," to finally "Your Next . . . Purchase." In a similar vein, a recent article in the *IBM Systems Journal*, entitled "Techniques for Assessing External Design of Software," noted that "[software] development has primarily focused on advancing the state of the computer programming art . . . . These accomplishments have, for the most part, been attributed to technological innovation. Now, more attention is being given to the usability of software."[12]

The crux of the information problem for products with low levels of customer experience appears to be that customers do not know how to evaluate products and therefore do not know and cannot articulate their information requirements.

An Information Industry Marketing Strategy Matrix

Figure 15.2 displays the marketing strategy matrix formed by the dimensions of technological maturity and customer experience. I have somewhat arbitrarily divided the axes into two parts each, indicating "emerging" and "fully mature" technologies and "unfamiliar" and "fully experienced" levels of customer experience. The division into four quadrants is merely an analytical convenience rather than a description of a discrete process in either dimension.

The matrix allows for four types of marketing situations by designating products according to their relative positions along the two dimensions. From this description it is possible to identify basic marketing strategies that are appropriate to products in each quadrant. Further, it is possible to identify the strategic imperative that must be met in order to exploit fully the potential of products in each quadrant. By *strategic imperative* I mean the underlying theme or focus for overall management efforts, or the thrust of overall business strategy. Figure 15.3 provides a description of strategies appropriate to each theme. Figure 15.4 provides examples of products in each quadrant.

Quadrant I. "Curiosities" are the products of an emerging technology in applications with which customers have little or no expe-

Figure 15.2 Information Industry Strategy Matrix

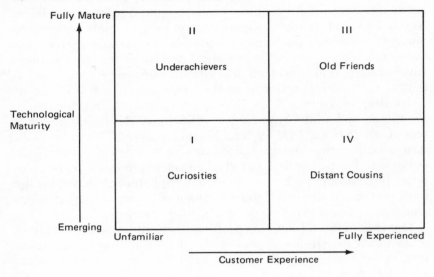

Figure 15.3 Fundamental Marketing Strategies (and Strategic Imperatives)

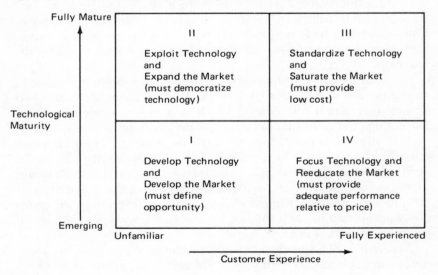

Figure 15.4 Product Illustrations

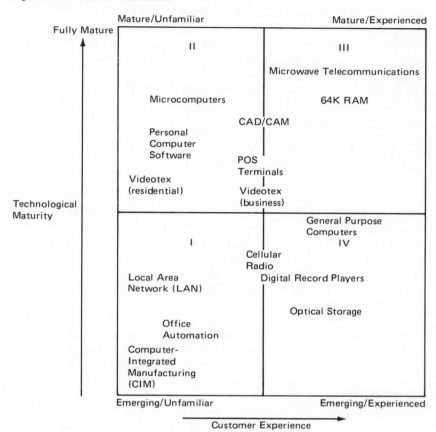

rience. The technologies that emerge tend to be of a revolutionary and sometimes dramatic nature, rather than the technological refinements of currently available products that are more likely to be familiar both to the technologist and the vendor firm as well as to the customer. The challenge of marketing these unfamiliar "curiosities" is to *define the opportunity*, and this provides the strategic thrust for the business. Defining the opportunity has two components: developing the technology and developing the market.

To develop the technology requires that the marketer determine its current limits of function and performance and identify the applications actually and potentially best suited to it. Another way of expressing technology development is to define the potential "supply space" that the products of the technology will or can occupy.

An important step in developing the technology is attempting to rank in order the applications of the technology, beginning with those with the greatest business potential. The second aspect of defining the opportunity, developing the market, follows from technological development. After defining the technological supply space and ranking its applications, the marketer must communicate the applications potential and the benefits of technology to an unfamiliar customer base. The marketer's task is, first, to adequately define the technology's application potential in terms of the customer's needs and, second, to educate the customer so that technological assimilation is facilitated. This task is generally difficult, usually time consuming, and always encounters planned and unplanned-for customer resistance.

The marketer of "curiosities" is the marketer of information industry products and services that potentially change the way customers do business, in a way that is unfamiliar and viewed (correctly or incorrectly) as costly and risky. Probably a good example of a "curiosity" is the local area network (LAN). LANs are data communications networks that allow word-processing, data-processing, and communications equipment to interact or "talk to" each other in a very limited physical environment such as an office building. LANs are frequently viewed as the backbone of further developments in office automation, since the office automation concept requires interactive processing. Currently several major firms have proposed their own versions of specifications for a LAN. Among the major competitors, Xerox Corporation has developed ETHERNET and Wang Laboratories markets WANGNET. To date, penetration of these LANs has been limited and customer experience in the market is very limited. ETHERNET, Xerox's pioneering LAN, had reportedly fewer than one thousand installations by the end of 1982.

There are numerous reasons for low penetration by LANs. First, there is contention among vendors over the choice of technology. ETHERNET, for example, is a base band (digital, single channel) transmission system, whereas WANGNET is a broad band (analog, multichannel) transmission system. These basic technological differences give rise to certain performance advantages and disadvantages, which neither Wang nor Xerox has yet effectively packaged in terms of applications for specific user segments.

Second, competition between vendors has focused on the technology issue almost to the exclusion of customer education and product definition. As a result, an ETHERNET coinventor noted that "our orders dropped off significantly because people got confused. They were analyzing, not acting."[13] A third reason why

LANs have not been adopted is that because of marketers' inattention to applications marketing, users have been required to identify and evaluate LAN applications through the use of customer-initiated pilot projects. As a result the knowledge of successful applications is localized and not rapidly disseminated. Customers, in general, are unfamiliar with LANs and experience levels remain low. In sum, so long as the LAN opportunity remains undefined, its potential will remain unrealized.

The marketing strategy appropriate to LAN and other "curiosities" involves a substantial investment in market definition and customer education. These efforts should be directly related to the issues discussed earlier (see Table 15.2). Marketers must facilitate the ability of potential customers to become aware of and to understand product benefits and to discriminate among vendors' technologies and brands. In order to do this, marketers must influence the information sources used by customers, and develop those sources. For example, pilot sites and showcase accounts are valuable for making information directly available to potential accounts. The marketer must not only influence the acquisition practices of customers but, because of the interdepartmental nature of the impact of LAN, also develop the ability to suggest to customers what constitutes an effective planning and acquisition process. And since LAN will affect the competitive position of adopting firms, the marketer must be in a position to pull top management into the picture to provide a LAN mandate to lower-level departmental managers. The marketer of "curiosities" must essentially influence two customer decisions: "the decision to," which is the strategic decision of a customer to commit to the new technology, and "the decision who," which is the customer decision of vendor selection.

Quadrant II. "Underachievers" are products for which initial key product technologies have matured and become base technologies. Yet although the product technology has matured, there is still a relatively low level of customer experience. This rapid maturation of technology relative to the level of customer experience can come about because of the narrow limits within which the technology can be applied, because a substantial and rapid investment in the technology has been made by the industry, or because marketing efforts have limited the rate at which customers could acquire experience. The strategic thrust for the management of products that are "underachievers" is to effect customer experience and build business volume. Building business volume must come about by extending the technology to the broadest range of customer applications and by expanding the market through aggressive marketing efforts.

A major task of the Quadrant II marketer is to build volume in order to take advantage of manufacturing scale economies and opportunities for automation that will ensure a favorable cost position relative to competitors. This volume building may be done by introducing product line extensions, undertaking measures to increase market penetration such as the introduction of product features, expanding distribution channels to reach larger numbers of customers, expanding geographic market coverage, and aggressive pricing. A particularly strong mandate for the marketer of "underachievers" is to maintain and increase relative market share in order to obtain and protect a strong low-cost position.

A good example of a product in the "underachiever" category is the microcomputer. Basic microprocessor breakthroughs accomplished by Intel and further developments by firms such as Motorola and Texas Instruments made the microcomputer a novelty in the mid-1970s. By 1980, further innovations by Intel in the development of the 16-bit 8088 microprocessor had defined the standard for the industry. The 8088 was compatible with the earlier 8086 processor and could be upgraded to the more powerful APX286 Intel processor that would follow. By 1981 small microcomputer manufacturers such as Sirius Systems and large newcomers such as IBM had selected the 8088 for their products. Nippon Electric Company, Fujitsu, and Oki were among the Japanese microcomputer producers who did not use Intel microprocessors in their 8-bit machines in 1981, but were expected to use the 8088 or compatible processors for their anticipated 16-bit computers.

In the four short years between the Apple II—defined as a product for the computer hobbyist—and the introduction of the IBM Personal Computer, base microcomputer technology had matured. Prices for the 8088 declined rapidly as it became widely adopted and manufacturing volumes increased. Between 1980 and 1981 the price per unit dropped from $78 to $14 in distribution quantities of one hundred or more. Although microprocessor technology developed and matured rapidly, consumer experience did not. Early purchasers, prior to 1980, were computer "experts"—enthusiasts and hobbyists with advanced college degrees, high incomes and an interest in learning and practicing programming languages. The marketing task for the vendors of microcomputers and other "underachievers" is to *democratize* technology through aggressive marketing efforts in order to broaden and deepen the customer experience base in the market.

Attempts to democratize microcomputer technology have developed rapidly since the onset of microprocessor maturity. First, manufacturers introduced scores of new products into the market as adequate supplies of microprocessors assured access to technology. These products ranged from small personal computers, such as those marketed by Sinclair and Timex for under $100, to those produced by toy and game manufacturers such as Mattel and Atari, selling for a few hundred dollars, to microcomputers sold primarily for business applications such as Apple's Lisa and IBM's XT. These last-mentioned models sell for almost $10,000. Second, new distribution channels were developed to reach potential users and provide them with products, information, presale and postsale service and product assistance. Third, advertising expenditures, in particular those made by industry leaders IBM and Apple, have increased dramatically. The media used have expanded from print to broadcast and a broader audience has been reached. Fourth, software development has broadened the range of microcomputer applications and widened the potential for the technology. Fifth, an infrastructure of information sources has been expanded and supported by the industry. Encouraged by the efforts of manufacturers, for example, Byte Publications changed the name of one of its microcomputer magazines from *On Computing* to *Popular Computing* in 1981. At the same time it changed the publication's frequency from quarterly to monthly. In 1984 microcomputer magazines constitute one of the publishing industry's highest growth areas. Sixth, product development efforts have evolved to the point of spending relatively more on enhancing the man-machine interface and less on enhancing base technology. This has made microcomputers more accessible—more "friendly"—and hastened the rate of customer familiarization with the product category.

Finally, the industry prices have declined dramatically. Standardization of the components of microcomputer products allowed manufacturers to automate and take advantage of scale economies in production. As costs have declined manufacturers have passed on these savings to customers in the form of lower prices in an attempt to expand the market and their products' shares. These industry attempts to expand demand have led to the beginning of an industry shake-out. This shake-out is the result of the competitive requirements for substantial marketing expenditures on the one hand and a favorable cost position on the other. Small volume microcomputer manufacturers, such as North Star, who do not have the leverage to match the price reductions of the industry leaders and support marketing and distribution channels are undergoing severe profit pressure.[14]

These comments are meant to suggest that nonprice marketing efforts to democratize technology and the expansion of demand through pricing moves must occur if "underachievers" are to meet their full potential. Additionally, steps to increase customer experience should logically precede pricing reductions. Unless customers exhibit the characteristics associated with high levels of experience (see Table 15.2), rapid price reductions can result in customer confusion about the basic benefits of the product category and differences among brands. Especially for technologically complex products, price reductions alone may not serve to facilitate the acquisition of customer experience.

Quadrant III. "Old friends" are those products that have become technologically mature, and for which there is a high level of customer experience in the market. These are products that have undergone the democratization process. Customers are completely familiar with their use. Investments in process technologies substantially outweigh investments in product technologies. The strategic imperative for the marketer of an "old friend" is to become the low-cost producer. The ability to become the low-cost producer involves two steps. The first is the selection and standardization of a specific product technology, which in turn requires the selection of customer groups or customer applications to serve. In the example of LANs noted earlier, this might involve the selection of a broad band or a base band solution. In the case of long-distance voice transmission systems, technology selection might involve cable, satellite, or microwave. The second step in becoming a low-cost producer is to saturate the market in order to derive the maximum cost reductions possible from scale and experience effects.

A good example of a Quadrant III product or service may be long-distance voice transmission. The telephone was made commercially available in 1879 and by 1950 over 90 percent of all U.S. households, and virtually all commercial establishments, were telephonically wired. As a matter of U.S. communications policy, AT&T was the sole provider of long-distance telephone services over a national network consisting primarily of cables and wires. Although the level of customer experience with long-distance voice transmission services was very high (billings to the Long Lines Department in the late 1970s amounted to over $23 billion), there was no incentive to lower costs and prices to expand demand. In fact, some observers argued that AT&T had maintained its long-distance rates at artificially high levels in order to subsidize local telephone services.

Through a series of regulatory and judicial decisions beginning in the 1960s and extending through the 1970s, AT&T lost its monopoly over long-distance communications. New entrants, including Southern Pacific Communication, U.S. Transmission Systems, and MCI Telecommunications, entered the market. Among them, MCI provides AT&T with its most aggressive competition. The company, originally called Microwave Communications Incorporated, selected microwave technology for its transmission medium. Microwave technology, by the 1960s, was fully mature and cost substantially less than AT&T's cable medium. By 1981 MCI had almost one-half billion dollars invested in its microwave system. With such substantial capital investment, the key to MCI's profitability was volume and the company drove for volume by leveraging the lower cost of its transmission system in the form of lower prices. The offer of lower prices to long-distance customers proved extraordinarily successful for several reasons related to customer experience:

- The customer did not have to change his or her equipment—any touch-tone phone could be used.
- Access to the MCI system was relatively easy, requiring the use of a numerical access and identification code;
- Benefits were immediate, as a result of paying lower prices per unit call;
- Benefits were apparent or obvious to users, many of whom had developed particular long-distance calling habits and had established budgets for them; and
- Quality of transmission was adequate for users.

AT&T's market response (as contrasted to its legal and regulatory response) was muted by a reportedly higher-cost transmission system, a policy of nationwide average pricing, and a share of long-distance revenues of over 95 percent. Thus a reduction by AT&T in long-distance prices of 30 to 35 percent to meet MCI's competition for 2 to 3 percent of long-distance business would result in a price cut on all its business equivalent to $7 billion in pre-tax income. AT&T recently announced that its proposed 1984 long-distance rate reduction of $1.7 billion would result in reduced revenues of $665 million. The principal customer education requirements for the marketer of "old friends" is to ensure that customers and potential customers are aware of the cost differences among alternatives and are able to make the appropriate cost comparisons.

Quadrant IV. "Distant cousins" are products that embody new or emerging technologies while functional product performance standards and product usage requirements remain essentially unchanged from those products using mature or aging technologies. Customers of "distant cousins" are familiar with product usage and features, have standardized their acquisition practices, and have identified and routinized information-gathering and information-processing procedures. Marketers of "distant cousins" must provide superior price-performance ratios for customers. The new technology that forms the technical basis for these products must provide performance equivalent to the existing technology at a lower price, or provide superior performance at an equivalent price. The fundamental marketing requirements for Quadrant IV products are to focus the new technology on specific applications and reeducate the market concerning superior price and performance characteristics.

For products of equivalent performance resulting from new technology, the simplest means of reeducating the market is through the pricing mechanism and efforts to communicate lower prices to customers. Although this approach seems a logical one, it is potentially difficult to execute effectively. New technologies have some, perhaps substantial, costs associated with their development and commercialization. Such costs must be recovered through pricing. At the same time, the old technologies that are being replaced have matured, process technologies are dominant, and manufacturing costs are low. In addition, old technology plants and equipment may be fully depreciated. As a result, a marketer of a new technology with equivalent performance and a cost (price) advantage over an existing technology may be met by stiff resistance and competitive pricing by firms with a stake in the existing technology. Such resistance may make the recovery of development and commercialization costs difficult or impossible. A critical factor deciding the suitability of a marketing strategy that focuses on providing equivalent performance at a price advantage is the relative cost position of firms offering the new and the existing technologies, as well as the sustainability of competitive pricing by vendors of existing technology.

The marketer who can offer superior performance at a price equivalent to the existing technology is in a potentially stronger competitive position for the long term. Vendors of existing technology products may meet the competition of new technology by reducing prices. But vendors of the new technology, in addition to having some price flexibility, also have the ability to promote their technology's superior absolute performance capabilities and thus establish a new basis for performance standards. Essentially, the marketer must reeducate the market to an enhanced level of performance.

The general purpose computer market provides an interesting illustration of these two approaches to price-performance marketing: one providing superior absolute performance, the other equivalent performance. The general purpose computer market is one in which customers, especially large commercial customers, are fully experienced. Many large commercial users gained initial experience with data-processing equipment and services in the 1950s and 1960s. By the mid-1970s, these customers had widely adopted general purpose computers throughout their organizations and were so well versed in computer usage that they acted as product consultants to mainframe producers. In 1975 Gene Amdahl, a former IBM computer designer, formed a company, which bears his name, to manufacture and sell large computers that would run on IBM programs and with IBM support and peripheral equipment. Amdahl's products were designed to provide superior performance through innovative technology at prices lower than or equivalent to IBM. Amdahl's marketing strategy was to target his offerings to the base of large experienced users of IBM equipment who could evaluate his price and performance claims. In 1980, for example, Amdahl offered the model 5860 central processor complex using a new air-cooled technology. The 5860 was designed to compete with IBM's large liquid-cooled 3081 processor complex. Industry analysts estimated that the Amdahl product, initially priced from $3.8 million to $4.5 million, had a 25 to 35 percent price and performance edge over IBM. Pricing adjustments by IBM subsequently narrowed the Amdahl edge, but did not completely erode it. Amdahl is, in 1983, the largest of the IBM plug compatible manufacturers. It has been able to succeed despite IBM's pricing moves by providing superior performance through technological innovations.

In 1976 Itel Corporation also manufactured an IBM plug compatible computer. Contrasted to Amdahl, Itel focused on large users of medium-sized IBM computers. The company provided products that were equivalent to IBM in performance but depending on the specific model, priced 10 to 30 percent lower than IBM. When IBM drastically lowered its prices on medium-sized computers in 1979 with the introduction of the 4300 line, Itel was unable to effectively respond. As a result of this and the impact that IBM pricing had on Itel's leasing business, the company went bankrupt in 1980.

Benefits and Risks

Figures 15.5 and 15.6 summarize the principal benefits and risks that can accrue to a marketer in each quadrant of the strategy matrix. There are several features of these syntheses that are noteworthy. First, there is a fundamental difference between the focus of marketing efforts in Quadrants I and II taken together and in Quadrants III and IV. In Quadrants I and II principal marketing empha-

Figure 15.5 Potential Benefits of Participation for Industry Marketers

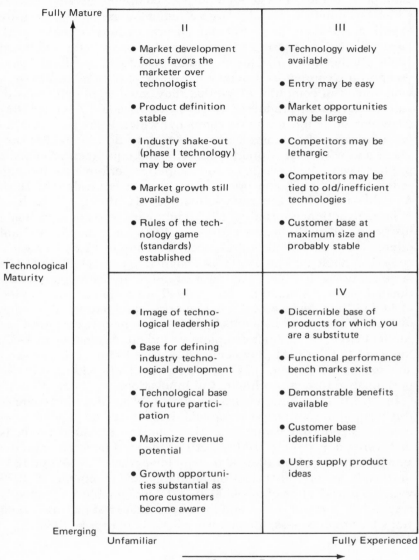

Fully Mature

II
- Market development focus favors the marketer over technologist
- Product definition stable
- Industry shake-out (phase I technology) may be over
- Market growth still available
- Rules of the technology game (standards) established

III
- Technology widely available
- Entry may be easy
- Market opportunities may be large
- Competitors may be lethargic
- Competitors may be tied to old/inefficient technologies
- Customer base at maximum size and probably stable

Technological Maturity

I
- Image of technological leadership
- Base for defining industry technological development
- Technological base for future participation
- Maximize revenue potential
- Growth opportunities substantial as more customers become aware

IV
- Discernible base of products for which you are a substitute
- Functional performance bench marks exist
- Demonstrable benefits available
- Customer base identifiable
- Users supply product ideas

Emerging

Unfamiliar

Fully Experienced

Customer Experience

Figure 15.6 Risks Facing Information Industry Marketers

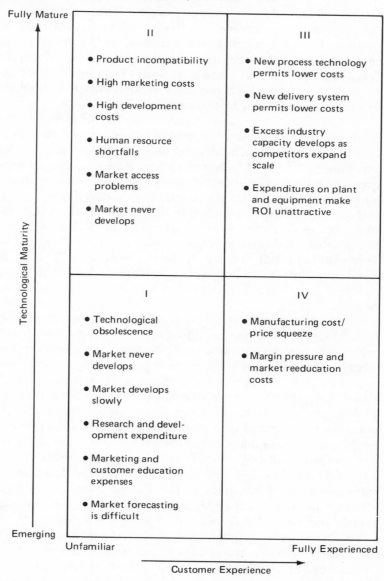

sis is placed on *customer* analysis and *customer* education as critical components of the marketing program. This is due, primarily, to the overriding requirement to effect greater levels of customer experience for the products being marketed. In Quadrants III and IV customers are technologically experienced and experienced product users; successful marketing strategies require a primary emphasis on *competition*. Both the costs of competitive technology and levels of competitive performance must be addressed.

Second, the nature of uncertainty facing information industry marketers differs among the various quadrants of the matrix. In Quadrants I and IV technological uncertainty engenders risks concerning the levels of product performance that can be expected from technological applications. As a result of this uncertainty, customers may resist adoption of the new technology's products unless and until they have confidence in the future developments that are likely to come about. Vendors of emerging technology products face a substantial investment in technological development as well as market definition and education or reeducation. The returns on these investments can be highly speculative. Specific strategies are required to manage the level of investment and the realization of returns.

One such strategy that has emerged in response to the substantial technology and market development costs of Quadrants I and IV is referred to as strategic partnering. Strategic partnering involves the shared exploitation of technological potential by vendors who are expert in various aspects of technological applications. An illustration of the extensive use of strategic partners is presented by N. V. Philips. Philips has, through various alliances (often with potential competitors), entered into numerous long-term agreements to develop specific technologies and markets. For example, the company has a venture with Siemens to develop speech synthesis technology, and with AT&T to develop digital voice and data communications systems for use outside the United States. IBM has used strategic partners such as Matsushita to manufacture videotex terminals and Texas Instruments to develop LAN circuits.[15]

The uncertainty facing marketers of products in Quadrants II and III results from the maturation of technology and its consequent widespread availability to potential entrants. A principal risk facing these vendors is that they will not achieve sufficient scale of operation to compete as a low-cost producer. A particularly critical decision facing an information industry vendor in Quadrant II is whether to attempt to participate broadly in the market and serve multiple segments by providing a standardized (low-cost) product to all segments, or to participate as a niche specialist serving a specific or limited number of segments. This decision turns not only on the resources of the firm and the goals management may have for the business but more broadly on how customer segments and customers' application needs will evolve in the face of declining costs of product technology.

Third, the matrix can be employed to match the requirements for successful participation in each quadrant against the marketing and managerial resources of the firm. For example, the firm with substantial assets in research and development, including specialized human resources, patents, laboratories, and testing facilities, is substantially more likely to participate in Quadrant I than a firm without these assets. Whether the technologically strong firm would choose to participate in Quadrants II or III as technology matures depends upon its strength in product development, applications management, and traditional marketing.

These brief comments suggest two related topics of importance to information industry marketers. The first is that an information industry vendor must decide whether to specialize in products at one stage of their evolution or to adapt to the changing requirements for success as the product evolves. The second is that products generally follow predictable technology and experience paths. Let me illustrate these notions with two examples.

It is frequently difficult to marshal the resources to market products effectively as they evolve along their technology and customer experience paths. It can also be difficult to market products at different stages of technological and experiential development, using the same marketing organizations and resources. Computer Devices (CD), a relatively small, but highly successful marketer of dumb computer terminals, is an example of the difficulties posed by marketing products at substantially different points in their evolution. CD successfully sold dumb computer terminals through a direct sales force in the late 1970s. During this time dumb data terminals became technologically mature and customers became very experienced in their use. The key technology for these products was large-scale manufacturing. Texas Instruments provided CD with formidable competition, selling a volume of terminals ten times greater than the smaller company. CD's margins came under substantial pressure and management undertook the development and marketing of a smart portable terminal in order to improve the company's financial performance. The smart terminal was a relatively new technology and customers were substantially less experienced in its usage. The purchasers and decision makers in customer organizations selecting dumb terminals were different from those selecting smart terminals. The uses to which smart terminals were put differed, as did their potential impact on the customer's organization. In short, smart terminals required a focus on customer usage, customer education, and the customer buying process, whereas dumb terminals required a focus on competitive costs and prices. The sales force viewed CD's introduction of smart terminals as an expensive sale for them to undertake. The selling cycle was substantially longer and the selling task more difficult. As a result, the company was unsuccessful in its initial efforts to market smart terminals.[16]

The second example is from the microcomputer software business. In 1979 the VisiCalc spreadsheet program was developed through the joint efforts of an MIT programmer and an MBA student at the Harvard Business school (HBS). The program was technologically new in terms of its advances in microcomputer software development and its spreadsheet application. VisiCalc was a prototypical Quadrant I product. The developers of the program recognized that their strengths were in programming and formed a development company, Software Arts. They also recognized their weakness in marketing and they licensed VisiCalc to a marketing company formed by another HBS graduate. That company was Personal Software (now Visicorp).

By 1981 one industry report noted the widespread acceptance of VisiCalc and the existence of thirteen "Visiclone" spreadsheet programs. This number grew rapidly as the basic microcomputer-programming skills became available to numerous software vendors. The proliferation of spreadsheet programs served to expand customer experience substantially. By 1983 access to the spreadsheet software technology served as "table stakes" to participate in the market. The continued success of VisiCalc among its competitors had come about as a result of continued product enhancements, expanded distribution, a well-publicized name supported by heavy advertising, and a strong, efficient manufacturing and distribution organization.

The value added in microcomputer software had shifted, in four short years, from development to marketing. In recognition of this dramatic shift the owners of Software Arts abandoned licensing as a strategy. Software Arts made a considerable investment in the development of an internal marketing organization with public relations, advertising, sales, and distribution functions prior to the announcement of new microcomputer software products in 1983.

Figure 15.7 traces the evolution of spreadsheet products through

Figure 15.7 Technology/Experience Paths for Stand-Alone Microcomputer Software

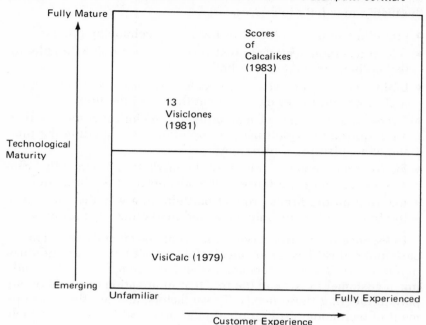

the marketing strategy matrix. I would suggest that its evolution is typical of many information industry products. The implication is that as VisiCalc and other spreadsheet software enter Quadrant III, cost will become a principal basis for competition and consequently scale considerations will become critical. Spreadsheet programs also face a technological obsolescence of a sort as stand-alone microcomputing software is threatened by integrated software packages, such as MBA or 1-2-3, that combine spreadsheet functions with graphics and communications capabilities.

Summary

The marketing strategy matrix described here can provide useful guidelines to marketers in the information industry. The identification of technological maturity and customer experience as bases for the selection of marketing strategy provides a focus for analyses that management may undertake by raising important questions that should be answered. Some of the more important issues that the matrix may help to address are:

- providing an overall focus for the firm's technology program;
- selecting product markets that leverage the firm's strengths in technology or marketing or both;
- timing the entry decision to coincide with changes in the technological and customer environment that favor the firm;
- forecasting the types of marketing and technical resources that are required to exploit market opportunities, including the timing of acquisition of resources;
- focusing on the key elements of the marketing program that can affect customer experience to the advantage of the firm; and
- focusing on the firm's product portfolio in a way that facilitates the budgeting for technological and marketing expenditures.

In essence the matrix serves to focus management's attention on basic but critical factors for successful competition in the information industry. These factors are a sound and complete understanding of customer needs and the role that information technology can play in meeting those needs. These factors, and not the development of technology itself, provide the principal basis upon which information industry participants can identify, develop, and sustain competitive advantage.

CHAPTER 16

Achieving System Cooperation in Developing the Market for Consumer Videotex

John A. Quelch
Harvard Business School

George S. Yip
Harvard Business School and
Management Analysis Center, Inc.

Videotex is one of the most important of the new communications technologies. It holds the promise of plugging the mass consumer market into the electronic information network. This network in turn has profound social and economic potential, perhaps returning us to the cottage in three generations—from the "cottage small beside a field of grain" via the freeway-dormitory Levittown back to the "electronic cottage."[1] Thus developing the videotex market is an important concern in its own right. In addition, videotex poses in heightened form a special development need of increasing interest to marketers and strategists. This is the need for system cooperation: That is, the development of the videotex market will depend not only on the individual efforts of participants (channel members) but also on how well the participants cooperate. Videotex seems to be an example of what Johan Arndt calls domesticated markets—markets that are of increasing importance.[2] Such markets do not handle transactions at arm's length, but emphasize long-term relationships and administrative processes on the basis of negotiated rules of exchange. They exhibit a degree of what Oliver Williamson terms "market failure," necessitating nonmarket organization to make these markets work.[3]

Other factors, particularly technological ones, are of course important for the development of the videotex market, but system cooperation remains the most important marketing factor. Furthermore, although generally recognized as important, this topic has not been thoroughly addressed. For example, one participant, Gerald Haslam of Southam Publishing, posits a stand-alone model as well as a partnership model as viable strategies.[4] We believe that the stand-alone model will not work. Videotex also seems to demand more system cooperation than previous comparable innovations. In this paper we take a two-level view of the videotex industry. First, we examine the need for cooperation among all types of participants—information suppliers, system information managers, system operators, network providers, hardware and software suppliers, investors, regulators, and business packagers. Second, we examine in detail one videotex service—teleshopping—in order to demonstrate the importance of cooperation and bundling in service design and execution.

What Is Videotex?

Definitions of an emerging service category obviously vary. One source defines it thus:

> Videotex can be described as the generic name for a new interactive mass medium that delivers text and visual information directly to consumers. The user interacts with the system via a handheld keypad, push button console, or full alphanumeric keyboard. Desired information is retrieved interactively from a Videotex center, through a telephone, cable, or regular television network, with text and graphics being displayed on a television screen or other video device.[5]

Videotex is, therefore, not so much a new technology as the polygamous marriage of several existing ones: computers, computer graphics, communication networks, television screens. It is the transformation of the familiar TV set from passive entertainer to interactive information supplier that provides the excitement about the potential of videotex. Television is in almost every American home and, via videotex, can be the Trojan horse that plugs the mass consumer market into the electronic information network.

The role of the television set accounts for the focus of this paper on the consumer market rather than the business one. Videotex is, of course, used by businesses as well as consumers. Indeed, the Prestel system in Britain currently has far more business than consumer users. For businesses, however, videotex is only a visual enhancement of already available computer-accessed data services.

In contrast, for consumers videotex is usually the first and only interactive information medium. As one participant put it, "Videotex is the Bastille Day of the home information revolution."

Where Is Videotex?

In the United States, videotex is probably the most heavily test marketed new product or service in history. In the last three years over twenty trials have been undertaken by different organizations. There are as yet no self-supporting commercial ventures.[6] In Europe, where videotex was "invented," and in Canada government involvement and support have blurred the distinction between trials and the real thing, and videotex usage is more widespread than in the United States.[7] Britain, the pioneer, has had an ongoing system, Prestel, since 1979, run by the state-owned communications company, British Telecom. France, in typical *dirigiste* fashion, already has a government policy to place a videotex terminal in every French home. Canadian farmers are already users of videotex services. Japan is in the second stage of testing the Captain system, launched in 1979. Japanese videotex faces the extra burden of needing to generate three thousand characters rather than twenty-six letters. Most Western European countries, Hong Kong, Brazil, and Venezuela are experimenting with videotex.

The Need for System Cooperation

The theme of this article is that videotex poses an unusual requirement for marketing and strategy: This requirement is "system cooperation." A successful videotex business appears to require the specialized skills and resources of participants from several different industries, and requires different roles to be played by participants. Several necessary roles have emerged in this young industry. While terminology varies, one set of names for these roles is information supplier (or provider), system information manager, system operator, network provider, and business packager. Other roles, not specific to videotex, include hardware supplier, software supplier, investors, and regulators. We sketch the relationship of these roles, and define them, in Exhibit 16.1, at the end of this chapter. (More complete and technical descriptions are available elsewhere.[8]) Three of the roles—information supplier, network provider, and hardware and software supplier—can only be performed by companies from existing industries with the requisite capability. Information can only be supplied (directly or indirectly) by those who create the information, networks by those in the network business, and hardware and software by those in the computer business. In theory, anyone can integrate into any role. But since these roles can already be performed by well-established companies in mature or near-mature industries, there is little short-term motivation to so integrate.

Although most roles require participants from existing industries, two roles—system information manager (or packager) and system operator—are sufficiently specialized to need "videotex specialists" (our term). Such specialists have typically been set up as independent operating units by companies participating in other videotex roles. For example, the Viewtron system is run by Viewdata Corporation of America, a subsidiary of Knight-Ridder Newspapers, which is a key supplier of information for the system. The business packager role—not an operating role but an entrepreneurial one—is also available to a participant from any industry.

Thus some roles have required participants, and others are "free" roles. In practice many participants have taken more than one role. In Table 16.1 are listed the generic roles and current types of participants in the United States and abroad. The complexity of roles and relationships is illustrated in Table 16.2, which presents a matrix of roles and participants in a selection of major current or recent projects. The general effect of this complexity is that a videotex participant must both choose the roles in which it will participate and manage its relationship with other participants in the system. This general effect comprises several specific aspects that pose spe-

TABLE 16.1 Required Roles and Current Participants

Required Roles	*Current Types of Participants*
Information supplier	Financial institutions
System information manager	Publishing companies
System operator	Retailers
Network provider	Telecommunications companies
Hardware supplier	Hardware manufacturers
Software supplier	Software creators
Investor	TV/entertainment companies
Regulator	Videotex specialists
Business packager	Miscellaneous companies
	Governments

Source: Adapted from Wayne W. Talarzyk and Robert E. Widing II.

cial problems and are also of conceptual interest to marketers and strategists. These specific aspects concern:

- specialist roles
- horizontal relationships
- multiple choice
- partners as competitors
- supply and demand "chicken and egg"

Specialist Roles

The many specialist roles required make it nearly impossible for any one existing company to create, single-handedly, a videotex operation.[9] Most trials have involved two or more participants in the major roles of system operators or service packagers. All trials, except for one or two pure banking ones, have involved many participants in the minor role of information suppliers. Furthermore all the solo-trial banks admit that a banking-only videotex operation will not be commercially viable, and all intend to involve other information suppliers.

This multispecialist-role aspect of videotex can be contrasted with the start-up situations of previous major innovations in communications and, its substitute, transportation: telephone, automobile, airline travel, radio, television and computers. Although all these earlier innovations required both industrial and public sector infrastructure, they were commercialized by companies acting more or less independently, organizing suppliers and subcontractors as necessary. Henry Ford could create the automobile industry with a few engineers and managers and a relatively unskilled labor force. IBM could create the computer industry with many engineers, managers, workers, and salespeople. Juan Trippe had to buy his seaplanes from Boeing, but then he could independently provide the Pan American trans-Pacific service. Indeed, an industry based on flying boats is, perhaps, the quintessential example of going it alone. RCA, which pioneered both radio and television, was jointly created by four companies—AT&T, General Electric, Westinghouse and United Fruit—but after receiving capital and patents from its creators, RCA could go it alone. That David Sarnoff was able to wrest independence for RCA is ultimate evidence of this point.

RCA, of course, needed cooperation from advertisers, program producers, and TV set manufacturers. Similarly, the computer in-

TABLE 16.2 Roles and Participants in Selected Projects in 1982

	Information Supplier	System Information Manager	System Operator	Network Provider	Hardware Supplier	Software Supplier	Investor	Packager/Promoter
Financial	Chase[1] Citibank[2] Banc One[3] Chemical[4] First Bank System[7]	American Express[23]	Chase[1] Citibank[2] Chemical[3]		Oak Industries[13]	Banc One[3]	American Express[6] Merrill Lynch[5] Equitable Life[5]	Un. Am. Corp.[14]
Publishing	Times Mirror[15] Dow-Jones[2,16-19] New York Times[22]		Times Mirror[15]	Times Mirror[15] Time, Inc.[21]		Dow-Jones[17]	Knight-Ridder[22]	
Retailers							Federated[5]	
Telecommunications			Manitoba Tel.[24]	Bell Canada[8] AT&T[22] Manitoba Tel.[24]	AT&T[25]		Bell Canada[8] AT&T[22] Br. Telecom.[10]	AT&T[22,25] Manitoba Tel.[24]
Hardware Manufacturing					Apple[1] Atari[4] Honeywell[7] Radio Shack[14] Digital[15]			
Software Time Sharing			OCLC[3]			OCLC[3] ADP[25] Telesystems[23]		
Entertainment	CBS[22]	Warner[6]	Cox Cable[13] Warner[6]	Cox Cable[13] Warner[6]			Warner[6]	Warner[6]

Videotex Specialists	Homserv[13] Viewmart[13] CompuServe[6] Comp-U-Card[15]	Infomart[8] CompuServe[14] Viewdata[22]	CompuServe[14]	Source[14] Infomart[15]	Compu-U-Card[5] Source[26]
Miscellaneous	Western Union[15]			American Can[2] H & R Block[6,14]	
Government					Canadian FDC[8] French[9] British[10] West Germany[11] Canadian[12]

V 1. Unannounced name for Chase project—New York area
V 2. HomeBase
V 3. Channel 2000
V 4. Pronto—New York area
I 5. Comp-U-Card—offers Comp-U-Store (shopping service via videotex systems)
V 6. Qube
V 7. First Hand
V 8. Vista—Canada
TN 9. Antiope
V 10. Prestel—project and technology
TN 11. Bildschirmtext—project and technology
TN 12. Telidon—technology only
V 13. INDAX
V 14. Express Banking
V 15. Gateway—Times Mirror Videotex Service: Southern California, Telidon, phone and cable
I 16. Dow-Jones News/Retrieval Service
I 17. Dow-Jones/Sammons Cable Information Service
V 18. Home Link Communications
T 19. Radio II—teletext
I 20. The Source
T 21. San Diego Teletext Service—Telidon
V 22. Viewtron—Coral Gables, phone
V 23. American Express will use Videodial software to become information provider and manager

V 24. IDA, ELI, Grassroots, FAST
V 25. CBS/AT&T—Ridgewood, N.J.
I 26. The Source

V = Videotex Project
T = Teletext Project
I = Information Supplier
TN = Technology

Subsidiaries
Viewmart—100 percent American Can
Viewdata Corp. of America—100 percent Knight-Ridder
Warner-Amex—50 percent Warner Communications, 50 percent American Express
Comp-U-Card—Federated, Equitable Life, Merrill Lynch
Infomart—joint venture of Southam Publishing, Torstar Corporation
CompuServe—H & R Block

Technologies
Telidon—owned by Canadian government, marketed by Infomart
Prestel—British Telecom., British government

dustry needed coordination among mainframe manufacturers, peripheral manufacturers, and software suppliers. This coordination was provided mainly, however, by compatibility with the dominant producer—IBM. Similarly, compatibility with AT&T was the mode of cooperation in telecommunications. Furthermore AT&T enjoyed a total monopoly for the first nineteen years of its existence, although its use of licensees—the future Bell operating companies—required some system cooperation.

There are two major reasons why the existence of specialist roles mandates greater system cooperation in videotex than in other new industries. As we said earlier, videotex is not a new technology, but rather an assortment of known, somewhat mature technologies already controlled by powerful competitors. Its newness is in the configuration of these technologies. In contrast, cars and computers were basically new technologies being exploited and defined by Henry Ford and Thomas Watson. Ford was also innovative in manufacturing process technology; by contrast, no videotex participant has yet developed a significant delivery process innovation.

We have cited Johan Arndt's "domesticated markets." The earlier innovations discussed here seem, in contrast, of the type that built "internalized markets." Alfred Chandler, Jr., has argued in *The Visible Hand* that it was the need for better coordination that led early industrial concerns, such as railroad companies, to internalize activities previously conducted by independent contractors.[10] When railroads began, there were no well-established suppliers of engines, coaches, tracks, stations, and signal boxes. The videotex equivalents, in contrast, are preexisting. The competitive strengths of the companies with these different required capabilities make integration dangerous. As one bank participant commented to the authors: "I have no desire to become a newspaper, nor a hardware vendor, let alone a hardware manufacturer." Thus videotex needs system cooperation to achieve the coordination done internally in integrated businesses. Conversely, videotex cannot rely on the *in*visible hand. Videotex operations are too new, complex, and existing in real time to allow for constant renegotiation of commercial relationships.

Horizontal Relationships

The railroad analogy highlights the second reason why videotex has great need for system cooperation. Like trains, videotex is a "horizontal" operation in real time. The required roles mostly do not relate vertically; that is, the role functions cannot all be performed sequentially as in the classic sequence: raw material providers → manufacturers → sellers → consumers. Inherent in an interactive system is that activities are simultaneous. The core roles of system information manager and system operator and network provider have to be performed simultaneously. Information suppliers also have to perform in real time to the extent necessary to keep their information current: by the minute for financial information, hourly for weather and travel information, and daily for shopping information. Business packagers, investors, regulators, and hardware and software suppliers can, by contrast, perform their roles in the traditional, vertical, off-line mode.

Thus a complex set of relationships has to be developed and made routine. Furthermore it is not only necessary to get the parts to work together, as in a railroad, but to create a greater sum. The CEO of one major videotex operation cited the analogy with television, which pioneers had to learn was more than radio with pictures (both in program content and business operation); analogously, videotex is far more complex than television.

The current uncertainty in relationships is evidenced by a banking system operator's comment that his contracts with information suppliers varied in length from one page to twenty. Negotiating arrangements with other banks would also take months, with new issues surfacing in each new deal. Indeed, the industry association is trying to design standard contract clauses for videotex banking.

Multiple Choice

Another unusual feature of the videotex industry is that most participants can choose more than one role (see Table 16.2). Although some roles can only be played by specific types of participants, others can be played by any participant:

"Dedicated" Roles and Participants	"Free" Roles
Information supplier—the relevant supplier	System information manager
Network provider—telecommunications (phone or cable)	System operator
Hardware supplier—existing manufacturers	Business packager
Software supplier—existing suppliers	Investor
Regulator—governments	

In contrast, as we argued earlier, because of mature technologies and entrenched competitors, it is unlikely that integration into a "dedicated" role will be profitable. In many cases, participants in "dedicated" roles have also absorbed one or more "free" roles. Thus potential participants have to decide how much of a system they will take on themselves.

In addition to the usual business considerations, the choice of roles should also depend on considerations of relative power—the obverse of system cooperation. This relative power is affected by both operating dynamics and by the nature of the consumer franchise. On operating dynamics, many in the videotex industry take as their model the traditional information industry in which it is said that 25 percent of revenues go to the creator of information and 75 percent to the distributor.

Greater power and revenues will also accrue to participants with a greater share of the consumer franchise. By franchise we mean consumer loyalty arising from perception of who adds value. Consumers are aware of all components of the system: network provider, system operator, system information manager, and information supplier. The key question is which role consumers will perceive as the most important one. Currently, the system operator probably has the greatest visibility in most operations. An operator can, however, lose its consumer franchise to more powerfully branded information suppliers or system information managers. Pure shopping services are in particular danger if consumers view competing systems as "commodity" channels that add little value. In contrast, full-blown videotex operations with a broad range of services are more likely to develop and retain a strong franchise. Learning and switching costs will probably lead to consumers identifying themselves as "Viewtron households" or "Pronto households" in the same way they may now be "GM households" or "Ford households."

System information managers will also have a choice in their level of salience and hence franchise. They can be low visibility, low franchise, passive "gateways" to their component services. Alternatively they can have high visibility and franchise by actively managing the consumer's use of the system. For example, for a consumer seeking a loan, a low visibility financial system information manager would merely list loan sources and rates. In contrast, a high visibility system information manager would identify the one or few best loan sources from an interrogatory sequence. The franchise that comes with high visibility can be used to negotiate better arrangements with one system operator, or to achieve multiple distribution through several systems.

Partners as Competitors

Closely related to the existence of multiple choices of roles is the unusual extent to which potential participants have to regard each other as competitors as well as partners. In any market, channel members face some threat of backward or forward integration by channel partners. The threat seems great in videotex. The threat of being cannibalized by a partner appears very high for participants in free roles. This may be one reason why there have been so many test markets: The test is not merely to evaluate consumer demand but also to evaluate the relative contribution and power of project partners. No one wants to be the Oyster who took the one-way walk with the Walrus and the Carpenter. Furthermore, participants have to be competitively alert, not just because of the new business opportunity posed by videotex, but because of the threat to existing businesses. Publishers and retailers, in particular, have to guard against the danger of videotex disrupting, if not replacing, their traditional modes of business. Thus, system cooperation in videotex has to be tempered by competitive fencing and wariness.

The general level of competitiveness is extremely high because of the high stakes involved and the many resourceful and diverse participants. Never before in the field of business conflict have so many behemoths, from such diverse bases, crowded into the same arena—AT&T, IBM, CBS, American Express, the *New York Times*, Sears, Roebuck, Merrill Lynch, Dow-Jones, Citibank, and others. Michael Porter's theories of competition would suggest intense rivalry among participants from so many different "strategic groups" and with conflicting motivations between offense and defense.[11]

Furthermore, not only can partners be competitors but competitors can be partners. As videotex systems expand their geographic coverage, more than one system will become available to individual households. In that case system operators may choose to become system information managers for rival systems thus:

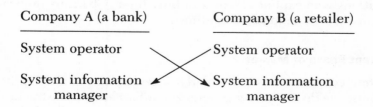

Company A (a bank)   Company B (a retailer)

System operator   System operator

System information   System information
 manager   manager

What a tangled web we will weave! New legal definitions of competition may be needed to cope with these reciprocal relationships.

The choice of partner will also be important. Many believe that a geographic franchise will develop around the system that joins with the leading local newspaper rather than the leading bank or retailer. Indeed, operators like Viewtron have rushed to sign joint venture agreements with newspapers in major cities. These agreements are locking up cities in which Viewtron's parent, Knight-Ridder, does not own the local newspaper.

Supply and Demand

Finally, the need for system cooperation on the supply side of videotex is complicated by a "chicken and egg" relationship with consumer demand. First, a videotex operation has very high fixed costs, and trial evidence suggests that consumers are sensitive to price. Hence there is the usual problem that videotex operators need to price low enough to generate the volume to cover costs. A second source of the "chicken and egg" relationship is more peculiar to videotex, although still related to the price dilemma. Because a videotex service provides a *bundle* of disparate information services, most consumers do not want to subscribe until there is a very large bundle of offerings. Conversely, operators cannot afford to provide a large bundle until they have a large number of subscribers. Similarly, information suppliers may not want to participate until there is a large consumer user base. The credit card industry faced this same dilemma in starting out. Whom should American Express sell first? Retailers or consumers? Airlines were crucial for American Express plans but were reluctant to be the first users. When they did sign up, consumer interest grew rapidly. Another issue between consumers and information suppliers will be the allocation of cost: Who will pay for it? This is the usual question with any new medium. One answer to this question may be that those banks and retailers, for example, who do *not* become information suppliers will pay in lost sales and market share. Prestel, in the United Kingdom, has found that it is small, regional, financial institutions who exploit videotex to breach entry barriers protecting the markets of national competitors.

Current Phase of Market

System cooperation is particularly necessary in the United States because we do not have a generalized information infrastructure as European countries do, nor is there a large government role forcing companies together in domesticated markets. The need for system cooperation is greatest now in this early development phase of videotex and should decrease as the market matures. This decrease will occur for several reasons:

- The relationships will have become systematized.
- Dominant participants will emerge, probably different ones at each stage of evolution, to take leadership roles.
- Increasing technical standardization (for example, the North American Presentation Level Protocol) will provide integration.

Meanwhile, however, the "strategic window" into this market will be open only to system cooperators.[12]

The Individual Service: Teleshopping

Let us consider system cooperation at the level of the individual videotex service. If we use teleshopping as our example, we can examine why the packaging or bundling role is necessary to deliver this service; the relative potential for manufacturers, retailers, and others to assume the role of the teleshopping packager; marketing challenges in delivering the package, in particular pricing; and, in a summary section, the likely characteristics of successful teleshopping packagers.[13]

Videotex Teleshopping

Videotex teleshopping is a new form of direct marketing. If we compare teleshopping via interactive videotex systems such as Viewtron with direct mail, direct response advertising, and other novel direct marketing approaches delivered via cable television, we find that the distinctive features of videotex teleshopping are, first, that the consumer controls the timing and content of the information delivered and, second, that purchases can be made directly from the comfort of an armchair via a hand-held keypad without the need for a telephone call (Table 16.3).

What information would the consumer ideally want a teleshopping service to deliver and how should the information be organized? We suggest that the consumer would wish to consult a *Consumer Reports*-style matrix of comparative attribute information on a comprehensive assortment of brands in a particular product category. Such comparative product information would probably be perceived as especially valuable for higher-cost, higher-risk purchases in categories such as automobiles and appliances, where product choices are based largely on objective rather than subjec-

TABLE 16.3 Comparison of Direct Marketing Techniques

	Consumer Control of Timing and Content of Information Delivery	Information Delivery Medium	Consumer Response Medium
Direct mail	No	Mail	Mail or telephone
Direct response advertising	No	Television	Mail or telephone
Cable shopping shows	No	Cable TV	Mail or telephone
Cable shop	Yes	Cable TV	Mail or telephone
Comp-U-Star	Yes	Cable TV/telephone	Keypad
Interactive videotex	Yes	Cable TV/telephone	Keypad

tive information. In addition, the consumer would probably wish to have price information on the products and brands presented on the teleshopping service. But purchases would probably be made only if the consumer were convinced that the prices were competitive with those available through other distribution channels. It is worth noting that the final prices for many products for which the comparative information matrix would be especially valuable— including automobiles and major appliances—are now typically negotiated at the point of purchase with a retail salesperson. Hence, it is possible that, in the case of high-risk, high-salience products with frequent new product introductions, the consumer would rather not make a purchase via the videotex teleshopping service, but would use it as a convenient source of prepurchase information.

Some would argue that consumers are so used to receiving *free* information (in the form of advertising) that they would be unwilling to pay for a teleshopping service unless it offered purchase capability. Yet only one in four users of Comp-U-Card's shopping information service actually makes a purchase through a participating Comp-U-Card retailer. The majority are apparently willing to pay a membership fee to obtain comparative attribute and price information, which they then use as negotiating leverage with traditional retailers. Either way, the consumer is likely to use a teleshopping service only if it offers sufficient net incremental value over alternative distribution channels on the following four dimensions.

Price Relative to the price of the specific product, is the cost to the consumer of the service and the cost of access time necessary to acquire information and make a decision reasonable? Is there a fair assurance that the prices offered are lower than or equal to store prices for the same item?

Convenience How easy is it to use the system and access the required data? Does it take less time than shopping around retail stores? Is the payment and product delivery system convenient?

Service Is the information provided complete, accurate, and up to date? Is the information as good as, if not better than, that available from a traditional retailer?

Assortment Is the breadth of assortment within a product category sufficient to reassure the consumer that he or she has received information on the prices and characteristics of a sufficient range of options?

Packaging a Videotex Teleshopping Service

Clearly, not all products will lend themselves to being marketed in videotex teleshopping and not all consumers will see a net value in using such a service. These barriers have been recognized in previous studies.[14] But an additional—and hitherto understated—barrier to the widespread availability of videotex teleshopping is the complexity of organizing and managing such a service.

There are two types of organization tasks to be considered. The first is the packaging of an individual teleshopping service that translates information from multiple information suppliers into a single data base. The second is the organization of an umbrella teleshopping service that offers consumers access to several teleshopping data bases, each provided by a particular manufacturer, retailer, or information packager. We believe that the first of these two tasks is the harder to execute, but that the resulting service may add more value in the consumer's view. Let us consider more closely the motivations and ability of manufacturers, retailers, and others to perform these organizing and packaging tasks.

Manufacturers No single manufacturer (with the possible exceptions of General Motors and General Electric) has such a broad product line or such a strong brand name that it could deliver a service of sufficient interest by providing information on, and an opportunity to purchase, its products alone. Most users of a teleshopping service will probably wish to compare the prices and performance of competitive products within the *same* data base

Figure 16.1 Teleshopping Service Comprising Two Manufacturer Data Bases

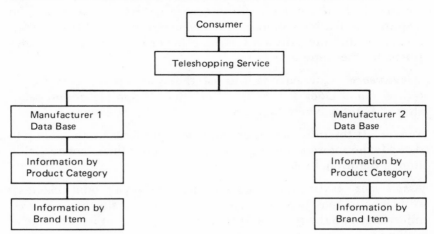

without the inconvenience of jumping from one manufacturer's database to another as would be required in a system comprising two manufacturers' data bases (Figure 16.1). An additional obstacle would be the difficulty that manufacturers would face in pricing their products lower than suggested retail prices; to do so would annoy their traditional channels. Yet suggested prices are often higher than actual prices, given retailer price promotions and customer-retailer negotiations. In addition, manufacturers of premium products might be reluctant to include price information in their data bases for fear of making consumers more price sensitive. For these reasons, we conclude that manufacturers will not act as information system managers for a videotex teleshopping service.

Retailers Many major retailers, but few manufacturers, are currently involved in teleshopping trials. Why is this the case? Both traditional retailers and direct marketing-catalog houses have the experience in assembling assortments of products and the direct contact with the end consumer that manufacturers lack. Both are potentially vulnerable to cannibalization of their existing sales by videotex teleshopping and thus have a defensive motivation for involvement, whereas manufacturers need not be quite as concerned since their products will be sold through one channel or another. Catalog showroom chains such as Service Merchandise, mail-order houses, and the traditional retailers who mail catalogs have particularly valuable experience in assembling information in a manner similar to that required in a teleshopping data base to facilitate browsing and catalog shopping. Even traditional retailers who only sell through stores have packaging experience in the sense that they organize merchandise product assortments. They could, if they wished, offer in-store videotex systems to help get customers used to a home-based teleshopping videotex service. Finally, many of the larger traditional retailers have their own van delivery systems, which can deliver items ordered via teleshopping from local outlets or warehouses, whereas manufacturers selling direct would have to use independently controlled services such as UPS.

There are, nevertheless, problems that may prevent many retailers from becoming aggressively involved as videotex teleshopping system information managers or even as information suppliers. First, still and moving picture capability on videotex is not well developed (more so in the case of telephone versus cable transmission), restricting the product categories that can sensibly be offered, and limiting the format in which information can be presented. The retailer will, therefore, have to decide which items in its product assortment are appropriate for teleshopping, and how to merchandise and manage "video shelf space" in a completely new medium. Second, only price-oriented retailers will be enthusiastic participants if, as seems likely, the consumer will use the teleshopping service to compare the prices of different items or to check the price of a preselected item on the teleshopping service against the store price. Upscale retailers may be willing to provide information about in-store events and promotions but, like upscale manufacturers, will not wish to encourage price comparisons or to increase the price sensitivity of consumers.

Third, some premium price and quality manufacturers might pressure the retail customers against involvement in a teleshopping service. They would be annoyed if retailers to whom they sold their products presented them on videotex in a purely price comparison fashion without sufficient additional product attribute information. Yet in the final analysis, few manufacturers would be willing to jeopardize their market shares and sales through traditional retailers by trying to prevent them from selling their products, perhaps at lower prices, through a teleshopping service. King Cullen was presumably able to overcome the objections of similarly reluctant manufacturers when he initiated the supermarket concept. Indeed, some manufacturers, viewing retailer involvement in videotex teleshopping as inevitable, might allow retailers to apply co-op advertising dollars against space on the videotex pages to present a fuller story about their products and reinforce their ongoing advertising campaigns in the traditional media.

Fourth, the ability and motivation of the retailer to become aggressively involved in videotex teleshopping will be greater the higher the percentage of its business that is accounted for by product categories appropriate to videotex teleshopping, and the broader and more complete the assortment of brands that it can offer (for purposes of consumer comparison) within each category. Most traditional retailers will probably become involved in teleshopping principally for defensive reasons, being primarily concerned with maintaining customer traffic to cover the fixed overhead of their store locations. Fifth, just as a manufacturer is likely to be reluctant and unable to package an information service including competitive manufacturers' products as well as its own, so a retailer is unlikely to package a teleshopping service that provides price comparisons of the same product through its operation versus the operation of a competitive retailer. In both cases, the second manufacturer or retailer would also be unlikely to tolerate the loss of control implied by such an arrangement. Thus, the individual retailer is unlikely to be able to act as a packager of information supplied by several competitors.

In conclusion, we believe that only the largest general merchandise chains, particularly Sears, Roebuck and Company and J. C. Penney, and catalog showroom chains such as Service Merchandise have the necessary financial resources to afford high start-up costs, the experience in catalog selling, the necessary price-oriented merchandising policy, the product line breadth and depth, the national name recognition, and the power versus their manufacturer-suppliers to become important information suppliers in a national teleshopping service. While they might also become system information managers integrating national and local teleshopping information, success would not depend on their packaging data from other retailers with their own. Many consumers would be interested in consulting and purchasing through a teleshopping service (see Figure 16.2) that included products offered by just one of these major national retailers.

But we also believe that there will be ample opportunity for large local retailers, especially department stores, to become involved as information suppliers, and possibly as teleshopping system information managers, at the local level. The attractiveness of national teleshopping services will be enhanced if they are offered by a local videotex system operator in conjunction with a local teleshopping service (see Figure 16.3). Larger local or regional retailers, including supermarket chains, might even take a financial stake in local system operator consortia in order to exert some control over the nature of the teleshopping service offered to consumers. We

Figure 16.2 Teleshopping Service Comprising Two National Retailer Data Bases

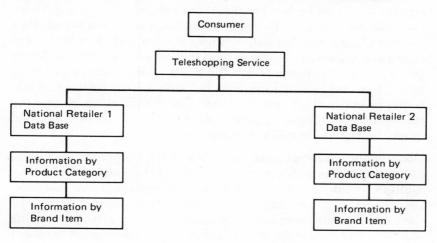

Figure 16.3 Teleshopping Service Comprising National and Local Retailer Data Bases

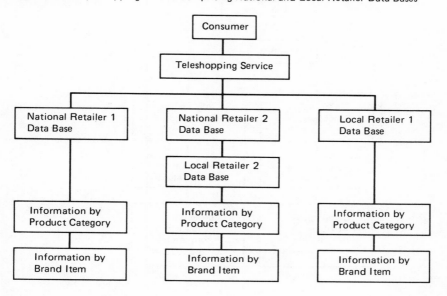

believe that, particularly in the case of local supermarkets, the principal goal will not be to make direct sales via teleshopping services, but to increase store traffic by announcing price specials and other in-store promotions that will require a smaller and, therefore, more cheaply maintained data base than that which we envision being provided by the national teleshopping system managers. Once again, however, we believe that individual local retailers, while acting as information suppliers, will find it difficult to assume the role of system information managers because of the reluctance of other competitive retailers to cooperate.

Other Information Packagers If videotex teleshopping data bases, either national or local, are to incorporate information provided by multiple retailers or manufacturers in an organized and easily accessible manner, it seems that some other party will have to assume the role of system information manager (see Figure 16.4). The value of having the system information manager or information packager deliver a teleshopping service is threefold. First, like any middleman, economies of scale permit the packager to manage the data bases more economically than individual manufacturers or retailers could. Information packagers concentrating all of their efforts on a teleshopping service should be able to do a better job on software

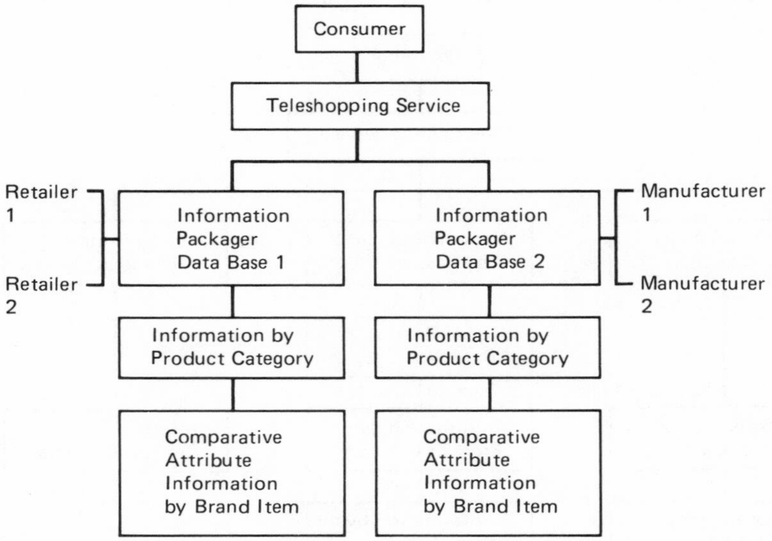

Figure 16.4 Teleshopping Service Comprising Two Information Packager Data Bases

development, page design, standardized effective presentation, and organization of the data base content into a coherent whole. Second, individual manufacturers and retailers can purchase videotex pages from the packager with assurance that they are not part of a service controlled by a channel competitor (as in the case of manufacturer and retailer managed teleshopping services). Under these circumstances, they will be more willing to supply information for the packager to translate into a comparison shopping format more valued by the consumer than a series of an individual listings. In addition, the involvement of an independent packager will result in fewer disputes over the order and placement of individual information supplier's material. Third, information packagers can perhaps best organize "gateway" systems by which a consumer's information request or order can be routed to a participating company's own computer for processing and fulfillment.

Would-be videotex teleshopping information packagers will also have to confront several problems. First, manufacturers, retailers, and other information suppliers may not be willing to provide the necessary information if the packager is then going to reorganize and collate the information into a form that would permit easy consumer comparisons, particularly if the information suppliers are expected to pay for page creation and maintenance. Thus, the teleshopping information packager may well be able to provide a higher added value information service to the consumer (at the extreme, making purchase recommendations) the stronger its financial resources and ability to maintain its independence. Second, if the names of the packagers are not well known, their teleshopping services may lack consumer credibility and require significant promotional investment. Third, the consumer may wonder whether she or he can obtain redress from the manufacturer or retailer in the event of a postpurchase problem. The responsibility of the information packager in the transaction will need to be more clearly defined, and will depend partly on the degree to which information supplied by retailers and manufacturers is modified by the packager rather than being merely presented on a videotex page paid for by the information supplier. Fourth, while the number of competitive teleshopping data bases will be fewer if they are organized by packagers than if offered by individual retailers, packagers may be equally unlikely to cross-reference each other's services, particularly if they are offering competitive merchandise.

Publishers and Broadcasters Who might these videotex teleshopping packagers be? Because of the financial resources required to support start-up costs and early losses until a critical mass of both consumers and information suppliers can be generated, the packagers in this category are unlikely to be entrepreneurial start-up companies, but, rather, independent subsidiaries of major corporations. Even so, the best-known information packager in the teleshopping area at the moment is an entrepreneurial company, Comp-U-Card of America, Inc. Comp-U-Card offers on a subscription basis access to its data base on prices and product information. Comp-U-Card also charges participating retailers a percentage of the sales revenues on merchandise purchased through the system. One would think that most videotex system operators would be eager to add the Comp-U-Card service, but Comp-U-Card has experienced significant product delivery problems with a number of its participating retailers. In addition, prominent videotex system operators in publishing and broadcasting number among their most important clients many manufacturers and retailers who are less than enthusiastic about encouraging consumer use of data bases like Comp-U-Card.

Another well-known information packager is Infomart, not least because of its development of the software needed to execute a teleshopping service. It is a joint venture of the two largest Canadian publishing companies—Torstar Corporation and Southam Publishing. Publishers are well placed to assume the system information manager role in this area. They are long-established and experienced information gatherers and processors. Since the advent of television, the larger publishers have always defined their businesses broadly in terms of communications rather than narrowly in terms of publishing; they have a propensity for diversification.

In addition, newspaper and magazine publishers often have a local market presence as well as a national organization. Individual newspapers in major chains like Knight-Ridder are in contact with local advertisers who might be interested in participating in a teleshopping service. And since their traditional print advertising revenue may be threatened by the advent of the videotex medium, they have a strong defensive motivation for assuming the roles of both system information manager and local system operator. As a system information manager, a large newspaper publisher could organize a national videotex teleshopping service, supplemented in each city by a local teleshopping service organized by the local newspaper. A similar case can be made for the involvement of network, but especially cable, television companies as teleshopping system information managers, particularly if cable television rather than the telephone line emerges as the dominant vehicle for delivering interactive videotex to the consumer.

Financial Institutions Because telebanking will be the lead videotex service, financial institutions will be well placed to become involved in the packaging of videotex teleshopping services both nationally and locally. Why will telebanking be the lead service? First, most consumer research studies show greater demand among consumers for the added convenience of telebanking versus teleshopping. Second, transaction productivity savings from telebanking can be readily quantified. In addition, telebanking presents banks constrained by regulations on the scope of their operations with a clearer market and product extension opportunity than retailers might perceive to be associated with teleshopping. Third, packaging a telebanking service will be easier than packaging a teleshopping service. Not only do the banks have stronger motivations and financial resources than retailers, but there is already an established tradition of cooperation between local banks and the national banking system, making it easier for the local bank to join a national telebanking service organized, for example, by Chemical Bank or Citibank. At the same time, banks generate a high percentage of their services in-house, whereas retailers are more dependent on their suppliers; an individual local bank would be better placed to develop a telebanking service on its own than would a local retailer in developing a teleshopping service.

What implications does the lead role of telebanking in the development of consumer videotex hold for teleshopping? First, the offerings of a teleshopping service will have to be targeted initially at the videotex customer base attracted by the telebanking service. Second, financial institutions, particularly American Express, which is already heavily involved in product merchandising, may be strongly interested in organizing a teleshopping service that would add to the consumer appeal of the overall videotex system incorporating the telebanking service. Both the Chase Manhattan Bank's Paymatic videotex system and Chemical Bank's Pronto system include teleshopping services.

In addition, teleshopping and telebanking are similar in that both are transactional services. Bankers want to ensure that they, rather than retailers like Sears, Roebuck, control the payment systems associated with teleshopping. Banks can make money on teleshopping through financing teleshopping purchases and through having payments made by bank credit cards or electronic funds transfer systems.

Finally, banks have the funds to become investors in local videotex system consortia and to absorb start-up losses on a teleshopping service. They typically enjoy a solid, reliable image among their customers and would, therefore, add credibility to a teleshopping service. Unfortunately, banks have limited experience in product assortment selection and merchandising. Rather, they are currently concerned with becoming full financial service suppliers; consequently, trying to organize teleshopping services might be a relatively unprofitable distraction. Thus, while banks have a strong interest in investing in the development of teleshopping services, they will wish to delegate the information system manager function, particularly at the local level. For example, a recently announced videotex field trial sponsored by nineteen banks will offer not only telebanking but also teleshopping to be provided by Videotex America, a joint venture of Infomart and Times Mirror, the communications company.

Network Providers In addition to communications companies and financial institutions, a third group of possible system information managers for teleshopping services are network providers such as AT&T. AT&T could easily run the centralized data banks of a national videotex teleshopping service. It has the base to move into information gathering and advertising from its *Yellow Pages* operation (although AT&T has lost control of this source of revenue to the recently divested operating companies). Its Western Electric subsidiary is developing home terminals. And, of course, AT&T has the funds to invest to become a system information manager, not only in teleshopping, but across the range of videotex services. Since the divestiture of the operating companies, AT&T's motivation to act as an information manager has been enhanced, since it will no longer be a network provider able to collect revenues from connect time. But as a packager of a teleshopping service, AT&T might experience some difficulty in understanding how consumers wish to use the data submitted by manufacturers and retailers and organizing them in a different form involving creative page design and merchandising. We believe that AT&T will wish to delegate the role of information system manager for a teleshopping service to its videotex partners such as CBS and Knight-Ridder.

Pricing the Package

In the final analysis, the development of videotex teleshopping services will be guided by those institutions willing to absorb the necessary start-up investment costs. The relative power of the actors in the system will depend on who absorbs the costs and risks of system organization and management and on how any profits from the teleshopping service are shared:

Information supplier	Data base organization costs
National system operator	Data base maintenance costs
National information system manager	Data base management costs
Local system operator	Data base usage costs
Network provider	
Consumer	

The allocation of costs will also influence the speed of market penetration. The consumer's trial and adoption rates will be more rapid if the costs to be borne by consumers are lower. Charges to consumers could include a one-time connect charge, a monthly flat fee, a charge each time the data base is accessed, and a connect time charge, which might be waived if a purchase is made. Charges to information suppliers could include a per-page creation and maintenance charge, a charge each time a page is accessed, and a percentage of the value of all merchandise ordered along with an order-processing charge. The pricing structure to consumers and information suppliers depends on whether additional roles are assumed by the system information manager. If, for example, the system manager is also the network provider charging consumers for connect time, the manager would not be at all concerned about consumers' using the system to browse and acquire information without making a purchase.

There are several other issues to consider in pricing the package. How will the pricing of the teleshopping service be related to the price of the entire videotex "system"? Will the teleshopping service have widespread appeal and, therefore, be a part of the basic product offering, or will it be so highly valued by only a limited segment of videotex consumers that it should be offered as an optional premium service? If the teleshopping service comprises several data bases, will a single fee permit the consumer to access all of them (in the interests of simplicity), or will different charges be assessed for the right to access individual data bases? For example, an information only service (without purchase capability) probably would not command as high a price (if any!) as a service offering that convenience. Is the pricing structure designed so that data base additions to the package can easily be accommodated without confusing or upsetting the consumer (as different manufacturers, retailers, and consumer segments enter the videotex teleshopping arena over time)?

Successful Teleshopping Packagers

The organizations most likely to emerge as system information managers of a teleshopping service have certain characteristics:

- They are at the forefront of developing and marketing the overall videotex package, either as system information managers or local system operators.
- They regard teleshopping as an important and potentially profitable element of the total videotex package.
- They can deliver a service that offers consumers the most incremental value over existing, competitive shopping channels.
- They can effectively use consumer research to understand what products should be offered on a teleshopping service and how they should be presented, given the preferences of the emerging customer base for the overall videotex system.
- They can most contribute to overcoming (or offer merchandise least affected by) the technological barriers (no motion pictures, no national standards, weak data indexing) and consumer barriers to widespread use (equipment costs, ease of using the service, concern about privacy of information and redress in the event of dissatisfaction, need for rapid delivery of "impulse" purchases).
- They have easy and reliable access to telephone or cable transmission networks.
- They currently have a significant percentage of sales in product categories susceptible to sales through videotex teleshopping, and thus have a strong defensive motivation to participate.
- They have the funds and commitment to support a developmental period during which consumer usage may be lower than the level needed to cover costs.

We conclude that retailers will act principally as information suppliers, though the major general merchandise chains may attempt to establish themselves as national teleshopping information system managers, albeit offering only their own merchandise. Local retailers will be involved as information suppliers to local teleshopping services and may, in some cases, also have a financial stake in the local videotex system, along with local banks and publishers. We believe that both communications companies and financial institutions will take the initiative in packaging national teleshopping services, but that communications companies with a national and a local presence, such as Knight-Ridder, will be better able to execute the service to the satisfaction of both consumers and information suppliers. In either case, it is likely that important aspects of organizing and managing the teleshopping service will be delegated to specialist packagers such as Comp-U-Card and Infomart, especially in the early stages of market development.

Summary

System cooperation is crucial for the successful development of the consumer videotex market because of specialist roles, horizontal relationships, multiple choice, partners as competitors, and supply and demand problems. As is clear from the teleshopping example, individual participants have to recognize that they cannot develop a system on their own. They will also have to choose roles and partners carefully, bearing in mind how industry evolution may affect the wisdom of those choices. They will have to learn to live with new and complicated partner relationships—sharing enough to make the system work, but not enough to make divorce dangerous. Maximizing their share of the consumer franchise will be crucial in building bargaining power within the system. The leader of a system, the business packager or system operator, will have to do more than coordinate the parts. The successful leaders will create new business paradigms, such as the network system created in television.

The nature of relationships will be more like the semi-internalized domesticated markets described by Johan Arndt than either the fully internalized markets described by Alfred Chandler or the fully free "perfect" markets of classical economics discussed by Oliver Williamson. Videotex appears to be on the following continuum:

Free markets → Domesticated markets → Fully internalized markets
(Williamson)   (Arndt)   (Chandler)

continuum of increasing systematization and cooperation
↑
Videotex?

Thus, an overall issue for videotex is where it should be on the continuum, and how its position on the continuum will shift over time.

EXHIBIT 16.1 Definitions of Required Roles

As is inherent in being a new industry, there are no agreed-upon definitions of roles. We provide here definitions of videotex terms that appear to have wide usage and acceptance.

The *system operator* is the central role in a videotex system. This role links the suppliers of information with their users. As manager of the system, the system operator is typically responsible for the following:

- computer storage of the information data base
- terminals for updating data
- switching capacity for other data bases
- hardware and software development to channel products through the system
- interface with customers of services
- marketing and distribution of products in subscriber contact
- packaging and control of mix of services offered

The *network provider* supplies the communications vehicle linking the user with the system operator. Network providers are primarily telephone companies or two-way cable systems. (For teletext, which is one-way and noninteractive, network providers can be broadcast media.)

The *information supplier* provides information or markets products or services through the videotex system. Using frame creation terminals, the suppliers create and maintain pages of information to be stored in the system's data base.

The *system information manager* performs the same functions as a system operator, but on a specialized basis. The managers concentrate on a small segment within the wide range of information sources, such as financial information. The presence of system information managers reduces the number of information suppliers that the system operator has to deal with, and reduces the amount of specialist expertise to be developed.

The *business packager* (or promoter) does not refer to an operating role but is nonetheless essential. The packager provides the entrepreneurial glue for the entire system by making the key business decisions. Frequently the system operator takes on the packager role, but not always. Important packager or promoter roles are being played by network providers (e.g., AT&T) and by regulators (e.g., French and Canadian governments).

EXHIBIT 16.1 (continued)

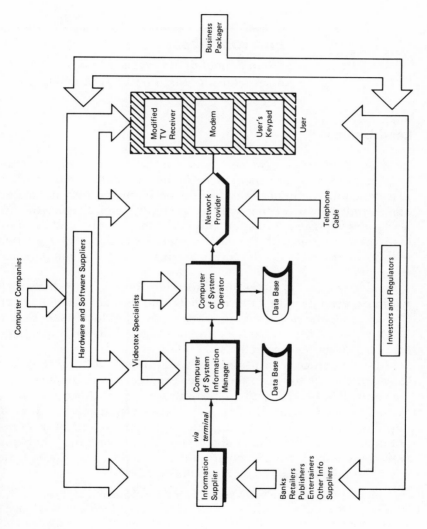

CHAPTER 17

Learning from Lead Users

Eric von Hippel

Sloan School of Management
Massachusetts Institute of Technology

Lead Users

Lead users are users who face needs that will be general in a marketplace, but they face them years before the bulk of that marketplace encounters them. Thus, firms experimenting with automated offices today in ways that will be generally useful tomorrow are lead users of office automation. Similarly, those individual consumers experimenting with personal computers at home in ways that will become general in the future are lead users of home personal computers.

Lead users can aid marketing researchers because they have real-world experience with "future" needs, and thus are in a good position to evaluate proposed new responsive products (see Figure 17.1). Indeed, they can serve as a kind of need-forecasting laboratory for marketing research.

Moreover, since lead users may well attempt to fulfill the need they experience, they can sometimes provide new product concept data as well as need data to properly attuned marketing researchers. Sometimes lead user problem-solving activity takes the form of applying existing commercial products or components in ways not anticipated by their manufacturers—sometimes the problem-solving activity involves actually developing new products. Consider the following published examples:

> Since 1957, when a North Carolina trucker, Malcolm McLean, discovered that he could save time and cut down on theft and breakage by hoisting his goods-laden truck rigs directly aboard ship, containerization has completely transformed the shipping industry. . . .
>
> Says Robert Calder, executive director of the Boston Shipping Association: "The shift from freighters to container ships is no less a revolution than the transition from the sailing ship to the steamship."[1]

Figure 17.1

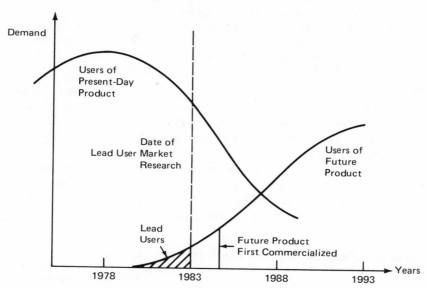

Indeed, even young lead users can assemble components in novel ways that prove commercially significant:

> In the early 1970s, store owners and salesmen in southern California began to notice that youngsters were fixing up their bikes to look like motorcycles, complete with imitation tailpipes and "chopper-types" handlebars. Sporting crash helmets and Honda motorcycle T-shirts, the youngsters raced their fancy 20-inchers on dirt tracks.
>
> Obviously on to a good thing, the manufacturers came out with a whole new line of "motocross" models. By 1974 the motorcycle-style units accounted for 8 percent of all 20-inch bicycles shipped. Two years later half of the 3.7 million new juvenile bikes sold were out of motocross mold.[2]

The line between adapting an existing product to new uses and actually designing and building a new product is a thin one—and sometimes lead users cross it, as in the following case:

> Every year Americans throw away enough oil to fill 15 supertankers. The waste, which runs to 1.1 billion gallons, is the glop that is drained from industrial machinery, buses, trucks and the crank-cases of cars at every oil change. The gunk is so grimy that it is usually just sold for pennies per gallon to waste oil dealers.
>
> In Europe, many gas station owners sensibly save the used oil and burn it to heat their workrooms. Now a growing number of U.S. gas stations and auto salvagers are doing the same. They are installing so-called junk oil furnaces that utilize an idea pioneered 17 years ago by

a West German garage owner, Walter Kroll, who developed a waste oil burner to save on heating costs for his shop.

At least half a dozen U.S. manufacturers are now rushing to bring out competing products. Tri-State Products of Fombell, Pa., has sold 1,800 of its $1,200 "Hooter" furnaces. Bigger waste oil furnaces are being marketed by Pittsburgh's Dravo/Hastings Corp.[3]

The real-world significance of product development activity by lead users has been explored in several careful empirical studies. These show lead users to be the actual developers of most commercially successful product innovations in some product categories (see Table 17.1).

Since problem-solving activity is an expense that will be undertaken only by those who can expect to gain from it, marketing researchers can expect lead users to engage in product development only when this course of action pays.[4] Otherwise they must content

TABLE 17.1 Empirical Data on the Source of Product Innovations

Study	Nature of Innovations and Sample Selection Criteria	n	Innovation Product Developed by:[a] Lead Users	Manu-facturers	Others
Knight	Computer innovations 1944–1962:				
	• systems reaching new performance high	143	25%	75%	
	• systems with radical structural innovations (level 1)	18	33	67	
Enos	Major petroleum processing innovations	7	43	14	43%[b]
Freeman	Chemical processes and process equipment available for license, 1967	810	70	30	
Berger	All engineering polymers developed in U.S. after 1955, with 10mm pounds produced in 1975	6	0	100	
Boyden	Chemical additives for plastics: all plasticizers and UV stabilizers developed after World War II for use with four major polymers	16	0	100	
Lionetta	All pultrusion-processing machinery innovations first introduced commercially 1940–1976, which offered users a major increment in functional utility	13	85	15	
von Hippel	Scientific instrument innovations:				
	• first of type (e.g., first NMR)	4	100	0	
	• major functional improvements	44	82	18	
	• minor functional improvements	63	70	30	

TABLE 17.1 *(continued)*

Study	Nature of Innovations and Sample Selection Criteria	n	Innovation Product Developed by:[a]		
			Lead Users	Manu-facturers	Others
von Hippel	Semiconductor and electronic subassembly manufacturing equipment:				
	• first of type used in commercial production	7	100	0	
	• major functional improvements	22	63	21	16[c]
	• minor functional improvements	20	59	29	12[c]
Peck	New product or production techniques described as advance in state of art by industry trade journals 1946–1957[d]				
	• in aluminum joining (w)	52	17	50	33
	• in aluminum finishing (x)	27	33	48	19
	• in aluminum fabricating (y)	76	30	49	21
	• in aluminum alloys (z)	39	3	79	18

[a]NA data excluded from percentage computations.
[b]Attribute to independent inventors/invention development companies.
[c]Attribute to joint user-manufacturer innovation projects.
[d]Data categories were translated from those used by Peck as follows:
Mfr. = Equipment manufacturer for (w,x,y); primary and secondary aluminum producer for (z).
User = End product manufacturer for (w,x,z); primary and secondary aluminum producers, commercial R&D companies, government labs, and foreign sources for (w); primary aluminum producers, commercial R&D companies, and individual inventor for (x); end product manufacturers, commercial R&D companies, government labs, and foreign sources for (y); independent fabricators, end product manufacturers, government labs, and foreign sources for (z).

The studies cited are:

K. E. Knight, "A Study of Technological Innovation: The Evolution of Digital Computers" (Ph.D. diss., Carnegie Institute of Technology, 1963). Data shown in Table 17.1 are from Knight's Appendix B, parts 2 and 3.
J. Enos, *Petroleum Progress and Profits* (Cambridge, Mass.: MIT Press, 1962).
C. Freeman, "Chemical Process Plant: Innovations and the World Market," *National Institute Economic Review*.
A. Berger, "Factors Influencing the Locus of Innovation Activity Leading to Scientific Instrument and Plastics Innovation" (S.M. thesis, MIT Sloan School of Management, 1975).
J. Boyden, "A Study of the Innovation Process in the Plastics Additives Industry" (S.M. thesis, MIT Sloan School of Management, 1976).
W. G. Lionetta, Jr., "Sources of Innovation within the Pultrusion Industry" (S.M. thesis, MIT Sloan School of Management, 1977).
E. von Hippel, "The Dominant Role of Users in the Scientific Instrument Innovation Process," *Research Policy* 5 (1976): 212–39.
E. von Hippel, "The Dominant Role of the User in Semiconductor and Electronic Subassembly Process Innovation," *IEEE Transactions on Engineering Management*, May 1977.
M. J. Peck, "Inventions in the Postwar American Aluminum Industry" in *The Rate and Direction of Inventive Activity: Economic and Social Factors*, a report of the National Bureau of Economic Research, New York (Princeton, N.J.: Princeton University Press, 1969), p. 279.

themselves with need data only.[5] Need data from lead users can be extraordinarily useful to marketing researchers, however, and we now focus on this issue.

Incorporating Lead Users into Marketing Research Methods

In essence, I propose that a simple substitution of lead users for average users in many of today's marketing research methods will allow marketing researchers to identify many potential new product opportunities that are invisible today. To illustrate why this is so, I will first outline a "typical" modern quantitative marketing research method—perceptual mapping—and will review how consumer data are gathered for use in it. Limitations on data collected from average consumers will next be pointed out, and, finally, the advantages gained from employing lead users in such methods will be discussed.

Method Limits—Absent Lead Users

Perceptual mapping is a quantitative marketing research tool that is often used today to assist in the identification of profitable new product opportunities. As the name implies, perceptual mapping shows in a quantitative way how a consumer perceives a given product or product type.[6] Consider, for example, the product category of personal cameras and, within this category, two specific cameras—the Kodak Disc Camera and a Nikon 35mm camera. Clearly, a consumer's global perceptions of these two cameras will be quite different, but how can we encode these different perceptions so that they can be compared and quantitatively analyzed? Perceptual mapping performs this task by expressing a consumer's global perception of personal cameras in terms of a number of attributes. If this list of attributes is complete, a consumer's perception of any particular camera can be expressed in terms of the amount of each attribute the consumer perceives it to contain—and the difference between any two cameras can be expressed as the difference between the attribute profiles of these two products. If we then factor analyze this attribute data, we may express consumer perceptions of the product being studied in terms of a few underlying dimensions on a "perceptual map." Finally, we may add preference information to a perceptual map by asking consumers to rate the importance to them of the various product attributes identified previously, and to express their preferences for products that offer them in varying amounts. Preference information can be added to the perceptual map generated earlier in terms of the product positioning that customers feel would be ideal (the "ideal point") or in terms of the market share that a product positioned at any given point on the map could be expected to garner.

Perceptual and preference mapping clearly provide powerful tools to the marketing research practitioner attempting to specify new products. They allow him or her to see the market share consequences of designing a new product to fit a given position on a perceptual map and suggest what attributes must be designed into the product to obtain any desired position. Furthermore, consumer data gathered on product concepts or prototypes can show whether proposed new products will in fact be perceived by consumers as intended. All this analytical power and possibility, however, can only potentially characterize new products or services accurately and completely if, first, a complete set of relevant product or service attributes is provided as input to the method and if, second, consumers accurately assess their perceptions and preferences regarding these. Let us therefore consider in greater detail methods for attribute generation and evaluation.

Two types of methods are used to generate product attributes for marketing research methods such as perceptual mapping: similarity-dissimilarity ranking and focus group methods. The similarity-dissimilarity method generates the underlying dimensions that consumers use to characterize a product category by inviting a sample of consumers to rate pairs of products that already exist in that category in terms of their similarity and dissimilarity. Thus, if cameras A and B are seen by consumers as very similar in terms of picture quality, ease of use, and other attributes they felt important in a personal camera, they would rank these two cameras as similar. If consumers felt the cameras were different in important ways, on the other hand, they would rank them as dissimilar. Note that the method assumes that the consumer is motivated to rank the pairs of products as similar or dissimilar because of differences in underlying product attributes, but the method does not require him or her to specify—or even be aware of—the particular attributes that are influencing the rankings. This task is performed later by the market analyst, who looks at the products judged similar by the consumer sample, contrasts them with the products judged different, and "identifies"—based on his of her personal knowledge of the product type in question, its function, the marketplace, the consumer— the underlying dimensions of the products that "must be" motivating the consumer judgments examined. The analyst's conclusions then become the attribute set assumed to characterize the product category.

The similarity-dissimilarity method clearly depends heavily on an analyst's qualitative ability to interpret the data and characterize the attributes of the cameras (or of the various brand names, advertising images, and so on associated with the cameras in the consumer's mind) that are causing the similarity-dissimilarity rankings obtained. But, in addition, there are some more explicit restrictions on the type of attributes that the method will identify. By its nature, the similarity-dissimilarity method can only identify attributes that *exist* in the products being compared, to *varying* degrees. Thus, if cameras are being compared and *all* in the set use identical film, the attributes of this film would not be contained in the set identified by the method. Also, if *none* of the cameras being compared had a particular feature—for example, instant developing—then this attribute would not appear in the set. (The method would have been blind to instant developing as a possibly useful camera attribute prior to Edwin Land's invention of the Polaroid camera.) On the other hand, ease of focusing, an attribute that does differ between cameras, would be perceivable.

The second type of method used to generate product attributes for perceptual mapping and similar quantitative techniques involves qualitative interactions—primarily focus groups—with consumers familiar with the product category under study. Typically, a market research firm will assemble a group of consumers of a type of product under study, for instance, amateur photographers in the instance of "personal" 35mm cameras. These consumers participate in a discussion of perhaps two hours' duration, on a topic set by a group leader employed by the market research firm. The topic of the focus group may be narrow or broad, according to the interests of the market analysts conducting the research. Thus, in the instance of 35mm personal cameras, the topic may be as narrow as "aspects of 35mm cameras of X type" or as broad as "the photographic experience as you see it." The ensuing discussion is typed and transcribed. Market researchers then study the transcript and identify what they feel to be the critical attributes of the product type according to the group discussion.

Clearly, this and related qualitative techniques (such as "in-depth interviews," in which analysts hold discussions similar to those carried out in focus groups, but with only one interviewee at a session) depend heavily on the qualitative ability of the analyst to accurately abstract the attributes consumers feel important in products from interview data. Just as clearly, however, the focus group technique need not be limited only to identifying attributes already present in existing products—as was the case with the similarity-dissimilarity method discussed earlier. A topic that extends the boundaries of discussion beyond a given product to a larger framework, for example, could identify attributes not present in any extant product in a category under study. Thus, the broad topic mentioned earlier—"the photographic experience as you see it"—embraces the development process as well as use of the camera. If discussion of the topic brought out consumer dissatisfaction with the time lag between picture taking and receipt of the finished photograph, the analyst would be in possession of the same information that reportedly induced Land to conceive of the instant camera. Just as Land did, that is, the perceptive analyst would be in a position to ask whether the attribute of film development and printing—not then an attribute of any existing camera—could be incorporated into the camera.

How likely is it that an analyst will take this creative step? Or, more generally, how likely is it that the focus group method will be used to identify attributes not present in extant products of the type being studied, much less a complete list of all relevant attributes? The method contains no mechanism to encourage this outcome, and discussions with some practitioners indicate that in current practice, identification of *any* novel attribute is unlikely.

In sum, we see that it is impossible to identify desirable product attributes not present in existing products via similarity-dissimilarity ranking methods that elicit consumer perceptions of existing products. We have also seen that it is possible in principle—but not likely and not commonly done in practice—to identify novel product attributes through analysis of focus-group discussions. The fact that these attribute generation techniques provide the attributes used in marketing research techniques such as perceptual mapping has the practical effect of restricting such techniques to the identification of product opportunities that contain all or a subset of the attributes contained in existing products, although perhaps in different proportions. This in turn means that many potentially profitable new product opportunities—those containing novel attributes—are currently not identified.[7]

Advantages of Lead Users

Scholars who develop new marketing research techniques are well aware of the missing attribute problem, and have devised some methods to address it. Thus, G. L. Urban and J. R. Hauser point out that consumers identifying and evaluating product attributes may usefully be given new product concepts as well as existing products to consider.[8] If these new product concepts (which they call stretcher concepts) contain novel attributes, the participating consumers have an opportunity to identify these. Next, a number of creativity-enhancing methods such as synectics have been devised to aid in the development of new product concepts.[9] And, finally, some techniques such as Kelley's Repertory Grid have been developed to somewhat systematize and improve the process by which consumers identify and evaluate the attributes of products and product concepts.

Although the methods and method types just noted are very useful, they do not address an underlying difficulty that hinders accurate consumer identification of novel product attributes and the evolution of these or of novel product concepts containing them. This difficulty is that consumers have only a poor *ability* to identify (accurately characterize) or accurately evaluate product attributes they have not experienced in real life. This is so because the marketing researcher who asks a consumer to identify, evaluate the importance of, or express preference regarding product attributes the consumer has not experienced in real life is posing a difficult problem-solving task to an individual whose mind-set militates *against* performing the task in a creative way.

First, consider that individual products are only components in a larger usage pattern that may involve many products. (For example, a toothbrush is used in conjunction with and must be compatible with toothpaste. Similarly, a computer's characteristics must be compatible with the type of problems being solved, the types of software being used, and so forth.) As a consequence, a change in one component in a multiproduct usage pattern can change the need specification for some or all other products involved in that pattern. Thus, the development of new tooth powders might necessitate a responsive change in the need for toothbrushes. And, similarly, a change in the operating characteristics of a computer will mandate related changes in the need specifications for the software used with that computer.

Next, consider that consumers who are asked to evaluate the impact of, for example, making a computer inexpensive and easy to use (e.g., the personal computer) must first identify *which* of their existing usage patterns it would make sense to incorporate the personal computer in, and how they would evaluate its role in these patterns. Next, these consumers must identify and evaluate the new (to them) usage patterns the personal computer makes possible for the first time. Finally, since substitutes exist for many of the usage patterns they have been considering (e.g., there are many forms of entertainment available, in addition to computer games), they must estimate how the new possibilities presented by the personal computer will compete (or fail to compete) with their existing options.

The problem-solving task just described is clearly a very difficult one. Conceivably some could solve it, but studies of problem solving suggest that average users of existing products—the type of consumer evaluators usually chosen—are poorly situated to perform this task well.[10] In essence, a number of studies strongly show that intimate familiarity with existing product attributes and uses interferes with the ability to conceive of novel attributes and uses when invited to do so. Thus, experimental subjects, being familiar with pliers as a tool for holding, find it difficult to solve problems requiring them to use pliers in some other way.[11] Furthermore, the more recently objects or problem-solving strategies have been used in a familiar way, the more difficult subjects find it to employ them in a novel way.[12] In sum, average users have a poor ability to identify novel product attributes accurately because they do not have real-world experience with them.

But *lead users* are *well* positioned by the very same reasoning: They have real-world experience with the needs that future profitable products must serve and with attributes they must contain. Clearly, therefore, systematic utilization of lead user data in marketing research will allow practitioners to identify profitable new product opportunities, attributes, and concepts that are invisible today. What must be done to achieve this promise? Primarily, as I have shown, the task for marketing research is to identify lead users. Once identified, they can participate in existing marketing research methods in familiar ways. And although identification of lead users is a novel task for market researchers, experience shows it is not a difficult one. I therefore look forward to—and encourage—the increasingly routine application of the lead user concept by marketing research practitioners in the 1980s.

CHAPTER 18

Strategies for Marketing the New Technologies: Commentary

Stephan H. Haeckel

International Business Machines

In thinking about the marketing of present and future information technologies, it is helpful to keep in mind that we are dealing with *derived* demands. The primary demand, of course, is for information: whether it be in the form of data, text, audio, or image; whether it be for education, entertainment, investment or business decision making, monitoring a patient, or automating a factory.

Everyone knows that knowledge is power, and that data is an asset; many are familiar with Daniel Bell's thesis that codified information and knowledge are replacing capital and energy as the primary economic resources. But after making the obligatory curtsy to the primary role of information, most authors hurry on to deal at length with the hardware, as though the future could be divined by gazing long enough into an array of silicon gates. Apparently, certain firms also suffer from hardware fixation. John Cady refers to a *Forbes* article that notes that some "companies are offering the technology simply because it's exciting." The prognosis for those companies is not good.

Why this almost exclusive focus on the technology? Why not on its *use*? We don't market technology, after all; we market its application. And its application is to get information from those who have it to those who need it, processing and transforming it to add value wherever we can along the way. Yet market research is still done in terms of the demand for computers, terminals, videotex systems, or software, rather than in terms of the demand for the information to which they provide access. Theodore Levitt makes an interesting observation that may provide a clue to why this is the case: "We do not what's important, but what's amenable to our technologies of inquiry, to the data that are easily at hand."

Technology is tangible. It can be counted and classified. But information? How do you deal with a resource the demand for which is infinite and the supply inexhaustible—at least in terms of quantity? How can you measure it, when its value is situational? How can you set up a double-entry bookkeeping system for an asset that is retained after being sold?

Pending the development of an economic value theory for information, the default metrics are those of the capital-centered economy: We add up the net amount of other resources that are conserved when the "right" information is available and acted upon under the "right" circumstances. Getting closer to economic order quantities, reducing inventories, and cutting out float are examples of this kind of valuation. This is the way information technology has been justified for three decades. It has the merit of being conservative, but it also has the drawback of most indirect measurements: certain dimensions of value are simply not counted.

According to Daniel Bell, our economy will be centered around a new resource. If so, we will require no less than a new economics, and from marketing theorists we will require the principles upon which to formulate marketing strategies. In the case of the information technology industry, these principles must take certain factors into consideration:

- an underlying technology whose unit costs will continue to spiral downward at 20 to 30 percent per year over the next decade;
- a mushrooming user community that understands, and takes advantage of, only a fraction of the function and power of the tools provided; and
- the conflicts inherent in the high values associated with both access to and privacy of integrated information.

It is hard to think of a more important area for conceptual thinking and fundamental academic research in the information age than the development of an economic value theory for information, for it would provide a direct way to rationalize and justify the technology that stores, communicates, and transforms it. This would allow the providers of information technology to base their plans and forecasts on an understanding of the market's primary need, as opposed to its derived need.

John Cady identifies the challenge of marketing new technologies as one of defining the opportunity. He asserts that "defining the opportunity has two components: developing the technology and developing the market" and that "to develop the technology requires that the marketer determine its current limits of function and performance and identify the applications actually and potentially best suited to it." The latter task is extraordinarily difficult for most new technologies, given the rapid rate at which technology tends to evolve in its early stages, and the fact that usable systems comprise many parallel and interdependent technologies. The job is impossible for some. Impossible at the outset, at least, because there is no customer "literacy" with the technology at that time. Aldous Huxley, among others, has noted that certain thoughts are unthinkable without a requisite literacy. Newton, for example, could not think thoughts that Einstein could, because Newton did not have the required literacy in quantum mechanics.

This observation explains the famous and wildly understated forecasts of total demand for computers in the early 1950s. It, and our experience of the last thirty years with the applications of information-processing technology, suggest an alternate way of mapping the stages of technology assimilation (see Figure 18.1).

Figure 18.1 Stages of Technology Assimilation, Application Evolution

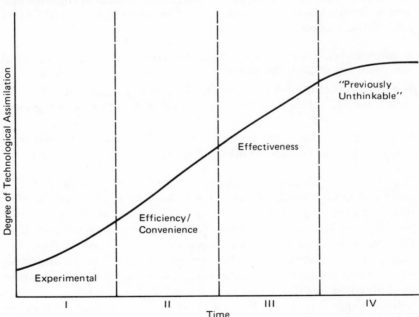

Note: Although the S curve probably applies to the demand function for new technologies as well, different technologies will experience maximum growth in different stages: the programmable calculator in Stage II, for example, and the personal computer in Stage III or IV.

TABLE 18.1 Examples of Application Categories for Selected Technologies

Technology	Stage II Efficiency/ Convenience	Stage III Effectiveness	Stage IV "Previously Unthinkable"
General purpose computer	Payroll billing Accounts receivable	Inventory mgmt. Airline reservations	Expert systems
Microcomputer	Word processing Backgammon	Networking VisiCalc Graphics	Intelligent games
	Drill and practice	Remedial instruction	New pedagogies
Videodisc	Movies	Catalogs Training sys. Encyclopedias	Games New pedagogies
Videotex	Stock quotes News	Teleshopping Telebanking	Telemedicine Telemusic

Stage I: *Experimental Applications.* This stage is roughly equivalent to Cady's "curiosity" stage, and McFarlan and McKenney's first phase.[1] In the mid-1950s it was characterized by prototype scientific application development, and in the early 1970s, by hobbyists building personal computers from kits.

Stage II: *Efficiency/Convenience Applications.* In this stage the technology is employed to do essentially the same work that was being done before, but at less cost or more conveniently. Payroll and automated inventory record-keeping systems in the late 1950s and word processing on personal computers in the early 1980s are examples. The distinction between efficiency and convenience is made in recognition of the fact that when the cost of a usable package of the new technology falls sufficiently to make its acquisition discretionary, there is no need for financial cost-benefit justifications.

Stage III: *Effectiveness Applications.* In this stage, old problems are addressed in new ways, with better results. Inventory management systems are evolved to deal with service levels, economic order quantities, and smoothing factors. Airline reservations systems expand from automatic booking to incorporate scheduling algorithms and package promotions. Personal computer networking, providing timely access to other experts and information bases, is a current example.

Stage IV: *"Previously Unthinkable" Applications.* In this stage, with the required literacy attained, truly innovative exploitation of the technology occurs. Inventory management systems are extended to provide decisions support systems; for example, what would a 20 percent reduction in inventory do to service levels? Flight simulators, "expert systems" to help diagnose pulmonary disease, and adventure games on personal computers are current examples. Weather-forecasting models, artificial intelligence applications, and new pedagogies are potential future examples.

This mapping has the strategic advantage of being sequential, and therefore of incorporating the dimension of time into marketing strategies. Early in the cycle, strategies should focus on identifying cost and expense-reduction applications. For products priced below the discretionary level, it will be important to identify meaningful uses of the product, and to ensure that the user's expectation levels are appropriately set and met. Selling the technology "because it is exciting" risks discouraging initial buyers from moving into the next stage. Reports of personal computers sitting unused in schools and collecting dust in executive offices are worrisome because of the potential backlash from disenchanted customers who don't know what to do with them.

Later on, marketing strategies involve work with users who, as von Hippel points out, will make new opportunities "visible," or at least "thinkable." This is accompanied by programs to disseminate the cutting-edge applications as rapidly as possible to the next tier of customers. IBM has found joint studies with customers to specify and develop major new application systems to be extremely valuable. Once successfully implemented, complex applications are disseminated through application transfer teams, who specialize in helping new customers install the new systems as expeditiously as possible.

Information technology can be viewed as a delivery vehicle for processing, storing, and distributing information. In order to function in this way, as Professors Quelch and Yip point out, hardware, software, and service components have to be coordinated so that they constitute a coherent information-provider to information-user system. Such a system, for lack of a better term, I call an information infrastructure.

The invention of the steam engine is often associated with the advent of the industrial revolution. But neither the steam engine nor the locomotive was sufficient to realize the industrial age. Not until railroad tracks were laid did the transportation infrastructure upon which the industrial economy was dependent come into being. It is worth mentioning that all the track had to be the same gauge in order for it to function as an infrastructure. Similarly, not until we have "laid the tracks" of an information infrastructure will we have the basis for realizing an information economy.

It is often assumed that the communications infrastructure serves that purpose, and it is certainly true that a communications network is a necessary ingredient. But not a sufficient one. Suppose you are a physician who needs to consult a specialist in Helsinki. The communications infrastructure will put you in touch with her, assuming that the phone jacks, dialing conventions, busy-ring conventions, and so on are of the right "gauge," and that you know the phone number. At this point, the information infrastructure takes over. First, you had better speak Finnish, or she English, or both of you German. Then you will have to identify yourself; establish your credentials and claim on the information you seek from her; and satisfy yourself that you have the right person on the other end of the line. Finally, you must both be adequately educated on the subject matter. All of the above is necessary before an exchange of information can take place.

If instead of you and the good Finnish doctor, two applications programs running in two computers have been linked together by the communications infrastructure, then the functions of the information infrastructure will have to be assumed by programming. This may not be too difficult for a single conversation, but it becomes extraordinarily complex when you attempt to generalize the information infrastructure functions to embrace conversations between many professionals in several disciplines, speaking a large number of different languages.

This "anybody to anybody in any language on any subject" capability can only be achieved if the programming to accomplish it is designed in advance to accommodate such generality. As one might imagine, the selection of the architect is a crucial decision: The selection determines the utility, longevity, and economics of the information network "house" customers will be living in for a long time to come. And it has to be designed to facilitate eventual information exchange with other houses, which, of course, is greatly simplified if the neighbors happen to have chosen the same architect.

Many large firms have made the architectural decision for their enterprise information infrastructure. Some of them now wish to expedite the rate at which the infrastructure permeates their organization. One promising way of doing this is to have the infrastructure architecture accommodate and support a large number of "local area" data communication networks situated in various buildings or departments. Local area networks provide for the exchange of data between a variety of local devices, but do not typically perform the functions of the information infrastructure described above. Incorporating them into the information infrastructure is greatly facilitated if they are designed from the start with this in mind.

I've almost exhausted the possibilities of my analogy, and still haven't covered additional complexities such as the need to handle pictures, text, and voice messages, as well as data. But it should be obvious that matters can easily get out of hand if the local area network, the telephone network, and the facsimile network are not architecturally encompassed by the enterprise's information network. Voice, text, image, and data are all information, but in different media. Each has different functional, capacity, and performance demands, which the information infrastructure must be designed to accommodate.

The *enterprise* information infrastructure must do more than encompass and support substructures such as multiple media networks, department-level information systems, and functional information systems. It should also provide for information exchange with the information infrastructures of other enterprises at the application-to-application level of generality. In addition to intraenterprise and interenterprise infrastructures, there remains the requirement of providing a *residential* information infrastructure that ties individual homes into the infrastructures of information and transaction providers. This will enable the end-to-end transactions (shop-at-home, bank-at-home, learn-at-home) of the information age. To accomplish this, some sort of bridge, or "gateway," to the residential infrastructure must be incorporated into the design of the information provider's system. Videotex is a promising technology for providing residential information infrastructures. (It also has considerable potential for use within an enterprise—yet another requirement for our overworked architect to incorporate into the grand design.)

It can be argued that the alliances and cooperation described as necessary by Professors Quelch and Yip are directly related to the fact that a sufficiently general residential information infrastructure does not exist. Therefore, a substantial amount of trade-off and cooperation is needed in order to create one, or several. In Europe, where several governments have defined and established national videotex infrastructures, the "domesticated market" phenomenon is apparently less necessary. In the United States, major alliances are taking shape to deliver services of information providers. The absence of technical standards is producing either fragmented,

TABLE 18.2 Seven Strategic Transitions

	1970s	*1990s*
Primary resource	Hardware	Information
Primary acquirer	DP executive	Individuals
Vendor differentiation	Products	Offerings
Strategic architecture	Hardware	Infrastructure
Fastest growth	Equipment	Services
Future growth	On-line data bases	Noncoded
Primary inhibitors	Hardware cost	Productivity
	Comm. cost	Regulation/public
	Complexity	policy
		Standards
		Ease of use
		Valuation schemes
		Social impacts
		Complexity

noncompatible offerings or higher prices, as manufacturers attempt to support multiple protocols.

Final approval of the AT&T proposed North American Presentation Level Protocol Syntax (NAPLPS), which is supported by the American National Standards Institute, the Electronic Industries Association, and the Canadian Standards Association, could occur as early as this fall. If so, it would go a long way (but not all the way) toward providing the basis for fewer, more general videotex infrastructure architectures in the United States.

The information age is predicated on the centrality of codified information as a resource. Access to, and exploitation of, that resource throughout society requires the establishment of an appropriate information infrastructure, which includes, but is much more than, a communications infrastructure.

For those involved in the management of information and information technology, the 1980s promise to be years of major transition—transition in the sense that several strategic questions will receive different answers in the 1990s from those accepted in the 1970s (see Table 18.2). The marketing strategies of technology providers must enable customers to manage this transition successfully. To satisfy the requirement, the strategies should

• be founded on a sound understanding and estimate of customer information needs;

- be tuned to the application sequence implicit in the staged assimilation of the technologies that will be offered; and
- encourage and facilitate the creation, maintenance, and extension of information infrastructures.

We will benefit greatly from academic research that extends our understanding of how to do any of these better—but most especially, the first. From industry will emerge the Jay Goulds, J. P. Morgans, Henry Bessemers, Henry Fords, and Andrew Carnegies of the information age; from academia must emerge the Adam Smiths, David Ricardos, and Joseph Schumpeters.

PART FIVE

Some Possible Futures

CHAPTER 19

Computer-Aided Decision Making for Strategic Business Portfolio Decisions

V. Srinivasan
Stanford University Graduate School
of Business

The new information technologies that have evolved during the late 1970s and the early 1980s have brought about substantial improvements in the cost and speed of processing information. The managerial decision-making environment is bound to be favorably influenced by the new technologies. It is now much easier to conduct "what if" types of computer-aided analyses of alternative decisions under different scenarios of the market and the competition, and to examine the sensitivity of the outcome to uncertainties regarding key inputs. The improved managerial interface through computer graphics and user-friendly software, and the additional confidentiality provided by personal computers are likely to enhance the adoption of the new technology for managerial decision making.

Computer-aided decision making offers several advantages. First, by transferring cumbersome and time-consuming evaluations to the computer, managers can give greater attention to the more qualitative issues involved in a decision. Second, a mathematical model, even if it is a simple accounting equation, organizes managerial thinking and minimizes the chances of mistakenly omitting important aspects of the problem. Finally, there is a substantial amount of empirical evidence stating that even simple models perform better than "clinical" decision making.[1] Decision makers are good at identifying the important aspects of a problem and at providing information on various components of the problem; but they perform less effectively than simple models when it comes to aggregating the information.[2] Thus, computer-aided decision making offers the ability to combine the best of both worlds by gathering information on components of the problem from the manager and by using the computer to combine the information. An important disadvantage of computer-aided decision making is that it may increase the emphasis placed on quantitative information more than may be appropriate under the circumstances.

Computer-aided decision making is gaining increased acceptance. VisiCalc, the electronic spreadsheet for financial planning, is the best-selling piece of software (other than games) ever produced for a personal computer.[3] Decision support systems have been successfully used in many tactical marketing decision-making situations.[4] Given the increased level of business activity in acquisitions, mergers, and divestitures and a greater tendency for firms to diversify, the time seems to be right for a computer-aided analysis of broader strategic decisions.[5] After reviewing the general concepts and previous approaches in the area of business portfolio analysis, I shall describe a decision support system called STRATPORT (for STRATegic PORTfolio planning) and discuss some important extensions to improve its implementability and validity.

Business Portfolio Analysis

For planning purposes it is useful to conceptualize a firm as consisting of a portfolio of business units. A business unit is usually defined as a unit of the firm with a distinct product line that serves a well-defined market. The overall philosophy of business portfolio analysis is to conceptualize the firm as a holding company of many business units. The operations of the firm are decentralized to the business units. Allocation of resources, which is believed to be key to the profitability and survival of the firm, is centralized. Synergistic effects across the business units are assumed to be largely unaffected by the strategies pursued by the different business units.

The business portfolio analysis approaches of General Electric/ McKinsey, Boston Consulting Group, Arthur D. Little, and Royal Dutch Shell share the broad overall philosophy outlined above. They difffer in the methods used to classify business units into homogeneous groups and in the resulting strategy prescriptions for business units in each homogeneous group.[6] For instance, in the popular Boston Consulting Group (BCG) approach, business units are classified on the basis of relative market share and market growth into Stars, Cash Cows, Question Marks, and Dogs.[7] Cash Cows correspond to business units with high relative market share (and hence, increased profitability because of "experience [curve] effects") and low market growth (and hence, greater market stability and low needs for financial investment), and produce an excess cash flow for the firm. The excess cash can be used to invest in Stars (high relative market share, high growth) or to improve the market position of Question Marks (low relative market share, high growth.)

The limitations of business portfolio analysis have been discussed by several authors.[8] The delineation of the firm into business units consistent with organizational structure but with few cost or marketing interdependencies is a difficult task. The BCG approach assumes that two business units with the same values for relative market share and market growth will have identical cash flow patterns. This assumption is untenable given the large industry differences observed in the relationships between strategic variables and profitability in the PIMS (profit impact of marketing strategies) studies.[9] The critical distinctions between cash flow and profit, and between relative and absolute profitability, are not made in the analysis. Furthermore, the roles of external financing and new business units are unclear in the growth-share matrix. Finally, differential risks across the business units are not taken into account in the analysis.

Given the limitations of business portfolio analysis, the convenient tendency is to abandon it.[10] But that is "throwing the baby out with the bathwater." The important relationship between market share and profitability is one of the few robust empirical results in the marketing strategy area demonstrated in the PIMS studies.[11] The same results are found in the Federal Trade Commission's line of business and other studies.[12] Experience curve effects have been repeatedly demonstrated in empirical studies.[13] The STRATPORT decision support system presented below utilizes these empirical findings in its design, yet provides for considerable flexibility in describing the environment for each business unit rather than being limited only to relationships between profitability, market share, and market growth.

The STRATPORT Decision Support System

STRATPORT provides computer-aided decision support for business portfolio analysis and as such, embraces the broad overall philosophy of centralized resource allocation for the firm's business units.[14] The difficult problem of delineating the firm into business units is present in STRATPORT as in the other approaches. Consequently, it is important to take into account the implications of the assumed business unit definition in interpreting the outcomes of the analysis.

STRATPORT conceptualizes strategies in terms of market share objectives to be achieved in each of the business units in the portfolio. It evaluates strategies in terms of both the short-term cash requirements needed to accomplish the strategy and the impacts on (long-term) net present value of the after-tax cash flows (i.e., the impact on shareholder value).[15]

The STRATPORT decision support system consists of a detailed mathematical model linking the strategic objectives to several intermediate financial quantities such as marketing investments, costs, revenues, capacity expenditures, and working capital. These intermediate financial quantities are, in turn, aggregated to yield short-term cash requirement and long-term profitability. STRATPORT uses empirical data whenever they are available. For components of the model for which empirical data are unavailable, subjective judgments of managers are obtained.

As a decision support system, STRATPORT has substantial input-output capabilities. It is easy to conduct "what if" analyses; given strategic objectives, STRATPORT can readily evaluate the bottom-line implications. It is easy to conduct sensitivity analyses, that is, examine the changes in outputs as some parameters of the system, such as the slope of the experience curve and the cost of gaining market share, are modified. STRATPORT has an optimization phase that generates the strategy that maximizes net present value for any given limit on short-term cash requirement. By repeatedly conducting such analyses for different levels of short-term cash limit, one can evaluate the long-term value of raising additional debt or equity (see Figure 19.1). The "optimal" strategies identified by STRATPORT, as well as any other proposed strategies, have to be examined on the basis of qualitative aspects that have not been considered in the computer-aided analysis. In this sense, the optimization phase can be viewed mainly as an idea generator.

The most important difference between STRATPORT and previous approaches to business portfolio analysis is that while the previous approaches are qualitative in nature, STRATPORT is a quantitative decision aid, that is, it gives bottom-line implications of proposed strategies. Other distinctions that overcome many limitations of the previous approaches are the following:

Figure 19.1 Net Present Value from Additional Debt/Equity

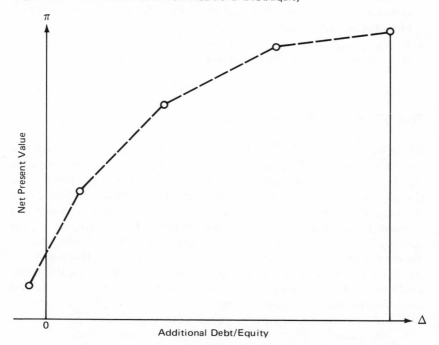

Source: Based on J. C. Larreche and V. Srinivasan, "STRATPORT: A Model for the Evaluation and Formulation of Business Portfolio Strategies," *Management Science* 28 (1982):996. Reprinted by permission of the Institute of Management Sciences, Providence, Rhode Island.

- Explicit consideration is given to marketing investments, costs, revenues, capacity expenditures, and working capital. Since all parameters are unit specific, there is considerable flexibility in describing the environment faced by a business unit.
- Acquisitions (new business units) and divestitures are readily handled in the framework. For instance, to examine the value of a new business unit, two analyses of the business portfolio need to be made, one with the new business unit, and one without. The analysis with the new business unit proceeds after subtracting the acquisition price from the short-term cash flow limit.
- The role of external financing is captured by examining the impact of changes in the short-term net cash flow limit.
- The explicit quantification of financial quantities avoids the confusion in previous approaches between relative and absolute

profitability; and between cash flows and profits. All financial quantities are discounted and expressed in present value terms after taking tax effects into account.

- Explicit consideration of differential risks across the business units is given as per the capital-asset pricing model.[16]

The STRATPORT Framework

STRATPORT considers a planning period and a postplanning period. The changes in market shares (increases and decreases) for the different business units are assumed to be accomplished during the planning period, which will typically last from two to five years, depending on the industries involved. The postplanning period is included mainly to capture the long-term impact of the strategies accomplished during the planning period. For this reason, market shares are treated as if they remained constant during the postplanning period. Typically, the postplanning period will last from five to fifteen years. The cash flow requirements are evaluated over the planning period, whereas the (long-term) net present value is evaluated over both planning and postplanning periods.

As illustrated in Figure 19.2, there is a planning period of T years and a postplanning period of S-T years. (The figure is not drawn to scale; T is usually only a small fraction of S.) Note that market share evolves from its initial value m_0 to the strategic goal m_T at the end of the planning period, and stays at m_T during the postplanning period. (The market share m_T may be larger than, equal to, or smaller than m_0.) The shape of the curve describing the evolution of market share over the planning period is under user control. The user is asked to estimate the proportion of the total market share change $(m_T - m_0)$ that will be realized at the midpoint of the planning period. For a firm with a business unit in the electronics industry and another in heavy metals, one would expect a smaller initial rate of change for the business unit in the heavy metals industry. Consequently, that business unit's proportion of market share change by the midpoint of the planning period will be smaller.

The different intermediate financial quantities are aggregated through the accounting equations at the bottom of the figure to lead to the short-term cash flow need and the long-term profit. (For simplicity of exposition, net present value is replaced by its undiscounted counterpart, i.e., long-term profit, and tax effects are not considered.) Given the strategic importance of marketing, the expenditures needed to achieve and maintain market share goals are

Figure 19.2 Components of Long-Term Profit and Short-Term Cash Flow Need for a Single Business Unit

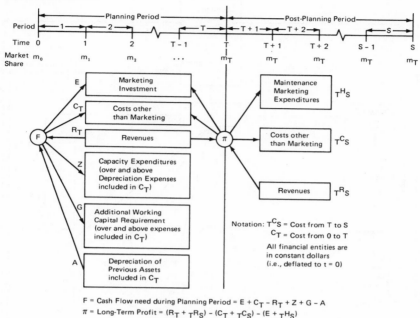

F = Cash Flow need during Planning Period = $E + C_T - R_T + Z + G - A$

π = Long-Term Profit = $(R_T + {}_TR_S) - (C_T + {}_TC_S) - (E + {}_TH_S)$

Source: From J. C. Larreche and V. Srinivasan, "STRATPORT: A Model for the Evaluation and Formulation of Business Portfolio Strategies," *Management Science* 28 (1982):982. Reprinted by permission of the Institute of Management Sciences, Providence, Rhode Island.

considered separately from all other costs. Capacity costs are included under the costs C in the form of depreciation expenses. To compute the cash flow during the planning period, one needs to take into account the total capacity expenditures, not merely the apportioned depreciation expenses. The quantity Z incorporates the difference between capacity expenditure and depreciation expense. The additional working capital G and the depreciation of previous assets A are similarly included to incorporate the difference between expenditure and expense.

Figure 19.3 presents in skeleton form the structure of the STRATPORT model. (The letters A through E in the figure refer to key relationships to be described subsequently using Figure 19.4.) To accomplish the market share goal, marketing investment is needed during the planning period. To maintain the market share during the postplanning period, marketing maintenance expenditures are needed. The market size, that is, the industry sales volumes, for years 1, 2, . . . , S, presumably obtained through standard forecasting procedures, are exogenous inputs to STRAT-

Figure 19.3 Structure of STRATPORT for a Single Business Unit

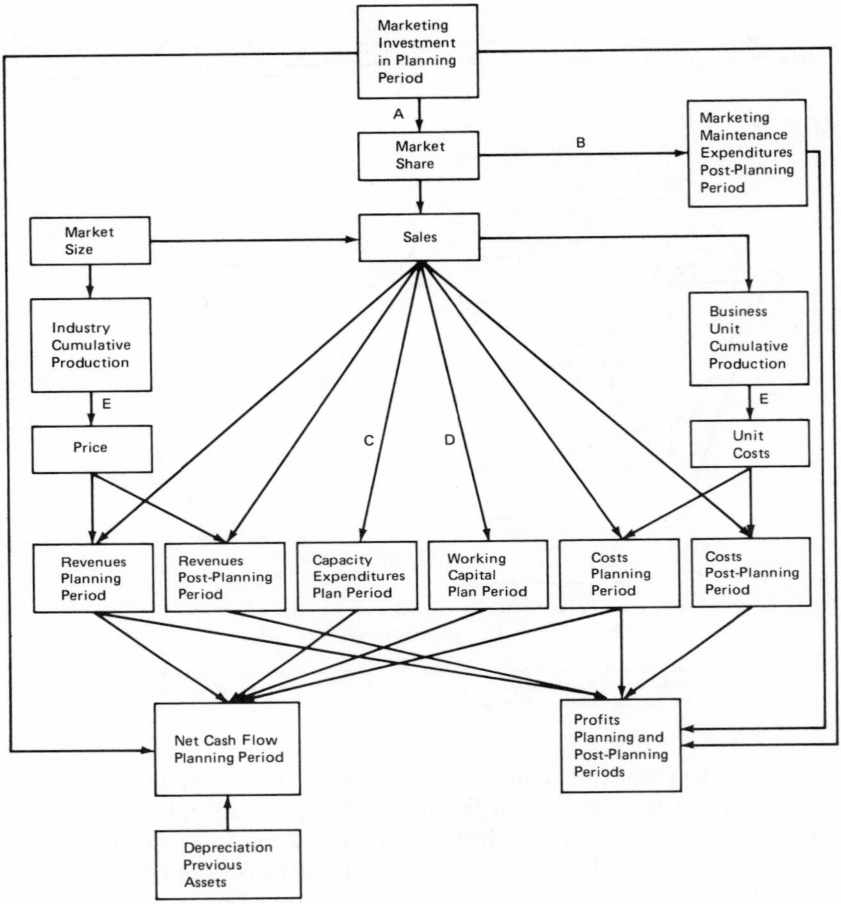

Source: From J. C. Larreche and V. Srinivasan, "STRATPORT: A Decision Support System for Strategic Planning," *Journal of Marketing* 45 (Fall 1981):45. Reprinted by permission of the American Marketing Association, Chicago.

Note: The diagram as drawn assumes no spillover effects of one firm's experience on another firm's cost. If spillover effects are present, there will be an additional arrow from Industry Cumulative Production to Costs.

PORT. (The potential changes in industry sales volume as a result of the strategy pursued in the business unit can be incorporated by an iterative application of STRATPORT.) By multiplying market share and industry sales, the business unit's sales can be computed. Unit costs (in inflation-adjusted dollars) are modeled through the experience curve as a function of both the firm's own experience (that is, cumulative production in the business unit) and industry experience (that is, cumulative production in the industry). The

Figure 19.4 Main Functional Relationships

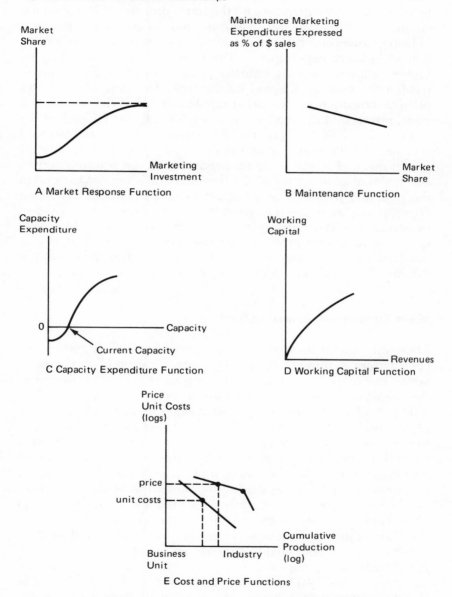

A Market Response Function

B Maintenance Function

C Capacity Expenditure Function

D Working Capital Function

E Cost and Price Functions

Source: From J. C. Larreche and V. Srinivasan, "STRATPORT: A Decision Support System for Strategic Planning," *Journal of Marketing* 45 (Fall 1981):46. Reprinted by permission of the American Marketing Association, Chicago.

latter term is included to take into account potential "spillover effects" of industry experience on the firm's unit cost.[17] Based on the empirical studies done by the Boston Consulting Group and others, industry price (in inflation-adjusted dollars) is modeled as a function of industry experience.[18] The price set by the firm may be higher or lower than the industry price, depending on the price-positioning strategy adopted by the firm. The ratio of the firm's price to industry price is another input to STRATPORT. Given unit costs, prices, and the business unit's sales volumes for each of the years 1, 2, . . . , S, STRATPORT computes the total costs and revenues for the planning and postplanning periods. Capacity expenditures and working capital needs during the planning period are modeled as functions of the business unit's sales at the end of the planning period. These various financial quantities are then appropriately aggregated to yield the short-term cash flow needed to accomplish the strategy in the business unit and the corresponding long-term profit. By aggregating these two bottom-line numbers over the business units, the corresponding overall implications of the portfolio strategy can be determined.

Main Functional Relationships

There are several main functional relationships (see Figure 19.4). (The letters A through E in this figure correspond to the same letters in Figure 19.3.) The market response function (A) describes the relationship between marketing investment during the planning period and the resulting market share at the end of the planning period. Following a procedure proposed by J. D. C. Little, this function is calibrated from four managerial inputs: (1) the market share that would result if no marketing investment is made; (2) the maximum market share resulting from an unlimited marketing investment; (3) the current market share and the marketing investment needed to maintain it; and (4) the expected market share for a 50 percent increase in marketing investment over that given under (3).[19] To supply the last one, the manager is encouraged to think about the best tactics (acquisition of small competitors, new product introductions, improvements in product quality, advertising and personal selling) to achieve the maximum effect for the additional investment, taking into account likely competitive reactions.

The maintenance function (B) indicates the marketing effort needed to maintain market share during the postplanning period. The downward sloping curve indicates that scale economies are present in marketing expenditures. This function is also calibrated using subjective managerial judgment. The capacity expenditure function (C) can usually be estimated from engineering cost estimates. Similarly, the working capital function (D) can usually be estimated from past financial records.

The behavior of (inflation-adjusted) price is described as a function of industry cumulative production (E). In this particular case, the curve is kinked to indicate that a period of rapid price decline (shake-out) is expected to follow the maintenance of a price umbrella. This curve may be estimated from past data or based on subjective judgments of how price is likely to evolve in the future, or both.

The behavior of (inflation-adjusted) unit cost is also seen here (E) as a function of cumulative production in the business unit. As indicated earlier, a more realistic formulation should take into account the possibility of spillovers, that is, the experience of one firm partly spills over to other firms. Consequently, one may model unit costs as a function of the cumulative production in both the business unit and the industry.[20] Assuming that the business unit has been in production for a long enough time, the spillover coefficient and the experience curve parameter can be estimated from past data.[21]

Using STRATPORT

In addition to obtaining from STRATPORT the bottom-line implications, all strategies, whether they be status quo or proposals made by management or generated by the optimization phase, need to be evaluated on qualitative dimensions not taken into account in the STRATPORT analysis, for example, the flexibility provided by the strategy under alternative scenarios. The promising strategies that remain need to be examined in detail for their robustness as the input paramaters are changed. One of the biggest advantages of a decision support system is the relative ease with which such sensitivity analyses can be carried out.

Large, multidivisional firms do carry out business portfolio analyses; in fact, a significant proportion of the management consulting business is of this nature. But there is also a substantial reluctance to carry out such analysis because of political considerations. Undertaking such a broad-based analysis usually requires the cooperation of most top managers, some of whose jobs may well be threatened by such an analysis. Thus, it is worthwhile to think of alternative methods that reap nearly the same benefits as business portfolio analysis, but are implementationally simpler.

A simpler method to implement can be devised by using traditional capital budget approval procedures. Let us assume that corporate approval requires that any strategic proposal from a business unit contain a net present value financial analysis. The STRATPORT analysis conducted at the business unit level (not at the portfolio level) would be useful for this purpose. In order to obtain nearly the same results as those obtained in a full-blown business portfolio analysis, two important modifications need to be made in the way financial calculations are done at the business unit level. First, the discount rate to be used by a business unit is specified at the corporate level as the sum of a base discount rate and a risk factor unique to the business unit. The base discount rate would be a weighted combination of the required rate of return on risk-free equity financing and the debt cost of capital; the risk factor would be based on the riskiness level of the business unit.[22] Second, the cash flows during the planning period should be multiplied by a factor (greater than one) to be specified at the corporate level.

Intuitively, the second modification takes into account the impact of the limit the firm faces on the amount of cash that it has available or that can be raised in the short term. The first modification ensures that riskier business units will be penalized accordingly. There are strong mathematical reasons to believe that the proposed alternative method will produce results nearly as good as a full-blown business portfolio analysis.

It should also be emphasized that the STRATPORT model and the decision support system are useful at the business unit level itself without having to do any broader business portfolio analysis of all business units of the firm. One may wish to simply evaluate the financial implications of proposed strategies for the business unit and the sensitivity of the bottom-line implications to changes in key input parameters. Implementation at this level is often easier, since it is merely strategic planning at the business unit level and as such does not require the cooperation from other business units or approval at the corporate level.

Synergy Effects

An important assumption in STRATPORT as well as in the previous approaches to business portfolio analysis is that there are no marketing or cost interdependencies between the business units of the firm; if synergy effects do exist, they are assumed to remain nearly the same, independent of the strategies pursued by the business units. The only interdependency taken into account is financial, that is, the total investment over all business units should not exceed the limit on short-term cash flow. A recent empirical analysis suggests that these assumptions may largely be valid.[23] The "relatedness" between the business units of the firm was not found to be significantly related to profitability, indicating that the hypothesis of the independent business unit cannot be rejected. Diversification was positively related to profitability, indicating that the investment limitation hypothesis may be valid and internal financing across the business units is valuable to the firm. These empirical results suggest that a STRATPORT-like analysis may be valid even if there is some relatedness between business units. But in many situations the interdependencies may be so large that an alternative modeling approach is called for. Additional benefits of taking into account interdependencies are that the errors created by delineating the firm into business units will be less serious and the resulting strategy recommendations more robust with respect to alternative specifications of the business units.

The alternative framework in the context of a firm with two business units is illustrated in Figure 19.5. (The extension to multiple business units is straightforward.) For simplicity of exposition, considerations such as capacity expenditures and working capital, and the breakdown into planning and postplanning periods, are omitted in this discussion. Marketing investment in business unit 1 affects not only the market share in that business unit, but also the market share of the other business unit. Such direct and indirect effects can be incorporated by redefining the relationship in Figure 19.4 (A) to be between market share and "effective" marketing investment; the latter is defined to be the sum of the marketing investment in the business unit under consideration plus some managerially specified fraction of the marketing investment in the other business unit.

Cost interdependencies are taken into account in Figure 19.5 by relating unit cost in business unit 1 to the cumulative experience in business unit 1 plus a proportion of the cumulative experience in business unit 2. The relevant proportion can be empirically estimated; failing this, it can be specified as a managerial input. Although spillover effects (the effect on unit cost of industry experience) are not shown in Figure 19.5, they can be taken into account as previously discussed. The remainder of Figure 19.5 is self-explanatory.

In an earlier section, some modifications to traditional capital budget approval procedures were suggested to ease the implemen-

Figure 19.5 Marketing and Cost Interdependencies for a Firm with Two Business Units

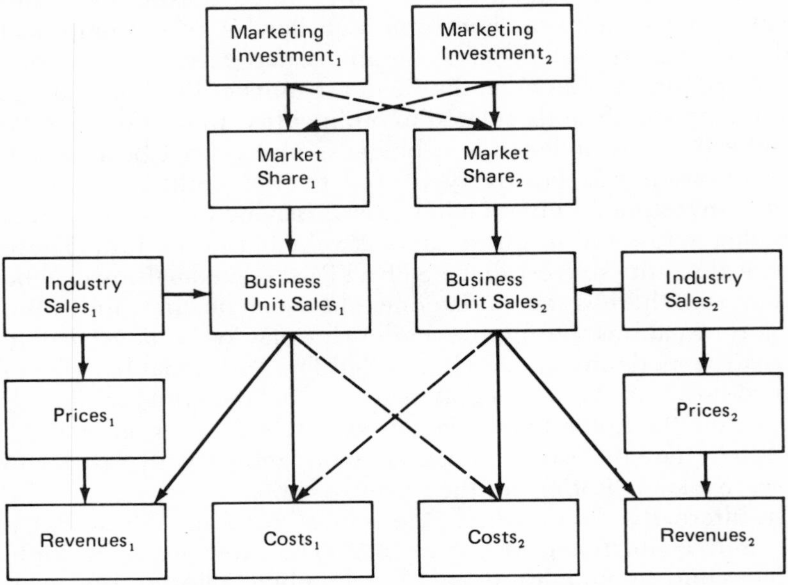

Note: Subscripts denote business unit numbers. Solid lines indicate direct effects, while dashed lines indicate indirect effects. For simplicity of presentation, the indirect effects of Industry Sales$_1$ or Prices$_2$, and conversely, are not shown. Similarly, the potential direct and indirect effects of marketing investment on industry sales are not shown. Profits are computed as (Revenues—Costs—Marketing Investment).

tation of a business portfolio analysis. To take into account the synergy effects discussed in this section, the firm should require additional information on the indirect effect of the strategic proposal of business unit 1 on the present value of cash flows in business unit 2. The direct as well as indirect effects have to be taken into account in approving or not approving budget proposals. Synergy effects also suggest that the capital budget approvals should be done simultaneously for all the business units.

Concluding Note

Computer-aided decision making provides the apparatus for systematically analyzing the relevant aspects of a problem. It also provides a convenient method to rapidly evaluate the implications of changes in assumptions regarding the firm, its markets, and the competition. Recent advances in computer graphics and user-friendly software are likely to improve the managerial interface with the computer. By better understanding the quantifiable aspects of a problem, managers can spend their time more fruitfully on the important qualitative issues that are not captured by the decision support system. All the above advantages are pertinent to strategic decision making for business portfolios. It is hoped that STRATPORT and the extensions provided here will facilitate the managerial use of the new information technology for major strategic decisions.

CHAPTER 20

The Coming Revolution in Marketing Theory

John R. Hauser

Sloan School of Management
Massachusetts Institute of Technology

Our modern civilization is due to the fact that in the year Galileo died, Newton was born. . . . This one a supreme experimentalist and enough of a mathematician, and that one a supreme mathematician and enough of an experimentalist.

Alfred North Whitehead
The First Physical Synthesis

On the occasion of the seventy-fifth anniversary of the Harvard Business School, we have been asked to examine the impact on marketing of new information technology. There is no doubt in my mind that this new technology will lead to greater precision with which to observe marketing phenomena and greater technological power with which to plan and implement marketing strategy. So expected is this information revolution that *Business Week* for April 25, 1983, claimed a new era for management with "the shrinking of middle management," "computer-run offices and factories," and an accompanying social revolution, "a disenchanted middle class."

For students in the history of science, it is clear that there will be a revolution in marketing, and that the revolution will result from greater precision and technological power, but also that the revolution will come from an unexpected source, mathematical theorists. Just as our understanding of financial strategy changed dramatically with the sudden onslaught of new theory, so too will marketing strategy. Even now at the leading business schools, mathematical theorists are building upon empirical data and questioning the way we view marketing phenomena.

In this essay I hope to persuade you that the revolution is coming. It will be resisted, but it will come. My thesis is not normative, but predictive. I draw this hypothesis partly from published essays on revolutions in science, partly from my experience as an editor and a member of editorial boards for technical marketing journals, partly from some of my own attempts at theory, and partly from my background and training in the physical sciences and engineering. (Curiously, such training is a common cultural bond among the majority of mathematical marketing theorists.)

Throughout this essay I provide examples of marketing theory, mostly based on consumer packaged goods. But you must understand that these are only a modest beginning, creative advancements that signal breakthroughs that will shake the foundations of marketing thought in many areas including durable and industrial products, tactical and strategic decisions, and domestic and international arenas.

Precision

It merely looked at data, and applied to it neither thought nor imagination—like the ethnocentricists in the Middle Ages who saw with everyday clarity the sun revolving in predictable ellipses around the earth, as opposed to Copernicus who interpreted a more compelling reality, having no more data than they, but a more searching mind.

Theodore Levitt
The Globalization of Markets

With information available instantly, decisions can be made faster—and with more precision.

Business Week
April 25, 1983

Any consumer goods market researcher worth his salt must today recognize the incredible precision of measurement possible with data collected from automated supermarket checkouts. We can now observe daily, potentially even hourly, responses to price changes, end aisle displays, and other marketing actions. We can record the in-store environment for our products and, of equal importance, our competitors' products. We can track a family over time and across multiple stores. With "split cable," we can add to this data base records of the television advertising the consumer sees and we can experiment with alternative formats and exposure levels. And researchers are still adding to this data base. For example, researchers at the University of Chicago have added information on print advertising exposure and format.[1] This measurement has spawned sophisticated analysis systems. For example, at MIT, Guadagni and Little have developed analytical computer models that use these data to uncover promotion and price elasticities with previously unattainable precision.[2] Using Bell System data bases, AT&T now has a system that can measure the impact of advertising copy at the level of one additional telephone call per year.[3] No longer must we continually live with large measurement error and unobservable outcomes. The outcomes are in plain view and demand explanation. Let us examine the impact of data on science.

Theodore Levitt alludes to the Copernican revolution. In A.D. 146, a Greek philosopher, Ptolemy, postulated that the earth was at the center of the universe and that the sun, the moon, the planets, and the stars rotated around the earth on celestial spheres. Of course, the planets were a bit eccentric, and Ptolemy and subsequent scientists added an amazingly complex set of spheres within spheres to explain deviations from perfection. Within the measurement system of the first fourteen centuries, the Ptolemaic system was sufficient to explain the motions of the heavens. But as measurement improved in the Renaissance, more and more "epicycles" were added to the Ptolemaic model to make it work. The model was in crisis. It had become too complex. Astronomers began to wonder whether there might be a simplicity in celestial motion that was obscured when such motion was interpreted within the complexity of the prevailing Ptolemaic model.

Then, in 1543, Copernicus, in a radical departure from established scientific thought, saw the sun at the center, with the earth revolving around it. The model was now simpler, though Copernicus had to retain "epicycles" in order to have the earth and the planets revolve in spheres.

Copernicus was a genius, but not the first. In the third century B.C., Aristarchus had postulated a sun-centered system. But the measurement capability in his time could not distinguish between the two theories and common belief held the earth to be the center of the universe. After all, it was plain to all observers that falling objects fell downward to seek the center of the universe. Poor Aristarchus; his theory was sound, but without the proper instrumentation, he could not demonstrate its validity. He could only stand accused of impiety.

Even in 1543, measurement was not yet sufficiently accurate to distinguish an earth-centered celestial system from a sun-centered system. But the Ptolemaic model was in crisis and measurement was improving. In 1576, Tycho Brahe persuaded Frederick II to underwrite improved measurement. Brahe spent the next twenty years collecting data he hoped would combine the Copernican system with the Ptolemaic system. He never achieved this synthesis, but "on his deathbed he solemnly confided his system to his celebrated pupil, Kepler, then but 28 years old."[4]

And He Set Forth Laws

Physics, however, does not consist merely in building up encyclopedic records of the motions of particles. Observations are a beginning, not an end in themselves. From them (as Newton said) we hope to infer laws of motion—generalizations that embrace all motions of a given type.

A. P. French
Physics: A New Introductory Course

An increasingly rich literature of empirical studies helps resolve these issues by revealing major advertising phenomena that models should encompass.

J. D. C. Little
"Aggregate Advertising Models:
The State of the Art"

Brahe's measurement was the most accurate one the world had ever seen. He became an international celebrity in his own time, entertaining philosophers, theologians, and princes at his observatory. But it remained for young Kepler to unify twenty years of data, to establish the dominance of a sun-centered system, to greatly simplify our understanding of the motion of heavenly bodies, and to spark the mathematical revolution in astronomy. He did it with the following three simple axioms.

1. The planets move in ellipses having the sun at one focus.
2. The line joining the sun to a given planet sweeps out equal areas in equal times.
3. The square of the planet's year, divided by the cube of its mean distance from the sun, is the same for all planets.[5]

From these axioms and analytic geometry, Kepler was able to reproduce Brahe's measurements. It must be remembered that Kepler set out to complete Brahe's unification, but he could not do so if he were to be true to the data. With his genius and his faith in the accuracy of Brahe's measurements, he was able to see simplicity where his contemporaries saw complexity.

Today, on a modest scale in marketing science, such laws are being set forth to synthesize and summarize the chaos of data. I choose as one example, Little's five postulates of advertising response. Before setting forth these laws, let me briefly summarize Little's reasoning.

Little has been studying advertising response for almost twenty years and has published extensively in academically respected journals.[6] But in 1979, he found that "ignorance of advertising response phenomena, inability to make good measurement, and a lack of theory to organize existing knowledge contribute to great waste in advertising. Contradictions abound."[7] Little presents a series of anecdotes to illustrate that managers often implicitly assume contradictory postulates to justify actions, and that hard, quantitative questions, such as "should a 'flight' be half as long and twice as intense?" are often not even asked.

But all is not lost. Advertising research has its Tycho Brahes and a large number of careful empirical studies have been documented. Little reviews the data and synthesizes them with the following five laws.

1. Sales respond dynamically upward and downward to increases and decreases of advertising and frequently do so at different rates.
2. Steady-state response can be concave or S-shaped and will often have positive sales at zero-advertising.
3. Competitive advertising affects sales.
4. The dollar effectiveness of advertising can change over time as the result of changes in media, copy, and other factors.
5. Products sometimes respond to increased advertising with a sales increase that falls off even as advertising is held constant.[8]

Once stated, these laws are self-evident. How could anyone not believe them? What manager would act in a manner that assumes they are false? Yet, in his review of analytic models, Little finds that famous economics models of advertising such as the Vidale-Wolfe and Nerlove-Arrow models are woefully lacking in their ability to be consistent with these laws and that many management science models and managerial actions do little better. Little does not condemn these actions and models; after all, Ptolemy and Copernicus were geniuses, even though their models were later modified. But Little demands that we listen to the data and modify our models if they cannot explain the data.

Little gives us hope. He goes on to show that modifications to the Lanchester model and his own Brandaid model can handle four of the five postulates. He closes on the optimistic note that "in the next 5 to 10 years there will be abundant opportunities for understanding advertising processes better and putting this knowledge to work in improving marketing productivity."[9]

I note that Little's postulates are being resisted; for example, they sparked a lively, productive debate among some of marketing's best scientists at the first marketing science conference, held in March 1983 at the University of Southern California, and the debate is far from over.[10] Furthermore, they are unlikely to be the final word, as researchers challenge, extend, and modify these simple postulates. They are, however, a beginning.

More Precision and Some Thought

> Alas, a few years ago, I should have said "my universe": but now my mind has been opened to higher views of things.
>> Edwin A. Abbott
>> *Flatland*

> It might have remained a toy, but in his hands it created a revolution.
>> Alfred North Whitehead
>> *The First Physical Synthesis*

Little's postulates explain how advertising responds to marketing actions, not why. To complete the revolution we must know why. With "why," we can generalize to new situations and develop creative ways to influence advertising response.

Let's return to Kepler. His laws tell us how planets move, not why. Newton's laws explain why, but before Newton came Galileo. It was obvious to the Greeks and to Galileo's contemporaries that a rock falls faster than a leaf. Surely, heavier objects fall faster. But Galileo thought more deeply and set forth the following "thought experiment":

> Suppose I have two identical balls. Then, by the above law, they must fall at the same rate. But suppose they were linked by some massless invisible string. They weigh twice as much and will fall, perhaps, twice as fast. But this appears to be a contradiction.

Galileo was led to the conclusion that all objects must fall at the same rate and conducted the famous Tower of Pisa experiment to demonstrate his law of gravity. We now believe the deeper truth that the leaf falls more slowly than the rock because of air resistance.

In the epigraph above, Whitehead refers to Galileo and the telescope. Galileo used the telescope to observe the heavens and asked why moving objects such as planets ever stop. "This question must have seemed like sheer effrontry, since anyone could plainly see that rest was the natural state of a body, a state which a body sought to recover as soon as it was put in motion."[11] Galileo insisted that bodies in motion tend to stay in motion. But to do so he had to abstract from reality and study, in his mind's eye, the frictionless plane, an entity that can never really exist. Such abstractions occur throughout science. Ask any chemist about Boyle's law, which defines an "ideal gas," or any electrical engineer about Ohm's law, which defines an ideal resistor.

To understand reality, we must abstract from reality. We model the world in its ideal case and only then do we work backward to incorporate troublesome everyday effects. For example, the transistor is the forerunner of the integrated circuits that make today's information technologies possible. Analysis of early transistor circuits relied on simple abstract models of ideal transistors. Effects were added and the models improved as circuits became more complex and the tasks they were called upon to perform become more demanding. The trained engineer knew which model to use for which situation.[12]

In marketing, such ideal abstractions are now being set forth. For example, two University of Chicago researchers, Blattberg and Jeuland, use a "micro-modeling" approach to examine the "why" of advertising response.[13] Little's postulates specify how the *market* responds to advertising; Blattberg and Jeuland ask whether this market response can be explained as an aggregation of individual consumers responding to advertising. They specify three assumptions:

1. Every consumer has a probability, q, of being exposed to advertising and that probability is the same across consumers.
2. The probability of being exposed to an advertisement is independent from insertion to insertion.
3. Once a consumer sees an advertisement, he or she forgets at a constant rate.[14]

We know that no real-world advertising response will satisfy all of these assumptions; but by studying the implications of these "ideal" assumptions, Blattberg and Jeuland understand the implications of the model and examine how well an ideal advertising response can approximate a real advertising response. Just as Galileo's model of the frictionless plane has been extended to a multitude of practical problems, so will Blattberg and Jeuland's "ideal" microresponse be applied to practical advertising problems. (They themselves suggest how one might deal with the heterogeneity, competitive effects, and varying copy effectiveness.)

With just these three simple assumptions, Blattberg and Jeuland are successful in reproducing observed aggregate effects. For example, their model is consistent with three of Little's five postulates (four if you use the competitive extension) and could readily be modified to handle Little's fifth postulate. More importantly, their model can be used to address Little's question: "Should a 'flight' be half as long and twice as intense?"

A special case of their model (probability of exposure, q, close to zero and equal spacing of advertising insertions) reproduces a model that is similar to the econometric models now in popular use. What's more, the micromodel provides a satisfying explanation of why Clarke found that the "observed" carry-over effect of advertising is heavily dependent upon the observation period (monthly, quarterly, yearly) used to measure the effect.[15] The micromodel demonstrates that this variation is a measurement artifact, not an actual lagged effect.

Thus, we see the progression of marketing theory from observation to more precise measurement to "how" postulates to a "why" theory. Of course, the theory needs testing, elaboration, application, and maybe, a rival theory, but we see in this example the clear interrelationships among empirical research, methodological research, and theory. Contributors, such as Little, Blattberg, Bass, Jeuland, and Clarke, who think deeply about data rather than simply cataloging them, are today laying the foundation for a comprehensive theory of advertising response.

Axioms and the Mathematization of Marketing

> While formal logic and pure mathematics do not in themselves establish any assertions about matters of empirical fact, they provide an efficient and entirely indispensable machinery for deducing, from abstract theoretical assumptions. . . .
>
> Carl G. Hempel
> "Geometry and Empirical Science"

> . . . the great successes of Galileo and Newton consisted in their mathematical analysis of physical events, the combination of them into physical postulates, or "axioms," and the deductive development, from the postulates and definitions of new concepts, of theorems which, since they stated consequences about the physical world, could be tested.
>
> Edward H. Madden
> "Making Sense of Science"

In 1686 Newton modified Galileo's law of inertia (bodies in motion stay in motion, bodies at rest stay at rest unless acted upon by an outside force) and added two mathematical postulates: (1) $F = ma$ for motion and (2) $F = Gm_1 m_2/r^2$ for gravitation where F is force, m is mass, a is acceleration, r is distance, and G is a fitting parameter. With these quantitative laws, or "axioms," and with his mathematical skill, Newton was able to obtain Kepler's "how" laws as just one of many implications of Newton's "why" laws. Newton was also able to explain the tides, falling bodies, and many other observed facts with his three simple axioms. Can we do the same for marketing phenomena? I believe that we can, and we are now trying.

I have already mentioned Blattberg and Jeuland. In their system they too set forth three axioms. They were able to obtain such powerful results because (1) the axioms had very specific quantitative implications and (2) they were able to call upon formal logic and mathematical skill to derive practical and testable implications from their axioms. It is for such applications that managers should examine the writings of the mathematical marketing theorists. For as Hempel points out, ". . . a mathematical theorem, once proved, is established once and for all; it holds with that particular certainty which no subsequent empirical discoveries, however unexpected and extraordinary, can ever affect to the slightest extent."[16]

Thus, if you believe our axioms, then you must believe our results. If the results do not make sense or can be shown to be false, then mathematical logic demands that you question at least one of our axioms. In this way we progress to more sophisticated axioms that better represent the world as we believe it to be.

Let me provide an example from some of my own attempts at theory (in collaboration with Steven Shugan of the University of Chicago). I have written extensively on new product development and the importance of innovation to today's corporations.[17] But in this research it soon became apparent that while managers are interested in developing new products, they also fear competitive new products. For every new product launched, five or six managers must defend their profit from capture by new competitive products. Shugan and I began to study defensive strategy with four ideal axioms that are well supported in the empirical marketing literature.

1. Consumers maximize utility in a multiattributed space.
2. Consumers have heterogeneous tastes.
3. Utility can be approximated by a weighted sum of the product's attributes.

4. The relevant attributes are scaled by price, that is, "effectiveness" per dollar or "gentleness" per dollar.[18]

With these four axioms and an assumption that aggregate advertising response satisfies, at least, Little's second postulate, we were able to show that the following theorems are a necessary logical result. To maintain the best possible profit position, the defending firm should:

A. decrease spending on distribution;
B. decrease spending on awareness advertising;
C. decrease price in unsegmented markets;
D. perhaps, increase price in segmented markets; and,
E. improve the product (and support the improvement with advertising) in the direction of the defender's strength; that is, for the attribute(s) on which the defender's product is better than the attacker's product.

Furthermore, these results are true (if you believe our axioms) no matter what specific details you measure about the advertising response function or no matter what the exact positions are of the attacking and defending products. Of course, how much you decrease distribution spending does depend upon these details.

Steven Gaskin of MIT and I have applied this model to a consumer good category with over $100 million in annual sales. Interestingly, the firm was doing about the best they could before the new product attacked the market. They could have maintained approximately $500,000 more annual profit and three more share points after the attack if they had followed the model's prescriptions. (They decreased advertising and distribution but increased price.)

But I Don't Believe Your Assumptions

The strangest phenomenon for the philosophical observer, however, was the fact that physical research was not paralyzed by these contradictions, that the physicist managed somehow to go on with two contradictory conceptions and learned to apply sometimes the one, sometimes the other, with an amazing success as far as observational discoveries are concerned.

Hans Reichenbach
"Are There Atoms?"

. . . the early developmental stages of most sciences have been characterized by continual competition between a number of distinct

views of nature, each partially derived from, and all roughly compat-
ible with, the dictates of scientific observation and method.
Thomas S. Kuhn
"The Structure of Scientific
Revolutions"

Reichenbach refers to the 250-year-old debate among physical
scientists about whether light was a particle or a wave. Light has
momentum, like a particle, but exhibits interference, and is seen in
waves resulting from two pebbles thrown side by side into a pond.
(Newton was the founder of the particle theory and his contemporary, Huygens, the founder of the wave theory.) Both theories existed side by side, fading in and out of popularity as new phenomena were discovered; both theories fit some, but not all, of the facts
of observation; and both theories led to tremendous technological
developments in optics and related engineering application. In
fact, it was the dominance of the wave theory of light in the
nineteenth century that led scientists to postulate a medium,
"luminiferous ether," through which light travels like waves
through water. But which theory was right? It remained for twentieth-century quantum theorists to provide an answer.

Let us return now to the defensive marketing theorems. Many
managers and some academics find theorem A to be counterintui-
tive. Surely an aggressive defense must entail strengthening your
distribution chain. Since the theorems are a logical result of the
axioms, this must mean that at least one axiom is wrong. The favorite target is axiom 4. After all, who ever heard of dividing "gentleness" by price to get "gentleness per dollar"? It is common knowledge (pick up any textbook on market research) that gentleness is at
most an "interval" scale, not the required "ratio scale."

Actually, with all mathematical theories, each theorem does not
require all the axioms and theorem A does not depend upon axiom
4. It depends only on Little's second postulate applied to distribution response. To better understand theorem A, recognize that the
defending manager faces a smaller demand for his product than he
did before the attack. It is no longer in his interest to invest in the
marginal distributor. What the theorems really say is that price and
repositioning are better weapons for defense than distribution and
awareness advertising.

Theorem A does not depend upon axiom 4, but the pricing
theorems, C and D, do. Should we reject them because common
belief holds that "gentleness per dollar" is an unmeasurable construct? Many have said we should. But economic theory and deductive reasoning from the postulate that consumers maximize utility

subject to a budget constraint suggest that consumers should use "gentleness per dollar," not "gentleness," to evaluate a product such as Tylenol.[19] Rather than throw out this strange notion, Gaskin and I set up an experiment in which we used two alternative models—(1) attributes scaled by price and (2) price as another attribute—to forecast the share of a new product.[20] Model 1, based on axiom 4, predicted a market share of 7 percent. Model 2, with price as an attribute, predicted a share of 18 percent. The actual share observed one year later was 7 to 8 percent. Success! Or is it?

Good arguments can be made in favor of model 2.[21] And such models have also predicted well.[22] Because our model 2 was only one of many potential ways to model price as an attribute, we have not shown the dominance of model 1, but rather the feasibility of model 1.[23] We can say from our empirical experiments to date that the four defensive axioms make some empirical sense and that they should not be rejected simply because the results suggest departure from intuition. Perhaps, price should be modeled sometimes as an attribute and sometimes as a scaling factor, just as light, for 250 years, was modeled sometimes as a wave and sometimes as a particle.

Such a duality theory was extremely powerful for the advancement of optics. It was only in 1924, when Louis de Broglie set forth a theory that light *and matter* have the properties of *both* waves and particles, that the two contradictory theories could be reconciled. De Broglie's theory was subsequently demonstrated empirically and led to revolutionary ideas in quantum mechanics. Axioms are important, but they cannot be taken entirely on faith. Successful axioms are (eventually) tested and empirically grounded in an iterative process of theoretical and empirical research.

Researchers in consumer behavior argue strongly that experiments that attempt to falsify theory are important in guiding theory.[24] But falsification is a complex philosophical point. "Ideal" models are difficult to falsify. How can you falsify "bodies in motion stay in motion unless acted upon by an outside force"? Not only is it physically impossible to rule out all forces—for example, the gravitational pull of the sun—but if anything stops the object, it is, by definition, a force. Nonetheless, the (definitional) law of Galileo and Newton led to a scientific and technological revolution.

Even theories that are eventually rejected are valuable in helping us understand empirical phenomena. Consider Lorentz contraction. The chief spokesman of the falsification philosophy of science, Karl Popper, has cited Lorentz contraction "as an auxiliary hypothesis which should be excluded from empirical science by the falsifiability criterion."[25] But it was Einstein providing, in part, a "microtheory" to explain Lorentz contraction who developed the special theory that led to the twentieth-century revolution in physics.[26] Thomas Kuhn cautions us: "No process yet discovered by the historical study of scientific development at all resembles the methodological stereotype of falsification by direct comparison to nature."[27]

I believe in a middle ground between the falsificationists and Kuhn. I believe that while falsification experiments can be important, they alone are not sufficient to the advancement of theory. They are part of a greater whole that includes exploratory data collection, theory formulation, deductive reasoning, and practice. I am uncomfortable with any claim that one component in the pursuit of knowledge is uniquely qualified to be called science.

We must be critical. We must question our axioms. But we must also proceed with caution. The implications of axioms, even axioms we question, help guide theory and, inevitably, lead to improved theory and more powerful and useful implications.

But Is Your Model Relevant?

Both in mathematics and astronomy, research reports had ceased already in antiquity to be intelligible to a generally educated audience. In dynamics, research became similarly esoteric in the Middle Ages. . . . Too little attention is paid to the essential relationship between that gulf and the mechanisms intrinsic to scientific advance.

Thomas S. Kuhn
"The Structure of Scientific
Revolutions"

Newton had, in the theory of universal gravitation, created what would today be called a mathematical model of the solar system. And having once made the model, he followed out a host of its other implications.

A. P. French
Physics: A New Introductory Course

It is the vogue to attack mathematical theory as being of no relevance to managers. Such attacks are unfortunate, because mathematical theory is relevant. For example, Little has demonstrated time and again that his models help real managers make real decisions and that such decisions lead to better outcomes than would have been obtained without the mathematical analysis.[28]

My MIT colleagues, Alvin Silk and Glen Urban, have developed a forecasting model, based on mathematical marketing theory, that has become a viable commercial enterprise.[29] In over three hundred applications, the model has performed well, providing extremely accurate predictions of a new product's market share, predictions that are made *prior* to test marketing. Recently, Glen Urban looked back at the three hundred applications and used scientific methods to evaluate the model in terms of its utility to managers.[30] According to Urban's estimates, the value of the model in incremental profit per new product launched could be as much as $11 million. That's relevance. Even if these estimates are inflated by a factor of ten, such an impact suggests that the Silk-Urban model cannot be ignored.

If such models are so valuable, why, then, are they attacked by otherwise brilliant managers? I believe the attacks come because managers do not speak "pure mathematics." If I write "Šitas sakinys yra aiškus tam, kuris skaito lietuviškai," I would expect few of you to understand me. But if you spoke Lithuanian, one of the world's oldest living languages, you would find the sentence perfectly clear. Further, if you do not speak Lithuanian, you would be willing to await translation before judging the relevance of the statement. On the other hand, if I write $\nabla \times \vec{B} = (1/c)(\partial\vec{E}/\partial t) + (4\pi\rho/c)\vec{J}$, I am inundated with questions about relevance to managers. I am not even allowed a translation. I am guilty until proven innocent. But an equation is a sentence; mathematical operators such as ∇x and $\partial/\partial t$ are verbs, and symbols such as $\vec{E}$, $\vec{B}$, and $\vec{J}$ are nouns. Once you know the language, the above equation becomes one of the fundamental equations of electromagnetism. It is of enormous relevance for the design of the information technologies that are the theme of this conference. But you must speak the language to use the equation itself.

There is no reason to expect managers to speak "pure mathematics" any more than Lithuanian. They can survive without either. For Lithuanian they can hire a translator; for electronics they can hire an engineer or simply use the technology created by the engineers. But an engineer is a doer for electronics just as a manager is a doer for marketing.

It is, in part, incumbent upon mathematical marketing theorists to translate their work. This will happen as they apply their work. But I also see more and more mathematically trained engineers being attracted to marketing management. Such engineers will be the first to use mathematical theory and manage better. With their success this theory will become attractive to all managers, as has today's computing and information technology.

But Your Theory Is Not Complete

> To be accepted as a paradigm, a theory must seem better than its competitors, but it need not, and in fact never does, explain all the facts with which it can be confronted.
>
> Thomas S. Kuhn
> "The Structure of Scientific
> Revolutions"

> He presented mathematicians with the astounding and melancholy conclusions that the axiomatic method has certain inherent limitations, which rule out the possibility that even the ordinary arithmetic of the integers (whole numbers) can ever be fully axiomized.
>
> E. Nagel and J. Newman
> *Gödel's Proof*

Newton's laws were not complete; some might say that they were wrong. But this does not diminish in any way the impact that they had on the technological and social revolutions they served to foster. Nor does Einstein's theory diminish Newton's genius. Without Newtonian mechanics there would have been no Einsteinian mechanics. As Einstein himself pointed out, "The old mechanics is valid for small velocities and forms the limiting case of the new one."[31] By small velocities, Einstein means that Newtonian mechanics will be within a percentage point for any velocity less than 94 million miles per hour. That covers a lot of practical cases and Newton's theory is much easier to apply.

It is not clear that even Einstein's theory is or ever can be complete. Not only did Einstein fail to achieve a complete unification of force fields, but developments in mathematical logic suggest that no set of axioms can ever be complete because there will always be propositions that can neither be proven nor disproven with the axiom.[32] This statement (for arithmetic) is the mathematical proof published in 1931 by Kurt Gödel to which Nagel and Newman refer. Gödel's proof is exceedingly complex, but its implication is that it is logically inconsistent to expect even the axioms of simple arithmetic to be complete, let alone a set of axioms that refer to empirical marketing phenomena.

Despite the warnings from the history of science and from pure logic, we all too often criticize mathematical marketing theories as incomplete. Such criticisms are valid to the extent that they caution us from blindly applying a theory beyond the boundaries of its axioms. But such criticisms are counterproductive if they prevent us from using our theories for the problems they can solve productively. It is the investigation and extension of axiomatic boundaries that makes marketing a science. For example, in proving the defensive marketing theorems, Shugan and I assume that the main actors are (1) the attacking firm and (2) the defending firm. We assume that the net result of all movements by other firms will not reverse the basic results. It is easy to advance intuitive arguments to suggest that this is true, but we have not yet proven this result from axioms. It is a challenge to which we will rise, but such proofs require time.

In the meantime, our theories are clearly valid for gaining insight into defensive problems. (When Newton demonstrated his law of universal gravitation, he knowingly ignored second-order forces such as the effect of Mars on the orbit of the moon. It remained for later researchers to complete such second-order analyses.) Let me illustrate, with the Farley-Srinivasan sales force compensation problem, the time scale and style of research necessary to elaborate axioms. In 1964, John Farley of Columbia University published a seminal article on sales force compensation.[33] In that article he showed that for a firm to maximize profit, it should pay salesmen an equal percentage of gross margin across all products. To derive his result, Farley assumed that the salesman's total time was fixed a priori, an assumption that Srinivasan would later question. With this assumption, for the next seventeen years Farley's insights led to elaborations of theory, empirical tests, applications, and most importantly, valuable insights into the problem.

In 1981, V. Srinivasan of Stanford University asked, "Does this result hold if we must also motivate the salesman to allocate his (or her) time to selling?"[34] This question had been asked by others. Srinivasan's contribution is that he was able to use his mathematical skill to provide an answer. The answer is yes, but only in two restricted cases, one of which is Farley's fixed time axiom. Thus, as Einstein asked a fundamental question, "Is the velocity of light constant for all reference frames?" and used his mathematical skill to generalize Newton's theory, so Srinivasan has asked a fundamental question and used his mathematical skill to generalize Farley's theory. There are other results in Srinivasan's theory, including a case where it is optimal to pay salesmen a fixed percentage of gross sales, but I need not elaborate them here.

Srinivasan's contribution is not simply that he generalized Farley's theory. He helped us to better understand the problem. He showed us the boundaries of the theory and directed us to the critical assumptions necessary to apply the theory in real applications. Managers must now decide which assumptions best approximate their situations. They can then apply the appropriate compensation scheme.

Is Srinivasan's theory complete? Of course not. Srinivasan himself suggests valuable new avenues of research and active research is being undertaken along these lines in at least three universities. For example, issues of uncertainty add a new perspective on the problem and lead to new insights, insights that add to, rather than detract from, previous results.

Theory advances with challenge, extension, modification, and sometimes, revolution. But it rarely springs forth without roots in other theories and in precise measurement of marketing phenomena.

Who Is the Horse and Who Is the Driver?

> Only very occasionally, as in the cases of ancient statics, dynamics, and geometrical optics, do facts collected with little guidance from preestablished theory speak with sufficient clarity to permit the emergence of a first paradigm.
>
> Thomas S. Kuhn
> "The Structure of Scientific
> Revolutions"

> [Einstein] seemed to know the answers without the benefit of anything more than a hint or two from nature; the rest was mere confirmation.
>
> A. P. French
> *Relativity: An Introduction to the
> Special Theory*

I have argued that information technology will lead to the greater precision necessary for a revolution in marketing theory. But how will that revolution come about? Should we thrash around in the data until we are shocked by the facts, or is there a better way? We have seen the role that the data of Tycho Brahe played in the revolution of celestial mechanics. But Tycho Brahe's data were not collected at random; they were collected with the purpose of unifying the Ptolemaic and Copernican theories.

Consider the famous Michelson-Morley experiment. The wave theory of light suggested that there exists a luminiferous ether through which light travels like waves through water. If there were a luminiferous ether and if the earth were traveling through this ether, then we should be able to detect an "ether wind" as we detect a wind when we thrust our hand outside the window of a moving car. An ether wind should manifest itself through a drag on the velocity of light. Unfortunately, the leading figure in electromagnetic phenomena, James Clerk Maxwell, demonstrated convincingly that the effect of the drag was too small to measure. It would be one part in 100 million. But in 1881 Michelson invented a new instrument of such accuracy that an ether wind would be detectable. Much to his dismay, he found no ether wind. Even with an instrument ten times as accurate, he and Morley could still find no effect.

The Michelson-Morley experiment led the Dutch theorist, Lorentz, to postulate a contraction of all objects due to motion, and an independent derivation of this contraction was a key component in Einstein's theory. Although Einstein claimed not to have had any direct knowledge of the experiment itself, the experiment obviously influenced contemporary physics theory, which in turn influenced Einstein.

But the Michelson-Morley experiment would not have been performed and would need no interpretation without the theory of luminiferous ether. *It was a null result.* It said only that light travels at the same velocity in all directions. It would have been of little relevance without theory.

Such anecdotes from the history of science suggest that perhaps we should not simply use information technology to collect data blindly and then try to interpret them, but rather, we should perhaps use mathematical theory to guide our investigations.

For example, in application of the defensive axioms we assume that they hold for all products that a consumer evokes and that evoking can best be modeled with a response function satisfying (at least) Little's second postulate.[35] Derivations based on the axioms suggest that a price-off promotion will have two effects: One effect will result because a promotion increases evoking, and will appear as a promotion response more or less independent of price. The second effect will manifest itself as would any change in price. Curiously, these are exactly the effects that Guadagni and Little found in their sophisticated analysis, using information technology, of in-store promotions.[36]

Thus, precision, measurement, experimentation, and observation are crucial for the advancement of theory. But the circle is complete. Theory is crucial for deciding which marketing phenomena to measure. For example, the most significant effect that Little and Guadagni identified with their data was an unexplained "loyalty" factor, that is, the tendency of consumers to continue to purchase products they already purchased in spite of price changes and promotion. Such an effect is predicted by the first defensive marketing axiom that each brand has its unique position in a multiattributed space. Predictions with respect to this phenomenon are specific and could be tested. Such research would be interesting and valuable to the advancement of theory, but information on positioning is not currently collected in electronic shopping panels.

How Should We Proceed?

Roughly speaking, we may distinguish, according to Max Planck, two conflicting conceptions in the philosophy of science: the metaphysical and the positivistic conception. Each of these regards Einstein as its chief advocate and most distinguished witness. If there were a legal case to be decided, it would be possible to produce satisfactory evidence on behalf of either position by quoting Einstein.

> Philipp Frank
> *Einstein, Mach, and Logical Positivism*

You, who are blessed with shade as well as light, you, who are gifted with two eyes, endowed with a knowledge of perspective, and charmed with the enjoyment of various colours, you, who can actually see an angle, and contemplate the complete circumference of a Circle in the happy region of the Three Dimensions—how shall I make clear to you the extreme difficulty which we in Flatland experience in recognizing one another's configuration?

> Edwin A. Abbott
> *Flatland*

It has become popular in marketing journals to argue how one should proceed with the science of marketing. I do not wish to enter that debate. My thesis is not that we should proceed with mathematical marketing theory, only that such theory is inevitable. It will result from increased precision, new information, and probing minds. There will be a revolution in marketing theory. The foundations are now being built. I have focused on mathematical theory, but marketing theory cannot stand alone in the absence of an empirical base. It is intimately related to a myriad of other scientific pursuits.

There is a role for everyone. We have seen that data collection (Tycho Brahe), experimentation (Michelson-Morley), and observation (Ptolemy, Copernicus, Galileo, Newton, Einstein), are critical components in the discovery of scientific knowledge. Such work is now proceeding in marketing science. I have not discussed engineering, but it is clear that those who use theory to solve real problems must themselves develop and modify theory to make it practical.

But what about doers, those managers who must every day solve complex marketing problems? If we only remember that it was the need to develop a practical calendar that was, in part, behind the Copernican revolution, we see that the doer, the person who demands, needs, and uses practical solutions, is at the core of theoretical development whether he knows it or not.

We are all in this together as we each pursue our own interests. Each learns from the other, and each in his or her own way is a necessary part of the coming revolution in marketing theory. Throughout this essay, I have provided examples of marketing theory. These examples are only a sample of the valuable work now being published.[37]

CHAPTER 21

Paradoxical Futures Versus a New Beginning

Theodore Levitt
Harvard Business School

The most significant aspect about the colloquium that brought these essays together was its reactive character. Rarely did we ask what it is that marketing knowledge and marketing practice can do to help the new technologies become more effective and useful. Mostly we asked how marketing will be affected by those technologies and what marketing can do to capitalize on them. In this way we conceded our dependence. We are not the agents of destiny, but rather its consequence. Technology is the acknowledged master, the engine that pulls all the rest along and determines where the future shall be, how fast it shall be attained, what we shall do within it, and who shall prosper, who languish, who fossilize. Our colloquium's purpose thus revealed itself as trying to help us get on technology's bandwagon, carrying us along somehow with its protean forces in a way that assures the marketing profession's relevance, utility, and influence.

There is no presumption that all sectors of society or all fields of knowledge are equal in importance or consequence. In all things there are hierarchies of importance. Their lineups vary according to our concerns. The derivative character of the concerns of the colloquium did not diminish their importance, nor reduce the productive possibilities of the colloquium's outcome. Far better that we should have been concerned with how the new technologies might affect or shape the work of marketing than to be painfully shaken into attentiveness when obsolescence lurks imminently in some future time.

No matter how constructively influential the colloquium may turn out to be, many blunders will surely lie ahead as new technologies are affected and used by marketing. Instead of mistakes, many of these should be viewed simply as probabilistic events—

inescapable and inevitable. Nor is it likely that if the colloquium had never been held it would be much missed. There are so many smart people in marketing (as elsewhere) that it is virtually assured that most of them will, by themselves, find the technologies that will help.

The world of practical affairs is characterized by its practicality. It does what needs to be done to achieve what's intended. The bracing pressures of reality destroy habit, decompose custom, and dissolve sentimentality. Opportunity will generally be grasped by others before it destroys the skeptics or the tardy. There are too many practical people in the world, too many hungry hustlers and intelligent functionaries, to keep adaptation and innovation at bay.

That almost certainly will be true of marketing practice. What will happen in the academy is more problematic. Understandably, and I believe, desirably, the work of the academy is contemplative and less intent on immediate utility than is the work of its practitioner counterparts. It seeks to understand and explain before it tries to prescribe, exploring crevices, relationships, and causations that are generally of little interest or apparent promise to practitioners. The new information technologies will almost certainly expand opportunities for the academy to do even more of all this, and that will produce, certainly in the short run, even more agnosticism by practitioners.

The founding fathers of the study of marketing in the academy were closely attached to practice—at the minimum in the sense of being in intimate and constant touch with marketing practitioners. All the original textbooks were based on direct field observation by their authors. Until the 1950s, almost all research was clinical or historical. It almost always required a lot of time in the field with practitioners at work. In the past twenty years, as the numbers of academic marketers have vastly expanded, so has their distance from practice. Few reach widely or deeply into the businesses and the operations that are the object of their concern. Seldom do they develop close or continuing associations with marketing practitioners. To the extent they have such associations, these tend generally to be with staff professionals rather than line managers, and if with line managers, mostly as lecturers to and prescribers for them rather than as intimate confidants or close observers of them. The result is that what is viewed as important and relevant by the academy is rarely held in the same light by practitioners.

Today's professional journals (and to a considerable extent even textbooks) exhibit a strong preference for research esoterica, theory, consolidating models, and formal methods to derive or test theories and paradigms. There is an obvious preference for exquisite refinement of new modes of inquiry and for questions or issues of rare interest and unobvious value to practitioners. Mostly this is justified in the name of science and pure inquiry, things that have worked so well in the hard sciences and to which we owe the modern world. Nor should we forget that it is through publishing in journals with these preferences that academic reputations are built and promotions made.

One wonders, therefore, whether in the future the academy will ever want to study in clinical depth what's actually happening in reality; whether it will study reality in any way that approximates certain important aspects of reality itself; whether with more and faster technologies and more data bases constantly available, ambitious young scholars will risk doing anything that departs from what is becoming the prevailing orthodoxy. And what has this orthodoxy in methodology and objectives achieved this past quarter century? What, as our tools of inquiry and analysis multiply, will the future bring?

Prediction, according to an old Confucian saying, is very treacherous, especially with respect to the future. For us, forecasting is both more comfortable and more sensible—that is, suggesting general outlines of possibilities and probabilities based on certain evolving patterns in the development of technology, its uses, and its effects. The futures of which we usually speak are those that are theoretically or practically possible and probable, given what we know, and making certain reasonable mediating assumptions. But we should also contemplate another set of futures—those that are unintended, unexpected, and unrealized. Who would have expected, for example, that the development of the incandescent lamp, by which we lighted our lives and our libraries, would now darken our lives with commercial pornography directed at our children and darken our libraries during prime-time television hours? Why is it that in looking back twenty to thirty years we see a whole series of extravagant claims in behalf of new knowledge tools that have been unfulfilled or have failed? Daniel Bell, in his book *The Social Sciences since the Second World War*, includes among these game theory, econometrics, general equilibrium theory, micromotive theory, monetarism, Keynesian disequilibrium, business cycle theory, theory of allocation, and theory of rational expectations.[1] And he points out, in addition, that most of these are contradictory to each other or have eclipsed some of the others. Would it help those of us in marketing who work with some of the new knowledge tools to make some assessment of these failures or shortfalls, and those of our own? Is it enough merely to assert that the development of science is a slow and painstaking process during which failures and shortfalls are inevitable and even necessary?

We were fortunate in having J. R. Hauser make the case for "science" in marketing, precisely because in hands like his, the search for the possibilities of science in the practice of marketing is marked by a first-rate intelligence and incorruptible integrity. In light of the unfulfilled or failed promises in the older social sciences, it may be useful in thinking about marketing's future if we look for a minute at some of the work of Frank Bass, who can be described as the founding father of marketing science.

First, Frank Bass's work is based, like all scientific work, on faith—faith that it is possible to know enough, and know it well enough, to derive general principles or laws about phenomena; in our case, the essentially "social" phenomena of marketing.[2] While the subject matters of the social and the hard sciences may differ, there is the animating positivistic *belief* that there must be a common logic of explanation if their theories and laws are to be "science." Stephen Toulmin and others have argued that the older sureties of the philosophy of science have been undermined as applied to the social sciences.[3] This is because it is becoming increasingly difficult to have a closed system in the social world, and unless you can have a closed system, you cannot have a science of that system. The epistemological significance of this argument is well illustrated by neoclassical economics, the most advanced prototype of science in the social sciences. Neoclassical economics specifies a powerful set of finite variables and the equations for their interaction. Yet its predictive power has become increasingly limited, precisely because the system cannot be closed. Variables exogenous to the system intrude constantly and ever more powerfully. And that partly explains why the economists are the originators of so many alternative or mediating models and analytical tools, such as game theory, econometrics, and others. Their inventive new constructions represent attempts to close systems that will not close, as in the hard sciences, attempts to make science out of conditions that refuse to yield.

Professor Bass, in trying to close the system as it applies in marketing, came up with the ingenious construction of combining econometrics with stochastic modeling. Econometrics, it is important to emphasize, is not a model. It attempts to be a map that describes precisely all the contours, involutions, and relationships of and in a market. But because he understood that the system is porous and constantly intruded upon by unexpected externalities, Professor Bass added the realistic idea of stochastic shocks to model their probable effects on his econometric maps. This makes for considerable complexity, particularly when compared to deterministic models, which tend to be mathematical, abstract, conceptual, and highly simplified. Their strength resides in their appeal, which is their simplicity and clarity.

If relationships in the social world are inherently unstable, and becoming increasingly less stable (which in itself is a testable proposition), then trying to model and thereby explain these relationships (which is one of the axial purposes of science) may become less and less useful. Or we may have to think of modeling in a different way.

Modeling existed before it was called by that name. Machiavelli had a model, as did Adam Smith, David Ricardo, Karl Marx, Max Weber, Vilfredo Pareto, and Talcott Parsons. Most of the models used by these writers were largely descriptive in nature, except for the economists' (Smith, Ricardo, Marx, and Pareto) model, which also had formal-analytic content. As to marketing, the work of its founding fathers was almost entirely descriptive. It represented making tangible the institutional economists' dissatisfactions with the dominant cognitive style of the economics profession. Description in marketing scholarship was gradually augmented with various taxonomies, some of which were strictly denotative, such as the various classes of trade (wholesale and retail), for example, and others more abstract, what Bell would call sociographic, such as classes of goods (shopping goods and convenience goods, for example). Then came, also from these founding fathers, the first stab at more formal-analytic models, such as the marketing mix.

Today's models tend, generally, to be formal-analytical, but incorporating concepts, knowledge, theories, and methods from other disciplines. Thus we have behavioral models laced heavily with mathematical representations, econometric models (really maps), and mathematical models. And it is these, their advocates, and their users who now lead and shape marketing in the academy.

It is interesting that so many of the most eminent and productive marketing scholars that we identify with these formal analytics have recently shifted their attention toward strategic planning. (V. Srinivasan exemplifies this shift at the highest level of methodological and analytical prowess and integrity.) Why is this shift occurring? Let me suggest some possibilities.

First, success in business requires the firm to be compatible with its environment, which means, largely, the marketplace. Since marketing is presumed to know the marketplace better than anybody, then marketing should define the strategy and planning for the entire enterprise. So, at least, influential marketing academics such as Yoram Wind, David Montgomery, and George Day fervently assert. Nor are they entirely wrong in this assertion, though, I would argue, they overstate their case.

Another possible explanation may simply be that modeling and formal analytics are easier to do in strategic planning than in marketing. The further removed from the messiness of institutional and operational realities, the easier it is to do the math. There are fewer variables, and they have a greater constancy. But the appeal of strategic planning may not really be that the math is easier or the realities of practical affairs less intrusive. Rather, the appeal may be that it covers ground that has greater appeal to the academic, because being further removed from practice than even marketing models and formal marketing analytics, it is more susceptible to theorizing, conceptualizing, and the production of elegantly plausible paradigms. Why should a person choose to become an expert in a field of practice (like marketing), and yet choose to disassociate himself or herself professionally from that practice by residing in the academy except for the latter's emphasis on study, theory, and conceptualization—unless, of course, it is the academy's three other great attractions, June, July, and August? Thus it is understandable that we find a shift of interest into activities more amenable to conceptualization.

There is perhaps a third possibility. Could it be that there is some sense of boredom and exhaustion among academic marketers with the work of these past two decades? So many of the journal articles have become little more than emendations or elaborations of minor research, and so few people in industry seem to care. Could it be, therefore, that dealing with bigger and more important things has greater appeal and, also, greater possibility for attracting the attention of practitioners?

It doesn't matter, except perhaps to consider our own marketing problems in the academy. Why do so few people in industry seem to care? Why, for example, did General Electric—whence originated the marketing concept, marketing research in its most advanced form, and the idea of the marketing vice-president, and a marketing staff—begin disassembling its central marketing consulting staff, throw out most of the marketing staffs in its business units, and insist that more market research be done in the Japanese fashion, namely, by having the designers, the engineers, and the salespeople spend a lot of time talking to the trade, going into stores and distribution centers, and talking directly with customers and users?

Unless General Electric is totally aberrant, the question must be answered. My discussions and experiences with people at GE and elsewhere suggest that bright and knowledgeable people of affairs simply don't get much help or satisfaction from most of what we see in our professional journals. And it is not for lack of having tried and having spent heavily to make the promised helpfulness work. It is not for lack of patience. Nor is it for lack of intelligibility of the articles in the journals. How many academics have lived handsomely these recent years off seminars explaining with audio-visual clarity and proclaiming with firm conviction the liberating possibilities of their published works?

There is also a problem of source credibility. Neither our business seminars nor our private conversations with business people convey enough practical familiarity with the businesses, or with the operations and the problems of our listeners. We speak at lofty levels, drawing for familiarity and credibility on what we read in *Business Week, Fortune,* and sometimes doctoral theses. Too often we talk *at* business people, not with them; they are treated as an audience, we operate as performers; they are expected to listen, we to speak. But who will listen with conviction to speakers who will not themselves listen? Who will, for long, listen to (or even for a moment believe) the nonlistener whose knowledge comes largely from the press, from laboratory experiments with graduate students, from second-derivative and third-derivative field research (questionnaires, test markets, product movement data) that is rarely shaped or nourished by any direct or extended contact with customers, tradespeople, salespeople, line managers; in short, with systemic familiarity with the troublesome realities of daily competitive and organizational life? The problem is not that practitioners don't respect solid technical experts from without. It's that the practitioners live in a world of high stakes, and therefore need to feel that these experts know more than what is yielded by data analysis and theory alone. Would you, for your cancerous mother, engage an internist who had never seen the inside of a cadaver, obviously never had an internship, who systematically avoids further contact with his patients after having turned them over to the surgeons, and also avoids speaking afterward with those surgeons? Do you suppose his private insulation from practice would somehow reveal itself as you interview him? Would you let him treat your ailing mother?

None of this by itself, or even in conjunction with other arguments, is an argument against the quest that was the subject of this colloquium. The academy exists in part precisely for that quest. It is a quest that is not easily, and perhaps not even desirably, the proper domain of operating firms. But it raises the question of how we should order our lives and our scholarship. Given that we will have, increasingly, more of certain quantitative data, better data, more rapidly available data, and more powerful tools with which to analyze them and help manage their use in practice, what should be our priorities for how we spend our academic lives? Should we be inside the academy studying the organism from the outside through the quantitative data that are collected, collectible, or creatable (via experimental work), or should we be studying that organism also from the inside by systematically spending observational (and even working) time in it and with its workers?

The biggest risk is that the academy will become increasingly driven by the insulating and trivializing possibilities that the new technologies unfortunately make possible. We can see already how this has happened just in the past decade. Consider only how little we see of industrial marketing and of global competition in our prestigious journals. We do not know what's important, but what's amenable to our technologies of inquiry, to the data that are easily at hand, and otherwise convenient and least troublesome. Field work is a lot of trouble, both in terms of access and understanding. Further, it is expensive, unwieldy, and, in untrained hands, "unscientific" and not easily replicable or subject to verification.

Thus we risk that marketing scholars will be increasingly distant from the day-to-day work of marketing and the lives of operating managers. We court an even greater insularity when we strive increasingly for the refinement of method rather than the cultivation of relevance. Consider the short and, I would say, wasted history of operations research. Born in World War II to solve logistical and tactical problems on sea and land, it did marvelously and flourished later in business and in the academy by being thoroughly practical and applied. As computers became more readily and powerfully available, and mathematicians more abundantly attracted to the field, operations research became incredibly abstract, theoretical, obsessed with refinement of technique, and, essentially, irrelevant.

Sir Isaiah Berlin divided classical Russian literature into two major parts. He compared the Dostoevski strain to the fox, the Tolstoy strain to the hedgehog. The fox, he said, knows a great deal about a great many things. The hedgehog knows everything about one great thing. He preferred Tolstoy, the hedgehog, because knowing everything required not only pure knowledge, but also practical knowledge—what works. The "possible future" to which I want to appeal is the future of greater functionality, of more functional knowledge and practical wisdom. In short, what works: to be hedgehog rather than fox, to avoid the fate of neoclassical economics in which the anointed scholarly few speak only to each other.

I spoke earlier of the declining stability of relationships in the social world, and hence their declining "modelability," and of the need perhaps to think of modeling in a different way. There is, on this score, a good example of one way that rigorous methods and the new technologies can be productively linked with practice and real problems. It is John Little's well-known decision calculus, his idea of decision support systems. It is a superbly responsible and functional construction, and that's why managers listen. I also spoke of Frank Bass and others like him who seek verifiable functionality and concentrate on what's important.

To be a functioning academic devoted to the work of a practicing profession is especially difficult. There is a constant tension between the incentive structure of the academy and the expectations of the practitioner—in our case, business. The academy believes, as an act of faith, in the liberating possibilities of truth—pure knowledge. Business requires and wants practical knowledge, whether it's true or not. (Everybody knows, of course, that things don't have to be true in order to be so.) The academy is thus populated with a great many knowledge workers whose preferences about their work almost necessarily diverge from the preferences of the constituency for which they largely labor.

No matter how earnestly the academy asserts the probable future (or even immediate) importance and usefulness of its research and its normative constructs, it will generally be seen by practitioners as too remote and abstract. "Knowledge" is a different commodity for the academic worker and the business worker. At the extreme, the academic worker considers knowledge as being or aspiring to "truth"—pure knowledge that takes, finally, the form of theory, concepts, even laws of the market. This is far removed from what business thinks knowledge to be, which is practical knowledge that can be put to immediate use.

Figure 21.1 depicts these tensions as they manifest themselves today in the academy and also indicates some suggestions. Along the horizontal plane it shows "knowledge" as being either practical or pure, in the same way that Kant distinguished philosophically between pure reason and practical reason. Along the vertical plane are the institutional orientations of the knowledge workers in the academy. Some are oriented toward the kind of knowledge that interests business (at the top), and some more toward the kind that interests the academy (at the bottom). These orientations reflect, at the extremes, different notions about what knowledge is or should be. The traditional academic worker functions most commonly and most comfortably in the world of theory and concepts. He resides, mostly, in the southeast (SE) quadrant of Figure 21.1. There reside the profession's gatekeepers. They tend, generally, to define the

Figure 21.1 Institutional Orientation of the Knowledge Worker

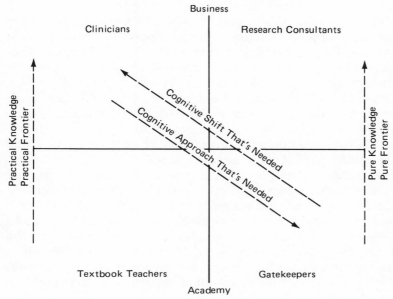

field, and defend and guard it against contamination. Contamination from what? From those knowledge workers whose orientations are mostly toward practical knowledge—what business easily understands, appreciates, and can put to easy immediate use. Those who would apparently contaminate reside cognitively in the northwest (NW) quadrant, the exact opposite and most distant point from the SE. They are the clinicians of the profession.

Academic knowledge workers who shift their interests and research laterally (westward) from the SE toward the development and teaching of practical knowledge distance themselves from what is purely academic work. To be thus interested in and researching what business regards as practical things, they are compelled to get close to business itself—at least, closer to its trade literature and to stories of its experiences and practices. They are drawn, as if by a powerful magnet, increasingly into the orbit of the work, interests, and cognitive styles of business, which not only wants practical knowledge, but also early results. As they move west, they are simultaneously drawn north. For them the scholarly research (and what comes from it) that has become de rigueur in the SE gradually looks less and less realistic and often irrelevant. They come to believe that the closed-system assumptions that drive scientific work in the hard sciences, and which they were trained and inspired to pursue in marketing, are simply inapplicable.

In their increasingly intimate association with practice, two other things often happen: First, they gradually shed the cognitive style of traditionally legitimate academic work—the deliberate, reflective attitude toward facts and a compelling personal need for deeper comprehension and fixed theory. Their research suffers, therefore, in both quantity and traditionally acceptable quality. It tends often to become, not research, but simply reporting—even often just storytelling. As a consequence, the second thing happens: These academics lose the respect of, and suffer declining repute among, traditional or orthodox academics.

Though these academic clinicians of business know, tell, and sometimes write a lot about practice, it is generally unacceptable to the gatekeepers, who seek seriously to protect what they believe is the scientific integrity and promise of science in marketing, and who establish the research agendas of the profession in the academy. The gatekeepers in the SE quadrant and the clinicians in the distant NE quadrant are driven, in the process, to the antipodes, increasingly alienated from each other, not speaking to or profiting from each other, as they should.

My colleague, Professor Thomas V. Bonoma, has written a very thoughtful paper on precisely how the two streams of research can complement each other.[4] He describes the process of field-based descriptive research and suggests that its particular place in the continuum of knowledge and theory-building methods may consist most powerfully in helping all research ask the right questions and include the right ingredients in its work. He shows that when the materials of the research are powerfully context driven, to miss, misunderstand, or avoid the complex context from which the materials arise is to hobble the conclusions drawn from the research. He demonstrates that in our branch of the social sciences, since "the system" can never be closed, to do research in it requires a deep understanding of the way its openness constantly confounds its operations and therefore, the generalizability of research findings that assume either a closed system or a system mathematically understandable by the introduction of probabilistic hedges.

The decision calculus is an important step toward helping to bring the "clinical" and the "gatekeeper" streams of research into closer proximity to each other. In this respect, the decision calculus is not important because of its sophisticated analytical tools and the data it employs analytically, but rather because of its closeness to practice. That it refers to itself as creating and using decision support systems is significant. It is and wants to be involved with practice and practitioners. It moves, generally, from the SE upward to the NE. This puts it into closer proximity with the clinical researchers who are involved with practice in a related way, sometimes even at a level of intimacy that enables them to understand business from the inside, to experience directly its reality, to know what managers really need and value, and to fully understand the forces that drive their lives and decisions. To understand those forces fully requires finally, however, for them to move westward to the NW. To presume to help with science those who operate in the NW, one must know the context of those who function in the NW. Because of this, the work of knowledge and science in the social sciences must transcend itself. It must become, also, the art of the possible. The profession's research consultants to business (who reside cognitively and operationally in the NE quadrant) know this very well, and that is why they are more comprehensible and more valued by practitioners than when they lived totally in the SE.

Mostly what is needed in the academy is a reciprocal shift of attitudes and cognitive styles. The academy's gatekeepers in the SE quadrant require more knowledge and intimacy with the practical affairs of business, so that the academy's methods, tools, and theories become more realistic, relevant, important, and employable. The close clinical partners of business in the academy, residing in the NW quadrant, require more employment of the formal methods and cognitive styles of the SE, a more generous attitude toward systematic inquiry and formal conceptualization. Both groups require greater and more wholesome interaction.

Nothing, said Peter Drucker, is more wasteful than doing with great efficiency that which should not be done. Nothing would be more wasteful than using the new technological facilitators becoming available in escalating abundance in the service of trivial, irrelevant, and unattainable ends. The dissent from economics that led to the creation of marketing in the academy must now shift to an accommodating and functional mode, serving sensibly both the standards of the academy and the requirements of the world of work. It is time for a new beginning.

Contributors

VINCENT P. BARABBA is director of market intelligence at Eastman Kodak Company and a former director of the U.S. Census Bureau. His experience includes the management of market research for Xerox Corporation, and he has held executive positions with Decision Making Information, Datamatics, Inc., and Communications Associates. An elected member of the International Statistical Institute, he has been a director of the Social Science Research Council and vice president of the American Statistical Association and the American Marketing Association.

DAVID K. BRAUN is director of media services at General Foods Corporation. He joined the company in 1964 as a sales representative in the desserts business and later moved into product management.

ROBERT D. BUZZELL is Sebastian S. Kresge Professor of Business Administration at Harvard Business School, where he has taught since 1961, chairing the marketing faculty from 1972 to 1977. Executive director of the Marketing Science Institute from 1968 to 1972, he is the author of several books, including *Marketing, A Contemporary Analysis* (McGraw-Hill, 1972). He has been a vice president of the American Marketing Association and a member of the Commerce Department's National Marketing Advisory Committee, as well as a director of several corporations.

JOHN F. CADY is associate professor of business administration at Harvard Business School, where he has taught since 1976. He has been a consultant to the Federal Trade Commission's Bureau of Consumer Protection and Bureau of Competition, as well as to a variety of business corporations. A member of the editorial board of the *Journal of Marketing*, he is the author of *Marketing and the Public Interest* (Marketing Science Institute, 1978) and *Drugs on the Market* (D. C. Heath, 1976).

E. RAYMOND COREY is Malcolm P. McNair Professor of Marketing and director of the Division of Research at Harvard Business School. He has been a member of the Harvard faculty since 1948. Executive director of the Marketing Science Institute, he is the author of several books, including *The Development of Markets for New Materials*, *Organization Strategy: A Marketing Approach*, and *Procurement Management: Strategy, Organization and Decision-Making*. Corey has also been a director of several corporations and a consultant to numerous others.

MICHAEL DREXLER is executive vice president and director of media and programming at Doyle Dane Bernbach, the advertising agency. A member of the American Association of Advertising Agencies Media Policy Committee and a director of the International Radio and Television Foundation, he has also been president of the Media Directors Council and cochairman of the Advertising Research Foundation Television Audience Measurement Committee.

STEPHAN H. HAECKEL is director of advanced market development in the corporate marketing department of IBM, with which he has been associated since 1960. He is a trustee of the Marketing Science Institute and a member of its executive and research policy committee.

JOHN R. HAUSER is associate professor of management science at the Sloan School of Management, Massachusetts Institute of Technology. Before joining the M.I.T. faculty in 1980, he taught at Northwestern University's Graduate School of Management. Coauthor of *Design and Marketing New Products* (Prentice-Hall, 1980), he is marketing editor of *Management Science*.

MARY GARDINER JONES is a partner in the law firm of Tedards & Jones. She has published widely on information technologies, consumer law, and policy subjects, and is coauthor of *Consumerism: A New Force in Society*. A commissioner of the Federal Trade Commission from 1964 to 1973, she has practiced law with private firms and served as a trial attorney with the Antitrust Division of the Department of Justice. From 1975 to 1982 Jones was vice president, consumer affairs, at Western Union Telegraph Co. She has taught at the College of Law and the College of Commerce and Business Administration, University of Illinois. President of the Consumer Interest Research Institute, she chairs the Council on Economic Priorities and is a director of the Consumer Research Foundation.

PATRICK J. KAUFMANN is an assistant professor of business administration at Harvard Business School. He received a Ph.D. in marketing from the Kellogg Graduate School of Management at Northwestern University, an MBA from Wharton, and a J.D. from Boston College. Before beginning an MBA program in 1978, he practiced law in Boston.

THEODORE LEVITT is Edward W. Carter Professor of Business Administration and head of the marketing area at Harvard Business School. His books include *Innovation in Marketing* (McGraw-Hill, 1962), *The Marketing Mode: Pathways to Corporate Growth* (McGraw-Hill, 1969), *The Third Sector: New Tactics for a Responsive Society* (Amacom, 1973), and *Marketing for Business Growth* (McGraw-Hill, 1976). He is a director of several corporations and has served as a consultant to many firms involved in manufacturing, finance, natural resources, and trade.

CHARLES M. LILLIS is dean of the College of Business and Administration at the University of Colorado. He was formerly manager of marketing consulting and research services in the corporate marketing department of General Electric Company. Before joining GE in 1980, he had been senior marketing scientist at Du Pont, senior research consultant for Boeing Computer Services, and associate dean for business and economics at Washington State University.

BONNIE J. MCIVOR is a corporate marketing consultant at General Electric Company.

MICHAEL J. NAPLES is president of the Advertising Research Foundation and a former director of marketing research at Lever Brothers Company. A former vice president (marketing research) of the American Marketing Association, he is a member of the Market Research Council and the Copy Research Council. He is the author of *Effective Frequency: The Relationship between Frequency and Advertising Effectiveness.*

JOHN A. QUELCH is associate professor of business administration at Harvard Business School, where he has taught since 1979. He has been a consultant to a variety of corporations and to U.S. and Canadian government agencies. He is coauthor of *Advertising and Promotion Management* (Chilton, 1983), *Cases in Advertising and Promotion Management* (Business Publications, 1983), and *Consumer Behavior for Marketing Managers* (Allyn and Bacon, 1984).

MICHAEL L. RAY is professor of marketing and communications at Stanford University Graduate School of Business. An academic trustee of the Marketing Science Institute, he has been a member of the editorial boards of the *Journal of Advertising Research*, the *Journal of Marketing Research*, and the *Journal of Consumer Research*, and served as associate editor of *Consumer Research*, and of *Communication Research*. His publications include *Advertising and Communication Management* (Prentice-Hall, 1982).

WALTER J. SALMON is Stanley Roth, Sr., Professor of Retailing at Harvard Business School. He serves on the boards of a number of U.S. corporations and is coauthor of *The Consumer and the Supermarket—1980* (National Association of Food Chains) and *The Super Store—Strategic Implications for the Seventies* (Marketing Sciences Institute, 1972). He is a frequent speaker and seminar leader for companies and trade associations in the field of retail distribution.

V. SRINIVASAN is professor of marketing and management science and director of the doctoral program at Stanford University Graduate School of Business, where he has taught since 1976. His research interests center on the application and development of quantitative techniques in marketing, measurement of consumer preference structures, and operations research. Srinivasan is an associate editor of both *Marketing Science* and *Management Science*.

LOUIS W. STERN is A. Montgomery Ward Professor of Marketing at Northwestern University, where he has taught since 1973. Earlier he was a member of the consumer marketing and business research staff at Arthur D. Little, Inc., as assistant project leader for the National Commission on Food Marketing, and a member of the Ohio State University faculty. A faculty associate of Management Analysis Center, Inc., and of the Hernstein Institute in Vienna, Stern is on the editorial boards of the *Journal of Marketing Research* and the *Journal of Marketing*. He is coauthor of *Marketing Channels* (Prentice-Hall, 1982), *Perspectives in Marketing Management* (Scott, Foresman, 1971), *Competition in the Marketplace* (Scott, Foresman, 1970), and *Distribution Channels: Behavioral Dimensions* (Houghton Mifflin, 1969).

RUDOLPH W. STRUSE III is director of the marketing research department at Carnation Company. Before joining Carnation in 1979, he was involved in market research at Oscar Mayer & Company and at Foote, Cone & Belding.

ERIC VON HIPPEL is associate professor at the Sloan School of Management, Massachusetts Institute of Technology, where he has taught since 1973. Cofounder and engineering manager of a firm manufacturing facsimile transceivers (subsequently acquired by Burroughs Corporation), he has a special interest in the management of technological innovation.

WILLIAM F. WATERS is director of international individual retail sales and marketing for Merrill Lynch Capital Markets. Except for a brief period as executive vice president of the Industrial National Bank of Rhode Island, he has been associated with Merrill Lynch since 1957, serving at various times as manager of the Providence and Baltimore offices, vice president of corporate and public affairs, and director of marketing services. Waters was one of the original regular panelists on the television program "Wall Street Week."

BORIS C. G. WILENKIN has been associated with Unilever Plc. and its subsidiaries since the mid-1950s. Formerly managing director of Unilever's French fats and dairy company, he is currently responsible for analyzing important trends in brand marketing that are likely to affect the parent corporation's policies and future strategy.

GEORGE S. YIP is a consultant at Management Analysis Center. His previous experience includes account management with the Birds Eye Foods division of Unilever Plc., and sales and business management positions in the consumer research division of Data Resources, Inc. He is the author of *Barriers to Entry: A Corporate Strategy Perspective* (D. C. Heath, 1982).

Notes

INTRODUCTION

1. The scenario was presented at the HBS 75th Anniversary Colloquium in the form of a slide presentation, with actors portraying the various scenes and a narrator describing it. This presentation has been converted into a videocassette, which is available from HBS Case Services (order number 9-884-004).
2. With apologies to David Montgomery and Glen Urban, who used a similar future scenario to introduce their book *Management Science in Marketing* (Englewood Cliffs, N.J.: Prentice-Hall, 1969). Their vision of the future, with respect to decision support systems, has proved to be an accurate one.

CHAPTER 1

1. An outstanding example is a series of cases that were developed by Darral Clarke of the Harvard Business School: "Clark Material Handling Group-Overseas" (A) and (B). These cases are available through HBS Case Services, order numbers 581–091 and 581–150.
2. Arthur Andersen and Co., *Future Trends in Wholesale Distribution: A Time of Opportunity* (Washington, D.C.: Distribution Research and Education Foundation, 1982), p. 7.
3. Ibid., p. 7.
4. This and several other specific suggestions for research appear in the original version of the paper prepared by Corey for the colloquium. See E. R. Corey, "The Role of Information/Communications Technology in Industrial Distribution" (Boston: Harvard Business School Working Paper, 1983).
5. Arthur Andersen and Co., pp. 16–17.
6. F. Warren McFarlan, "IS and Competitive Strategy," Harvard Business School Case Services, order number 184–055, p. 1.
7. Anne B. Pillsbury, "The Hard-Selling Supplier to the Sick," *Fortune*, July 26, 1982, pp. 57–61.
8. McFarlan, p. 1. See also "Trade Group Calls Automation Bias Issue Exaggerated," *Travel Weekly*, November 21, 1983, pp. 1 and 4.
9. See, for example, C. Glenn Walters and Blaise J. Bergiel, *Marketing Channels*, 2d ed. (Glenview, Ill.: Scott, Foresman and Company, 1982), Chapter 18.

10. The quotation is from a draft of Greyser's introductory comments for the colloquium session on advertising.
11. For an example, see "How Schweppes Used Satellite Broadcasting to Harmonize Its International Marketing," *International Management*, March 1983, pp. 78–79.
12. The quotation is from a written draft of Bass's comments for the colloquium session "Some Possible Futures."

CHAPTER 2

1. Alfred D. Chandler, Jr., *The Visible Hand: The Managerial Revolution in American Business* (Cambridge, Mass.: Harvard University Press, 1971) p. 209.
2. The declining participation of distributors in the hospital supplies market is an exception to the patterns observed in the case of the other four industries. A major reason, according to American Hospital Supply managers, is that over the past decade a very substantial part of industry growth has come through the development of new "doctor preference" items, which have high brand identity and tend to be sold directly to the hospitals by their manufacturers. These products are intended for use often in elective surgical procedures such as heart transplants, implantable cataract operations, reconstructive joint prosthesis, and kidney dialysis. The development of new surgical techniques has been made possible by medical specialty products, often highly technical and costly.
3. In a speech prepared for the National Tool Builders Association, an AT&T spokesperson for its telemarketing services estimated that the cost of making an industrial sales call had risen from $56 in 1971 to $178 in 1981.
4. This and subsequent quotations of wholesale company executives are drawn from interviews conducted by the author during 1982 and 1983.
5. Chandler, *The Visible Hand*, p. 236.
6. Alfred D. Chandler, Jr., "Global Enterprise: The Formative Years" (typescript), Chapter 1, p. 18.
7. Scott Moss, *An Economic Theory and Business Strategy* (London: Oxford University Press, 1981), pp. 110–11. Minimum efficient scale is one of several important concepts and definitions articulated and used by Moss. Particularly important are those that are spelled out in Moss's Chapters 6 and 7, on vertical integration.
8. Oliver E. Williamson, "The Modern Corporation: Origins, Evolution, Attributes," *Journal of Economic Literature* 19 (December 1981): p. 181.
9. Ibid., p. 1546.
10. Ibid.
11. Louis Stern and Torger Reve, "Distribution Channels as Political Economies: A Framework of Comparative Analysis," *Journal of Marketing*, 44 (Summer 1981): pp. 52–64.
12. Ibid., p. 8.

CHAPTER 3

1. Transportation Data Coordinating Committee, *The U.S. Electronic Data Interchange Standards*, vol. 1 (Washington, D.C.: Transportation Data Coordinating Committee, 1981).
2. Arthur D. Little, Inc., *Electronic Data Interchange for the Grocery Industry: Feasibility Report* (Washington, D.C.: Arthur D. Little, Inc., 1980), pp. 13–14.
3. Peter B. Evans, "Multiple Hierarchies and Organizational Control," *Administrative Science Quarterly* 20 (1975): pp. 250–59. See also, Howard Aldrich and David A. Whetten, "Organization-sets, action-sets, and networks: making the most of simplicity," in Paul C. Nystrom and William H. Starbuck (eds.), *Handbook of Organization Design*, vol. 1 (New York: Oxford University Press, 1981), p. 393.

CHAPTER 4

1. The research for this paper was conducted by a group of second-year students, under the supervision of the author, in fulfillment of the requirements of the Creative Marketing Strategy course at the Harvard Business School during the 1982–1983 academic year. The members of the student group were Jose Abete, Matt Czajkowski, John Hoagland, Laurence Lepard, Rich Schlesinger, and Dennis Wong. Marci Dew of the consulting firm of IAMCO also participated in the research. The author is deeply indebted to them for their assistance.
2. Electronic in-home retailing is defined, for purposes of this article, as a videotex system with several characteristics. It makes available to the user, in his or her home, information selected by the user when the user demands it. The system also allows the user to communicate with the information provider and to pay for products or services purchased. Furthermore, to the extent that the system offers for sale products that cannot be transmitted electronically, it must also include a fulfillment and delivery system similar to those operated by direct mail retailers.
3. See Chapter 16, by John A. Quelch and George S. Yip.
4. The studies in full are: *The New TV Technologies: The View from the Viewer* (New York: Benton and Bowles, 1981); Stephen B. Ash and John Quelch, "The Impact of Videotex Technology on Shopping Intentions," Harvard Business School Working Paper, 1983; and Roger Blackwell and Nancy Offnut, "The Impact of Electronic Shopping on Consumer Decisions," paper presented to the American Marketing Association Educator's Conference, Chicago, Illinois, August 2, 1982.

CHAPTER 5

1. John D. C. Little, "Decision Support Systems for Marketing Managers," *Journal of Marketing* 43 (Summer 1979):11.

2. Peter G. W. Keen and S. Scott Morton, *Decision Support Systems: An Organizational Perspective* (Reading, Mass.: Addison-Wesley, 1978), p. 97.
3. Little, "Decision Support Systems," p. 15.

CHAPTER 6

1. Everett M. Rogers, *Diffusion of Innovations* (New York: Free Press, 1962), pp. 25–27.
2. Everett M. Rogers with F. Floyd Shoemaker, *Communication of Innovations* (New York: Free Press, 1971), pp. 101–103.
3. Nigel Piercy, "Marketing Information Bridging the Quicksand between Technology and Decision Making," *The Quarterly Review of Marketing*, August 1983, p. 3.
4. Rogers, *Communication of Innovations*, p. 99.
5. Material in this section is drawn from the summary report of the actual responses to the nineteen-question survey that was carried out, under my direction, with a number of groups within the U.S. Census Bureau (Washington, D.C.) during March and April 1976. A particularly thorough report was submitted by the Table Generator Branch, Systems Software Division, Bureau of the Census, *Systems Software Division's Response to the Director's Nineteen Questions on Generalized Tabulation Systems at the Census Bureau* (Washington, D.C., 1976).
6. Rogers, *Communication of Innovations*, pp. 112–13.
7. Ian I. Mitroff, Vincent P. Barabba, and Ralph H. Kilmann, "The Application of Behavioral and Philosophical Technologies to Strategic Planning: A Case Study of a Large Federal Agency," *Management Science*, September 1977, pp. 44–58.
8. Richard O. Mason, Ian I. Mitroff, and Vincent P. Barabba, "Creating the Manager's Plan Book: A New Route to Effective Planning," *Planning Review*, July 1980, pp. 11–16.
9. For more information on group formation techniques, see Ralph H. Kilmann, *Social Systems Design: Normative Theory and the MAPS Design Technology* (New York: Elsevier, 1977).
10. For a more detailed description of how this technique was used in an initial attempt in designing an MDSS, see Gerald Zaltman, ed., *Management Principles for Nonprofit Agencies and Organizations*, "Management Information vs. Misinformation Systems" (New York: AMACOM, 1979).
11. I am indebted to my colleague George Nix for this basic definition of an MDSS, which was contained in a commentary on an earlier draft of this paper. He also pointed out that the subject of the Census Bureau GTS and the MDSS have much in common: the GTS is a generalized system that replaces a variety of custom programs. In a similar vein, the MDSS is a generalized capability that replaces large numbers of customized programs, while it also systematizes and enhances the informal procedures.

12. Rogers, *Communication of Innovations*, pp. 112–13.
13. For a more detailed description of the Kodak MAIN system, see Vincent P. Barabba, "Market Intelligence: The Critical Issues—And Some Answers," The Fifteenth Albert Wesley Frey Lecture (University of Pittsburgh Press, 1982). See also Vincent P. Barabba, "Making Use of Methodologies Developed in Academia: Lessons from One Practitioner's Experience," in Ralph H. Kilmann, K. Thomas, D. P. Slevin, R. Nath, and S. L. Jerrell, eds., *Producing Useful Knowledge for Organizations* (New York: Praeger, 1983).
14. I am indebted for many insights into this area to the work of Professor Gerald Zaltman and his model of knowledge utilization. See Gerald Zaltman, "Enhancing Research Utilization: Guidelines for a Funding Agency," prepared for the RANN Research Utilization Task Force, June 1976. An earlier treatment of this topic can also be found in Vincent P. Barabba, "The Future Role of Information in American Life," in Norman Cousins, ed., *Reflections of America* (Washington, D.C.: U.S. Government Printing Office, 1980).
15. Vincent P. Barabba, "The Kodak MAIN System: Progress Report Number 1," prepared for limited distribution within the Eastman Kodak Company (Rochester, New York, July 21, 1982).
16. John F. Rockart and Michael E. Treacy, "The CEO Goes On-Line," *Harvard Business Review*, January-February 1982, pp. 82–88.
17. Ibid.
18. G. R. Wagner, "DSS: Dealing with Executive Assumptions in the Office of the Future," *Managerial Planning*, March-April 1982, pp. 4–10.
19. Ian I. Mitroff, Richard O. Mason, and Vincent P. Barabba, *The 1980 Census: Policymaking amid Turbulence* (Lexington, Mass.: Lexington Books, D. C. Heath, 1983).
20. Ibid., p. xiv.

CHAPTER 8

1. This paper incorporates information and ideas developed by Doyle Dane Bernbach Senior Vice-President Watson "Jay" James and his colleagues in the Video Technology/Programming group.

CHAPTER 9

1. *London Financial Times*, April 27, 1983.

CHAPTER 10

1. Nielsen Station Index, *1982–83 Perspective on Working Women*, p. 19.
2. Larry Light, "Socioeconomic Changes: The Challenges Facing Us," speech given at the Media Decisions Media Day, New York, New York, November 1977, p. 2.

3. A. C. Nielsen Co., *Nielsen News Release*, February 1978 and February 1983.
4. John Hunt, "Take Me Back to Tulsa: Television in Transition," *The Changing Media*, November 1982, p. 2.
5. *PRIZM: The ZIP-Market Cluster System* (New York), p. 2. This is a sales brochure.
6. *Nielsen News Release*, February 1983.
7. Used by permission.
8. Used by permission.
9. Used by permission.
10. James L. Ferguson, remarks made at General Foods' Worldwide Management Meeting, Rye Brook, New York, May 10, 1983.

CHAPTER 12

1. The analysis of information expressed here is derived principally from Harlan Cleveland's writings about the information society. See Harlan Cleveland, "Information as a Resource," *The Futurist*, December 1982, pp. 34–39. See also the list of information properties identified by the U.S. representations to the high-level conference on Information Computer and Communications Policy at the Organization for Economic Cooperation and Development at Paris, 1980. Arthur Baskin and Jane Yurow, "The Foundations of United States Policy," NTIA, Paris, France, October 1980.
2. Cleveland, "Information," p. 2.
3. John Tydeman, Hubert Lipinski, Richard P. Adler, Michael Nyhan, and Laurence Zwimpfer, *Teletext and Videotex in the United States* (New York: McGraw Hill, 1982).
4. Ibid., p. 6.
5. See note 3.
6. *Business Week*, January 29, 1981, p. 4.
7. See Appendix A for Table 12, prepared by Tydeman et al., p. 224.
8. Tadahiro Sekimoto, president of Nippon Electric Co., in the *New York Times*, January 9, 1983. See also the issue for January 8, 1983.
9. In one three-year period (1977–1980), five newspaper chains plus Westinghouse and American Express made major acquisitions in the cable business, presumably to assure themselves of outlets for their software. *CableVision*, February 15, 1980, p. 129.
10. For example, New York University's Center for Alternative Media joined with WETA, the Washington, D.C., public broadcast station, to test a teletext system in Washington, D.C. Online Computer Library Center (OCLC) joined with Bank One of Columbus, Ohio, and the League of Women Voters to test a videotex system in Columbus, Ohio. The University of Kentucky, U.S. Department of Agriculture, Tandy Corporation, and Western Union joined forces to test a videotex system to deliver agricultural information to farmers in four counties near Louisville. AT&T, Consumers Union, and Knight-Ridder test marketed a viewdata system in Coral Cables, Florida, which was also par-

ticipated in by Sears, Roebuck and B. Dalton Booksellers. AT&T and Times Mirror are jointly testing a videotex system in San Diego.

11. *New York Times*, January 8, 1983, p. 1; *Washington Post*, January 20, 1983, p. E2.
12. *New York Times*, April 15, 1983, p. 1.
13. *Wall Street Journal*, January 8, 1983.
14. Bowen and Schneider, "Freeware—An Optimistic Approach to Software Piracy," *Today*, January–February 1983, p. 14.
15. Irwin Stetzler, president, NERA International, Inc., "Economic Defenses in Antitrust Litigation," London, England, April 12, 1983 (mimeographed).
16. A. Oettinger provides a dramatic example of the global nature of the information world of a Polish airline clerk in Warsaw who makes reservations using a computer located in Georgia and a satellite dish located on the Queen Elizabeth II. *Bulletin of ASIS*, October 1978, p. 16.
17. Eli Noam, "Towards an Integrated Communication Market: Overcoming the Local Monopoly of Cable Television," *Communications Law Journal* 34 (1984), p. 209–257.

CHAPTER 13

1. A detailed published anaylsis of the results of this study is not available. For an overview of the research using the research cover story, see M. L. Ray and Alan G. Sawyer, "Repetition in Media Models: A Laboratory Technique," *Journal of Marketing Research*, February 1971, pp. 20–30; M. L. Ray, "Marketing Communication and the Hierarchy of Effects," in Peter Clarke, ed., *New Models for Communication Research* (Beverly Hills, Calif.: Sage, 1973); M. L. Ray, "Applications of a Marketing Communication Research System" (University of Illinois Department of Advertising, Working Paper, 1983). For other uses of the data in a consumer information services setting, see note 2.
2. See Michael L. Ray and Donald A. Dunn, "Local Consumer Information Systems: The Market for Information and Its Effect on the Market," in Andrew Mitchell, ed., *The Effect of Information on Consumer and Market Behavior* (Chicago: American Marketing Association, 1978), pp. 92–96; Donald A. Dunn and Michael L. Ray, "A Plan for Consumer Information Systems Development, Implementation and Evaluation," in Jerry Olson, ed., *Advances in Consumer Research*, vol. 7 (Ann Arbor: Association for Consumer Research, 1980), pp. 250–54.

CHAPTER 14

1. "The New Magicians of Market Research," *Fortune*, July 25, 1983.
2. Paper presented at the Advertising Research Foundation's New Advertising Research Technologies Workshop, New York, December 1982, p. 9.

CHAPTER 15

1. "Technology for Technology's Sake?" *Forbes*, May 9, 1983, pp. 196–204.
2. Ibid.
3. John F. Magee, "Assessing a Company's Technological Program," *Financial Analysts Journal*, July-August 1982, pp. 56–59.
4. William Abernathy, Kim Clark, and Alan Kantrow, *Industrial Renaissance: Producing a Competitive Future for America* (New York: Basic Books, 1983).
5. Ibid., p. 22.
6. "The Strategic Management of Technology" (Cambridge, Mass.: Arthur D. Little, 1981).
7. See Magee, "Assessing a Company's Technological Program," and, for more extensive treatment of the subjects covered here, "The Strategic Management of Technology," from which this discussion is derived.
8. Nathan Rosenberg and W. Edward Steinmueller, "The Economic Implications of the VLSI Revolution," in Nathan Rosenberg, ed., *Inside the Black Box: Technology and Economics* (New York: Cambridge University Press, 1982), p. 180.
9. Everett M. Rogers, *Diffusion of Innovations* (New York: Free Press, 1965), p. 4.
10. F. Warren McFarlan and James L. McKenney, *Corporate Information Systems Management* (Homewood, Ill.: Richard D. Irwin, 1983).
11. Glenda G. Anderson et al., "IBM and Computer Integrated Manufacturing," Field Study Report, Creative Marketing Strategy Course, Harvard Business School, May 1983 (typescript).
12. R. J. Pearsall, "Techniques for Assessing External Design of Software," *IBM Systems Journal*, 21 (1982): 211.
13. "Battle of the Networks," *Datamation*, March 1982, p. 12.
14. "The Squeeze Begins in Personal Computers," *Business Week*, May 30, 1983.
15. "Strategic Partnering: A New Formula to Crack Markets in the 80s," *Electronic Business*, March 1983.
16. Computer Devices, Inc., "Selling Intelligent Terminals," HBS Case Services, 9-581-146.

CHAPTER 16

1. The "cottage small . . ." is from the song "There will always be an England."
2. Johan Arndt, "Toward a Concept of Domesticated Markets," *Journal of Marketing*, 43 (Fall 1979): 69–75.
3. Oliver E. Williamson, *Markets and Hierarchies: Analysis and Antitrust Implications* (New York: Free Press, 1975).
4. Gerald Haslam, "The Whole Business of Corporate Investment," in *Videotex: Key to the Information Revolution* (New York: Online Publications, 1982).

5. Brochure advertising a conference "Videotex II" at the Ohio State University in October 1982, chaired by Professor Wayne W. Talarzyk.
6. Viewtron has announced that it will launch the country's first commercial videotex system in September 1983 in three Florida counties. Times Mirror will launch its Gateway in spring 1984 in the greater Los Angeles area.
7. Videotex was "invented" by a British Post Office engineer, Sam Fedida, in 1965.
8. John Tydeman, Hubert Lipinski, Richard P. Adler, Michael Nyhan, and Laurence Zwimpfer, *Teletext and Videotex in the United States* (New York: McGraw-Hill, 1982).
9. The authors thank Professors Robert D. Buzzell, John F. Cady, and Richard Tedlow for their help on this section.
10. Alfred D. Chandler, Jr., *The Visible Hand: The Managerial Revolution in American Business* (Cambridge, Mass.: Belknap Press, Harvard University Press, 1977).
11. Michael E. Porter, *Competitive Strategy: Techniques for Analyzing Industries and Competitors* (New York: Free Press, 1980).
12. See Derek F. Abell, "Strategic Windows," *Journal of Marketing*, 42 (Summer 1978): 21–26.
13. Teleshopping is defined as a videotex service that provides consumers with an opportunity to make an interactive purchase transaction, not as a service that merely permits consumers to retrieve product or store information.
14. John A. Quelch and Hirotaka Takeuchi, "Nonstore Marketing: Fast Track or Slow?" *Harvard Business Review*, July-August 1981, pp. 75–84.

CHAPTER 17

1. "Container Woes in Dockland," *Time*, October 17, 1977.
2. *New York Times*, January 29, 1978, p. F3.
3. "Users for Gunk," *Time*, January 28, 1980.
4. E. Mansfield et al., "Social and Private Rates of Return from Industrial Innovations," *Quarterly Journal of Economics* (May 1977), pp. 221–40.
5. Determining the benefits users (and manufacturers) may potentially gain from new product development activity is a complex issue, which I have discussed elsewhere. (E. von Hippel, "Appropriability of Innovation Benefit as a Predictor of the Source of Innovation," *Research Policy* 11 (1982): 95–115.) The reader may get a flavor of the complexity by observing that neither the costs of a given innovation nor its benefits are immutable. Consider costs: Consumers A and B might both have an equally strong need for a special program for their home computers, but only consumer B is a programmer. Probably, therefore, B's out-of-pocket costs to develop the program would be lower. Analogously, two firms might be aware of a need for a new process machine,

but firm A invents a cheaper approach to the problem than firm B does, and, again, B's costs would be lower. Similarly, the benefit potentially obtainable from working toward the solution of a given need is not immutable. If the solution offers benefit in the form of a competitive advantage—as would be the case with a manufacturing firm improving its production processes, for example—benefit actually obtained would obviously depend on the speed and scale with which the solution was deployed, on lead time over competitors, and so on.

6. G. L. Urban and J. R. Hauser, *Design and Marketing of New Products* (Englewood Cliffs, N.J.: Prentice-Hall, 1980). Chapter 9, pp. 185–224, provides an excellent discussion of perceptual mapping.

7. Currently there are no data that would allow us to say what proportion of all the need specifications for promising future products is rendered invisible by this limitation, although such data could be collected. One approach to an analysis of the problem would be to identify a representative sample of today's "important" (by some criterion) new products, and then see what proportion of these have important functional attributes not present in products that preceded them.

8. Urban and Hauser, pp. 149, 159–60.

9. W. J. Gordon, *Synectics: The Development of Creative Capacity* (New York: Harper & Row, 1961).

10. T. J. Allen and D. Marquis, "Positive and Negative Biasing Sets: The Effects of Prior Experience on Research Performance," *IEEE Transactions on Engineering Management*, December 1964. Also, B. Berelson and G. Steinger, *Human Behavior: An Inventory of Scientific Findings* (New York: Harcourt, Brace and World, 1964), pp. 203–208.

11. K. Duncker, "On Problem Solving," translated by Lynne S. Lees in J. Dashiell, ed., *Psychological Monographs*, vol. 58, no. 5 (Washington, D.C.: American Psychological Association, 1945).

12. Robert E. Adamson and D. W. Taylor, "Functional Fixedness as Related to Elapsed Time and to Set," *Journal of Experimental Psychology* 47 (1954): 122–26. See also S. L. Abraham, "Mechanization in Problem Solving: The Effect of Einsellung," in *Psychological Monographs*, vol. 5A, no. 6 (Washington, D.C.: American Psychological Association, 1942).

CHAPTER 18

1. Warren McFarlan and James L. McKenney, *Corporate Information Systems Management* (Homewood, Ill.: Richard D. Irwin, 1983).

CHAPTER 19

1. Robyn M. Dawes and Bernard Corrigan, "Linear Models in Decision Making," *Psychological Bulletin* 81(1974): 95–106.

2. Hillel J. Einhorn, "Expert Measurement and Mechanical Combination," *Organizational Behavior and Human Performance* 7(1972): 86–106.

3. *Time*, January 3, 1983, p. 28.

4. John D. C. Little, "Decision Support Systems for Marketing Managers," *Journal of Marketing* 43 (Summer 1979): 9–27.

5. On the level of business activity, see *Fortune*, January 24, 1983, p. 48.

6. For a detailed review of the alternative approaches, see Harper W. Boyd, Jr., and Jean-Claude Larreche, "The Foundations of Marketing Strategy," in Gerald Zaltman and Thomas V. Bonoma, eds., *Review of Marketing* (Chicago: American Marketing Association, 1978), pp. 41–72.

7. Throughout this chapter, references to the BCG approach relate to portfolio planning via the market-share, market-growth matrix. The remarks do not apply to the more general views of the Boston Consulting Group with respect to strategic planning.

8. In particular, see Yoram Wind and Vijay Mahajan, "Designing Product and Business Portfolios," *Harvard Business Review*, January-February 1981, pp. 155–65; and Walter Kiechel III, "The Decline of the Experience Curve," *Fortune*, October 5, 1981, pp. 139–46.

9. Lynn W. Phillips, Dae R. Chang, and Robert D. Buzzell, "Product Quality, Cost Position, and Business Performance: A Test of Some Key Hypotheses," *Journal of Marketing* 47 (Spring 1983): 26–43.

10. Walter Kiechel III, "Corporate Strategists under Fire," *Fortune*, December 27, 1982, pp. 34–39.

11. Robert D. Buzzell, Bradley T. Gale, and Ralph S. M. Sultan, "Market Share: A Key to Profitability," *Harvard Business Review*, January-February 1975, pp. 97–106.

12. David J. Ravenscraft, "Structure-Profit Relationships at the Line of Business and Industry Level" (Washington, D.C.: Bureau of Economics, Federal Trade Commission, Working Paper, July 1981); and Malcolm B. Coate, "An Empirical Analysis of the Boston Consulting Group's Portfolio Model" (Washington, D.C.: Bureau of Economics, Federal Trade Commission, Working Paper no. 71, August 1982).

13. For a recent study, see Marvin B. Lieberman, "The Learning Curve and Pricing in the Chemical Processing Industries" (Stanford, Calif.: Graduate School of Business, Stanford University, Working Paper, May 1983).

14. For a detailed description of the mathematical models underlying STRATPORT, see J. C. Larreche and V. Srinivasan, "STRATPORT: A Model for the Evaluation and Formulation of Business Portfolio Strategies," *Management Science*, 1982; pp. 979–1001. A nonmathematical description with a numerical example is given in J. C. Larreche and V. Srinivasan, "STRATPORT: A Decision Support System for Strategic Planning," *Journal of Marketing* 45 (Fall 1981): 39–52. The present paper, in addition to making a shift in emphasis toward computer-aided decision making, proposes a critical modification in the way

experience effects are built into the cost function. Moreover, an important extension for easier implementation of STRATPORT and an alternative framework to consider cost and marketing interdependencies are presented here.

15. Alfred Rappaport, "Selecting Strategies That Create Shareholder Value," *Harvard Business Review*, May-June 1981, pp. 139–49.
16. William F. Sharpe, "Capital-Asset Prices: A Theory of Market Equilibrium under Conditions of Risk," *Journal of Finance* 19(1964): 425–42.
17. Marvin B. Lieberman, "The Learning Curve, Pricing, and Market Structure in the Chemical Processing Industries" (Ph.D. diss., Harvard University, 1982), pp. 45–46.
18. See *Perspectives on Experience* (Boston, Mass.: Boston Consulting Group, 1968), Appendix A.
19. John D. C. Little, "Models and Managers: The Concept of a Decision Calculus," *Management Science*, 1970; pp. B466–B485.
20. See Lieberman, "The Learning Curve, Pricing, and Market Structure," p. 46. The unit cost h_P of the Pth unit of production in the business unit is modeled as

$$h_P = c\, P^{-(1-s)\lambda}\, I^{-s\lambda}$$

where c denotes the cost of production for the first unit, I is the industry's cumulative production, λ is the experience curve coefficient, and s $(0 < s < 1)$ is the proportion of learning spilled over. If $s = 0$, all learning is proprietary, whereas $s = 1$ denotes total spillover.
21. In logarithmic form, the unit cost expression becomes

$$\log h_P = \log c - \lambda[(1-s)\log P + s \log I].$$

If the spillover parameter s is known, c and λ can be estimated by standard regression techniques. The parameter s is estimated to be the value of s $(0 < s < 1)$ that maximizes the coefficient of determination of the above regression.
22. The approach presented is an extension of Larreche and Srinivasan, "STRATPORT: A Model," p. 992. The base discount rate r would be given by

$$r = \left(\frac{1}{1+DE}\right) r_f + \left(\frac{DE}{1+DE}\right) r_d$$

where DE is the debt-equity ratio (in market value terms), r_f is the risk-free rate of return (e.g., short-term treasury bills), and r_d is the debt cost of capital (interest rate on debt times $(1 - \text{tax rate})$). The risk factor r' unique to the business unit would be given by

$$r' = \left(\frac{1}{1+DE}\right) \text{Beta}\,(r_m - r_f)$$

where Beta is the "beta coefficient" for the business unit under consideration (see William F. Sharpe, "Capital-Asset Prices"), r_m is the expected rate of return on a well-diversified investment portfolio (e.g., *Standard and Poor's* 500) and DE and r_f are as defined before.

23. Coate, "An Empirical Analysis of the BCG Portfolio Model."

CHAPTER 20

1. R. C. Blattberg and K. J. Wisniewski, "Sales Response Estimation Using UPC Scanning Data," paper read at the First Marketing Science Conference, University of Southern California, Los Angeles, March 16–18, 1983.

2. P. M. Guadagni and J. D. C. Little, "A Logit Model of Brand Choice Calibrated on Scanner Data," *Marketing Science*, vol. 2, no. 4, Summer 1983.

3. A. Kuritsky, J. D. C. Little, A. J. Silk, and E. S. Bassman, "The Development, Testing, and Execution of a New Marketing Strategy at AT&T Long Lines," *Interfaces* 12 (December 1982): 22–27.

4. *Encyclopedia Americana* (1967), vol. 4, p. 393. All dates and descriptions of the Copernican revolution are from the *Encyclopedia Americana*.

5. A. P. French, "Particles and Newtonian Mechanics," in *Physics: A New Introductory Course* (Cambridge, Mass.: M.I.T. Science Teaching Center, 1965), pt. 1, pp. 11-17, 11-18.

6. For example, see J. D. C. Little, "A Model of Adaptive Control of Promotional Spending," *Operations Research* 14 (November-December 1966): 1075–98. Interestingly, Little's doctorate is in physics and he is also well known for his work in queuing theory and traffic signal optimization.

7. J. D. C. Little, "Aggregate Advertising Models: The State of the Art," *Operations Research* 27 (July-August 1979): 629.

8. Ibid., p. 644.

9. Ibid.

10. F. M. Bass, "A Discussion of Different Philosophies in the Analysis of Advertising-Sales Relationships," and J. D. C. Little, "Comments on Bass." Papers read at the First Marketing Science Conference, The Institute of Management Sciences, University of Southern California, Los Angeles, March 16–18, 1983.

11. E. H. Madden, "Making Sense of Science," in E. H. Madden, ed., *The Structure of Scientific Thought* (Boston, Mass.: Houghton-Mifflin, 1960).

12. See P. E. Gray and C. L. Searle, *Electronic Principles: Physics, Models, and Circuits* (New York: John Wiley, 1969).

13. R. C. Blattberg and A. P. Jeuland, "A Micro-modeling Approach to Investigate the Advertising-Sales Relationships," *Management Science*, September 1981, pp. 988–1005.

14. Ibid., p. 989.

15. Clarke demonstrated this phenomenon in an insightful review of the econometric literature on advertising lag effects. See D. G. Clarke,

"Econometric Measurement of the Duration of Advertising Effects on Sales," *Journal of Marketing Research* 13 (1976): 354–357.

16. C. G. Hempel, "Geometry and Empirical Science," *American Mathematical Monthly* 52 (1945), pp. 7–17. Reprinted in Madden, *The Structure*, pp. 71–80; quote is from p. 71.

17. See, for example, G. L. Urban and J. R. Hauser, *Design and Marketing of New Products* (Englewood Cliffs, N.J.: Prentice-Hall, 1980).

18. J. R. Hauser and S. M. Shugan, "Defensive Marketing Strategy," *Marketing Science*, vol. 2, no. 4, Fall 1983, pp. 319–360. See also the detailed discussion and empirical justification of the axioms.

19. For example, K. Lancaster, *Consumer Demand: A New Approach* (New York: Columbia University Press, 1971). But such ideas are classical as well. See marketing interpretation in J. R. Hauser and P. Simmie, "Profit Maximizing Perceptual Positions: An Integrated Theory for the Selection of Product Features and Price," *Management Science*, vol. 27, no. 1, January 1981, pp. 33–56.

20. J. R. Hauser and S. P. Gaskin, "Application of the 'Defender' Consumer Model," *Marketing Science*, vol. 3, no. 4, Fall 1984.

21. See, for example, V. Srinivasan, "Comments on the Role of Price in Individual Utility Judgments," in L. McAlister, ed., *Choice Models for Buyer Behavior* (Greenwich, Conn.: JAI Press, 1982).

22. See, for example, predictive tests in A. M. Tybout and J. R. Hauser, "A Marketing Audit Using a Conceptual Model of Consumer Behavior: Application and Evaluation," *Journal of Marketing* 45 (Summer 1981): 82–101; and J. R. Hauser and G. L. Urban, "A Normative Methodology for Modeling Consumer Response to Innovation," *Operations Research* 25 (July–August 1977): 579–619.

23. There are other confounding factors to consider in our experiment. For example, model 1 is based on axiom 4, but it also relies on axiom 2, heterogeneity of consumer tastes. Our model with price as an attribute did not use the full power of axiom 2. Thus, one can also interpret our experiment as favoring heterogeneity of consumer tastes over heterogeneity of consumer perceptions. A later test using a model combining axiom 2 and price as an attribute showed that the effect is still there but somewhat mitigated. See Hauser and Gaskin, "Application of the 'Defender' Consumer Model."

24. See, for example, B. J. Calder, L. W. Phillips, and A. M. Tybout, "Designing Research for Application," *Journal of Consumer Research* 8 (September 1981): 197–207. For example, they state on p. 198: "Theory applications call for falsification test procedures" and "Theories that survive rigorous attempts at falsification are accepted and accorded scientific status."

25. J. Losse, *A Historical Introduction to the Philosophy of Science* (New York: Oxford University Press, 1972), p. 192.

26. Einstein's derivation, however, was independent of Lorentz's derivation. Such contraction is still known as Lorentz contraction, or, occasionally, Lorentz-Einstein contraction. See A. P. French, *Physics*, pt. 2, chap. 3. One can argue that Einstein would have discovered this con-

traction anyway without Lorentz, but who can really say that Lorentz's work did not indirectly influence Einstein or that Lorentz's work did not facilitate the acceptance of Einstein's radical theories. (Lorentz contraction is the phenomenon that objects in motion with a velocity, v, relative to the frame of reference appear to be shorter by a factor of $(1-v^2/c^2)^{1/2}$ where c is the velocity of light.)

27. T. S. Kuhn, "The Structure of Scientific Revolutions." Reprinted in *Foundations of the Unity of Science: Toward an International Encyclopedia of United Science*, vol. 2, no. 2 (Chicago: University of Chicago Press, 1970), p. 139.

28. J. D. C. Little, "Decision Support Systems for Marketing Managers," *Journal of Marketing* 43 (1979): 9–27.

29. A. J. Silk and G. L. Urban "Pretest Market Evaluation of New Packaged Goods: A Model and Measurement Methodology," *Journal of Marketing Research* 15 (1978): 171–91.

30. G. L. Urban and G. M. Katz, "How Accurate Are Simulated Test Markets and How Should Managers Use Them?" in R. K. Srivastava and A. D. Schocker, eds., *Analytic Approaches to Products and Marketing Planning: The Second Conference* (Cambridge, Mass.: Marketing Science Institute, 1982).

31. A. Einstein and L. Infeld, "The Evolution of Physics" (1938), in French, *Physics*, pt. 2, chap. 1, p. 1.

32. For example, you can neither prove nor disprove the existence of an infinity larger than the number of integers (countably infinite), yet smaller than the number of points on a real line between 0.0 and 1.0 (uncountably infinite). For nonmathematical readers, there are as many points in the one-dimensional interval between 0.0 and 1.0 as there are in a three-dimensional universe that stretches to infinity in all directions. At infinity we must rely on deductive logic, not intuition.

33. J. U. Farley, "An Optimal Plan for Salesmen's Compensation," *Journal of Marketing Research* 1 (1964): 39–43.

34. V. Srinivasan, "The Equal Commission Rate Policy for a Multi-Product Salesforce," *Management Science*, July 1981, pp. 731–56.

35. By *evoking* we mean that the consumer has enough information about the product so that he or she can evaluate it. This is a stronger condition than awareness of the product.

36. See note 2.

37. The thoughts expressed in this essay are the result of many stimulating discussions I have had with my colleagues. Those who have influenced my personal philosophy include John Little, Glen Urban, Al Silk, and Leigh McAlister of M.I.T.; Steve Shugan and Abel Jeuland of the University of Chicago; Brian Sternthal and Alice Tybout of Northwestern University; Lynn Phillips and Seenu Srinivasan of Stanford University; Ted Levitt of Harvard University; Rheinhard Angelmar of INSEAD: Claes Fornell of the University of Michigan; Frank Bass of the University of Texas at Dallas; and Jehoshua Eliashberg of the University of Pennsylvania. My thanks in particular to my friend and fel-

low M.I.T. EE graduate, Dr. Edward McHale of the Foxboro Company, *mano geras draugas.*

I have been greatly influenced by the M.I.T. research culture in the Sloan School, through my undergraduate and graduate training in science and engineering at M.I.T., and by the ideas set forth by Thomas S. Kuhn of M.I.T.

CHAPTER 21

1. Published by Transaction Books, New Brunswick, New Jersey, 1981.
2. In the specific case of Bass, we should note that his quest has been marked mostly by a desire to help guide actions rather than to discover laws.
3. Stephen E. Toulmin, *Foresight and Understanding: An Inquiry into the Aims of Science* (Westport, Conn.: Greenwood Press, 1982). Originally published by Harper & Row, New York, 1963.
4. Thomas V. Bonoma, "A Case Study in Case Research: Marketing Implementation," Harvard Business School, May 1983 (mimeograph).

INDEX